Also by Victor S. Navasky

Naming Names
Kennedy Justice

A Matter of Opinion

A Matter of Opinion

VICTOR S. NAVASKY

Farrar, Straus and Giroux | New York

Farrar, Straus and Giroux
19 Union Square West, New York 10003

Copyright © 2005 by Victor S. Navasky
Distributed in Canada by Douglas & McIntyre Ltd.
Printed in the United States of America
First edition, 2005

Droodles used by permission of Tallfellow Press, Los Angeles, © 2000.

Library of Congress Cataloging-in-Publication Data
Navasky, Victor S.
  A matter of opinion / Victor S. Navasky.— 1st ed.
      p. cm.
  Includes index.
  ISBN-13: 978-0-374-29997-2
  ISBN-10: 0-374-29997-8 (alk. paper)
  1. Navasky, Victor S. 2. Editors—United States—Biography. 3. Nation (New York,
N.Y.: 1865) 4. Journalism—United States—History—20th century.
I. Title.

  PN4874.N285A3 2004
  070.5'1'092—dc22

                         2004059395

Designed by Jonathan D. Lippincott

www.fsgbooks.com

1   3   5   7   9   10   8   6   4   2

To Annie, whom everybody loves,
including me

The week has been singularly barren of exciting events.
—First sentence in first paragraph of first story of
first issue on first page of *The Nation*, 1865

Every maniac in the world that ever brought about the murder of people through war started out in an attic or a basement writing poetry . . . The thing to do is to have more magazines. Hundreds of them. Thousands. Print everything they write, so they'll believe they're immortal. That may keep them from going haywire.
—William Saroyan, *The Time of Your Life*, 1939

When a very great many, very important pundits all agree that something terrible will happen if we depart a hair's breadth from orthodoxy, the time has come to say, "Oh Yeah!" The ease with which people can nowadays be stampeded by the mass media gives a new importance to the role of the journal of opinion.
—Kingsley Martin, editor, *The New Statesman* (1931–1960)

I have the impression that every man, woman and child in the United States has an idea for one magazine that is "needed" (which is stronger than "wanted") by the American people.
—James B. Kobak, magazine consultant, 2003

CONTENTS

PREFACE

There is a man at Ole Miss, Samir Husni, who calls himself Mr. Magazine. Born in Lebanon, he was a sixth grader when he saw the first issue of *Superman* in Arabic, and he has been in love with magazines ever since. Every year he publishes a list of new magazine start-ups. Last year, according to Mr. Husni, 949 new magazines started up. Each of these magazines is or was somebody's dream. (I know, I know, some of these are the dreams of corporations, but the U.S. Supreme Court tells us that corporations are persons. What are you going to do?)

To start a new magazine, they say, you must develop a business plan describing the concept, the editorial need, the potential advertisers, the legal status of the company, the competition, the people involved, five years' worth of financial projections, and you may have to raise capital (including seed capital), undertake a direct-mail test, convene a focus group, put the arm on friends and relatives.

These days the smart money says that if you want to start a new magazine make it a niche magazine—like *Weight Watchers*. I don't really believe that. (What ever happened to *Max*, the magazine for tall people?) The smart money also says that the age of the "stand alone" independent magazine is over. I don't believe that, either.

This is the place to declare my interest. In the republic of conventional journalism, journals of opinion are considered second-class citizens. Objectivity is said to be impossible to achieve, but it is an ideal to be pursued. It is not that I am against objectivity (although the conventions of objective journalism do seem to have a way of strengthening the status quo); it is simply that I have a hard time understanding why we should seek that which we can never attain.

My heroes, the journalists who meant the most to me, were not objective. To name only the dead, they were crusading investigators like Lincoln Steffens, whose autobiography ought to be assigned reading; the sometimes indecipherable prophet-poet Murray Kempton; idealistic skeptics like I. F. Stone, and as you will see, Carey McWilliams, the rebel-radical who defined *The Nation* magazine from 1950 to 1975.

At Columbia University's Graduate School of Journalism, where I teach, entering students must declare one of four main concentrations: newspapers, magazines, broadcasting, and new media. In the 1970s investigative reporting was the glamour concentration. In the 1980s television was the thing. In the 1990s it was "new media." These days it seems to be magazines. When I started teaching at Columbia, I looked around for a usable textbook and couldn't find one. This is not that textbook, although it may be in the tradition of learning from one's own mistakes as well as those of others. This is not a personal memoir, but at times it feels like one, because I have felt free to draw on my adventures (mostly misadventures, really) in the magazine trade. I have also felt free to draw on what I have written elsewhere, because when I have written elsewhere I have felt free to draw on this, and I am no longer sure which is/was which. And this is not a biography of *The Nation*, although, because I have worked there for a quarter of a century, a disproportionate number of my examples, anecdotes, citations are from and about *The Nation*.

When I showed my book to my son, Bruno, he said, "I get it, it's a How-Not-To." And so it may be.

A Matter of Opinion

PROLOGUE

THE WAKE-UP CALL

Arthur Carter never called before 8:00 a.m. unless something was bothering him or he had some news. It was not quite 7:30 on a Monday morning in the spring of 1994, and I was lying in bed waiting for the alarm to go off in my Cambridge sublet on Memorial Drive, when the phone rang. It was Arthur, my friend, boss, and sometimes bane, and this morning something was bothering him or he had some news (depending on how you look at it). He made some small talk about the date for a benefit *The Nation* was planning in his honor, and then he said, "Oh, by the way, the transaction is on again."

"What transaction?" I asked.

"You know," he said, "that matter we talked about last year. Have Landey draw up the papers."

Bear with me while I tell you about that matter, about last year, about Landey and the papers, not to mention *The Nation* and what I was doing in Cambridge. They're all related.

I was in Cambridge because the year before, after sixteen years as the editor of *The Nation*, America's oldest weekly magazine (it was founded in New York City in 1865 by the great Anglo-Irish journalist E. L. Godkin, with the support of visionaries and malcontents in and around the abolitionist movement), I had persuaded Arthur I could use a sabbatical. Actually, Arthur didn't seem to need that much persuading, which probably should have given me pause. But it didn't, because I had a plan.

My plan was to spend six months, starting in January 1994, as a fellow at the Institute of Politics at Harvard University's Kennedy School of Government, where I would ruminate and run a seminar on the role of the journal of opinion in our times, and then spend the next six months writing a book on that subject.

There was a lot to ruminate on. Although *Nation* columnists indulged in occasional intramural sniping, and one of them indulged in more than occasional editor-bashing, only a few years earlier there had been a consensus in our community on most of the issues facing the country. For better or worse, our people were against the supply-side economics that Reagan-era Republicans believed in, in favor of a freeze on the production and development of nuclear weapons; against the death penalty, in favor of *Roe v. Wade*; and we believed that the Gulf War of 1991 had been a moral disaster and political mistake. Now there seemed to be only debate. For example, *The Nation*'s staff was split down the middle on what U.S. policy should be toward the war in Bosnia—half believing the United States should lift its arms embargo there and bomb the Serbs, the other half arguing that such intervention would only escalate the conflict and cause more blood to be spilled; almost half favored intervention in Haiti to restore the democratically elected President Jean-Bertrand Aristide to office after his ouster in 1991, those opposed maintaining that the racist history of past actions in Haiti disqualified the United States from present intervention; nobody thought that President Clinton's health-care proposal was adequate, but half the staff supported it because at least it incorporated the principle of universal health care, while the other half opposed it as inevitably discrediting that principle; the magazine endorsed the Oslo peace accords between the Israeli government and the Palestine Liberation Organization, but also ran a strong dissent from that position by the scholar and activist Edward Said (my guess is that at least a quarter of *The Nation* community concurred in Said's analysis), and so forth. These debates had erupted onto our letters page, among our columnists, in the articles section, and even spilled into book reviews.

Parallel debates were going on in William F. Buckley, Jr.'s conservative magazine *National Review*. There it was hawks versus isolationists, whereas at *The Nation* it was human-rights activists versus noninterventionists. The difference between the two was no mere matter of semantics. The underlying core values were jingoistic nationalism on the right and what some would call a woolly-headed internationalism on the liberal left. (This could not have referred to me, because not only was I not woolly-headed but, as I pointed out in a letter to the editor of *The New Yorker* at the time, it was wrong for a Talk of the Town item to call me "balding." "In fact," I wrote, "I am bald, period.")

The book I hoped to write would deal not merely with *The Nation* but with journals of opinion writ large. My working title was "Reflections on the Role of the Journal of Opinion in the Age of Electronic, Conglomerated, Transnational Communications, and if I can only come up with a subtitle my job is done." The idea was—without calling for a return to the good old days of Addison and Steele, when the production and consumption of opinion was limited to Grub Street hacks and the landed gentry—to answer the question: How does society protect, conserve, and encourage the sort of discourse that served the eighteenth century so well? Can a journal of opinion, in other words, help to reconceive the public sphere as one in which ideas flow freely, in which a dramatically enlarged, critically engaged public emerges? I wanted to explain the effect of these journals, their role in the birth of our nation, their relationship to the new technologies, the way they influenced mainstream media, and much more. But Arthur's telephone call five months into my year off changed all that.

I quickly figured out it was a wake-up call. "That matter" had reference to a conversation we had had over lunch the year before, when Arthur told me he had something to tell me that I wouldn't like.

Unlike *The Nation*'s previous owners, who had been attracted to the magazine because they shared its politics, Arthur Carter had no known politics. A maverick on Wall Street, he had founded a firm, Carter, Berlind & Weill, which by the 1990s had matured, by way of takeovers, into Shearson-Lehman–American Express. When in the mid-1980s he first approached Hamilton Fish, *The Nation*'s previous publisher, about buying the magazine and Ham asked him about his politics, he said he was a "registered opportunist" and uttered a nervous laugh, almost as nervous as Hamilton's. He said he was in the process of divesting himself of his various businesses, and now that he no longer had to worry about money—*The New York Times* put his net worth at "somewhere between one and two-hundred million"—he was interested in devoting himself to his first love, journalism. He had been business manager of his college paper at Brown, he had founded a prize-winning country weekly, *The Litchfield County Times*, near his home in Connecticut, and he admired what we had done with *The Nation*. He told us that his mother, a high-school French teacher, used to subscribe to it, and this meant a lot to him. He didn't mention the reading habits of his father, an internal revenue agent. But he did pledge a hands-off editorial policy and said that with his money and business background, and our, our . . . as a matter-of-fact, I don't remember what he said we brought to the table . . . we ought to make an unbeatable team.

Now here we were, at Gino's, one of Arthur's favorite watering holes. What used to be weekly lunches, by 1993 happened only once every two or three weeks. Instead of driving downtown (with his chauffeur sitting in the death seat) to *The Nation's* Thirteenth Street office as he used to do, we dined within walking distance of his East Sixty-fourth Street office. Arthur had a new journalistic love, *The New York Observer*. A weekly newspaper printed on peach-colored newsprint, it reported on the preoccupations—power, status, media, money, sex, and real estate—of Arthur's rich and famous neighbors in Manhattan's East Side, Connecticut, and the Hamptons. *The Nation's* circulation had moved from 75,000 to 100,000 on his watch, we had had our share of newsbreaks and coups, and even picked up an award or two along the way, but for Arthur the action had moved uptown. Besides, while the high-school French teacher in him scrupulously honored his hands-off-editorial pledge, he was under no such constraints at the *Observer*, his creation and brainchild.

Here is what Arthur told me: He had an offer to buy half of his business. As part of the deal he intended to spin off *The Nation* into a nonprofit and cut his $500,000 annual subsidy in half. "I know you won't like this," he said again.

The part I didn't like was less the part about cutting the subsidy in half (although that wasn't pleasant) than the nonprofit part. *The Nation* was an unprofitable for-profit company that had lost money for all but three of its then 130 years. All money-losing journals of opinion like *The Nation* at one time or another look at the nonprofit option, and we had, too, for it has a number of obvious financial advantages. First, since nonprofits are eligible for charitable donations, donations to them can immediately be deducted from the giver's taxable income, and this makes it easier to raise money. Second, nonprofits enjoy lower mailing rates. We calculated that *The Nation* would save a minimum of $250,000 per annum on mailing costs alone if it went nonprofit. Any number of American journals of opinion—*The Public Interest, Mother Jones, The Progressive, Commentary*, and *Commonweal*, to name only a few—were organized in this way. But as Arthur knew, because we had discussed it any number of times, I was adamantly opposed to the idea, because nonprofits can't endorse candidates for political office and, more important, because the law forbids them to devote more than a small percentage of their resources to trying to influence legislation. I didn't like the idea of leaving the tax status of our subversive weekly vulnerable to challenge by hostile political administrations in Washington. Conceivably, a journal that focuses on matters of public policy and issues can survive without endorsing political candidates. That's what *The New Leader, Commentary, Mother Jones, The American Spectator*, and others do. But to me the idea that a political weekly, whose raison d'être is almost by definition its intention to influence public opinion, might bargain away its right to influence the Congress or anyone else in exchange for favorable tax treatment was a bad idea, doubly so for a dissenting weekly.

"Let me get this straight," I said to Arthur. "According to what you told *The New York Times*, and me too, you have a net worth of maybe two hundred million. You are about to receive a cash windfall of maybe a hundred million. And *therefore* you want to cut your *Nation* subsidy in half?" I asked, doing my best to keep any note of incredulity out of my voice.

"That's right," Arthur said. He pointed out that now it would be *his* money rather than his corporation's money. I decided then and there that I had better reread Scott Fitzgerald. The very rich *are* very different from you and me, or at least from me. I thought it best not to pursue that line of inquiry.

"Arthur," I said, "you have done a noble thing in helping to build *The Nation*. You have scrupulously kept your pledge to honor the principle of editorial independence. You clearly don't identify with the magazine's editorial policy. *If* you are tired of the magazine, why don't you sell it? Or why don't you do what every other proprietor in the history of the magazine has done: if you don't want to bear the entire burden of the subsidy yourself, bring in some partners to bear it with you?"

Arthur didn't say anything. "Or," I said, taking a hefty sip of my Stoli on the rocks, "why don't you turn it over to me and I'll find the other half?"

Arthur looked up. "You mean I give you half the stock and I'll continue to put in half the money and you find the other half?"

"Something like that," I said.

He said, "You mean I give you 49 percent of the stock and—"

"No," I said. "I mean you give me 51 percent of the stock. If you control it, I'm going to have trouble raising the money." I had already had the experience of one potential backer of a *Nation*-related project declining the honor on the grounds that "I don't want to make Arthur Carter richer than he already is."

"Let's do it," Arthur said.

"Say what?" I said, checking both of our vodkas to see if the glasses were empty, full, half full, or half empty.

"Have Landey work it out with Tom." Landey is my brother-in-law Landey Strongin, the lawyer whom everybody loves. Tom is Tom Sheinman, Arthur's in-house counsel, whom everybody respects—sort of the Robert Duvall of the Carter empire.

"Let me get this straight," I said, repeating myself. "Are you telling me you are giving me one-half of *The Nation* and that we will be fifty–fifty partners but I will have control?" Arthur smiled and nodded his head, we clinked glasses, and I headed for the airport—I was on my way to a Rockefeller Foundation–funded conference on "Journals of Opinion" (as part of its series on Institutions of Civil Society)—but not before I called my brother-in-law the lawyer, that's Landey, to tell him the good news.

I flew to Bellagio, on Lake Como, Italy, where, it turned out, with the exception of me and Nikki Keddie, an American Islamicist who had founded a new, California-based periodical called *Contention: Debates in Society, Culture, and Science*, all the other editors were from the Muslim world. And the unstated agenda of the conference had to do with persuading fundamentalists that there was something to be said for democracy, pluralism, and the free exchange of ideas.

I learned a thing or two. For example, where I had always thought of the journal of opinion and the dissenting journal as interchangeable designations, in a politically chaotic and fluid nation like Lebanon, where there really was no establishment to dissent from, the editor of *The Beirut Review,* Dr. Paul Salem, saw his paper's purpose as "building a bridge" between Lebanon's intellectuals and its government. I also learned that in Pakistan it was permissible to publish things in English that one was not allowed to talk about in Urdu, the language of the masses. I was grateful for these lessons on the problems of disseminating opinion in the world of Islam.

By the time I returned to New York a week later, Landey had called Tom and had even done some paperwork. Tom, having spoken to Arthur, reported back that there were "tax problems." Landey didn't see any tax problems. Summer was upon us, and Arthur's sense of urgency seemed to have passed.

Then came the fall. I suggested to Arthur that we invite Landey to our unweekly lunch to clear up whether we had tax problems, Arthur problems, or what. Again, I found myself at Gino's, but this time Arthur's shoulders weren't hunched, and when we arrived at dessert, Arthur still hadn't raised the matter of "The Transaction," so I did. His vague response led me to observe, "Arthur, you seem to have lost your enthusiasm for this deal, at least at this time."

"Maybe that's right," he said, and the talk turned to *The East Hampton Star,* in which he had recently purchased an interest, and that, I assumed, was that. Four months later I arranged for my sabbatical at Harvard and forgot about it.

Now, in the spring of 1994, I was in Cambridge and it seemed "The Transaction" was on again, so I called my brother-in-law the lawyer and reminded him we had never settled the 49 percent vs. 51 percent question. I also told him that whatever the deal, we should do our best to get Arthur's signature on an option sooner rather than later, since Arthur had been known to change his mind. Otherwise it would be difficult for me to persuade potential investors that we were going forward.

"There's no hurry," Arthur had said. "We can do this by the end of the year."

Landey soon called Tom, and this time Tom called back within minutes. Landey gave me the news. "The deal Arthur wants to give you is this—not forty-nine percent and not fifty-one percent, but one hundred percent."

This, I thought, was too good to be true. And it was.

Landey continued with the "details." "He wants a million dollars for *The Nation,* but he asks nothing down and has proposed a payment schedule of $100,000 per annum at six percent interest." Arthur's further idea was that I could continue my sabbatical until the end of the year. "Tom asked me to ask you whether this accords with your understanding."

Of course it was a million dollars more than my understanding, but actually the price seemed if not generous then at least fair.

Some years before, I had asked Jim Kobak, everybody's magazine consultant and my old friend, what is the worth of a magazine that has been around for 130 years and has 85,000 subscribers, the hard core of whom renew at a rate of 80 percent, but that loses an average of $500,000 a year? He said it was worth whatever anyone would pay for it. "But if you asked me what it would cost to start such a magazine from scratch, it could take more than $10 million and you still couldn't guarantee the renewal rate or the brand identification."

I asked my brother-in-law the lawyer what he thought, and he said that on a million-dollar purchase, $100,000 a year with nothing down at 6 percent per annum was "cheap money."

Economics is not my strong point, but I did know two things: the magazine was losing $500,000 a year and I didn't have $500,000 to lose that year or any other year. Nor did I have a spare $100,000 per annum for Arthur, cheap money or uncheap money.

So on the assumption that I would spend the remainder of my sabbatical trying to raise the money to make the deal possible, I asked my brother-in-law the lawyer to draw up a draft agreement which provided that at any time between then and the end of the year I could give Arthur ten days' notice and he would thereupon turn the magazine (and its debts) over to me as of January 1, 1995.

"What is this ten days' notice crap?" Arthur asked. "Either he [that's me] wants to do it or he doesn't."

He wants to do it, I told Landey, but he doesn't know if he can raise the money. Having done business with Arthur for a half-dozen years, I believed/knew/assumed that his response was not an invitation to negotiate. It was more like a take-it-or-leave-it-and-if-you-don't-take-it-by-Friday-(you shmuck)-I-might-well-take-it-off-the-table.

There was still the little matter of how I would explain to my wife, Annie, who lacked her brother the lawyer's understanding of higher mathematics, that buying a magazine that was losing $500,000 a year for $1 million I didn't have was a deal worth grabbing by Friday. Especially since we both knew that journals of opinion almost never make money. Even that avatar of capitalism William F. Buckley, Jr., when asked whether his own journal of opinion might ever make a profit, had responded, "A profit? You don't expect the church to make a profit, do you?"

But I had an idea. Across the Charles River from the Kennedy School stood the world-famous Harvard Business School, and on its faculty was my friend Samuel L. Hayes III, who held the Jacob H. Schiff Chair in Investment Banking. Well, he wasn't exactly my friend, but we had served on Swarthmore College's Board of Managers together, where Sam was one of the key overseers of the college's investment portfolio, which that year was the No. 1 performer in the country. Over baked scrod at the business school's faculty club, I told Sam I might have the chance to acquire *The Nation*, and I explained the idea I had. Was there a way that he could turn our little company into one of those famous case studies? Suppose I opened *The Nation*'s books to a class of Harvard's brilliant young M.B.A. candidates. The final exam and class problem would be simple but challenging: How would they take a magazine and, without changing it, turn around its economics?

Sam gently reminded me that although he didn't read *The Nation* regularly (or irregularly either, for that matter), he suspected that his politics were not exactly *Nation* politics. But, he said, he would think about it, and I should send him its "financials."

I signed with Arthur, and not long after, I sent Sam the numbers, along with a business plan I had worked up. Although I had confidence in the projections I had developed with the help of Jim Kobak, which called for an investment of $3 million—this would cover the first few years of my Arthur payments and the annual deficit, with enough left over to invest in circulation growth until we reached the break-even point four years down the road—I feared that Sam, who sits on the board of Tiffany's, might regard our modest projections as pedagogically irrelevant to the needs of the nation's future industrial titans-in-waiting. Whatever Sam's verdict, I had to start raising money before he handed it down.

On the one hand, the prospect of raising $3 million was daunting. On the other, I believed the money was out there—over the years at least four well-heeled well-wishers had told me that if Arthur Carter ever wanted to sell the magazine, they were interested in buying. And I also knew that regardless of its value in the marketplace, this great cultural treasure, a part of America's heritage, was worth more than $3 million. All I had to do was sign up three out of my four potential investors and I was home free. Of course what my well-wishers forgot to mention—and naïf that I was, it never occurred to me—was that their interest had as its premise that they would be in control.

My idea, which I worked out with my brother-in-law the lawyer, was that we should set the thing up like a Broadway show. I, as the "producer," would have all the votes, and the angels, the investors, would put up all the money. What are investors for, if not to invest? Right? The difference between *The Nation* and Broadway, however, was this: although nineteen out of twenty Broadway shows flop, everybody expects that when a show is a hit they will get rich, whereas *The Nation*, paradoxically, was America's longest-running weekly magazine and yet, as far as I could establish, it had never made money. (This is not quite true. As I have already mentioned, most histories of the magazine say that it has lost money for all but three years; but they can never seem to agree on which three years! My favorite rumor is that it was during World War II, when, because of paper rationing, issues were only eight pages. The only trouble with this rumor is that when I checked, I found that the issues were twenty-six pages then.) Oswald Garrison Villard, the editor-publisher from 1918 to 1935, once got in a dispute with his successor, Freda Kirchwey, when he claimed that throughout his publishership *The Nation* made profits. Kirchwey, calling his bluff, pointed out in a letter that that's like a child who gets an allowance of fifty cents and ends the week with ten cents living at home with no rent, free meals and clothing paid for by doting parents saying that he/she made a profit.

The question whether a journal of opinion—especially one in the business of raising questions about capitalist exploitation—should be expected to or can ever realistically expect to justify itself in the marketplace is a fascinating one in its own right, and believe it or not, the economics of the journal of opinion is not as boring a subject as it ought to be. But I should mention what Carey McWilliams, who ran *The Nation* from 1955 through 1975, once said about the secret of its survival: "It is precisely because *The Nation*'s backers cared more about what it stood for than what it earned that the magazine has survived where countless other publications with circulations in the millions have gone under." This wasn't true merely about *The Nation*. It seemed to be true about the genre.

Most people do not acquire or found journals of opinion primarily for profit. I was going to say most sane people, but most sane people don't get involved with journals of opinion. I had better explain my own reasons for doing so, as well as my personal relationship to the world of finance and, while I'm at it, explain how I came to enter the world of journalism in general.

A PERSONAL NOTE

I am the first member of my family to earn a college degree (A.B., Swarthmore 1954).

My father, Macy, should have gone to college but couldn't because he had to go to work for his father, who had come to New York from Russia in the 1890s and founded a small clothing manufacturing business in New York City's garment district. "Students and Young Men's Clothing," it said on the pencil advertising "Navasky & Sons," which later became the Sturdybuilt Company. Although he subscribed to *The Nation* and *The New Republic*, my father was no radical, and my grandfather never had a kind word to say about labor unions, even in Yiddish. The other sons, my father's brothers, were Alex and Abe. That's Alexander Hamilton Navasky and Abraham Lincoln Navasky. My mother, née Esther Goldberg, was my father's secretary until she married him and "retired."

My father, who went to New York City's High School of Commerce, where he was an A student, hated business. He wanted to be a writer, but the closest he came to getting published was letters to an occasional editor. His specialty was writing letters to Dan Parker, a New York *Daily Mirror* sports columnist who thought all fights were fixed. My father, a fan, thought none were:

> 9/15/50 Dear Parker: What this town needs are sportswriters who know that athletes reach a peak and then pass it, and when past it are not as good as when at it. Those strange things sur-

rounding La Motta's recent fights were the key-pounders who hadn't assimilated this elementary truth . . . Occasionally an admirer, Yours, Macy.

Parker would reply on the back of Macy's notepaper: "You certainly are a smart guy, Macy, even if you do say so yourself." When his father died, my father sold his share of the family business, at least partly, I always assumed, so that I would never have to go into it. At age forty-six, dragging my mother along, he enrolled in a short-story-writing seminar at our local public library, where as far as I could figure out, he was the star student. Each week he would be asked to read his story, and after comments and revisions, he would put seven copies of his story in seven envelopes and send them off to seven magazines, like *The Dial,* the *Saturday Review*, and *Collier's*, along with self-addressed return envelopes. Over the course of the semester he received no acceptances but three or four encouraging letters, including one from the editor of *The Dial*, who wanted to know if he was working on a novel, and if so, asked to see it. Eventually he threw in the towel and spent the remainder of his days outwitting the stock market, writing letters to Dan Parker, and working his way through Faulkner, Dostoevsky, and the rest of the masters. It wasn't until years later that I discovered that each week my father had been sending out one original typed copy and six increasingly illegible carbon copies of the same stories, and that 100 percent of the encouraging notes were in response to the original manuscripts.

I had by accident what I later came to feel was an ideal education: From age five to eleven I attended the Rudolph Steiner School, whose aim was to cultivate the spirit by way of the arts;* from eleven to seventeen I went to the Little Red School House and its high school, Elisabeth Irwin, whose mission, through community engagement, was to imbue students with a social conscience; and from eighteen to twenty-

---

*At the time, my older sister and I felt discriminated against because everyone else on our block went to public school. When she graduated from the Steiner School and was accepted by the elite (public) Julia Richman Country School (famous because the actress Lauren Bacall had gone there), and by coincidence it turned out that I was going to be the only boy in my class at Steiner, I too left.

one I attended Swarthmore College, which focused on the intellect and the life of the mind in a Quaker context. For dessert, and as a correction to all of the above (age twenty-two to twenty-four), I served in the U.S. armed forces, after which I attended Yale Law School, which served as a bridge to the so-called real world.

My father chose the Rudolph Steiner School because, based on his own experience, he believed that public school "broke the spirit." Little did he know that Rudolph Steiner the man, founder of something called anthroposophy, literally believed that two weeks after the body expired the spirit surveyed the arc of its life and then was reincarnated in another vessel. (This I discovered only many years later—we were not taught reincarnation in school.) I chose Little Red because the best stickball player on my block went there. When I enrolled, neither I nor my parents knew that it had started as an experimental public school based on John Dewey's theories of progressive education and broke away when Elisabeth Irwin discovered that the Board of Education couldn't tolerate its independent ways. My parents knew mainly that it meant my taking a daily subway ride down to Greenwich Village, then still a bohemian redoubt, where the school was located.

Swarthmore chose me in the sense that it was the only college to which I had applied that accepted me.

At none of these institutions did I take a course in journalism or writing.

At Rudolph Steiner I learned my vowel sounds by acting them out in eurythmy classes ("O is for oak tree, tall and strong"). But I remember that after a third-grade field trip to a farm in upstate New York (an organic farm, of course—Rudolph Steiner was light-years ahead of the curve), our assignment the following week was to write 300 words on the trip. I chose as my topic "A Day in the Life of a Farmer" and dutifully turned in my paper. When it came back my teacher had written, "This is lovely, Victor. But what about the milking of the goat and the cows, and what about making the fire and dinner around the family table, and what about that tractor you rode on?" I had also forgotten to mention pitching hay. "Please fix."

So I dutifully fixed and a few days later turned in my much expanded paper. This time my teacher wrote, "This is wonderful, Victor.

You have really captured what it is like to be a farmer. But it is far longer than 300 words. Please revise, keeping in all the facts, but don't use more than 300 words."

And so I did and so I didn't.

At Little Red I remember putting out a lame, mimeographed parody of the high school's photo-offset paper, *Info*, which was called, with sublime eighth-grade imagination, *Ofni* (*Info* spelled backward, get it?). But my real literary education came from an inspirational high-school English teacher, Mr. Marvin. Mr. Marvin would spend much of his time reading aloud from his favorite poems—and not only would his heart leap up when he beheld a rainbow in the sky, but his whole body seemed to follow, and depending on the poem, like a ballet dancer he would often end up *en pointe*.

He also taught us about literary standards. The day we returned from summer vacation, he went around the class asking what we thought of the suggested summer reading, *Moby-Dick*. When my friend Richard Atkinson courageously (I thought) said he thought it was "boring," Mr. Marvin said, "*Moby-Dick* isn't on trial, Mr. Atkinson, you are."

At Elisabeth Irwin I learned about politics less through what we were taught in the classroom than from the songs we sang and the hootenannies featuring such subversives as Pete Seeger, Woody Guthrie, and Sonny Terry. They and we sang the anti-Fascist songs of the International Brigade in Spain, the labor songs of the CIO PAC ("Which Side Are You On?"), the freedom songs of the civil rights movement ("Lift Every Voice and Sing"), the protest songs from the Warsaw Ghetto, and yes, of the Chinese, Soviet, and American revolutions; and just for the fun of it, love songs and ditties like "Newspapermen Meet Such Interesting People."

Over the years, I have learned from George Orwell, from Khruschev's revelations at the Twentieth Party Congress, from Gorbachev's and other memoirs, from the Venona decrypts and selected Soviet archives, some of the many things wrong with this particular naïve internationalist vision of "the new world a-comin'." But as the democratic socialist Michael Harrington wrote in 1977 in *The Vast Majority*, although the popular-front vision was sometimes manipulated to rationalize cruelty rather than to promote kindness, "for all its confusions

and evasions and contradictions, it was a corruption of something good
that always remained in it: of an internationalism that is still the only
hope of mankind. My heart still quickens when I hear the songs of the
International Brigade." Mine, too.

At Swarthmore, a nondenominational college founded by liberal
Quakers (the Hicksites, followers of the early-nineteenth-century pas-
tor Elias Hicks, who believed, among other things, in coeducation), I
co-edited the weekly *Phoenix,* the student paper, and contributed to an
upstart student periodical called the *Lit.* Although I didn't understand
it at the time, my real magazine education came from the college's honors program, modeled by Frank Aydelotte after Oxford's tutorials. If
you entered the honors program, in your junior and senior years you attended no lectures, took no exams, and received no term grades. Instead, you took eight small-group seminars (two per semester), at the
end of which you were subjected to a battery of written and oral exams
from "outside" examiners; i.e., professors from other institutions, who
knew nothing about you other than what had been on your reading list.
The theory was that the weekly seminars would be unpolluted by students trying to impress professors.

For me, though, the requirement of writing a weekly, unfootnoted,
six-to-eight-page paper worked well, the equivalent of writing a weekly
journalistic essay on deadline; the give-and-take in the seminars was
the equivalent of an editorial conference; and the sharing of one's
weekly paper with fellow students (we each compiled each other's papers along with our own in ever-thickening spring binders) was a form
of pseudo-publication. The honors program still survives, albeit in a di-
luted form. In the late 1960s, new generations of students attacked the
honors seminars as elitist (only about 40 percent of the students were
admitted to them), sexist (professors were expected to provide refresh-
ments for the home-based seminars, a responsibility that frequently
fell upon their mostly female spouses), and the formula of four seminars in one's major and two in each of two related minors seemed too
narrow and inflexible. Many of the students now prefer to take a year
overseas.

At Swarthmore one of my favorite professors was Murray Stedman,
who taught political science. He told us if we remembered nothing
else we should commit to memory Robert MacIver's definition of myth

("a value-impregnated belief"). I also remember his line about why the student-run commons store, which dispensed hundreds of cups of coffee a day, nevertheless lost money. "Because," he said, "Swarthmore students have an anti-business bias. Put three City College business majors in charge of that store and in six months they will be making money hand over fist." I told him that the anti-business bias was a myth, but in my case at least was factually correct. It wasn't until decades later, after I entered the Harvard Business School, that I tried to do something about it.

"It's always better, when job hunting, to apply to a specific person rather than to an anonymous title," I tell my students, "and if possible to come with a connection to that person." I secured my own first job in the journalism business that way, although it wasn't until I had it that I learned that the old cliché—it's not what you know but whom you know—was not quite right.

During a break in a Shakespeare seminar at Swarthmore, my classmate Pat Bryson and I got to talking about our summer plans or, in my case, lack of them. "What would you like to do?" Pat asked. "Work on a newspaper or magazine," I said. "Well, maybe Daddy can help you," Pat said, in her cute upper-class Brit accent, "but it would have to be in England. Would that be all right?" "Would it!" I said.

Pat suggested that I call Daddy over the Christmas holidays and see whether he might help.

George Bryson had for fifteen years been the founder and managing director of the world-famous advertising agency Young & Rubicam's London office. In that capacity he dealt with—placed ads for and otherwise represented Y&R in—British newspapers, magazines, and television, and perhaps had some contacts he could put at my disposal. Now he was back in New York, though all his press contacts were in England. I called Mr. Bryson over the holidays. He invited me for a drink at his posh East Side apartment and we discussed two papers: the *News of the World*, which was a weekly with a circulation in the millions, and the *Daily Mirror*, a Labour daily, which seemed more my speed.

When I mentioned the conversation to Larry Lafore, my history professor, who had spent the previous year on sabbatical in the U.K., he said, "Oh, if you have a choice by all means do *News of the World*." He explained that a typical *News of the World* article might be an in-depth report on a parish priest who raped eight of his parishioners, but it would appear under a heading like "Clergyman Commits Indiscretion." Larry taught diplomatic history, but he was a gifted social historian, novelist, and world-class teacher. He taught one class on the history of England by having each student write for his term paper a chapter in a collective novel. He reeked of credibility and savoir faire. He lectured without notes, but his perfectly structured talks always ended a second before the bell, after which he would disappear out the door. Only on the last class of the semester did he end his class at the window, rather than the door. With nonchalant aplomb he proceeded to open the window and make his exit onto the fire escape.

A few months later I found myself on a student ship, Holland America's *Groote Beer*. After six rocky days at sea, I disembarked at Southampton, and once in London headed right for the offices of *News of the World*, where after a half-hour wait the editor saw me. He explained that he was seeing me as a courtesy to Mr. Bryson, but that the chapel (the British equivalent of the union local) would have his head if a nonchapel member "so much as lifted a pencil." But I came all the way from New York, I began to whine, when he continued. "Now," he said, "the provinces are something else again. Would you mind going to Worcester? If we presented you to The *Berrow's Worcester Journal* as an American who was studying the British press—that's really what you're doing, isn't it?"—he asked, as he began writing what I assumed to be a letter of introduction to a Mr. Jack Worrell, proprietor of the *Berrow's Worcester Journal*, the world's oldest weekly. "Well, yes, if you say so, although I was hoping to get some experience," I volunteered tentatively.

"Oh, you will, you will," he assured me as he handed me a sealed envelope on *News of the World* stationery and a ticket to Worcester, about an hour and a half from London by rail.

The next day I presented myself to Mr. Worrell, a nattily attired if somewhat stodgy gent. (Later I discovered he was a key member of the local gentry, when he invited me to accompany him on an otter hunt, but that is another story.) He ushered me into his office, opened the envelope I handed him, read it, and peered at me over his spectacles with what I took to be a quizzical look.

"Have you read this?" he asked.

"No," I said.

"Well, I think you had better."

Here, if memory serves, is what he handed me:

Dear Jack,

   This is to introduce Mr. Victor Navasky, an American student interested in learning by working on a British newspaper. Mr. Navasky is a friend of Miss Pat Bryson. Miss Pat Bryson is the daughter of Mr. George Bryson. Mr. George Bryson is the founder and Managing Director of Young & Rubicam's London office. Young & Rubicam owns 80 percent of *News of the World*. *News of the World* owns 100 percent of *Berrow's Worcester Journal*. Please help Mr. Navasky in any way you can.

                                                              Yours, etc.

It turned out to be not only my first job in the business but one of my best. I got to do everything from running cricket scores to writing advertising copy. For the Worcester Home Loan and Savings Association, for example, I suggested the following:

Polonius said, 'Neither a borrower nor a lender be.' But Polonius was a senile old fool whom Shakespeare killed off in the second act. Join the Worcester Home Loan and Savings Association and you can borrow and lend at the same time!

I even got to review *East Lynne*, which was playing at the local rep. I also learned something about the different press cultures at home and in England. The British tabs seemed more blatant (with their page-2 bathing beauties), but the more serious papers like the Manchester *Guardian*, which mixed interpretation with reporting, seemed more thoughtful than their U.S. counterparts. And in a premature glimpse at the media concentration to come, I discovered the economies-of-scale principle behind small-town chain-owned weeklies: The *Droit-*

wich Guardian, the *Evesham Standard*, the *Kidderminster Times*, and the *Berrow's Worcester Journal*, all owned by *News of the World*, all had different front pages and local news, but shared the same features from the Midlands. Years later, when I read about the letter of recommendation that enabled Lincoln Steffens to study philosophy abroad, I was reminded of how I got my job at the *Berrow's Worcester Journal* (which I did subsequently make the subject of a college paper). When Steffens applied to study in Berlin he ran into two obstacles. First, he was told he had to apply for a degree. And so he became a candidate for a Ph.D. in philosophy. As an undergraduate at Berkeley his habit had been to study only the subjects that interested him. Now he was in danger of flunking physics, a requirement for doctoral candidates. He was summoned to the office of his professor, a Colonel Edwards, who specialized in conic sections. Steffens confessed that he did not understand it and could not care less.

After pondering the matter, the colonel asked him if he could prove any propositions. "Yes," Steffens said, "some seven or eight. I know them by heart. All right,' Edwards said. 'I don't want you to cheat; I won't let you cheat. I'll give you a private examination right now. You do two out of three propositions and I'll give you a pass.' Going to the blackboard, he wrote up one. 'Can you do that?' I said I could. He wrote another. 'That too?' 'No,' I said, and he wrote another that I did not know. 'We'll make it three out of five,' he suggested, and he wrote up one more and looked at me. I laughed and nodded; I could do it, and slowly he chose the fifth, which I knew. I wrote them out in a few minutes, handed them in, and—he passed me, after a long and very serious lecture on ethics, which I told him was to be my specialty. I was going to Germany on purpose to find if there was any moral reason for or against cheating in cards, in politics, or in conic sections—'either by the student or the professor,' I added."

Professor-Colonel Edwards, who knew no one in Berlin, gave him a letter of recommendation anyway.

Moral: It's not what you know but whom you know, and whom who you know knows.

After my summer in Worcester, I signed up for a special program called The Washington Semester at the American University in the nation's capital, a sort of roving seminar including interviews with Supreme Court Justices, congressmen, legislative and administrative assistants, and more bureaucrats than you could count. Because I was the first Swarthmore student to sign on (a political science major named Michael Dukakis was the second), and because I was in the honors program and didn't have to worry about exams (yet), I could more or less write my own ticket. What I did was arrange to write a thesis in place of one seminar and to audit American U.'s course equivalent of Swarthmore's "Politics and Legislation" seminar for another.

And I also answered an ad in *The Washington Post* for a part-time job as tour guide, which I got. The "training" for the job consisted of my going on the tour two or three times myself and taking notes on what the other tour guides said. They would, naturally, start on the top floor (where the production department was), point out personalities along the way, like the famous cartoonist Herblock and other *Post* celebrities, and proceed floor by floor and department by department ("There's the newsroom where the reporters sit, there's the bullpen where copy is processed") until they reached the basement, where the presses rolled. The fun part was when a light started flashing or a bell went off signifying an important story on the AP wire.

I was not satisfied to do things the way they had always been done. I thought I had a better idea, and since each tour guide seemed to be more or less on his own, I implemented it. Instead of starting on the top floor, I'd take the tourists out onto the street where, I would say, the story starts. The reporters report, say, "Man Bites Dog." Then I would take them to the city desk on the fifth floor to see where the reporter wrote the story, then to the copy desk, where it was copy-edited, then to the makeup department on another floor. Then, in case it might generate editorial comment, I'd take them to the editorial floor, all the time going up and down the back stairs, introduce them to the great Herblock, and eventually we'd get to the basement, where the presses were located, and end up where we had started on the street, where a line of trucks awaited bundles of papers to drop throughout the District of Columbia. After two weeks (I worked part-time three afternoons a week), this ingenious system resulted in confusion, much traffic on the *Post* stairs, some loss of weight, lots of out-of-breath customers, and my getting to know Herblock (which served me well in later years, when I enlisted him to contribute an introduction to an anthology of political satire). It also resulted in my being transferred from my tour-guide role to a position of greater responsibility—tabulating entries in the *Post*'s weekly football pool. When I went into the Army and sought a job in Troop Information and Education, I was able to list on my résumé as "last employer" *The Washington Post*.

At Swarthmore I got in trouble for superimposing a photograph of college president John Nason's face peering through the open door of a coed's room, and putting this on the front page of the *Phoenix*, with a caption that said *Peekaboo!* We were trying to satirize what the college administration called its "intervisitation experiment," whereby men and women were allowed to visit each other in their dormitory rooms (albeit only on Sundays and only between the hours of 2:00 p.m. and 4:30 p.m. and only with the door open a minimum of 12 inches). The peg for our story was a closed door. When the hall proctor had gone to summon a young woman who had received a phone call and found a closed door, she opened it, and there was a male buttoning up his shirt, under which was brown skin. (The young woman was white.) Our article, as I remember it, didn't mention skin color. Those were the days. The punishment for our color-blind impudence was that my innocent co-editor and guilty I were summoned to the president's office for biweekly meetings to go over the articles in each issue. Because the meetings occurred *after* each issue had been published, it was explained to us that this was not censorship. And one of the deans raised the question of whether a sophomore (that was me, my co-editor was a senior) was mature enough to be editor. Only when a visiting political science professor, Philip Jacobs from the University of Pennsylvania, called me aside after class and told me, "Keep it up—that's what a college paper is supposed to be, a thorn in the side of the administration," did I begin to have an inkling that maybe immaturity had its compensations.

At Swarthmore in the early 1950s, with its classic liberal arts curriculum, a course in something as "practical" as journalism was unthinkable. And when, after graduation, I was drafted into the U.S.

Army, in the penumbra of the Korean War, the last thing I expected was that my military service would enhance my education as a journalist. I was wrong.

At first I hoped to do an exposé of the brutal nature of basic training at Camp Gordon, just outside Augusta, Georgia, where the sadistic Southern noncoms liked nothing better than to lord it over the recently arrived doughboys from New York City. I even wrote to the *New York Post* on the mistaken theory that they would assign an anonymous infantryman to write such a series.

But on reflection I decided (even if the *Post* had not already decided for me) that the story was no story. My most memorable experience was the day we had bayonet training. The instructor, a gung-ho sergeant, explained that in order to get our adrenaline up it helped, after fixing the bayonet, to leap from the trenches, point it at the dummy some fifty yards away, and, running at full speed, yell "Kill, kill, kill!" before plunging the bayonet into the dummy's heart and twisting it. Here, I should acknowledge, the sergeant then paused and confided that the post commander had heard from members of the Congress who had heard from the mothers of some of the more sensitive soldiers objecting to the brutality of the exercise. In an apparent concession to his commanding officer, our sergeant told us in his most syrupy Southern accent, "Those of you whose mommies object to your yelling 'Kill, kill, kill!' are allowed to yell 'Lollipop!'" (And that is what my buddy Private Hughie Thurschwell, a graduate of the University of Chicago law school, and I did, in unison. As ferociously as we could, we yelled "Lollipop, lollipop, lollipop!" and then plunged the bayonet in.)

Robert Sherrill once wrote a book called *Military Justice Is to Justice as Military Music Is to Music*. The same thing might be said about military journalism. In the 1954 about-to-be-peacetime Army, at least they had the decency not to call military newspapers "the press." Instead, the papers were put out under the rubric of "Troop Information and Education," which had about it the vague odor of an East European Ministry of Education. But that didn't mean I had nothing to learn from the experience.

At the end of the first eight weeks of basic training in Camp Gordon, Georgia, they asked what I had done and what I wanted to do. In reality I had done nothing but go to school, but I made a big deal of having edited the Swarthmore *Phoenix,* having "worked" at *The Washington Post,* not to mention the prestigious *Berrow's Worcester Journal,* and I said I wanted to work on an Army newspaper. So, of course, they sent me to train as a medic at Fort Sam Houston, Texas.

At the end of my second eight weeks of basic training, the personnel officer asked where I would like to serve out the remainder of my two years. Phil Landeck, one of my old Swarthmore roommates, was working at the military press office at Fort Meade, just outside Washington, D.C. This seemed to me ideal duty, and Phil told me that if I succeeded in staying off an overseas roster he would arrange to requisition me for Stateside duty. So I said I'd prefer to serve in this country. Somehow my friend Phil's request must have gotten lost in the mail, because everyone in my unit who requested overseas duty was sent to a NATO post just outside Paris. Every coward who requested domestic duty—bear in mind that although the Korean War was officially over, we all believed it could erupt again at any moment—was shipped off to a medical company at Fort Richardson, just outside Anchorage, Alaska.

On my second day at Fort Richardson I paid a visit to the one-room, three-person office of *The 53rd Inf. News,* a mimeographed weekly that chronicled the doings of the 53rd Infantry Regiment, and told them I was available for duty in my off hours. They looked at me as if I was loopy, but the editor, a corporal with a nice Southern drawl named Max Kennedy, deputized me Medical Company correspondent and told me I should send in ad hoc notes of Medical Company news, which I proceeded to do every week. I guess because I was the *only* company correspondent who sent in regular weekly reports—what else was there to do, Alaska being much of the time too cold to go outside?—when Max was ready to rotate back to the States, where he had been accepted at the University of Virginia Law School, I received a call from the second lieutenant who ran the office asking whether I'd be interested in replacing Max. Although I was on the fast track at the Medical Company, where I was the number-two company clerk and in line to be a Specialist 3rd Class (which had the equivalent in pay of a corporal, with no KP!), I opted for what I thought was the glamour job (albeit with KP) and agreed to the transfer.

No sooner had I arrived than the lieutenant who had hired me (and who couldn't have been a nicer guy) informed me that his time would soon be up and he would be going back to North Dakota to run the family's printing business. His replacement, a Lieutenant William Kelly, was Regular Army. Now this was not great news. It was drummed into us that Alaska was America's first line of defense, for if the Russians were to invade the United States, they would do so by crossing the Bering Strait from Big Diamede (which they owned) to Little Diamede (which we owned) and then proceed to invade us by way of Canada. This was why, periodically, a whistle would blow and we would all put on our snow-shoes (technically we were in the ski troops, but members of headquarters company, which controlled Troop Information and Education, were issued snowshoes) to attend maneuvers at Big Delta, where temperatures sometimes ran to 70 degrees below zero. The high point of my military career, as a matter of fact, came on the last day of Operation Moose Horn, where I was editor of *The Moose Hornblower*, an ad hoc daily information sheet about life on maneuvers. As a fan of the radio comedian Jack Benny, who had famously starred in a B movie, *The Horn Blows at Midnight*, I got to write, and run as our farewell headline on the last day, "Moose Horn Blows at Midnight."

Presumably because of the weather, which routinely went down to 20 or 30 below in winter, unmarried troops lived where they worked and played where they lived. In the two-story barracks, the bunks were on the second floor, the offices and mess hall were on the main floor, and in the basement was a "playroom" with a TV, Ping-Pong, and pool tables and magazines. The post library, post PX, and post movie theater (which changed features nightly and charged 25 cents) were all within a few hundred yards, and for much of the year, life was primarily indoors. As a consequence, military discipline was lax, boots were not shined except for special occasions, and rising and saluting when an officer came into the room (SOP, according to the manual) would have been regarded as peculiar.

Lieutenant Kelly didn't like any of this. In fact, he hated it almost as much as his number-one grievance: West Pointers. "If you want to get anywhere in this man's Army," Kelly complained virtually every day, "you have to have gone to the Point. They discriminate against guys like me." Lieutenant Kelly, whose boots were always spit-shined, was a graduate of Gettysburg College.

He never said much about what went in the paper, maybe because he was too bored to read it. But he was always after the Troop Information and Education noncom (who, like Max, was on his way home) to have his weekly report ready ahead of time, to have the office "shaped up for inspection," and such.

Then one day word came down that we had a new TI&E man. "Navasky," Lieutenant Kelly said, "you're going to love this. Our new TI&E noncom has an M.A. from Harvard and he speaks Mandarin Chinese. A real intellectual," he added, his eyes rolling upward as he shook his head from side to side. What was this man's Army coming to? He seemed to like the idea of having a Harvard man to push around.

One sleepy afternoon around three o'clock, just after the sun had gone down, we heard an uncharacteristic knock on the already mostly open door. We looked up and there, in pressed uniform, heels on spit-shined boots conspicuously clicked together, stiff-armed salute executed in perfect form, was a ramrod-straight, blond, crew-cut young man sporting starched fatigues and belting out for all the world to hear, "Specialist 3rd Class Lynn C. Noah reporting for duty, SIR!!!"

Lieutenant Kelly returned the salute, a growing grin on his face as he nodded his approval and welcomed Specialist Noah to his command. "At ease," he actually said.

For the next half hour I couldn't help eavesdropping—it being a three-desk, three-person office—as Lieutenant Kelly briefed his new charge on what was expected of him in general, and in particular what he wanted from him by the end of the day. Noah kept "Yes, sir-ing" him, and when Lieutenant Kelly left, Noah was again on his feet saluting.

I was somewhat concerned that I was going to be outnumbered in what used to be a laid-back informal office by two spiritual RA's* (even if one of them was a Mandarin-speaking draftee with a Harvard degree). I needn't have worried. As soon as Kelly left, Noah put his spit-shined boots up on his desk and we proceeded to get to know each other. He was smart, funny, from Pittsburgh, with a wife who was returning from a Fulbright in India. As 5:30 approached, I couldn't help noticing that he had not done even one of the three tasks Kelly had as-

*Regular Army types.

signed him, and thought I should remind him, as a new friend, lest he incur the lieutenant's wrath unnecessarily.

Noah listened respectfully and chuckled. "Thanks for the reminder," he said, "but those things make no sense. We already have the data in reports prepared by Division headquarters."

Yes, I acknowledged, but Lieutenant Kelly asked for them, and my experience with Kelly told me that you had better do what you were asked.

Noah smiled. "I believe with Confucius," he said.

"And Confucius says?" I said.

"Confucius says that you should always be agreeable, but then you should do what is right."

Noah got along fine, and Lieutenant Kelly came to appreciate that he had someone he could rely on.

While still in the Army Noah applied for and got a job with USIA, but it was not until twenty-five years later, after serving in Beijing and throughout Southeast Asia, that he, along with Confucius, again appeared on my radar screen.

Don't let me mislead you. I did not spend all my time in Alaska imbibing spiritual wisdom from Specialist 3rd class Lynn Noah. I also secured some practical experience. I worked weekends as floor sweeper and bottle washer for a short-lived weekly called *The Alaska Nugget* (printed on gold-colored paper), a job I found out about through the *Anchorage Times* classified section. And when I saw the ad for a writer for an Alaska-based TV series, I sent off my idea to "Bailey Bell, c/o Movies, Inc." at the appropriate *Anchorage Times* P.O. box. Imagine my thrill a week or two later when Bailey Bell himself called and said, "We like your idea. Come on downtown and let's talk."

That Saturday I presented myself in the modest cabin in downtown Anchorage which he shared with his wife.

Bailey told me they had received many responses to their ad, but they liked mine best. As he explained, "Jack Webb and I used to be cameramen together in Hollywood. We were drinking buddies. We would hang out and talk about our dreams. And now," he said, "he's got

Dragnet, the number-one hit on television. And I just read in the papers that his wife is suing him for a $2 million divorce. This could happen to me!" Bailey's wife asked if she could get me a cup of coffee.

"All you need," he explained, "is an exotic locale, and we've got that right outside our window—Alaska—and you need some sex and violence. Just add some sex and a little more violence to your great idea and we're ready to go. When can you start?"

I had not yet read—although I knew about—Nathanael West's much celebrated novel *Miss Lonelyhearts*. The film *Lonelyhearts*, starring Montgomery Clift, didn't come out until 1958. Nevertheless it was the "inspiration" for my proposed series, working title "The Adventures of Emory Mack." Emory Mack, under the mentorship of his editor in chief, starts breaking front-page stories right out of college. At age twenty-four he wins a Pulitzer Prize for his investigation of municipal corruption. His boss is involuntarily retired for reasons of age and is now running an Alaska-based daily. Emory, having won the most coveted award in journalism in his early twenties and lost the boss who had taught him all he knew, feels burned out. He needs time off to think about what to do next. His canny old boss persuades him to move up to his own cabin in the woods in Alaska, where there are no distractions, and to pay his bills by writing the weekly advice-to-the-lovelorn column for *The Nugget*. He need never even come into the office. The formula for the series was that every week Mack would choose a letter to answer, and to answer it properly, he would conduct his own little investigation of the matter under consideration. Somehow, by mistake, week after week he would end up with a front-page story. Of course I could throw in a little sex and violence, and to make me feel less guilty, I would make sure that each show had its own built-in social message.

Bailey and his wife told me again that they loved it and they wanted to sign me up to write six episodes. Their idea was to film three of them and then use the tapes to try to sell the series. Bailey explained to me that I had a choice: I could get a flat fee on acceptance of my work or I could take a share of the profits, which might well be in the millions.

I harbored no illusions that I was gifted at business, but if I do say so myself, on this occasion I displayed mature business judgment.

"What would the fee be?" I asked.

"Twenty-five dollars," Bailey said.

"Per script?" I asked, like a seasoned negotiator.

"Yep," Bailey said.

"I'll take it," I said.

I had never written television scripts before, but I felt a sense of fulfillment in my work, partly because I persuaded myself that the little social homilies I smuggled into my scripts lent them some sort of moral dignity. One script was about hunting deer out of season, and the moral was "Be safe while hunting." In another, I wrote about a Miss Alaska contest (the ratio of men to women in Alaska those days was something like 19–1; what's a single soldier going to do?), and the moral was "Alaska should be a state." The only script Bailey turned down was one where I had the villain hide some stolen diamonds by implanting them in the bellies of live salmon (who according to the laws of nature would return to their spawning ground a year later). Even though I invented an ichthyologist who cited chapter and verse from the salmon literature, Bailey thought the idea was "far-fetched."

I offered to take the cans of film Bailey had shot and show them to a friend in the television business (my friend Phil again, by now out of the Army and making commercials and industrials) while visiting New York on my two-week Christmas furlough. Bailey thought that was a splendid idea.

Which is what I did. Phil arranged a screening. I was only mildly disappointed when he reported they were out of focus. But my $25-a-script was in the bank. Who said I wasn't a business ace?

One reason I had not been reluctant to be drafted was the G.I. Bill. My theory at the time was that while I might well eventually make a living as a writer, given what I had to say, the world could wait another three or four years to hear it while I carried on my education. And my real question was which sort of school did I want the government to pay for? Business school didn't occur to me. I thought I found in Yale Law School a way to carry on my liberal arts education while getting a law degree, which would keep my options open, because while part of me was interested in the literary life, the other part was interested in politics and public affairs. There was a second, complicating factor. The trick for draftees in the peacetime Army of those days—especially for those in Alaska who yearned to return to the States (remember, Alaska was not yet one)—was to get accepted by a school whose starting date was three months *before* one's ETS (Estimated Time of Separation). (Under the law your military service could be reduced from twenty-four to twenty-one months in the interests of education, but no more than that.) As a result, half the USARAL (U.S. Army, Alaska) command seemed to be attending Oneida College in Oneida, New York, because Oneida was one of the few colleges on the quarterly system. In my case I got accepted by both the University of Chicago Law School (on the quarterly system) and Yale Law School, which wasn't, and I accepted both. My plan was to attend Chicago for the first quarter, starting in June 1956, and then transfer to Yale in September.

I had applied to Yale, Harvard, and Chicago, and Yale was my first choice, based on a comparative analysis of catalogues, including the following warning in the entry for one Fred Rodell's writing workshop called "Law and Public Opinion": "Several alumni of this seminar have ended up in journalism instead of law."

Also, according to the reigning folklore, Yale was small (682) and Harvard was big (1,683); Yale trains judges, Harvard trains lawyers; Yale doesn't teach you any law (few requirements, many electives), Harvard teaches you nothing but (few electives, many requirements); Yale turns out socially conscious policy makers, Harvard turns out fastidious legal technicians; Yale thinks that judges invent the law, Harvard thinks that judges discover the law; Yale is preoccupied with social values, Harvard is preoccupied with abstract concepts; Yale is interested in personalities, Harvard is interested in cases; Yale thinks most legal doctrine is ritual mumbo jumbo, Harvard thinks it comprises a self-contained logical system; Yale cares about results, Harvard cares about precedents; Yale thinks the law is what the judge had for breakfast, Harvard thinks it is a brooding omnipresence in the sky. Chicago, as I saw it, was simply a great law school (and philosophically someplace in between).

Of course, once I arrived in Chicago and explained my intention to the dean of the University of Chicago Law School, he kicked me out or, rather, requested that I withdraw, pointing out that neither Chicago nor Yale would appreciate my plan: Chicago, because it did not want to waste a much-sought-after place in the entering class on a ne'er-do-well like me who had decided in advance that Chicago wasn't good enough for him, and Yale, because it would want to introduce me to the majesty of the law in its own way and not have my legal education contaminated at the outset by the Chicago school.

The meeting was slightly traumatic, but the outcome was fine by me. Before leaving Alaska I had taken the precaution of securing a letter from the editor of the *Anchorage Daily News* deputizing me to cover the upcoming 1956 Democratic Convention for his paper.

When I'd been editing (and writing) the *53rd Inf. News,* Headquarters Public Information Office would occasionally send out one of our stories to the local press. And one day "Old Knick," the pseudonymous columnist of *The Anchorage Daily News,* had plucked out something I had written in rather purple prose about a nighttime firing exercise and reprinted it in his column as a "textbook example" of either good or bad writing, I'm still not sure which. I had stopped by his Anchorage office to thank him for the plug and we became friends, sort of. When I learned I was going to Chicago, city of the big shoulders and of the Democratic Convention of 1956, I had fallen by Old Knick's office to see whether Old Knick could introduce me to the editor, whom I planned to ask whether it was conceivable to cover the quadrennial carnival (or at least get credentials to see it).

Old Knick had turned out to be a pseudonym for the editor himself. He couldn't have been a nicer guy, told me it was too late to apply for convention credentials and that they planned to rely on wire service coverage, but gave me an informal letter (a Letter of Introduction: I knew about those!). If I saw anything that I thought would be of special interest to Alaskans, the Eskimo crowd, I should send it on.

And that's what I did. In 1956 the nomination of Adlai Stevenson as presidential candidate was a foregone conclusion. But perhaps to add spice for the delegates and also because of his famous Hamlet-like capacity for indecision, Stevenson, unwilling or unable to decide on a running mate, opened up the process for the vice-presidential slot to a free-for-all, which in practice meant a horse race between the relatively unknown dashing young senator from Massachusetts, John F. Kennedy, and the populist, anti–organized-crime crusader and senator from Tennessee, Estes Kefauver. I contacted the Alaskan delegation, each member of which agreed to cooperate, i.e., let me follow them around as the Veep candidates' entourages did their lobbying. (In the end, Kefauver with his coonskin cap carried Alaska, with its frontier mentality, as he carried the convention.)

Now for the embarrassing part. What struck me, a penniless veteran and out-of-work student, about the convention was something I had read about nowhere: Everything was free. Beautiful young women in candy-striped miniskirts poured free Pepsi-Cola at all the convention hotels. Corporations, especially Bell Telephone, gave lavish cocktail parties and hosted hospitality suites with hors d'oeuvres fit for, well, a delegate. Helicopters and buses ferried delegates and members of the press to the convention hall. With my letter I had talked my way into "perimeter" credentials, which meant I had access to a rotating press pass for periodic visits to the convention floor.

On my first day, when I ran into a college friend, Franz Leichter (he went on to become a state senator from the West Side of Manhattan), we naturally went off for a free lunch. He told me his father was covering the convention for an Austrian news service, and he was there because it was his dream to participate in a demonstration on the floor. I told him what I was doing and confessed that my only problem was that I had no place to type my stories without going home (an hour away). He said, no problem: The Western Union office has free typewriters. Sure enough, there in the basement of the convention hotel was a room full of tables, chairs, and scores, hundreds maybe, of free typewriters.

I sat down at one to type my first story, and I was about halfway through and thinking about my next sentence when a man with a Western Union badge tapped me on the shoulder and asked me, "Ready to go yet?" And being only halfway through I said quite naturally, "Not yet." When I finished, about a half hour later, the same man asked me if I had finished. I said yes and he asked, "Where is it going?" And I said to Anchorage, Alaska, the *Anchorage Daily News.*

"Hey, Joe!" he yelled to a man behind the counter near the entrance to the great hall, "Do we go to Alaska?" Joe took out a thick book from his drawer, looked something up, and said, "Yeah, sure."

The day after I filed my first story, when the Anchorage newspapers arrived by airplane for the Anchorage delegates, they contained no evidence of my work. I assumed my copy had arrived too late for inclusion, which didn't deter me from what became a daily ritual for the remainder of the convention. Every afternoon around 4:00, I would go down to the Western Union office and type my story and file it with Joe, who would send it via Western Union to Anchorage. The wonders of modern technology never cease to amaze.

As the daily paper arrived, each unaccountably missing my story, my credibility with the delegation seemed to suffer some slippage. I don't know why it didn't occur to me to call Old Knick, but it didn't. It was inconvenient, and calls to Alaska were, by my standards, by *any* standards, exorbitantly expensive. (I think I had one long-distance call from or to my parents during my entire Alaskan tour of military duty.) I guess, somewhere in my subconscious, I also feared he would not take the call.

On the fourth day of the convention I ran into Franz Leichter again. Having taken part in a demonstration on the floor, he was in the highest of spirits. He introduced me to his father, the Austrian correspondent, who asked me what I thought of the convention.

I said a few things about how the Kennedy camp seemed better organized than the Kefauver one, yet in the Alaskan delegation that same no-nonsense Kennedy efficiency seemed to spur resentment rather than affection. Then I said as a joke, "But my *real* discovery at this convention is how much you can get for nothing. Pepsi's are free. Dinner is free. Helicopter rides are free. Western Union is free—"

"Western Union is free?" he asked skeptically. "Are you sure?" he added diplomatically.

His son Franz was the man who had tipped me off to it, so why was he asking? And then it occurred to me for the first time that Franz had mentioned only free typewriters. "Excuse me," I said, mumbling something about an urgent appointment and making a beeline for the basement.

I boldly walked up to the counter and with fingers crossed asked, "How much does it cost to send a wire to Anchorage, Alaska?"

My heart sank as he took out his thick blue book and traced his finger across the pages. "Eleven cents a word," he said.

"For the *press*?" I said.

"Oh," he said, "our press rate is . . ."

I didn't hear *what* he said. I was crestfallen and humiliated at the same time. As far as I was concerned, it could have been thousands of dollars or hundreds, it made no difference. I didn't have the heart to ask whether my copy had been sent collect, whether it had been accepted or rejected (before or after it was read), or what.

Instead, I went to one of the free typewriters, put a piece of paper in, and started typing. Six pages later I had told Old Knick the whole story of my failed escapade, apologized, offered to reimburse the paper for all costs, and asked if he had even read my stories, and if so, what did he think of them. This time I did not give my copy to Joe. I put it in an envelope, bought the necessary stamps, and sent it by airmail.

To this day I do not know whether Old Knick's silence speaks for itself or whether, since it hadn't occurred to me to register my letter, he never got it, either.

2

"IN THE LAND
OF THE BLIND . . ."

In the 1950s it seemed possible to go through Yale Law School and not learn any law. The curriculum included a course on "Freud and Jurisprudence," which I took, and "Law and the Behavioral Sciences," which I took, and "Law and the Arts," which I took (okay, it covered copyright law and intellectual property), and "Law and Public Opinion," that course on writing about the law for non-lawyers which was one of the reasons I had wanted to go to Yale in the first place. It was taught by Fred Rodell, who in 1936 had written an article for the *University of Virginia Law Review* entitled, "Farewell to Law Reviews" that began: "There are two things wrong with all legal writing: One, its content and two, its style." He vowed never to write another footnote and didn't. I not only took his course but in my third year worked for him as his legal research instructor. His seminars met down the street from the law school at Mory's, the place where the Whiffenpoofs assembled.

Another course I took was "Law, Science and Policy." (Fred called it "Law, Science and Polisyllabics" because its teachers, Harold Lasswell and Myres MacDougall, saw law as a "policy science" requiring a language of its own.) Lasswell, a past president of the American Political Science Association, was a leading lay analyst and gourmet cook. MacDougall, president of the World Law Association, who was virtually blind and held his reading materials within an inch or two of his thick glasses, nevertheless saw things whole. (On the side, they also taught a noncredit seminar for selected faculty from within and outside the law school on how the Supreme Court makes up its mind, which I and one other law student were permitted to sit in on.)

The year I got to New Haven, Yale inaugurated an experimental program whereby each law student had to "concentrate" in one or another division (corporations, taxes, contracts, etc.). I chose public (or constitutional) law, and I'm glad I did. We got to go to a weekly seminar at the homes of the professors who oversaw our division—Rodell, Thomas Emerson, Louis Pollack (who later became dean and then a federal judge), and the young Alexander Bickel, who famously had clerked for Justice Felix Frankfurter and was fast becoming the country's foremost exponent of Frankfurterian judicial restraint.

Since the controversial Fred Rodell, who exchanged dirty limericks with the Supreme Court's leading judicial activist, William O. Douglas, helped First Amendment fundamentalist Justice Hugo Black select his law clerks, and liked to boast that he had been described as a "pathological critic of Justice Felix Frankfurter, in the Neanderthal wing of the visceral school of jurisprudence," we students always looked forward to the jurisprudential fireworks. From our perspective, these weekly seminars were more dramatic than opening night at the Shubert Theatre, which featured out-of-town try-out plays on their way to Broadway. The chief antagonists were Yale-trained Rodell and young Harvard-trained Bickel. A typical exchange between the cowboy-hatted, tieless Rodell and the three-piece-suited Bickel, who sported an F.D.R.-style cigarette holder, was, it seemed to me at the time, an ideal introduction to the niceties of jurisprudence. (In retrospect, I realize that it was not a bad introduction to the culture and subcultures of the journal of opinion either: Rodell was a contributing editor at *The Progressive*, the populist monthly based in Madison, Wisconsin, and Bickel was a contributing editor at *The New Republic*, the insider, establishment-liberal weekly based in Washington.)

When Bickel cited an opinion by Justice Douglas as an example of shallow judicial thinking, Rodell's riposte was that while those were Justice Douglas's words, what he "really meant" was much more radical:

BICKEL: I may be naïve, Fred, but when a Justice of the United States Supreme Court says x, I believe he means x.
RODELL: You're right, Alex, you are naïve.*

*Floyd Abrams, who went on to be a distinguished First Amendment lawyer, was another student in this seminar. He later was instrumental in bringing Bickel onto the *Times*'s legal team in the Pentagon papers case.

Along with Rodell, the legendary Tom Emerson was another of the magnets who drew me to Yale. He called himself a First Amendment absolutist, was perhaps the leading First Amendment scholar of his day, and had assembled the first casebook on political and civil rights and liberties. He was president of the controversial National Lawyers Guild, a McCarthy-era target, and he had been a candidate for the governorship of Connecticut on Henry Wallace's Progressive Party ticket, but withdrew when the Democrats put up Chester Bowles, for whom he had worked in the federal Office of Price Administration (OPA) during the war. He taught the first-ever course in an American law school on political and civil rights (which I took). He was known affectionately as "Tommy the Commie" (he wasn't), perhaps to distinguish him from his fellow civil libertarian the tax professor Boris Bittker, known as "Borey the Tory" (which he wasn't; he was head of the local chapter of the American Civil Liberties Union, whose newsletter I came to write and edit).

When, after my first day of class in Administrative Law with Emerson, a classmate asked me to sum it up in one word, I said, to my own surprise, "dull." And it was dull. Here was this old Turk, in a faculty said to be made up of Old Turks and Young Fogies, sticking to the boring facts, and what's worse, he was understated, had a tendency to mumble and laugh nervously, and was fair and reasonable. Yet it was through this modest, well-mannered man, who parted his white hair neatly in the middle and wore three-piece dark suits to class, that I got not just my introduction to the constitutional law of civil liberty but also a taste of the Cold War culture on the civil-liberties left, and the behind-the-scenes dramas that formed the backdrop for the struggle to preserve the legal rights and liberties of the rest of us.

I knew a little about the ACLU because when I was at Swarthmore, Patrick Murphy Malin, an economics professor, had resigned to become the ACLU's National Executive Director and had taken the occasion to explain the importance of protecting the right to free speech in the age of McCarthyism. What he had neglected to say, however, was that at that very moment the ACLU was under attack from its *left* for its failure to represent Communists at the trial level and, more generally, for its timidity where the rights of Communist Party members were concerned. The ACLU had kicked Elizabeth Gurley Flynn, an open Communist, off its board (years later it was to posthumously reinstate her). As a result, in 1953 non-Communists and fellow-travelers like Emerson, Carey McWilliams, and I. F. Stone, with a healthy assist from the progressive philanthropic humanist Corliss Lamont (one of whose ancestors had edited *The Nation* way back when), gave birth to a new old-left organization, the Emergency Civil Liberties Committee (ECLC), dedicated to protecting the rights of all, Commies included.

By and large, the two organizations had little use for each other. The leadership of the ACLU identified itself with the anti-Communist ethos of the day, which ECLC was organized to resist. But New Haven was an early exception to this antagonism, and therein lies my tale.

One day a sign went up on the law school bulletin board. The subject: "The Ten Things Wrong with the House Un-American Activities Committee." The speaker: Joseph L. Rauh, Jr., a well-known liberal and anti-Communist lawyer. The sponsors were listed as the Yale Law Forum, a student group, and the New Haven Civil Liberties Council, which I later discovered was an amalgam of the ACLU and the ECLC. It seems that New Haven was the only community in the country where the active members of the ACLU and the ECLC spoke to each other. Not only that, they got on so well that to avoid jurisdictional overlap they merged. The reason New Haven was able to do that, a veteran New Haven civil liberties activist explained to me, was that there was this fellow on the law faculty, Tom Emerson, who belonged to both organizations! So how could they not talk to each other?

Rauh had recently won a major victory on behalf of a client, the playwright Arthur Miller, who had been indicted for contempt of Congress when he declined to answer questions put to him by the House Un-American Activities Committee about a Communist Party meeting he had attended many years earlier. Arthur Miller was scheduled to introduce Rauh, and the rumor was that Miller's new bride, Marilyn Monroe, would accompany him to the lecture. The auditorium was packed. Never in the history of the Yale Law School had so many budding young corporate lawyers shown such interest in civil liberties, not to mention the ten things wrong with the Un-American Activities Committee.

Unbeknownst to the throngs, a tense drama was playing itself out offstage. Only after he accepted the invitation to speak (which he had received on the innocent stationery of the Yale Student Law Forum) did Rauh discover that the Emergency Civil Liberties Committee, which he regarded as a Communist front (in the parlance of the day) was co-sponsor of the event, and worse, on the platform would be Rabbi Robert Goldburg, chairman of the ECLC, who also happened to be president of an organization called the American Committee for the Protection of the Foreign Born, which had recently won itself a place of pride on the list of subversive organizations kept by the Attorney General's office ever since 1948.

Since the ECLC, unlike the ACLU, had no explicit policy forbidding Communists from being on their board, Rauh let it be known that while he would honor his speaking engagement, he would feel compelled in the course of the evening to disassociate himself from ECLC sponsorship. When Miller heard this, he was in a tough spot, because Rabbi Goldburg, among other accomplishments, had performed the marriage ceremony between Miller and Ms. Monroe. Reluctant to choose between his lawyer and his rabbi, Miller decided to solve the problem by staying home. This left only Rabbi Goldburg to introduce Rauh, and he did so with one of the shorter introductions on record. It went something like: "Whatever you think about Joe Rauh, he's a helluva lawyer."

For his part, Rauh proceeded to enumerate the ten things wrong with the House Un-American Activities Committee, but when he finished he added, that although of course he disapproved of HUAC, "which gives anti-Communism a bad name, occasionally they do something useful. For instance, they bring to public attention the true background and politics of organizations (like ECLC)." At this point Professor Emerson stood up and said, "I rise to say a few words in defense of the Emergency Civil Liberties Committee," which he proceeded to do by pointing out that the two organizations had differing perceptions about the threat that Communism posed to the United States; that ECLC thought the Communists posed little or no "clear and present domestic danger"; and that, in any event, the New Haven Civil Liberties Council believed in defending the rights of all, Communists included.

At Yale I perfected an art form I had begun at Swarthmore and carried forward at Fort Richardson: the art of procrastination-by-browsing, preferably in an open-shelf periodical room. At Fort Richardson I had gotten in trouble when I put in a request that the post library subscribe to *The Reporter*, Max Ascoli's liberal fortnightly. I was summoned to explain myself when it turned out that a newsletter of the same name was the house organ of an institution on the Attorney General's list of subversive organizations. Luckily for me, although I didn't know it at the time, Max Ascoli was famously anti-Communist (I knew only that I enjoyed the sophisticated contributions from writers like Douglass Cater, Dan Wakefield, and the young Meg Greenfield, who went on to be editor of the *Washington Post*'s editorial page). It wasn't as if I knew what I was looking for.

Then one day in New Haven in May 1957 I hit the jackpot. The magazine was *The Nation*, the writer was Dalton Trumbo, who had gone to prison as a member of the Hollywood Ten, the article was about the Hollywood blacklist. I had seen the Oscars (I was a multimedia procrastinator) and been mystified when a screenwriter named Robert Rich had failed to pick up his Oscar for a movie called *The Brave One*. Trumbo's essay explained (by not explaining) that when people asked him if Robert Rich was or wasn't his pseudonym, he "cannily" declined to say. He did point out that he had no known means of employment, yet he managed to maintain a house with a swimming pool, a wife and three children, and a ranch in the country. Yet nobody ever accused him of writing lousy B pictures under a pseudonym, and every time the authorship of a masterpiece was in question, his name would be rumored. Under these conditions, only a fool, he said, would affirm or deny authorship.

I had long been interested in the blacklist. At Elisabeth Irwin I had had friends whose parents were blacklisted. In the summer between my first and second year at Swarthmore I had worked as a bellhop at the Seven Keys Lodge in the Adirondacks, where one day we were visited by FBI agents who wanted to know about a guest, the actor J. Edward Bromberg (scruffy luggage, I could have told them). This former member of the Group Theatre had been subpoenaed before the House Committee on Un-American Activities, but had been excused on the basis of his doctor's certification that such an appearance would put too great a strain on his heart, already weakened from heart disease. When the agents discovered that he engaged in daily water sports, his subpoena was reissued, he was forced to appear, and a few months later he died. Someday, I had thought, maybe I would write something about it. At the time, however, it was enough to peruse *The Nation*. Anything to avoid my law school studies.

But my real interest in my years at law school was a magazine. We called it *Monocle*, "a leisurely quarterly of political satire," which meant it came out twice a year. Its motto was "In the land of the blind the one-eyed man is king," and our editorial policy was that "the views of our contributors, no matter how conflicting and contradictory, are the views of the editors." Tailgunner Joe McCarthy and his ilk were still very much in the news and our object was to question the official line but also to launch some trial balloons (at *Monocle* we had our own Trial Balloon Factory), while we punctured the pretensions of others.

As Carey McWilliams once observed about investigative journalism, it takes just one pinprick to collapse a balloon.

I quickly learned that if you wanted to start a magazine of political satire and you had limited resources, the Yale Law School was the place to be. The Yale Graduate School of Design was only a couple of blocks away and numbered among its students the future art directors of some of the most elegant magazines in America, all eager to fill their portfolios, while its faculty was willing to grant course credit for the students' work for *Monocle*.

The law school was also down the block from the department of philosophy, where my friend Jacob Needleman, who was to become one of the country's leading metaphysicians, was doing his graduate work. When I asked him whether he would join me in launching a magazine of political satire, his only reservation was nonmetaphysical. He had applied for a Fulbright scholarship to study abroad, and he was concerned that his affiliation with a politically subversive magazine, even one in the innocent guise of a satirical journal, might jeopardize his application.

Luckily for us, he overcame his qualms, and as a result, our first number featured a series of cryptic if intentionally pretentious parables under the simple heading "A Fable."

He stood on the street corner waiting for the light to turn green and permit him to cross. But the light remained red. The traffic was indeed heavy running against him, but considering even this, the light was taking an inexplicably long time to change color. Still, he waited. Many hours passed and the light failed to become green. The traffic had long since died away and now, in the small hours of the morning, there had appeared no automobiles for ten minutes. The light remained red and he did not cross—only waited. At length the sun began to rise: the streets were clean and clear with an occasional milk truck accentuating the silence and desolation. He stood up and gathering all his courage inside him dashed across the street against the light, which had not changed. At that precise moment a black automobile wheeled in a frenzy around the corner and struck him. He was rushed to a hospital where he soon died of internal injuries.

MORAL: Never disobey the law.

Needleman took off on his Fulbright after our first issue (and Larry Pearl, a law student classmate far better organized than I, took his place on the masthead). But my civil liberties education took another great leap forward when Needleman returned from Europe on the same ship as the beat poet Allen Ginsberg, who a few months earlier had made national headlines for having disrobed at a poetry reading in Los Angeles. Ginsberg wanted to read at Yale and sent Needleman a postcard asking if he could arrange it. Needleman made a few inquiries and got no takers, so he asked me if I had any ideas. Well, I said, I pass this place called the Jewish Community Center every day on my walk to school. They always seem to be advertising one or another cultural event. Maybe they would be interested. I knew from an article I had read in *Time* magazine that Ginsberg was a Buddhist (he kept sending Needleman Zen koans on postcards—my favorite was "Even the minimum smells of garlic"), but I figured he sounded Jewish.

The next day Needleman called to tell me the bad news. At his meeting the executive director of the JCC expressed concern that Ginsberg might do something that would be offensive to its members. Needleman said not to worry, he would ask Ginsberg to promise not to take his clothes off. But suppose he says something offensive? They then proceeded to have a discussion about what would and wouldn't offend the center's upper-middle-class Jewish constituency. As Needleman explained it, "He wanted me to guarantee that Ginsberg wouldn't say anything worse than 'shit,' and I didn't feel I could do that." (Eventually, Ginsberg did receive an invitation from an undergraduate society, the reading was a great success, and he and his friend the poet Peter Orlovsky spent the night on my floor. Twenty-five years later, when we served together on the Board of American PEN, the writers' organization, it was hard for me to get that image out of my head.)

We chose a unique format for *Monocle* (tall and thin, with bookjacket-type flaps), literally used wrapping paper for our first cover, and illustrated all the articles with variations on woodcuts in the public domain, lending the proceedings a nineteenth-century air which an English professor writing in the *Yale Daily News* found reminiscent of the famous *Punch* cartoonists Leech and Tenniel. The look was so arresting that we were able to persuade a local printer to provide free paper in exchange for our giving him permission to use a press overrun of fifty copies (we printed only five hundred) as free samples to attract new printing customers.

The law faculty itself turned out to be a source of unexpected talent. We knew that Rodell could write, but it was not until he shared with us one of the dirty limericks that he famously used to exchange with Justice Douglas that we made him our limericks editor. Here are two clean ones he tossed off for our pilot number (eventually he wrote one for every member of the Warren Court):

> A Connecticut Senator Dodd
> Has a habit a little bit odd—
> Since to speak for his State
> Wouldn't carry much weight
> He purports to be speaking for God.

> If the medical care bill won't pass
> So the aged are paid for en masse,
> Then the halt and the lame

Will know just who to blame—
The American Medical Ass.

I knew that Charles L. Black, Jr., who taught constitutional law, had helped draft the NAACP Legal Defense and Educational Fund's brief that led to the historic *Brown v. Board of Education* decision, and I knew (because he said so in *The New Republic*, to which he was a sometime contributor) that this Texas-born white professor felt closest to his black students. What I didn't know until I wrote a profile of him for the *Yale Law Report*, a glossy bimonthly aimed at alumni, was that writing under the name Charles Lund, he was a secret poet. So we got him to write a poem for *Monocle*: "This White Citizen Considers a Fearful Possibility":

> If a colored man should carry
> Some relation who was dear to me
> Out of the middle of an edifice aflame,
> What on earth would I say
> If he wanted to live near to me,
> Or objected when I called him by his Christian name?
> . . .
> So my feeble distaff kindred, let it ever more behoove you
> To go easy with the kerosene,
> And never smoke in bed,
> But if conflagration happens,
> And a black man would remove you,
> Send him packing, please, I'm begging you,
> And burn to death instead.

Even my fellow law students turned out to be something of a talent pool. Richard Lingeman, who ultimately left the law for *Monocle*, then left *Monocle* for *The New York Times Book Review*, and years later (in 1978) defected from the *Times* to become executive editor of *The Nation*, took time out from studying for his tax exam to write a parody of T. S. Eliot ("April is the accrualist month"); and Charles J. Levy, who eventually left the law for sociology, footnoted Emma Lazarus's poem at the base of the Statue of Liberty with appropriate passages from the most repressive anti-immigrant legislation of the McCarthy period, the McCarran-Walter Immigration Act:

> *Give me your tired* unless they are aliens who are polygamists or who practice polygamy or advocate for the practice of polygamy,
> *Your poor* unless they are aliens who are paupers, professional beggars or vagrants,
> *Your huddled masses yearning to breathe free* unless they are aliens who are afflicted with tuberculosis in any form . . . etc.

On the business side there was my classmate Charles J. Prentiss, the most successful ad salesman I've ever met. Chuck, a graduate of Queens College in New York City, had a foolproof sales technique, halfway between a sit-in and a filibuster. He would, for example, go into Rosey's Cleaners and wait patiently for Rosey himself, then he would tell Rosey about *Monocle* and perhaps even immodestly quote to Rosey, who couldn't have cared less, from his own modest contribution to the magazine: "Oh, why has the radical/Taken a sabbatical?" Then, without quite saying so, he would make clear that since he gave Rosey more than $300 worth of dry-cleaning business in the course of a semester, it wouldn't be smart business for Rosey not to take out one $100 half-page ad per semester. And then the clincher: He would whip out a prototype ad custom-made in advance for Rosey (by a graphic-arts graduate student working for credit), saying, "The art work is free of charge." Every time a new customer came in during this performance, Chuck would graciously suspend his pitch, only to resume when the customer left. After an hour of this, Rosey or Chuck's other targets would get the message. If they took an ad, Chuck would leave. These days Chuck Prentiss, a genius who made the law review and graduated near the top of his class, sells health insurance and spends his nights singing his ditties at piano bars around town.

Volume I, number 1, which I had typed on an Olivetti, was barely off the photo-offset presses when I received a pink summons from the New Haven postmaster informing me that the 400 copies we were attempting to ship to various parts of the country were on hold pending my appearance at the New Haven post office.

I of course immediately assumed that the copies were impounded for

seditious libel and proceeded to assemble my case: Supreme Court
opinions by Justices Hugo Black and William O. Douglas, the great First
Amendment absolutists on the Warren Court; copious references and
citations to John Peter Zenger, the eighteenth-century printer who had
been imprisoned for seditious libel in 1734 but won an historic jury verdict in 1735 because, as his eminent attorney Andrew (Alexander's
brother) Hamilton argued, for the words to be libelous they must be
"false, malicious and seditious or else we are not guilty." I put on my
J. Press tie, packed my toothbrush, and went downtown to face the music.

Imagine my disappointment on discovering that we were not the
victims of McCarthyite censors, after all. Rather, according to the
postmaster, we had improperly declared ourselves to be "second-class
matter." To that, I had to plead guilty. When I was typing up our masthead, I noticed that *Harper's* magazine, under *its* masthead, had called
itself "second-class matter," and since *Monocle*, like *Harper's*, was a
magazine, I had blithely assumed, and entered in tiny type on our
masthead, that we were, too.

But I now learned that to obtain second-class mailing privileges one
has to publish at least four times a year at regular intervals, the publication must have an established list of subscribers and a known office,
and it must meet sundry other bureaucratic requirements (including
payment of an application fee), none of which we had met. In fact, it
was somewhat tactlessly explained, we were fourth-class matter.

I briefly tried to argue that we were a first-class magazine. I cited
Oliver Jensen's Gettysburg address in Eisenhowerese ("I haven't checked
these figures yet, but eighty-seven years ago, I think it was . . ."), but to
no avail. I didn't even get a chance to make the case that Karla Kuskin's
send-up of a Billy Graham ad asking readers to send 10 cents to his
Kingdom Come, Inc., and find salvation was a valuable exposé of
mail fraud. The postmaster wasn't interested, but I know you would
have been:

> Incorporated Lord above
> Whose slogans end with light and love,
> Enclosed find dime
> Accept it please
> And in exchange send hope and ease
> A message honeyed, balmed and planned

To rhyme, that we many understand
From darkness unto light we go
Praising BBD and O
Clipping coupons so that we
Might dwell one day our Lord with Thee.*

We lost the argument, and my fellow miscreants and I were sentenced to countless hours of manual labor as we laboriously crossed out, copy by copy, the line about our nonexistent postal status, using the blue pencils thoughtfully provided by the New Haven postal authorities.

Second-class matter is no laughing matter, and has a long glorious history, I learned later. And ironically, in 1996, after I became *The Nation*'s publisher, I found myself testifying before an obscure Washington-based agency called the Postal Rate Commission, pleading with the commissioners not to abolish this category that *Monocle* didn't qualify for but that *The Nation* and virtually all other journals of opinion depend on for their survival.

But at the time, the intervention of the New Haven post office seemed but a bureaucratic irritant. I had naïvely assumed that magazines were primarily about writers and readers, about editorial and artistic content. The post office, advertisers, printers, and all the rest I thought of as mere facilitators. But I learned otherwise. Putting out this modest little journal of political satire and social criticism taught

---

*Karla wrote under the transparent pseudonym of k*s*k, Karla Seidman Kuskin; she went on to a career as a prizewinning children's book author. For *Monocle*, she also wrote and illustrated a series of political allegories. *The Rocky Road Upward* told the heartwarming story of two little fellows. One was "very rich and handsome." The other "has tasted poverty." The rich little boy "had an awful lot of beautiful sisters and smart, handsome brothers and he went to the very best schools." The poor young man "had a couple of siblings, one of whom got fat and borrowed money. He struggled against tremendous odds and went to second-rate schools." The rich little boy returned from the wars "covered with medals and glory." When the war was over the poor young man "came home." The rich young man's "hair fell over his eyes and he had a splendid smile." The poor young man's "hair receded and on the advice of friends he smiled infrequently." On January 20, 1961, the rich young man became President of the United States of America. "His beautiful wife was there to see him take the oath of office. So were his mommy an daddy and sisters and brothers and masses of glorious people like statesmen and humanitarians. Robert Frost and Tony Curtis were there." The poor young man "was forty-seven years old and he went home with Pat." The moral (presented in an elaborately embroidered frame): "Think it over, Horatio, baby."

me that virtually every aspect of magazine publication is dictated either by a bureaucracy like the post office, or by a specific business interest or by what my Harvard Business School colleagues would call market considerations.

At *Monocle* our theory had been that a magazine's price should reflect its value. Thus, if one issue was worth $10, we should charge $10, but if we deemed the next issue inferior, thinner or whatever, and only worth 50 cents, we should charge only 50 cents. But we soon learned that in the traditional magazine business the price is the same for every issue, so that newsdealers don't get confused. It makes life easier for them.

At *Monocle* we believed that the ideal magazine ought to permit its contents to determine its look—including its shape, size, and paper quality. Why not look like what you are? If you really think what you are publishing won't endure, newsprint isn't bad for wrapping fish; but if you think what you have published should be part of the reader's permanent collection, how about perfect binding on special, heavy paper stock? But in the conventional magazine business one orders paper in bulk to achieve economy of scale.

At *Monocle* at first we thought we could beat the system with our tall, skinny 5 x 11 format, but one prints in standard sizes to accommodate printing presses, and later we had to make an adjustment.

At *Monocle* we thought a magazine should come out when it has something to say rather than have its frequency dictated by moon cycles as interpreted by the post office. But magazines are published weekly or monthly or quarterly to conform to postal regulations.

We didn't see any editorial reason why books and arts coverage had invariably to appear in the same place, but we learned that magazine sections, like the book reviews and the arts coverage, always appear in the same relative position, to enable advertisers to buy position.

Meanwhile, there was law school to get through. At Yale, once one finished the first semester it was possible, through adroit selection, to take only courses that required papers rather than exams. And this, too, although I didn't think of it at the time, helped to launch me on a writing-editing career in the direction of *The Nation*.

The issue of racial quotas was barely bubbling up (the term "affirmative action" had not yet entered the national vocabulary), and I wrote my thesis on "The Benevolent Quota in Housing," the attempt to integrate housing through so-called benign quotas. Were they legal? Were they desirable? Did they work? Without my knowledge Fred Rodell had submitted it to the *Yale Law Journal* for possible publication, though it had a policy against publishing student work under student bylines.

And one day he gave me the good news. If I was willing to work with the editors over the summer, they might be interested in publishing a revised, unsigned version of my paper as a "comment" (a term of art for student scholarship of some length), and my name would appear on the journal's masthead as one of the (student) editors. This was no small matter, as it meant that forever after I would be eligible to attend the prestigious annual law journal banquet and my résumé would gain an ornament much in favor among the hiring partners of the top Wall Street firms. Since I already had summer plans and since I doubted that my destiny lay on Wall Street, I passed up the opportunity. Instead, on the theory that an article about racial quotas might find a home in a journal whose main focus was race, I submitted it to the *Howard Law Journal*, confessed that it was a student paper (threw in that it had won the Benjamin Scharps Prize for best paper by a third-year student), and *mirabile dictu*, it was accepted more or less as I had written it. A year later it appeared with my name on it, no less.

Besides, editing *Monocle* turned out to have some unexpected fringe benefits. I got a job offer from Roger Price, a talented stand-up comic and inventor of Droodles. The only way to explain a Droodle is to show one:

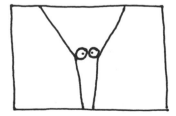

The above is either a dry martini with two olives or, if you turn the page upside down, a cross-eyed member of the Ku Klux Klan.

Here's another:

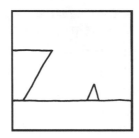

Ship arriving too late to save a drowning witch.

He was starting a publishing company, Price Stern Sloan, and they were interested in publishing either *Monocle* or a new magazine, which he called *Grump*. And if that didn't work out, his lawyer Charles Rembar, who turned out to be a leading practitioner of literary law, told me I could always go to work for his firm. (His clients included his cousin Norman Mailer and the avant-garde publisher Barney Rossett.) And when Dean Eugene V. D. Rostow discovered that *Monocle*, which he had picked up at a local newsstand, was the product of Yale Law students, he took parental pride in it. So when a friend on the staff of Michigan governor G. Mennen "Soapy" Williams, the darkest of horses in the upcoming 1960 Democratic presidential sweepstakes, asked Rostow if he could recommend a speechwriter, and the dean asked his assistant to pass on the résumés of possible candidates, his assistant—who also happened to have gone to Swarthmore (it does get incestuous, doesn't it?)—threw in mine; and because I was the only candidate with no speechwriting experience, when the dean sent the résumés to Michigan, he said nice things about me, which Soapy's people mistakenly read as making me *primus inter pares*. Also, I was younger and less expensive than the others, and it didn't hurt that the latest issue of *Monocle* included a parody of presidential politics in the form of a Monopoly game (which the instructions said "should be played in a smoke-filled room") whose object was "to get from log cabin to White House." The opening square read: "You do not choose to run. All you want is to be a good governor. Go ahead 4." I got the job.

Not counting a paper I wrote for Tom Emerson's civil liberties seminar on "Deportation as Punishment" that appeared in the *Kansas City
Law Review* (also one of the few law reviews in the country at the time
willing to publish law student work under law student bylines), the first
article I wrote that was ever published in a national magazine appeared
in *Frontier*, a small California-based journal of opinion, in October of
1958. It derived from a paper I'd written for my seminar on Law and the
Arts about the legality of a Jack Benny spoof of the Boyer-Bergman
movie, *Gaslight*, called "Autolight." I argued that in ruling against Benny
because of similarities in "characters," "dialogue," "climax," etc., the
California court of appeals had counted what it couldn't comprehend,
and that its decision, which confused parody with plagiarism, was itself
a parody of the judicial process. I added that parody was a legitimate
form of social criticism and as such was entitled to First Amendment
protection. (Despite my Steiner background, I am not a theosophist or
any other kind of mystic, but am I really supposed to think it is a mere
coincidence that eight years later a small box appeared in the February
27, 1967, issue of *The Nation* announcing: "As of this issue, *Frontier*
Magazine has merged with *The Nation*"?)

Six months after I went to work for Soapy, I had an idea for an article
he might write. It called for an invigorated Democratic Advisory Council,
a progressive counterpart to today's centrist Democratic Leadership
Council. I did a draft, Soapy made his adjustments, and his press secretary sent it off—surprise!—to *The Nation*, whose enterprising editor
Carey McWilliams had asked him the previous year for a submission.
Carey liked it. *The Nation* published it. So my first article in *The Nation*
appeared in the summer of 1960, on the eve of the Democratic Convention in Los Angeles, under the byline of G. Mennen Williams.

Simultaneously—on the theory that whether or not it's true that
you can't take it with you, but you can always give it the old college try—
we Yale Law students who had started *Monocle* tried to take it with us
when we graduated. This was shortly after a young man named Hugh
Hefner had an idea for a new magazine, *Playboy*, which he claimed to
have started with an investment of $500. We didn't have $500, but on
the strength of *Monocle* I had won a scholarship to the Radcliffe Publishing Procedures summer course my last year of law school. I witnessed there a parade of circulation, direct mail, publishing, and other

guest speakers. My fellow students who were job hunting thought of the passing parade as potential employers, but since I already had *Monocle*, I regarded them as free consultants.

When Abner Seidman, circulation director of *Look*, lectured, I asked him how one got on newsstands in New Haven, for example. His advice couldn't have been more practical. "Call my friend So-and-so, who is New Haven's (monopoly) newsstand wholesaler, and tell him Abner said to put you on his newsstands." I did and he did.

And when *Playboy*'s associate publisher, A. C. Spectorsky, came through, I asked him how much it would cost to make *Monocle* a monthly magazine. He said—this was 1958—it would cost $500,000, "but if you have $500,000, why would you want to start a magazine?"

Incidentally, on my first day in Cambridge, I opened up an issue of the *Harvard Crimson* only to find a dazzling assault on *Monocle* by one John Leonard, who appeared to be a sophomore. He attacked our patronage (Yale), he attacked our tall and thin shape (in Freudian terms no less), he attacked our content (as warmed-over anti-McCarthyism), and I don't recall what else he attacked, but he did it with wit and pungency. I naturally sent him a note, thanked him for his brilliant parody of a review, and invited him to contribute to *Monocle*, which he finally got around to doing some five years later.*

We kept *Monocle* going through the mails. And in my travels with "Soapy" he didn't seem to mind that I sold subscriptions along the way (among others to a young Illinois publisher named Paul Simon, who went on to become a state senator and then a U.S. senator; and the wife of Avern Cohen, later the distinguished U.S. District Court judge for the Eastern District of Michigan). But when J.F.K. got elected and "Soapy" went to the State Department as Kennedy's Assistant Secretary of State for African Affairs (J.F.K.'s first appointment), I returned to New York to see if I could make a go of *Monocle*.

Now why, you may ask, would a serious young man like me want to give up a promising legal career (or life as a New Frontiersman, for that matter) for a satire magazine?

*Fourteen years after our meeting in Cambridge he signed me up as a monthly columnist for *The New York Times Book Review*, and twenty-two years after that, Katrina vanden Heuvel and I hired John and his wife, Sue, as co-literary editors of *The Nation*. Stay tuned.

First, I guess I was not that serious. Second, the career was not that promising. Third, I believed in satire as a kind of social criticism and I saw our countertrendy, irreverent magazine as part of an irreverence boomlet, a modest voice of protest from within the so-called Silent Generation, which the historian Arthur Schlesinger, Jr., called "the bland leading the bland." With a newspaper as his only stage prop, the stand-up comic Mort Sahl was inventing a new kind of political humor at the hungry i in San Francisco ("Is there anyone I haven't offended yet?"), and Lenny Bruce seemed to invite the local cops every time he appeared onstage (either because of what he said or what he smoked). Harry Golden, editor of *The Carolina Israelite*, whose book *Only in America* was number one on the bestseller list, containing such proposals as his vertical integration plan, which would thwart segregated seating in public places by removing all chairs; Mike Nichols and Elaine May were improvising their way from Chicago's Compass Theater, to the big time. Jules Feiffer's "Sick, sick, sick" cartoons in *The Village Voice* mocked the avant-garde itself, and Paul Krassner's *The Realist* ("Freethought, Criticism and Satire") hilariously violated the conventional canons of good taste, but, as Malcolm Muggeridge once observed, "All great satire is in bad taste." P. D. East's anti-segregationist *Petal Paper*, *Monocle* pointed out, was read and praised throughout the world except in Petal, Mississippi, where it was published. And okay, I'll admit, it was more fun publishing Sidney Zion's Runyonesque "The Day They Put the Snatch on Orval" (Faubus, the segregationist governor of Arkansas) than learning the Federal Rules of Civil Procedure or studying Negotiable Instruments.

After we moved *Monocle* to New York, we made a brief alliance with the improvisatory actor Peter Cook, then appearing on Broadway in *Beyond the Fringe*, who had also helped found London's *Private Eye*, and for a while there was talk of a merger. But one stumbling block was *Monocle*'s appearance. Cook felt it looked too beautiful. *Private Eye*, with its typewriter type and photo-offset appearance, including an amateurish joke-photo on the cover, looked as if it had been slapped together the night before by a bunch of madmen typing through the night. On the other hand, in the days before it was common for even so refined a periodical as *The New Yorker* to use an occasional obscenity, Cook confessed that it was his dream to devote two pages to the single word "fuck," set in the most ornate type available in full color, and under it, the caption: *Who says it's a dirty word?* We never could get together.

Although I didn't appreciate it at the time, putting together a prospectus and trying to persuade potential investors in the face of playwright George S. Kaufman's famous definition—"Satire is what closes on Saturday night"—that political satire was a good investment turned out to be ideal training for my subsequent life as publisher of *The Nation*.

Through Soapy Williams I had met Adam Yarmolinsky, a lawyer-writer–foundation consultant (who ended up at the Pentagon), and through Adam I met Robert Yoakum, former city editor of the Paris-based *International Herald Tribune*, who (with the help of Adlai Stevenson, George Ball, and others) had raised two-thirds of the money he needed to start what he called "a liberal *Time*" and then struck out. Yoakum taught me how to write a prospectus and introduced me to Jim Kobak, then a partner at J. K. Lasser and accountant to the Magazine Publishers of America, and to the late great circulation consultant Bert Garmise. When he was not signing up high-priced clients on one or another putting green, Garmise taught me the a, b, c's and the x, y, z's of direct mail subscription solicitation, including how to test price, copy, and "list." And Kobak taught me how to work with a computer program that would project expenses and revenues.

Friends and relatives were soon subjected to a *Monocle* prospectus that projected two stages for the magazine. In stage one we would raise $30,000 seed capital, in order to do three things (and pay modest salaries while doing them): a direct mail test, a pilot issue of the "new" *Monocle*, and an offering circular. (Even though we didn't have an underwriter, we figured that since by this time *Monocle* had 1,487 paid subscribers, we might want to recruit investors from states throughout the union, and this required registration with the SEC.) In the end, we produced an offering circular—I suspect the only one in history that began—with some lines from John Dryden:

> Satire has always shown among the rest,
> And is the boldest way, if not the best,
> To tell men freely of their foulest faults,
> To laugh at their vain deeds and vainer thoughts.

If it all worked out, we would raise the rest of the capital we needed and move to monthly publication. On the mistaken theory that the most likely people to invest in magazines are people in the magazine business, one of the first things I did in my attempt to convert *Monocle* from a hobby to a business was to attend the annual meeting of the Magazine Publishers of America, at the Greenbrier resort hotel in White Sulphur Springs, West Virginia.

Of course the people in the magazine business, when they were not on the Greenbrier's putting green or attending a seminar, were quick to point out that with its mini-economics *Monocle* was not really a business; it was more of a hobby. But even though I raised not a penny, even though the seminars on magazine economics were too technical, too obvious, or too mass-market-oriented, and even though the only exercise I got was on my daily walk to and from my inexpensive motel two miles down the road from the Greenbrier, meeting Bernie Yudain alone was worth the trip. I had been told to look up Bernie by his brother Sid, who published a Capitol Hill weekly called *Roll Call*, which in those days was little more than a hometown paper featuring cheesecake shots of the secretaries who worked on the hill. (I always thought Sid was sitting atop a valuable franchise, and many years later so did Arthur Leavitt, Arthur Carter's former partner, who bought the name *Roll Call* and converted it into a serious and sometimes news-making sheet, before selling it when he became head of the SEC under President Clinton.) Bernie, who hailed from Connecticut, where his brother edited *The Greenwich Time*, was something else. He offered to buy me a drink. He got a great kick out of our draft prospectus, which described *Monocle* readers as "the sub-influential"—the guys who wrote rather than delivered the nightly news, for example. He told me he was a friend and fan of one of our writers, Calvin "Bud" Trillin (though he kept calling him Trilling). On Bernie's MPA badge it said in big letters that he worked for *Time* magazine in Washington. When I asked him if he was with the Washington bureau of *Time*, he said, "Not exactly." What did he do for *Time*? I asked. "Well," he said, "I take the postmaster to lunch."

"Seriously," I said, "what do you do?"

"Seriously?" he repeated. "Seriously, I also take him for drinks and dinner. And not just the postmaster. Anyone who works in the post office I will take to lunch or drinks or dinner, and I have even been known to spring for an occasional breakfast, although personally I'd rather sleep late and read the papers."

"What do you discuss at breakfast, lunch, and drinks and dinner with these people?" I persisted.

"I tell jokes," said Bernie, which I could easily believe. I knew his brother Sid was at the time moonlighting from *Roll Call* by serving as agent-cum–gag writer for an up-and-coming but still unknown Washington-based stand-up political comic called Mark Russell.

I never could get Bernie, who was sweet, funny, and decent, to tell me much more about what he did, only that the postmaster indeed held one key to successful magazine economics. And it wasn't until thirty-five years later, when I testified before the Postal Rate Commission as *The Nation* magazine's new publisher, that I found out how right he was.

My other initial forays into fund-raising were no more successful, but they were instructive, especially those that didn't work out. Take the case of Mr. V.

"I love your smile," said Mr. V. when I sat down at his table for our prearranged appointment at his club in New York, sixty stories up. My Swarthmore friend Paul Gottlieb's new bride, Linda, who was working at our office over the summer, had met Mr. V. at a suburban cocktail party and told him about our magazine, and he told her he would get us the $30,000 we needed, no problem. So here I was at a plush East Side eatery. "I like your smile," he repeated. "I like your smile, I like you, I like your idea, and I like your timing . . . *But*," he continued, "I don't like your magazine. I haven't read it, but I don't like it. And I'll tell you what I don't like about it: the shape! Change the shape," said Mr. V., "and you've got yourself a deal."

Before I could protest, he was on to his next point.

"Now," he said, "exactly how much money are you looking for?"

I told him.

"That makes me sick," said Mr. V. "Think big, think big. Let me tell you something. I'm in on a deal with a man who has bought and sold the Empire State Building. If you're going to jump, jump off the Empire State Building. Are you married?" I shook my bachelor's head. "Well," he pointed out, "if you're going to get slapped, get slapped by a society woman. What have you got to lose? The worst that can happen is that you'll fail, and you're a failure already."

I couldn't argue with that.

"Okay," said Mr. V. "Now, I'm going to give you an idea—a Big Idea—and I'm going to give it to you at my usual rate, for nothing. Why am I giving you this for nothing? For the same reason I do everything— fun and options. Fun and options. You have a good idea, but it's bigger than you thought. You need an international satire magazine—a *world* satire magazine. And it should be published . . ."

At this point he shifted in his chair and peered about the room, pre-sumably to make sure that there were no rival international satire maga-zine entrepreneurs listening. Then he continued: "It should be published in Bermuda! Or the Bahamas! Do you realize how many businessmen have retired to Bermuda (or the Bahamas) for tax purposes? You publish from Bermuda, and you publish the kind of magazine I'm talking about and I'll get you your money."

"If you can raise the money for a truly international satire maga-zine—offices in Rome, Paris, London, Tokyo, São Paolo, New York, and Washington," I said, thinking as Big as I could, "and you under-stand that we run the magazine, we're certainly willing to consider publishing from Bermuda. Although I must confess," I confessed, "this is a slight departure from what we had in mind."

Mr. V. then proceeded to outline the "three *real* reasons he was do-ing this: "One, to make money; two, to make money; and three, to have fun—but I can't have any fun unless I make money."

I left Mr. V. feeling that he was either the greatest promoter of them all or a particularly entertaining phony. I went back to my office, did some checking (memo to self: next time check before lunch rather than after), and learned that Mr. V. made his first million when a man walked into his office with this idea of playing music in elevators. Mr. V. told the fellow to Think Big. I don't know if that story is true. I do know I saw Mr. V. three or four times thereafter, until finally he was supposed to make a presentation to our board of directors (one of whom suggested that the meeting be in Bermuda), and the afternoon came and passed with no Mr. V. He didn't show and didn't excuse him-self. I guess we didn't think big enough.

At one point I thought I needed $10,000 to close phase one of the deal, and I journeyed out to Hollywood to see George Axelrod, the highly successful screenwriter brother-in-law of our attorney, my Yale Law School classmate David Dretzin. My strategy was to ask him not for money but rather for suggestions of others whom we might approach, on the erroneous theory that once he heard what a great thing we had going, he would find the temptation to invest on his own irresistible.

Axelrod arrived an hour and a half late for our appointment on a note of triumph. He had just closed a deal with Frank Sinatra on *The Manchurian Candidate*. "Our lives have just changed," he told his wife. "I've got the movie. I've got the star. I've got the money. I've got the distribution, and I've got Irving [that was Irving "Swifty" Lazar, the agent], who is coming at 9:30 to make all the arrangements. Now," he asked, turning to me, "what can I do for you?" He seemed so up from the day's events that for a moment I thought my ship had come in. As I described our plans for *Monocle* he kept nodding enthusiastically. "So," I finished with a flourish, "here I am looking for one man with $10,000."

"I wouldn't give you a quarter," he said. "Don't think I don't have it. Not only do I have $10,000—I have $12,000. I could make you out a check right now, but I won't—let me show you why." He led me back through a kitchen and out into the patio adjacent to his Olympic-sized swimming pool.

"No, don't look at it, feel it." We kneeled down and dipped our hands in the water. As I held my hand in the water, he continued: "Notice, 82 degrees. Not 81, not 83, but 82 degrees. That means I can go in anytime—morning, noon, or night—and it's always 82 degrees. Now let me tell you something. I believe in that swimming pool. And if you're any good, you will attack me. And why should I pay my hard-earned money to have you attack me? Join me and I'm with you. Fight me and I'm for you. But don't attack me and expect me to subsidize you. Go hungry. Hate me. Fight me. That's the only way you'll ever make it."

I left without dinner.

There are those who prefer to give their capital only to people who are in genuine need of money, yet seem to feel better if you look tanned, prosperous, and confident, i.e., as if you don't really need it. On the other hand, a certain type of investor wants to make sure that you are not too greedy or too mercenary, but will also guard against investing in someone who lacks the instinct for profit. As the Philadelphia banker Albert Greenfield so colorfully put it when I gave him an opportunity to join *Monocle*'s elite group of shareholders, "I'm not interested in throwing my money down the sewer." Another seasoned financier put it slightly more diplomatically. Like Mr. V., he told me he gave money for three reasons, but different ones: "I give for business—but you haven't demonstrated you can make a profit, so you're not a business; I give to charity—but you're not a charity; and I give because I'm charmed—but you haven't charmed me."

Eventually, I learned that investors, even rich, smart investors who have no illusions about profitability, want structure. As long as I told people that I was looking for $30,000 in seed capital and we would organize our business in a way that would maximize their tax needs, I raised not a penny. As soon as I told them that I was looking for ten people who would put up $3,000 each and would be given a certain percentage of the business for their money, I raised my $30,000. Through friends and friends of friends and relatives of friends and readers of the old *Monocle,* we recruited an eclectic group that included, among others, Philip Stern, an heir to the Sears, Roebuck fortune who was also the author of *The Great Treasury Raid* (about the need to reform regressive tax laws) and went on to write *The Best Congress Money Can Buy,* a premature call for campaign finance reform (years later he became an investor in *The Nation*); Lionel I. Pincus, an investment banker with a social conscience who went on to found Warburg Pincus; Bob Worth, a music and science publisher whose son was to intern for *The Nation* at the start of his distinguished career in journalism at the *Washington Monthly* and *The New York Times.* Even my old family law professor, Fowler Harper, came in. Fowler lived in a house he called Hearst's Folly because he built it with the proceeds of a successful libel action against William Randolph Hearst, whose papers had called him a red (which he was at heart but not in fact). And then there was Ruth Field, the widow of Marshall Field, who had put up the money for *PM,* the ad-free progressive paper of the 1940s (its motto was "We're against people who push other people around"). Mrs. Field told me that her late husband had warned her against investing in publications because they could be an endless drain, but she knew from past personal experience that Jack Kaplan, another potential investor, was a hardheaded and difficult businessman, and said that if we persuaded him we had persuaded her. And so we come to Jack Kaplan himself, who almost brought down the whole house of cards.

When I was in Alaska I had read an article in *Time* about Kaplan, who had turned the Welch's grape juice company back to the workers and was said to be interested in funding a string of liberal newspapers. Through my Swarthmore friend Christopher Lehmann-Haupt, who had gone to high school with Kaplan's daughter Mary, we got to see Jack. He was a bow-tied dapper man in his seventies, legendarily difficult, who strolled to work daily from his home in the East Nineties to his office on lower Fifth Avenue. Kaplan advised us for tax reasons to set *Monocle* up as a Sub Chapter S corporation, which would give its shareholders corporate protection against lawsuits and yet, in the event of losses, permit them to deduct their share as ordinary income, as if it were a partnership.

We did as Mr. K. suggested, everyone signed on, and I returned with the good news. This time Kaplan was accompanied by his aide Ray Rubinow. He said he had forgotten to mention one little detail: he would sign, but only if we set up a three-person executive committee (two of whom would be himself and Rubinow) to whom the editor would report.

I started to object.

"Don't worry," he said, "the other shareholders will all be for it. Ask them. You'll see."

I worried, and I worried for a number of reasons. The first I didn't share with him. The J. M. Kaplan Fund, his family foundation, had recently been in the news as having been a conduit for the CIA, in connection with its passing money to anti-Communist trade unionists in Santo Domingo. Despite all his other worthy philanthropic labors, I thought it would look and be bad for a man with such a pedigree to have veto power over our future. Second, and fundamentally, the whole idea of having a broad base of support was to guarantee the editor's (my!) independence.

Also, as I explained to Mr. Kaplan, "It took me six months to get an appointment with you. It took me three months to get an appointment with Mrs. Field. We have in anticipation signed a lease on an office. This deal will never happen if I have to track down every one of my shareholders in the next two weeks, our deadline. But here is what I will do. I will introduce your idea at our first shareholders' meeting. If you are right and everyone thinks it's a great idea, we can make it happen then." Kaplan relented, to Rubinow's astonishment. (Later Rubinow told me that had never happened before.) And since most of our shareholders, including Kaplan himself, couldn't be bothered to show up for the first shareholders' meeting, the proposal for an executive committee was put on the shelf, and so, for a while at least, *Monocle* was in business.

It had been explained to me that while small-circulation magazines invariably lose money, newsletters, which charge more and give the reader less, invariably make money. Since I had a small staff already lined up, brimming with ideas but no place to put them, why not, the entrepreneur in me asked, start a newsletter? After all, we had already begun publishing occasional Emergency Bulletins, as we called them. For example, when J.F.K., who had campaigned on the slogan that "with a stroke of his pen" Eisenhower could integrate publicly assisted housing, had been in office three months, and not yet gotten around to signing such an executive order, we started a campaign of our own. On the theory that the White House had run out of ink, we started an "Ink for Jack" campaign. We sent out an Emergency Bulletin in the form of a blotter, instructing our subscribers to send bottles of ink to the White House. Although like everything else we did, these bulletins did not make a profit, they had a modest effect on public life: James Farmer, executive director of the Congress for Racial Equality, ordered copies in bulk to send as a premium to new members; and we even received a call from Pierre Salinger, J.F.K.'s press secretary. On the other hand, Pierre was calling to ask us to cease and desist, because so many bottles of ink were arriving broken and messing up the White House mailroom. (In 1962 President Kennedy did sign Executive Order 11063, integrating public housing.)

In those days, a "hot" newsletter, published by Cowles Communications, which also published *Look*, was *The Insider's Newsletter*. It got its information (which it claimed was entirely new news) from a series of invisible investigators: anonymous stringers, some of them whistleblowing insiders, others entrepreneurial outsiders, one of whom was

Ralph Nader. We decided to have an *Outsider's Newsletter*. The theory of *The Insider's Newsletter* was that people were yearning to be on the inside and to get inside information (perhaps even act on it to their financial benefit before it was generally available). But, we argued, what with *The Insider's Newsletter*, I. F. Stone's newsletter, *The Kiplinger Letter*, and such, the problem was not too little information but too much. Information overload, we called it. It would take "persistence, courage, and intelligent ignorance to get the outside story—the story of what is not going on." Our job would be to shepherd our readers through the morass of overreported news and "facts" by telling them what was not going on. Or by telling them what was wrong with everyone else's journalism. A. J. Liebling aside, virtually nobody in those days wrote about the press. But Calvin Trillin, whose day job was working as a reporter for *Time*, in a fit of premature press criticism proposed an *Outsider's Newsletter* feature called "Letters to Other Editors," where he told them in our periodical what was wrong with their periodicals.

Then came the New York newspaper strike of 1962. We didn't yet have the loot for *Monocle*, but we had another moneymaking idea which didn't make anybody any money. We would publish one-shot parodies of all the morning papers, so that when people went to work one morning they would see perfect likenesses of the *Post* (we called it the *Pest*), the *News* (we called it the *Dally Noose*), etc. We actually did manage to find a publisher who would put up the money for two of the papers. It was Arthur Frommer, who had not yet quit his day job as a lawyer with Paul, Weiss, Rifkind, Wharton & Garrison for his career as publisher of *Europe on $5 a Day* (and eventually every other continent). Trillin's headline for the *Pest* read COLD SNAP HITS NEW YORK/NEGROES AND JEWS SUFFER MOST. (He claims I opposed the headline because there was no story to go with it.) The main consequence of the parodies was that Mrs. Dorothy Schiff, whose editors wanted her to sue, instructed them instead to hire our best writers. Those who accepted jobs with the *Post* were Nora Ephron (who had done a send-up of its gossip columnist, Leonard Lyons) and Sidney Zion (who did a parody of the legendary Murray Kempton entitled "Goodbye, Mrs. Chipps"). They both had successful runs at the *Post*—then Nora went on to literary and Hollywood success and Sid to *The New York Times* and everywhere else, where he continued to make constructive trouble.

The parodies were a hit and our newsletter was a *succès d'estime*, but since the reason subscribers paid hundreds of dollars for a Wall Street newsletter like *Kiplinger's* was that they expected to make hundreds of thousands of dollars from stock-market transactions based on (legal) insider information, it should have been no surprise that our newsletter, which by definition gave our readers less, somehow lost as much money as *Monocle* itself. So we revamped *Monocle's* format (keeping it tall and skinny, but now it was 5½ x 11), which meant it was, as our ad salesmen pointed out, "as tall as *Time* and as wide as *Reader's Digest*." That way a full-page ad prepared for *The Reader's Digest* could be a three-quarter-page ad in *Monocle*, and a single-column ad in *Time* would be a half page in *Monocle*. Not that it helped us sell ads. Of course, as Trillin liked to point out, our ad salesman was opposed on principle to selling ads, or rather, he refused to engage in the industry-wide practice of inflating our circulation numbers by 50 percent. But since we didn't tell anyone, the advertising people tended to discount our numbers by 50 percent. This was too bad, since our numbers were real, in the sense that whereas most magazines are sold on consignment (which means that if they are not sold, the retailer can return them), *Monocle* was sold (to bookstores) outright—a creative innovation of a Simon & Schuster vice president and *Monocle* fan, Tony Schulte. This was smart publishing on Tony's part. By giving bookstores a steep discount (70 percent off the cover price), Simon & Schuster didn't have to worry about or pay for returns. But critics might claim that it was dumb publishing on our part. We were so elated to have Simon & Schuster as our distributor that we accepted a deal that never quite covered our printing costs, thinking we would make up the difference in advertising (we didn't), if not through our increasingly popular and equally mispriced newsletter. Maybe I wasn't such a business ace, after all.

Most people thought of *Monocle* as a humor magazine. Actually, most people didn't think about *Monocle* at all, but those who did thought of it as a sophomoric humor magazine. Our literary reputation and finances improved over the years, especially after we stopped publishing "regularly" in 1965. But from the beginning I thought of it as a satire magazine, and I would pompously explain the difference between humor (harmless) and satire (poisonous). Or I would quote Gilbert Cannon, that wise old Englishman who said, "No tyrant, no tyrannous idea ever came crashing to earth but it was first wounded by the shafts of satire; no free man, no free idea ever rose to the heights but it endured them." I also wrote, "The difference between humor and satire is the difference between attacking Ike [who satirized himself] and attacking Jack [who seemed to require a sharper scalpel]."

In the spring of 1959, I had met one person who had a unique feeling for the social uses to which satire might be put. I was sitting in the dormitory room of Jack Waltuch, editor of the *Yale Law Report*, when there came a knock on the door. It was a student from Harvard Law, editor of the *Harvard Law Record*. He thought there might be ways the two journals could collaborate to raise the social consciousness of our respective institutions, and he was especially interested in *Monocle*. Satire, he thought, was a valuable tool of social criticism. That was my introduction to Ralph Nader.

By 1961, when I was back in New York trying to convert *Monocle* into a business from my apartment on West Sixty-ninth Street, again there was a knock on the door. Remember me? asked the same lanky Harvard man. Nader was by this time writing freelance for *The Christian Science Monitor*, and he had just come back from the Soviet Union, where he had written about *Krokodil*, the Soviet satire magazine. Did you know, Nader asked, that there are many *Krokodil*s? They're not called that, but each republic seemed to have its own satire magazine, and while political censorship existed all over the U.S.S.R., Nader reported that these magazines functioned as ombudsmen, exposing corruption and sloth in the local bureaucracies. Amazing. Why didn't we have that? We discussed his writing for *Monocle*. He had another hobbyhorse. While still at Harvard he had written an article published in, of all places, *The Nation*, about the Corvair. But "The Safe Car You Can't Buy" was more than an article. It was a cause, a crusade. Dividing his time between Washington and New York, he wrote, he phoned, he demonstrated, he mobilized, he picketed. (Once a year an invitation would come to join him on a picket line. The target: the annual automobile show at New York's Coliseum. "It will only be a few hours. Put on a suit and tie and if you have an attaché case bring it. The important thing is to look respectable. We'll provide the placards.") When not picketing he was on the phone. But unlike your average unemployed citizen, somehow he was on the phone to Connecticut's former governor, now Senator Abraham Ribicoff, or to Daniel Patrick Moynihan, then at the Department of Labor.

Contrary to his image, Nader has a keen sense of the absurd. He once told a story about how he got around every secretary's opening question: "You know. You call a senator's office or a vice president at Ford and the first thing the secretary asks is 'Who are you with?' So I was on the phone one day and I was at home in Connecticut and the secretary asked who are you with and I thought what do I say? 'I'm not with anyone'? No, that won't do it. 'I'm with my mother'? I didn't think that would fly. And just then my dog wandered in and I said, 'I'm with my dog.' And I got through."

In 1962 Ralph wrote an article for *Monocle*. It was a parody of a speech by a CEO of one of the big three automobile companies, patiently explaining to shareholders how they went about the business of planned obsolescence. We mistakenly turned down the piece as heavy-handed, which it was. We told Ralph Nader, "You ought to turn this into a book—it's too heavy-handed for a satire magazine piece." Ha! Now, of course, we claim credit for his book *Unsafe at Any Speed*, which, like Rachel Carson's *Silent Spring*, raised the national consciousness. As it happened, through Robert Ockene, whom I had met at the Radcliffe Publishing Procedures course, he had already signed a contract with Grossman Publishers, a small firm founded by Dick Grossman, who had quit Simon & Schuster so that he could publish handsome-looking books of social and cultural significance with the care, attention, and integrity that the mainstream publishers couldn't give them. Each book would be its own event. He had a vision.

After *Unsafe at Any Speed* was published, Nader came to fame— partly as the result of an article by James Ridgeway in *The New Republic* detailing how General Motors had put a gumshoe on his track and tried to entrap him by hiring a prostitute to lure him into a compromising situation. GM's chairman issued a public apology. So his career was launched in one journal of opinion, *The Nation*, and his book was catapulted onto the bestseller list via another journal of opinion, *The New Republic*.

In 2000, when Nader ran for President on the Green Party ticket, *The Nation*'s position was "Vote your conscience where you can" (support Nader in states where your vote won't tip the election), "but vote for Gore where you must" (states too close to call). I don't think Ralph thought it was funny when I said that *Monocle* would have supported him without qualification. And he really got upset with us in 2004, when in an "Open Letter" *The Nation* urged him to forgo the presidential race, lest he simultaneously play the spoiler in the election and spoil his own splendid reputation as the country's number-one consumer advocate.

After we turned *Monocle* from a "leisurely" quarterly into a quarterly, we decided to keep publishing our weekly *Outsider's Newsletter*, in order to stay on top of the news, despite the fact that it didn't have any. A typical item comes from 1964: After Michigan's Republican governor George Romney fasted for divine guidance before announcing his (ultimately unsuccessful) run for the presidency in 1964, *The Outsider's Newsletter* ran this, ghostwritten by one Calvin Trillin:

MICHIGAN STANDS FAST ON FAST!

East Lansing, Michigan—Ronald M. Rutherford, still undecided on whether or not to become the Christian Action Party candidate for Governor of Michigan, died today of starvation. He was 64.

Mr. Rutherford, like Republican Gov. George Romney, began a fast for divine guidance last spring. But, unlike Mr. Romney, Mr. Rutherford did not receive an answer within 24 hours, and was still waiting for a reply at his death.

Although some of his supporters interpreted this delay as tantamount to a negative reply—a "divine pocket veto," in the words of one ward leader—Mr. Rutherford insisted on maintaining his 238-day fast, even though he was too weak for prayer and press conferences after his first four months.

Dick Lingeman "translated" a mythical book by Ichiro Kuichi, a Japanese author, entitled *Destiny's Deckhand: The Autobiography of a Seaman on the Japanese Destroyer That Rammed Kennedy's PT-109*. According to Lingeman, Kuichi came to the United States to plug his book, but his offer to commit hara-kiri on the *Today* show was turned down. (He was the only kamikaze pilot ever to fly ten missions.) He went home to campaign to be Japan's first astronaut.

Since our newsletter was by this time losing as much money if not more than our magazine, smart-ass accountants might well ask what we thought we were doing. This is a good question. But we thought the newsletter was functioning as a sort of farm team for the magazine (not unlike some Web sites of today's hard-copy magazines), and that eventually the magazine would "grow into profitability," as the phrase went. In the meantime, the talent we were developing might find a mass audience.

With the help of C.D.B. Bryan, we invented a new form of poetry, the poem of Protest. Here's one:

> Okay, Bird! (prod) Get
> Outta my way you
> Dumb bird (kick)
> Whattsa matter you,
> You stupid (scuffle)
> Bird? Getta outta here and
> Take all those (Lunge!)
> Goddam Bird Eggs with
> You, BIRD (FLAPPITY—
> FLAPPITY, flappity)

And we even launched two comic strips: *Captain Melanin*, Bob Grossman's running account of Billy Bootblack, a shoeshine boy who turns himself into a black Captain Marvel by shouting not "Shazam" but "Booker T. Washington" and "Modern Jazz Quartet." The other, drawn by Ed Koren, who later came to fame via his fuzzy creatures in *The New Yorker*, featured a peacenik hero who recited the magic equation and turned into a fat superman who looked suspiciously like the Hudson Institute's Herman Kahn as he flew over the metropolis with obscure mathematical formulas filling the clouds above his fertile brain.

C.D.B. Bryan had written a brilliant parody of J. D. Salinger while at Yale, so we commissioned him to plagiarize himself, only this time politicize it and make it about the new Kennedy couple in the White House. A month later "A Perfect Day for Honeyfitz" arrived in the mail:

In the first place you've probably read a thousand goddam stories about them already. I mean every time you pick up a magazine there's some phony article about them written by a seamstress, or an ex-roommate, or a sailor on a PT boat, for Chrissake. And I'm sick and tired of all those phonies who say they could tell by the way he brushed his *teeth* at *Choate*, for Chrissake, that he would become President of the United States. In the first place he hardly ever brushed his teeth—I don't mean he *never* brushed them, or anything. I mean he didn't brush them any three goddam times a day, that's all . . .

Then there was David Cort, who wrote for us what he called "A Simpleton's Notebook." His original and sometimes hilarious essays had recently been published under the title *Is There an American in the House?* Cort, an elderly fellow who had served as associate editor of "the original" *Vanity Fair*, book review editor of *Vogue*, all departments writer at *Time*, and executive editor of *Life*, told me that the only periodical that regularly published his maverick essays, even though they were conspicuously nonpolitical in the conventional sense, was—what else?—*The Nation*. *The Nation* had once published an essay of his called "Once Upon a Time, Inc." where he elaborated his theory that Henry Luce's original vision—that it was possible to synthesize the truth about an event quite briefly the very week it happened—had been lost. The only reason *Time* now had armies of correspondents "was for the PR, so they could claim it was based on original reporting." The fact was, you could do what Luce originally had proposed from AP reports.

David once told me that there were five joys in the life of a freelance writer: "When you get an idea; when you are in the midst of typing and the story is zinging along so that you are hardly able to keep up with what you have to say; when you put the manuscript in the envelope and send it off; when the article is accepted; and when you get your check." What about when it appears in print? For David that was no special thrill, though for most writers that was what it was all about.

One day, while casually browsing through *National Review*, I came across a movie review whose wall-to-wall imagery and jam-packed literary allusions and ideas caused me to check the byline: John Leonard. At first I thought his *National Review* connection explained the hidden politics behind his summer 1958 *Crimson* evisceration of *Monocle*. But as I was soon to discover, not all inmates of this right-wing nuthouse shared Buckley's right-wing politics—certainly not such originals as Joan Didion, Garry Wills, Renata Adler, and, not on staff but also politically unreliable, the writers Noel Parmental (a Goldwater speechwriter who moonlighted for Carey McWilliams's *Nation*) and John Gregory Dunne.

After a year at *National Review*, Leonard had completed his education at Berkeley, worked for the Pacifica Radio Network, written a novel, and made a living as a writer of technical texts. In 1963 *Monocle* persuaded John to write "Confessions of a *National Review* Contributor," which he did as a parody of Whittaker Chamber's foreword (in the form of a letter to his children) to his bestselling memoir *Witness*. By the time of Leonard's parody (in the form of a letter to his grandchildren), Chambers was a contributing editor at *National Review*. It was dazzling, along with most things Leonard wrote, and so when Christopher Lehmann-Haupt, who had been on *Monocle*'s original masthead as a consulting editor (he had been a waiter at the Yale Law School dining room while studying to be a playwright at the Yale Drama School) and was now working for *The New York Times Book Review*, told me about an opening for a young editor, and asked if I had anyone to recommend, I threw Leonard's name into the pot. In what seemed like twenty minutes, Leonard's career at the *Times* took off: He was the youngest editor ever of *The New York Times Book Review*.

And in 1964 we ran our "News Managing" editor, Marvin Kitman, for President. I had met Marvin in 1959, when he was researching an article about monocles. He was writing a column for *The Morning Telegraph*, a racing sheet, at the time. He'd come across a reference to the magazine *Monocle* in the card catalogue of the New York Public Library (we had donated a copy), and sent me a note asking about the climate for political satire. I'd written back that there was more strontium in the air, and we were off to the races.

Although we were in the satire business, we hadn't invented the idea of running or supporting one of our own for public office. It has long been part of the American tradition. For example, in 1897, when one Julius Wayland moved his socialist paper *Appeal to Reason* to Girard, Kansas, he let it be known that the purpose of the paper, whose single-issue printings were to reach over a million copies, was twofold: "to war against oppression and vast wrongs, dispelling the tears, blood and woes of capitalism; and to imbue Americans with actively egalitarian, non-exploitative values." But *Appeal* also supported its most famous columnist, Eugene V. Debs, for President of the United States. In 1909 Fighting Bob La Follette, who later ran for President himself, founded *La Follette's Weekly Magazine*, billing it as "a publication that will not mince words or suppress facts when public utterance demands plain talk." It survives to this day as *The Progressive*, a monthly that mixes populism with pacifism but, ironically, made its loudest noise when, in 1979—based on the reporter Howard Morland's study of available documents in the public record—it published a recipe for making a homegrown atom bomb and successfully (albeit expensively) mobilized a campaign to resist the government's attempt to suppress its publication.

They say that the office seeks the man, and in 1964, at age thirty-five, Marvin was the only man in the *Monocle* office old enough to run for President. Besides, as he pointed out, the mainstream candidates were all campaigning on their personality, "and my friends tell me I have a winning personality." Cynics may claim that the Kitman candidacy was nothing more than a circulation-building gimmick, and it is true that inside many small-circulation magazines there is a mass-circulation magazine struggling to be born. But it is also true that in Marvin, the *only* registered Republican in the *Monocle* office, we had the perfect foil to challenge Barry (*The Conscience of a Conservative*) Goldwater in the Republican primary of 1964. Marvin claimed that despite all the talk about Goldwater's conservatism, in truth he was a McKinley (or was it Teddy Roosevelt?) Republican, whereas Kitman was a true conservative, since he was running on a platform that went all the way back to Abraham Lincoln. The year 1964 was the year of "Freedom Summer," of "Bull" Connor's police dogs, of the Mississippi voter-registration campaign, so Kitman ran on Lincoln's 1864 platform, which had three main planks—it called for "freeing the slaves, the unconditional surrender of the South, and the reinforcement of the garrison at Fort Sumter."

On Kitman's behalf, we actually trudged through the snows of New Hampshire for its presidential primary, where we discovered it was possible, on payment of a $15 filing fee, for a would-be party convention delegate to file in a candidate's name, which is what one local photographer, a *Monocle* subscriber, did. Kitman, for his part, gained more votes (76) than the noncampaigning but prominently mentioned dark horse William Scranton, governor of Pennsylvania. And we went to the Republican Convention at the Cow Palace in San Francisco. We formally attempted to put the 1864 Republican platform before the 1964 Republican platform committee (they said it was too radical); we produced our own version of campaign paraphernalia (campaign buttons for "Veterans of the Abraham Lincoln Brigade" and special ribbons that said "spontaneous demonstrator" and "paid volunteer"); we took advantage of the facilities to stage daily press conferences. (Sample question from a real reporter: Mr. Kitman, what is your ethnic background? A: "You are trying to raise the religious issue, and I prefer not to discuss the issues since I am campaigning on my personality and my friends tell me I have a winning personality. But I will say, I am twice as Jewish as Goldwater.") We even got Kitman's name put in nomination (well, half of it) before the security police intervened.

We had gotten the rogue nominator on the floor of the convention by giving him one of our official convention press badges. Once on the floor, however, he substituted for his press badge a badge artfully altered by a *Monocle* graphic artist: Where the original said *Press*, the words *Microphone Technician* were substituted. As per our instructions, our man Larry Hankin, a member of the San Francisco improvisational comedy group called The Committee, made himself a familiar figure in the vicinity of the Virgin Islands delegation by ostentatiously adjusting and tapping microphones. We knew from preliminary research (it always pays to do preliminary research), also because we had been introduced to Bruce Raab, the young man in charge of convention electronics (in the years ahead he went on to a distinguished legal career), that each delegation's mikes went live only when the chair recognized the relevant delegation. So as soon as the chairman recognized the chair of the three-person delegation from the Virgin Islands, Hankin was at the microphone, ostensibly to adjust it. Holding the microphone in one hand and holding off the chairman of the Virgin Islands delegation with the other, he actually got as far as putting in nomination "The next President of the United States, Marvin Kit . . ." when armed security guards seized him and spirited him out of the arena. As Larry was dragged toward the exit, puzzled delegates could hear his protests: "Hey, I've got an 8:30 curtain."

While Kitman might not agree, had there been no *Monocle* there would have been no Kitman campaign. And had there been no *National Review*, the conservative journal founded by William F. Buckley, Jr., in 1956, there might have been no Goldwater campaign (or indeed, the Reagan presidency, which came sixteen years later).

Before the *National Review*, there were conservatives but there was no conservative movement—no body of ideas that could provide the basis for such a movement. But under the banner of what it called "Fusionism," the *National Review* brought together Milton Friedmanesque free-market economics, Russell Kirk–type, traditionalist Burkean conservatism, and good old-fashioned anti-Communism, the Elmer's Glue of the Cold War years. Not that it was alone on the right. *The Freeman, Human Events*, the post-Mencken *American Mercury, Modern Age*, and later, *The Public Interest*, the Heritage Foundation's *Policy Review*, and in their neoconservative phase *Commentary* and even *Partisan Review*, among others, provided space for traditional conservative reflection. Nevertheless, by the time the Goldwater movement had transformed itself into the Reagan-for-President movement, it seemed evident that *National Review* more than any other institution had nourished and cultivated the writers and ideas—cuckoo though they seem to me—that gave substance to right-wing politics in America.

When Buckley announced his candidacy for mayor of New York City (in 1965), we invited him down to the *Monocle* office, and he agreed to come, perhaps on the theory that the Buckley campaign had something to learn from the Kitman campaign of the year before. A few days earlier *The New York Times* had published an editorial objecting to *National Review*'s criticism of Hunter College, which was permitting Alger Hiss to speak on campus; the *Times* said everyone from Hiss to Buckley should be welcome to air their views, no matter how unpopular; and Buckley, in a letter to the editor, had taken exception, contending that while he himself should of course be permitted to share his views, Hiss was a convicted perjurer and traitor to his country and therefore should be disqualified. So I began our session by welcoming

Buckley but noting that the last occupant of the chair he sat in had been Alger Hiss, our guest speaker the previous month. He took the occasion to display his peculiar combination of wit and viciousness. "What's Alger doing now?" he asked, affecting the *faux* familiar. Answer: "He's selling stationery." Buckley, without missing a beat, responded, "It just goes to show the Soviet Union hasn't solved its unemployment problem yet."

Asked how he proposed to deal with the water shortage then afflicting New York, Buckley riposted, "Let them drink wine."

Buckley's magazine may be said to be exhibit A in my proof that journals of opinion are not eighteenth-century relics. It's instructive and some might even say inspirational to look at the mini-economics that was making a magazine like *National Review* possible in those years leading up to the Goldwater and Reagan candidacies, when crackpot ideas like supply-side economics and such were under development. And Buckley himself had been good enough to deconstruct small-magazine economics in the October 16, 1959, issue of *National Review*.

It may seem unseemly to invoke *National Review* statistics on behalf of the case for—as model for—journals that may have only contempt for its politics. But *National Review* itself had no such compunction. As one of its writers acknowledged when it was launched in 1956:

> It was the ideas developed in *The Nation* and *The New Republic* and the *Masses* (long since defunct) thirty and forty years ago that seduced a generation and laid the foundation for the New Deal and what has followed. The circulation of these magazines were not large, but they spoke to the younger generations, in and out of the universities, and won them—to devastating effect.

Not only that, but in his 1959 essay "Can a Little Magazine Break Even?" Buckley wrote that it could—and furthermore even make a profit. But how many subscribers would it take? After some hemming and hawing around about its not being an easy question to answer because of how costs and advertising revenues change with increases in volume, and all the rest, he proved with brio and Buckleyan precision that "assuming our subscription list continued to grow in the same proportion as in 1958, i.e., half by renewal, half in response to promotion, and the deficit stayed at $135,000, we would break even with an additional 62,719 subscribers. Added to our present subscription list of about 29,000 this could give us a total mailing of 91,791." Being Buckley, he could not resist adding, "It is probably not an exaggeration to say that when there are that many literate and aroused conservatives in the land the country will break even too!"

As I write, for what it's worth, *National Review*'s circulation is 154,800 and its deficit, according to Buckley's last funding appeal, was substantial. Even with a compassionate conservative in the White House, although the country did better than break even under his predecessor, conservative economists project a deficit in the hundreds of billions for years to come.

But I digress. Here is Buckley's 1959 quantitative logic: First, like all good logicians, he stated his premise—that a journal tailored to the tastes of the "thinking few" must depend for its survival on what readers are willing to pay, since advertisers will not come in numbers high enough to cover the bill. He then proceeded to blame *The New York Times* for the resulting problem. In 1958 the daily *Times* charged a nickel.

> It is very hard, let's face it, while the *Times* costs five cents a copy and *Life* twenty-five for *National Review* to charge thirty cents . . . let alone sixty cents—which is what we should be charging, given the costs of publishing, and what we *would* be charging if the average American reader were prepared to pay as much more, relatively, for periodical reading matter over the price in 1933, as he is prepared to pay, today, for a hamburger, or a movie, or an automobile, or a pencil.

The dilemma for the small magazine, according to Buckley, is that it cannot behave as mass-circulation magazines do when the cost of manufacturing goes up, say, by 10 percent. The mass-periodical publisher can raise his ad rates by 10 percent and the advertiser can raise the price of his products. But small-magazine publishers are at a disadvantage because periodical consumers are used to subsidized prices. "The reader of *National Review* or the *New Leader* or the *Nation* is, with his left hand buying *Life*, and *The Saturday Evening Post* and the *New York Times*; or if not, he is aware consciously or semi-consciously of their prices at the newsstand, and it is from them that he derives the standards of value by reference to which he passes judgment on the asking price of the 'competitive' product."

Since most advertisers "will not extensively patronize journals written for the few," the only way for these journals to survive would be to let their prices keep pace with inflation, which would mean charging two or three times as much as they do. "In other words, if the reading public had allowed periodicals to keep pace with the rise in price of automobiles, rolls, dog collars, or cigarettes, publisher's hair would not turn white so early in life."

Okay, so besides saying *National Review* would break even with another sixty-odd thousand subscribers (assuming income and costs would remain constant), Buckley answered another question, or tried to. What profit does *National Review* make from a single subscription?

A. None, of course, if you count the overhead.
But taking overhead as a fixed cost, then how much?
A. It depends. It depends on how much money was spent in attracting the attention of the subscriber—on the so-called promotion cost of his subscription; or, if he is already a subscriber, on how many letters (they are costly) need be sent before he gets around to renewing.

But by the Reagan years *National Review* not only got its 62,719 new subscribers (at one point, with Reagan making TV commercials for *National Review*, circulation went up to 276,756), yet, as I reported above, was still losing money, and the country was not breaking even, either. What went wrong?

For years when people asked me how far away *The Nation* was from breakeven, I would answer (based on our latest projections): "Other things being equal, about three years." And based on our latest projections, I was right. We still expected to break even in three years. But of course "other" things are never equal.

In *National Review*'s case, way back in 1959, management was trying to develop "corollary commercial enterprises" capable of taking on a share of the load. At one point, they even tried their own newsletter! Meanwhile, Buckley explained, it would continue to depend for its survival on the kindness of strangers, i.e., friends of the magazine or, as he artfully put it, those who

> can afford to contribute to the political education of their nation and are generous and dutiful enough to do so. Journals of opinion are both educational and political enterprises and I know of no political enterprise that is self-supporting and very few educational enterprises: so that it is not so very striking that *National Review* should have to turn for assistance to those it seeks to serve, educationally and politically.

How does he reconcile this with his magazine's free-market rhetoric? He doesn't. Instead, with a little fancy footwork, he charmingly changes the subject.

> If the editors, feature writers, contributors and book reviewers of *National Review* don't offer more education than all the teachers' colleges combined, we volunteer to spend the rest of our lives studying Life Adjustment. If *National Review* does not contribute more to the political sanity of the nation than the League of Women Voters and the Ford Foundation combined, we offer our services, free of charge, to Americans for Democratic Action.

At *Monocle*, aside from our money-losing newsletter, we didn't know from corollary enterprises, but we did know that like *National Review* we were losing money, and unlike *National Review*, we didn't have Buckley bucks to back us up. So I went back out on the street to try to refinance the magazine, with or without the newsletter. By now we were subletting some of our space at 80 Fifth Avenue to freelance writers and editors, and one of them—irony of ironies—was the erstwhile head of *The Insider's Newsletter*, a bright Yale graduate named Pete Hunter. *Look* had decided to discontinue *The Insider's Newsletter,* and Hunter, who was a fan of *The Outsider's Newsletter*, had approached us for office space, having heard from our mutual acquaintance Ralph Nader that we were subletting. Hunter had an idea for a new newsletter which he thought "couldn't miss." He would resurrect his old network of surreptitious researchers but this time providing research on demand—custom-made research, as it were—and would charge not tens or hundreds of dollars per subscriber but thousands. For this to work, he would need not thousands of subscribers but fewer than a hundred.

Once again I made my *Monocle* rounds. After many phone calls, much correspondence, more than a few two-martini lunches, and much twisting of Phil Stern's aching elbow, I had secured everybody's agreement to go along provided everyone else went along (that old trick). When I went back to the charming Mrs. Field, as before, she once again hitched her decision to that of Jack Kaplan. "I tell you what," she told me, "if you can persuade Jack Kaplan to come back in, I will, too." It remained only to persuade Mr. Kaplan, whose Fifth Avenue office by coincidence was across the street from *Monocle*.

His philosophy was fine—"If you have a lot of money, you should spread it around to help things grow." But as I already knew, the trick was to get him to act on his philosophy. Years later James Wechsler, longtime crusading liberal editor of the *New York Post*, told me of his own troubles with Kaplan, who had been part of a consortium to buy the *New York Post* from Dorothy Schiff (this was long before Rupert Murdoch actually bought it). The idea was that the consortium would enable Wechsler to get out from under Mrs. Schiff's shadow and liberate him to run an independent paper in his own way. At the last moment Kaplan came forward with a minor detail: Wechsler would have to report to a three-person executive committee, one of whom would be Kaplan and the second of whom would be a nice fellow named Ray Rubinow, who worked for Kaplan and did his bidding. The deal was undone. It seemed to me I had heard that song before.

Now Mr. Kaplan told me that his oldest daughter, Joan Kaplan Davidson, had moved back to New York and was now running the Kaplan Fund. She was the intellectual in the family, and if I could persuade her, I had persuaded him.

I thanked him and took my leave with a heavy heart, because I had been told by a mutual friend that the dynamic Joan Davidson—who had great energy and great politics—she went on to run for the state senate and become head of the New York State Council on the Arts, a personal friend, and a *Nation* supporter—had only one drawback: We were told that she did not really believe in satire as a legitimate agent of change. It was strictly for laughs, and since the assassination of John F. Kennedy and other recent events, politics were not so funny.

Still, I wrote Joan for an appointment, told her what I wanted to see her about, and urged her not to take the matter lightly, since on her decision rested not only the $10,000 investment we were asking of the Kaplans but the whole deal. She called, and we had lunch. It turned out she had a sense of satire, after all, and she proposed that the Kaplan Fund, instead of "investing," buy and distribute $10,000 worth of magazines. I knew this would be fine by Mrs. Field and her fellow shareholders. *Monocle* was back in business . . . I thought.

Whew. But just as I was getting ready to call in our new round of funding, who should I meet strolling down Fourteenth Street but Jack Kaplan. He was shaking his head. "So you convinced my daughter," he said. "What does *she* know?"

"She's the intellectual in the family," I reminded him.

"Look," he said, "you're a bright young man. Part of being a bright young man is knowing when to quit, when to move on. It's time for you to move on."

By this time we had moved on to the revolving door in front of his office building. "Besides," he said, "you're not seeking enough capital. Instead of looking for $100,000, you need $350,000. I tell you what I'll do. Phil Stern is a nice young man. He's heir to the Sears, Roebuck fortune and he has just written that book on taxes, *The Great Treasury Raid*. He doesn't know what he's talking about. He doesn't understand money. You tell Phil Stern I said if he'll put up half of the $350,000 I'll put up the other half."

This was a fine idea, except that I had already talked to Phil Stern and he understood money well enough to balk at putting up another penny, no less another $10,000, although he had said, "If everybody else is in, I guess I'll be in, but reluctantly."

If I knew then what I know now, I'd have stayed with it. But my battery had run down, and I guess I must have been ready to move on, because that's what I did.

Editorially *Monocle* was rocking, as they say now but didn't yet then. And sales per issue were so good that instead of our usual print order of 25,000, Simon & Schuster had agreed to take 75,000 copies of our upcoming special CIA issue and treat them like paperback books and, instead of simply taking sales orders, to "force" them out into the stores. This special CIA number, which had been scheduled to come out on November 19, 1963, had something to do with our eventual demise. Because of President Kennedy's assassination, most of the 75,000 copies never left the warehouse. Actually, although its timing could not have been more dismal, I thought the issue, which included Marvin Kitman's failed attempt to sell an advance copy of our CIA exposé to the Agency itself, was pretty funny.

It included Dick Lingeman's version of a CIA house organ ("For Your Eyes Only") complete with classified ads ("Shabby 2 Rooms on back street in Zagreb. Candy store front. Excellent cover business . . ."); Dan Greenburg's interoffice memorandum on how the CIA might change its image ("I think it's pretty clear to all of us by now just what kind of trouble we at the CIA are in imagewise— The three little words that kind of bring it home to me are: South Viet Nam . . ."); and Eleanor Dienstag's diary of an unwitting CIA hausfrau ("I Was the Wife of a Polish Ham Importer in Hungary"). But that was before I discovered via a Freedom of Information Act request twenty-five years later that the CIA had acquired its own copy of "subject publication" and had it "reviewed by a group of individuals in the Office of Security." Happily for us, they kept their literary opinion to themselves. But in the interest of full disclosure, I now, for the first time, disclose it: "Regarding the current issue, it is the opinion of the reviewers that the issue does not reflect any brilliant talent; that it is not entertaining or humorous; and in fact several of the cartoons are vulgar and in extremely poor taste. The professional level of style, composition, grammar, etc., appears to be deliberately low, and the same few themes are constantly replayed."

When *Monocle* ran out of money, as we saw it we had two choices: We could do the honorable thing and in the great tradition of American capitalism declare bankruptcy, go into Chapter 11, and pay our creditors one cent on the dollar; or, in the jargon of the mid-1960s, we could sell out. And incidentally, *Monocle* had some expertise in the art of selling out. Just before we went out of business we sent out a questionnaire asking 347 intellectuals, novelists, and activists—using as our database the index to Norman Podhoretz's book *Making It*, the latest list of Guggenheim fellows, and other ephemera—why they sold out.

The four-question survey was easy to follow.

1. Name
2. I have   ❑
                    Sold out (check one)
   I have not ❑
3. Reason for selling out (if extra space is needed use back of the page or other sheets)
4. Recommendations for other interviewees

We received responses from, among others, Norman Podhoretz, who told us that he threw our questionnaire in the garbage, "where it belongs"; Norman Mailer, whose name had been mistyped and who wrote that "I, kid Integrity, have only been tempted to sell out when wise-ass crypto-faggot types in the mailing offices of magazines like *Monocle* spell my name Normal Mailer" (and suggested that we change our name from *Monocle* to *Doughnut*); and Dwight Macdonald, who wrote that "I've sold but not, with one large exception, out." The exception was during 1929–36, when he was a staff writer on *Fortune*, "a hack in Luce's stable" who wrote on assigned subjects in "house" style rather than his own. He left because "it had become neurologically impossible. I kept falling asleep in the act of prostitution."

We published an entry from *Harper's* magazine editor Willie Morris, even though after his submission he cast doubt on his credibility as a sellout by noisily quitting as editor of *Harper's* magazine rather than sell out to the money men there. We decided to print his response anyway, "in the interests of scientific integrity." Some of the entries were funny, some angry, and some, like that of Julian Bond, then "the first Negro to sit in the Georgia state legislature," now the head of the NAACP, were bittersweet.

I sold out on March 15, 1959, while on a bus trip from Atlanta to Florence, Alabama. I took a seat near the front of the bus, and some few miles out of Atlanta, the bus driver pulled to the side

of the road to allow some white gentleman to negotiate a change
in my seating.

After some brief discussion, I acquiesced, and took a seat in
the rear. There I was met by some brothers of color, who re-
monstrated with me.

"We were behind you all the way."

And so they were.

And in order to write an appropriate introduction to the symposium (it
later appeared in *The Antioch Review*, to which *Monocle* itself sold
out), Kitman took a job in advertising.

As for the rest of us, we decided we would each write our own book
on our own time. Simultaneously we had an idea for a new enterprise
whereby we might use the revenue to pay *Monocle's* debts to society,
not to mention our creditors, our writers, and ourselves. But first we
had our own work to do.

In 1964, when Robert Kennedy resigned as Attorney General to run for
the U.S. Senate from New York, as the man from *Monocle* I naturally
became a charter member of an organization called Carpetbaggers for
Kennedy. Its motto was "Vote for the Man of Your Choice from the
State of His Choice." But a year later, as an alumnus of the Yale Law
School and a soon-to-be alumnus of money-losing *Monocle*, I signed
up to write a book on R.F.K. as Attorney General. Since the rumor was
that he was thinking of running for President, and since his attorney
generalship was his only significant executive experience, and since no
one had ever written a book on the role of the Attorney General before,
the project seemed to me a no-brainer. Not that it was my idea originally. No, it was a fellow Yale law student, Michael Meltsner (who
went on to be an NAACP Legal Defense Fund lawyer, a professor of
constitutional law, an author of both fiction and nonfiction, a law
school dean, and a sex therapist), who asked me what I thought of the
idea and I said I thought it was capital. Then when Michael decided
he did not have the time to do it by himself (he was also taking acting
lessons on the theory that good litigators must be good performers), I
volunteered to be his co-author, and when he decided that he did not
have the time to do his half, with his blessing I decided to do it myself.

The way I proceeded on *Kennedy Justice*, lurching from magazine assignment to magazine assignment, was in accordance with my triangulated theory of freelancing: To make ends meet, one has to average at least three pay days for the same research. When interviewing a book subject for a magazine piece, this system can have its hazards (if you pull your punches, your article will suffer; if you don't, your access will suffer). It can also have its advantages. Busy people may not want to see a first-time author for a book he's composing about the past which won't appear until some distant future, especially if they play less than a starring role, yet they have a motive to cooperate on an article about themselves scheduled to run in the short run; and then there is the added plus of expenses paid. Nevertheless, I reviewed books about Robert Kennedy for *Book World* and the *Times Book Review*, and I wrote profiles of Under Secretary of State Nicholas deB. Katzenbach and Robert Morgenthau, U.S. Attorney for the Southern District of New York, for *The New York Times Magazine*. Seven years after the first freedom ride, in 1968, I persuaded *The Atlantic Monthly* to let me retrace the freedom riders' route from bus station to bus station all over the South, to see what progress if any had been made in desegregating public facilities. (The answer was some, but in a place like Jackson, Mississippi, not all that much.) *The Atlantic* was happy to foot the bill, by the way, but I suspect that was because they were mainly paying for bus tickets.

I'm not complaining, especially since freelancing also provided a cost-free continuing adult-education course in the way real-world magazines worked. Consider the 1967 article I wrote for the *Saturday Evening Post*, the first and last time I wrote for Ben Franklin's old magazine. The subject was Ramsey Clark, whom L.B.J. had just appointed as Attorney General. Clark had served as head of the Justice Department Lands Division (in charge of Indian land claims, among others) under Kennedy, and I wanted to talk to him about that; Kennedy had used him to mediate some difficult interracial situations in the South, and I wanted to talk to him about that; and I had been told that despite the fact that he was the youngest assistant attorney general in the department, he had consistently raised principled objections to its position on wiretaps and other incursions on civil liberty in the pursuit of organized crime, and I wanted to talk to him about that. Lastly, as Attorney

General he was taking actions that seemed calculated to declare his ideological independence from his father, Justice Tom Clark, who as Harry Truman's Attorney General had brought some major Cold War political cases, and I was interested in that, too.

Also, I expected to learn about the power relationship between the President and his chief law enforcement officer, but the lesson that stayed with me longest turned out to be about the power relationship between the art director and the editor of an American mass magazine.

The *Post* had commissioned an article of 2,000–2,500 words. But as occasionally happens, space that week was available for only a 1,500-word short (they had a word for it), and I was told it was my choice: Either they could cut 1,000 words (more than a third of the piece) or we could put the article on hold and it might never run. Never having been published in the *Post* and concerned that my article was not imperishable, I voted to proceed and showed up in the editor's office to do the deed.

The first few hundred words were easy. In fact, one might argue, as Tom Congdon, my editor, did, that cutting actually improved things. The next five hundred words were more difficult, and Tom was gracious enough to say things like "I hate to lose that grace note." Cut. Or "A subtle qualification it would be nice to include. Too bad," as he shook his head sadly and bit his lip. Cut.

Then there was nothing more to be cut, but the piece was still thirty words too long. What to do? "This is going to mean blood," Tom conceded, shaking his head sadly. "We are going to inflict a wound on your piece. All we can do is try to do as little damage as possible."

At which point I had what I thought was a bright idea. If we had been in a cartoon, a little lightbulb would have popped up over my head. Speaking of cartoons, there, in the middle of the page, was a cartoon, a *Saturday Evening Post* staple—*Hazel,* the wisecracking housekeeper who always put the middle-class Mr. and Mrs. for whom she worked in their place.

The year was 1967, violence was in the air, there were riots in the slums and a presidential election around the corner. Washington, D.C., was coming off a 100,000-strong anti–Vietnam War demonstration, and thanks mainly to the restraint of Ramsey Clark, the subject of my profile, the whole affair never erupted into one of those violent physical confrontations that later came to mark the era. I thought I had made that point in thirty reasonably well-chosen words, and now my gentlemanly editor was painfully about to erase them. Yet even I was not so naïve as to think that he might eliminate *Hazel* in the interests of a more accurate, nuanced portrait of the nation's controversial chief law enforcement officer. Still, *Hazel* appeared in a box which ran 4" x 5" and was set off by what seemed to me more than ample white space. "What about cutting back on some of the white space?" I asked in my most tentative voice. Congdon smiled, as if to say, We're in this together, kid. *Hazel* stayed, and the bloodstains on her pristine white-spaced environment were noticed only by me.

Space, says my friend Milton Glaser, the world-famous magazine designer, is power.

Meanwhile, Dick Lingeman was at work on a book about the home front during World War II, which became *Don't You Know There's a War On?* Courty Bryan wrote *P. S. Wilkerson*, which won the *Harper's* prize for best first novel. Kitman, whose short-lived career in advertising didn't stop him from writing something called "George Washington's Expense Account by General George Washington and PFC Marvin Kitman," was now composing a sequel about George Washington's presidential campaign, working title, "The Making of the President, 1789." (When Theodore White's publisher contacted him to complain that White had taken out a trademark on *The Making of the President* title, Kitman told him not to worry, he would call his own book *The Making of the Prefident*.)

Monocle books, which we decided to call Pentacle Books (thinking to name our burgeoning conglomerate Tentacle), were something else entirely. We thought of *Monocle* books as un-books that would never bear our names. Their purpose was to do what our newsletter had failed to do—to bail *Monocle* out. We got the idea for *Monocle* books from an experience we had with one of our writers, Dan Greenburg, and an experience I had on the radio.

Dan, with whom I had been in correspondence when *Monocle* was still at Yale, came into our New York office one day early on, when it was still one room in my two-room apartment, with an idea for a book, which he called "A Jewish Mother's Strategy." It was a funny idea. But, like many young writers, he didn't know any book publishers, did we?

I sent him to the one publisher I knew, Roger Price, who was now launching his new novelty-book publishing business. The next thing we heard was that at Roger's suggestion Dan had changed the name of his book to *How to Be a Jewish Mother*, and before too long, it was number one on the *New York Times* bestseller list.

The idea for *Monocle* books came one evening when I was on Casper Citron's radio interview show promoting *Monocle*. Bill Adler was a co-guest, promoting a book he had compiled called *More Kennedy Wit*, a sequel, in case you haven't figured it out, to *The Kennedy Wit* (which also eventually gave rise to *The Stevenson Wit* and *The Johnson Wit*. I'm still waiting for *The Eisenhower Wit*). *The Stevenson Wit* I could understand. He was always telling self-deprecatory stories about himself. Kennedy I could understand. But *The Johnson Wit*? It occurred to me that in order to understand the outbreak of wit books one needed not a theory of charisma but a theory of publishing. And Adler provided it when he told me (off-mic) that *The Kennedy Wit* had sold 100,000 copies in hardcover and close to 1,000,000 in paperback. I noticed on my own that these wit books were each priced at $3, were 5½" x 8¼", with black-and-white cover photos and the title in red 42-point News Gothic in the upper-right-hand corner. In other words, they had a formula, which was to imitate what worked.

Our basic idea was to imitate their idea—to come up with ideas for books that didn't require writers and to find trade-book publishers willing to pay for and publish them. Then we'd hire researchers, whom we would pay by the hour to research them, and use the vast profits to pay our bills and ourselves. Since the idea was to make money, and some of our best, i.e., worst, ideas were calculated to appeal to the largest possible audience, i.e., the lowest common denominator, we not only had no pride of authorship but had shame of authorship, preferring to be anonymous and behind-the-scenes. This was before the words "book packager" had entered the publishing world's vocabulary. But as we saw it, we'd be doing the nonbusiness side of the books we published: come up with the idea, oversee the research, guarantee the quality of the editorial content. In that capacity we were responsible for more than thirty un-books, on none of which did we put our name. Now it can be told that although they were published under such eminent imprints as Simon & Schuster, the Dial Press, Bantam Books,

G. P. Putnam, Workman, and so forth, *Monocle* was the real perpetrator behind such classics as *The McCarthy Wit* (Eugene, that is); *The Beatles: Words Without Music* (transcripts of Beatles press conferences); *Barbed Wires*, a collection of famous funny telegrams (like Robert Benchley's on arriving in Venice: STREETS FULL OF WATER, PLEASE ADVISE); *The Illustrated Gift Edition of The Communist Manifesto* (the manifesto was in the public domain and our back cover blurb said, "Revolutionary!" V. I. Lenin); *The Algonquin Wits*; dictionaries such as *Drugs from A to Z, Witchcraft from A to Z,* and so forth.

Weary of nonbooks and wary of real books, we missed the opportunity *Monocle* had afforded to comment on the passing scene. And there was much on which to comment. *The Royal Canadian Air Force (RCAF) Exercise Plans for Physical Fitness* had barely hit the bestseller list when Stein & Day published our own *The RCAF Diet, Exercise and Sex Manual* (our RCAF was the Red Chinese Air Force) by William Randolph Hersch (a pseudonym for Lingeman, Kitman, and me). Those were the days of the Vietnam War, when our military and political leaders kept assuring us that there was "light at the end of the tunnel," that our boys "will be home by Christmas." We put out an entire book of such assurances from L.B.J., General Westmoreland, Secretary of Defense Robert McNamara, and greater and lesser evil characters predicting the imminent end of the war. Grove Press, the publisher, worried that the war would be over before they went to press, but needless to say, the war—and the predictions—continued long after this particular un-book was published.

In the end, we were unsuited to follow our own formula: having inexperienced, low-priced young people research books based on our clichéd ideas that we would edit into shape and then sit back and clip coupons. Call it hubris, call it boredom, or call it incompetence, I prefer to think that our instincts were insufficiently base. For instance, when a lawyer friend told us that Delacorte had sold on supermarket counters alone more than 2 million copies of a little, 25-cent chapbook he had tossed off called *A Wife's Rights*, our immediate thought was to produce a quickie on *Kids' Rights*. But the researcher we recruited, who was Jean Strouse, claimed that it was impossible and perhaps even unethical to reduce the complexities of children's rights to hornbook-law one-liners. She persuaded us that the subject called for a real book and proceeded to research and write it, under the snappy title *Up Against the Law*. She also, rightly, believed she was entitled to a share of the royalties, which we gave her. Of course the book received respectful reviews, and instead of selling in the millions, it sold in the tens of thousands.

That book may have been a turning point for us, however. We continued to spawn collections, anthologies, and other ephemera, but somehow they got more and more ambitious and sold fewer and fewer copies. Under our aegis James Boylan, the former editor of the *Columbia Journalism Review*, put together a thoroughly scholarly, annotated selection of articles from what was arguably the best newspaper this country ever produced, the old *New York World*. Two Berkeley graduate students collected the most interesting essays written about the campus free-speech movement and what followed, under the title *Revolution at Berkeley*, and Irving Howe wrote a smart and prescient introduction that anticipated the campus turmoils to come in the early 1970s. As a result of Susan Sontag's essay on "camp" in *Partisan Review*, Milton Glaser and Avon Books publisher, Peter Mayer, asked us if we wanted to do a book on the subject, and we put together *The Camp Follower's Guide*, but we were violating our own rules, creating new materials rather than collecting old ones.

In this context our one bestseller, *Report from Iron Mountain: On the Possibility and Desirability of Peace*, was born. The year was 1966, and one morning *The New York Times* featured a short news item about how the stock market had tumbled because of what the headline called a "Peace Scare." The news item had no byline, but it seemed to Marvin, Dick Lingeman, and me to be worthy of Jonathan Swift, H. L. Mencken, Mark Twain. We, of course, had naïvely believed that the prospect of peace would be as welcome on Wall Street as in *Monocle's* low-rent Greenwich Village offices. All of which got us thinking. Suppose the government had appointed a task force to plan the transition from a wartime economy, and the task force concluded that we couldn't afford it because our entire economy was based on the preparation for war and without this threat it would collapse? And suppose, as a result, the report was therefore suppressed? In the spirit of Mencken's famous hoax about the introduction of the bathtub to the United States (he claimed that only after Millard Fillmore introduced one into the White House did Americans, who previously regarded them as unsanitary, start to bathe regularly), we decided to publish an account of the suppression of this report.

To give the book credibility we needed an ultrarespectable mainstream publisher with a sense of humor and the pluck to pull off a hoax. This publisher should also share our belief in the importance of putting the subject of economic conversion from a military to a peacetime economy on the national agenda.

Luckily for us the ideal candidate was at hand. Our collection of essays about the free-speech movement at Berkeley had been published by Dial Press, whose list included such prestigious writers as James Baldwin, Norman Mailer, and Richard Condon. As a result, we came to know Dial's maverick publisher, Richard Baron, and its imaginative editor in chief, author of a little-known novel called *Welcome to Hard Times*, one E. L. Doctorow. Later, he came to fame as the author of *The Book of Daniel*, *Ragtime*, and other novels that demonstrate that fiction can be a path to deep historical truths. Sight unseen, Dial signed on, and even listed the book in their catalogue as nonfiction, neglecting to mention to their salesmen that the *Report* was a hoax.

We had equal luck with our choice of author. We knew that Leonard Lewin, who had edited an anthology of political satire (under the pseudonym L. L. Case), was a student of the genre. We knew that he cared passionately about issues of war and peace. And his wicked simultaneous parody of the historian Arthur Schlesinger, Jr., and Eisenhower's speechwriter Emmet Hughes's memoir *The Ordeal of Power*, which *Monocle* had published under Lewin's title "The Ordeal of Rhetoric," showed him to be a sophisticated observer of what Ike had called in his farewell speech (written with the help of Hughes) the military-industrial complex.

There was one problem: Lewin insisted he couldn't write the story of the suppression of the so-called report until there was a report to be suppressed. And so, with the discreet input of his *Monocle* colleagues and people ranging from Arthur Waskow, then at the Institute for Policy Studies in Washington (who was at work on what he called "A History of the Future"); W. H. "Ping" Ferry of the Center for the Study of Democratic Institutions in Santa Barbara, California; John Kenneth Galbraith, who was back at Harvard after his stint as J.F.K.'s Ambassador to India; and a cadre of *Monocle* interns to track down original sources, Lewin wrote the report. *Report from Iron Mountain* was a brilliant imitation of think-tankese, rendered in impenetrable, bureaucratic prose, replete with obfuscating footnotes, all of them, except for two trick ones, to real if esoteric sources, in a variety of languages.

When we read the report, we all agreed that it had to be published in its entirety. Thus the report became the body of the book, and the narrative of its "suppression" appears in an explanatory foreword.

As it happened, our carefully planned cover story (or "legend," as they say in the CIA) paid off. When John Leo, then a reporter for *The New York Times*, spotted the nonfiction listing of *Report from Iron Mountain* in Dial's catalogue, he made the traditional round of calls to determine whether it was real or a hoax. At Dial he was told if he thought it was a fraud he should check the footnotes, virtually all of which, of course, checked out. No advance reviewer in the trade publications had labeled it a hoax, and the State Department's Arms Control and Disarmament Agency only said carefully, "To our knowledge no such special study group ever existed." When Leo called the White House, instead of a denial, he got a no-comment—we'll have-to-check-it-out-but-don't-quote-us. (For all the L.B.J. White House knew, the J.F.K. White House *had* commissioned such a study.) The upshot was that the *Times* published on the front page a well-reported article by Leo with a headline that itself could have been a parody of *Times* style. It said, "Some See a Book as Hoax/Others Take It Seriously." Who could ask for anything more?

Then John Kenneth Galbraith, who had been writing a series of spoof articles for *Esquire* under the pseudonym Mark Epernay about a fictitious "psychometrist," Professor Herschel McLandress (creator of the McLandress Coefficient, a theory about how long famous people can go without thinking about themselves—e.g., Henry Kissinger achieved a coefficient of 6.0 minutes on the scale), wrote a review in *Book World* under the name of McLandress. The professor concluded: "As I would put my personal repute behind the authenticity of this document, so I would testify to the validity of its conclusions. My reservations relate only to the wisdom of releasing it to an obviously unconditioned public." The review led to speculation that Galbraith himself had written *Report from Iron Mountain*. He called a press conference to deny he had anything to do with it. There were only two conceivable authors, he said: Dean Rusk or Clare Boothe Luce.

A number of people—most of them in government and regular readers of bureaucratese—came to believe *Report from Iron Mountain* was the real thing. Some reviewers praised it as a satire. *Transaction* magazine devoted the better part of an issue to a sober discussion of the questions the *Report* raised. The symposiasts, in addition to editor in chief Irving Louis Horowitz, included the economist Kenneth Boulding, the sociologist Herbert Gans, and other distinguished policy intellectuals. Most interesting were the reactions of Herman Kahn and Henry Kissinger, who took the satire personally and angrily dismissed it as sophomoric and idiotic; and Fletcher Prouty, a national security aide in the Kennedy Administration (the model for the Donald Sutherland character in Oliver Stone's *JFK*), who said he believed it was the real McCoy. In 1972 Lewin confessed his authorship in *The New York Times Book Review*. He had intended, he wrote, "to caricature the bankruptcy of the think-tank mentality by pursuing its style of scientific thinking to its logical ends." He defended the hoax technique as the best way to gain attention for the book and its underlying message.

In a weird coda, Lewin discovered in the mid-1980s that the ultra-right-wing Liberty Lobby and others, believing that the report was a government document and as such in the public domain, had disseminated thousands of copies without bothering to request permission, and some of these copies were being sold through Liberty Lobby's hate-filled newspaper, *The Spotlight*. He sued, and the case was settled out of court, resulting in the withdrawal of thousands of copies of the bootleg edition, which came to reside in Lewin's living room. But well-worn copies continued to circulate along with a six-hour video based on the book.

One might have thought that the hoax, having been confessed, proclaimed, and even adjudicated, would have been laid to rest. But no, like a radioactive substance it seemed to have a half-life of its own. On May 9, 1995, *The Wall Street Journal* published a front-page story headlined:

A CAUSE FOR FEAR
Though Called a Hoax
"Iron Mountain" Report
Guides Some Militias

Iron Mountain, it seemed, had returned. And this time, to the loonies in the boonies, it was evidence of a government plot so sinister it would make Waco look like a panty raid. *Aux arms, citoyens!* Along with *The Turner Diaries*, a novel of right-wing revolution, and Pat Robertson's *The New World Order*, a nonfiction exposé, with anti-Semitic undertones, of how a cabal of international bankers runs the world, the Michigan militia and other far-right groups apparently regarded *Iron Mountain* as a sort of bible. To us, its acceptance by superpatriots and conspiracy theorists of the far right is roughly akin to the Irish Republican Army considering Jonathan Swift's "A Modest Proposal" proof that eating babies is official British policy.

So although *Monocle* was no more, *Iron Mountain* wouldn't go away. In 1996 it was republished, this time by Basic Books, with a new introduction telling all. Perhaps this was partly because pied piper Lewin, with his perfect pitch, had stumbled on a netherworld for paranoids— the black hole of government secrecy and deception, where Kennedy assassinationologists march in lockstep with white supremacists, neo-Nazis, and militiamen. By exposing their exaggerated fears and suspicions, he also taps into our own unresolved political conflicts.

And undoubtedly it was partly because claims of national security are all too often a cloak for government lies, cover-ups, and bureaucratic disinformation. But the real relevance of Lewin's skillful parody of think-tankese and think-tank-think is that it underlines the folly of confusing moderation of tone with credibility, and of assigning so-called value-neutral prose a sacrosanct place in public discourse.

The *Report from Iron Mountain* also raised the perennial question of reality outdistancing satire. As Lewin later wrote: "The Pentagon Papers were not written by someone like me. Neither was the Defense Department's *Pax Americana* study (how to take over Latin America)." That ultraright conspiracy theorists, reinforced in their paranoia by governmental abuse and secrecy, take Lewin's scenario as seriously as the think-tankers take themselves is, of course, the scariest proposition of all. Every time Lewin or others in on it acknowledge that *Report from Iron Mountain* is a hoax, the conspiracy theorists regard it as further proof of a cover-up.

We wrote about this phenomenon in *The Nation*, after the *Wall Street Journal* article on militia reading habits. We said that perhaps the only way to put a stop to this speculation would be to tell them: "Guys, you're right! *Report from Iron Mountain* is a real document. Remember: You read it here in the pro-Commie, pro-government, pro-Jewish, anti-American *Nation*."

The physicist Alan Sokal is the scholar who in May 1996 revealed in the late *Lingua Franca*, a lively journal covering the trials and tribulations of academic life and letters, that his article on postmodern science that had just appeared in the Spring/Summer 1996 issue of *Social Text*, a respected if esoteric journal of cultural studies, was, like *Report from Iron Mountain,* both a parody and a hoax. Its title was "Transgressing the Boundaries: Toward a Transformative Hermeneutics of Quantum Gravity." Tom Frank, editor of the Chicago journal *The Baffler*, elucidated how the sophisticated editors of *Social Text* were taken in:

> With a hilarious studied slavishness Sokal carefully includes the usual pious references to the subversive power of interdisciplinary; he takes pains to flatter and agree with the editors of *Social Text* and goes out of his way to assail their usual targets; he summons the usual barrage of references and quotations, many of them predictably impenetrable; and he closes with confused calls for an "emancipatory mathematics" and "a libratory postmodern science."

Sokal's prank was aimed not at political enemies but rather at his fellow leftists, and what offended him was not their politics but what he called the "sloppy thinking" of their critique of science. His method was not unlike Lewin's: "I took the silliest things written about physics and mathematics by the most prominent peoples . . . [and then] concocted an argument relating it all" in their preposterous jargon. But whereas the militia rose to Lewin's bait even after he confessed, refusing to accept the hoax as a hoax, the left professoriat denounced Sokal for his "betrayal" of professional ethics and academic good faith.

I cheered Sokal on for any number of reasons beyond the sharpness of his skewer. As Tom Frank noted, there was a sweet irony in Sokal's target of the jargon of so-called poststructuralism. "It's a jargon with a curious twist, a professional language that celebrates anti-professionalism." It seemed to me that language was and is important, and like Lewin, Sokal performed a public service by exposing the social function of jargon—to keep outsiders out. (This is a delicate business, since the ostensible purpose of professional terminology is to permit the making of fine distinctions that would otherwise be lost. But the abuse of such entitlements deserves exposure, and if there is a little humiliation involved, so be it.)

Notwithstanding the success of *Iron Mountain*, as *Monocle's* book publishing business took off, we got more and more depressed: Our "serious" books took too much time and earned too little money, and our un-books were unserious and in the end not worth it. Besides, we had books of our own to write and other magazines to write for. With my family I moved down to Washington to work on that book about Robert Kennedy and the Justice Department. Then one day back in New York on business, I ran into a friend who said to me, "Hey, I read a letter from you last week."

"How's that?" I asked. I hadn't written him a letter last week.

"No, not to me," he said, "to some writer."

"Where did you find it?" I asked.

"In the gutter," he said.

The rest of the story is almost too depressing to tell. But it turned out that in a manic burst of expansive enthusiasm, without telling me, Pete Hunter had put the *Monocle* files in storage to provide space for expected expansion of his newsletter business. And then, when the expansion contracted, in a fit of depression he neglected to pay the storage bills, and after the third notice, which he forgot to tell us about, our files were apparently dumped. There is nothing like having one's magazine's files dumped in the gutter to concentrate the mind on what's next!

There are two theories about freelance writers, even triangulated ones like me. One, put forward by Don McKinney, an editor at *The Saturday Evening Post* (quoted in *Time*), is that a forty-year-old freelance writer is by definition something of a failure, since the best writers go on to become editors. The other, held by Elizabeth Young, a British arts journalist, is that editors are freelance writers who couldn't hack it. Depending on whether it is Monday or Wednesday, I believe they are both right (or wrong). In any case, I took on plenty of assignments during my *Monocle* and *Kennedy Justice* days because I thought it would help pay the bills, and if I was going to edit and publish my own magazine one day, it couldn't hurt to see how others did it. Harold Hayes, the legendary editor of *Esquire*, had seen and claimed to admire *Monocle*. He also had an idea. As he explained it, a brilliant young Random House editor named Jason Epstein was said to have a theory that you needed only six people to make a book a bestseller. My assignment was to buttonhole Epstein, find out who the six were, and, in the course of a profile, explain how the system worked.

I found Jason, who denied he had any such theory, but I also found a group of writers whom I thought of as the New York intellectual establishment (Norman Podhoretz was later to dub them "the family") and instead of the original assignment wrote my piece about them with Jason at its center.

Unbeknownst to me, *Esquire* had been quietly planning an issue on what it called the literary establishment (complete with charts on who was in, who was out, who was up, and who was down, who was in the red hot center, and so forth). *Esquire*'s establishment chart caused something of a hubbub when it appeared, and what with one thing and another, my article didn't.

Maybe it didn't appear because *Esquire*'s establishment chart preempted my belated establishment article. Maybe it was because the article didn't measure up (or down, depending on your perspective). Or maybe it was because I made the beginner's mistake of showing the article to its subject. When I showed the piece to Jason, I thought I heard him laugh out loud (I think that's where I wrote something about how he cared less about his Jewish heritage than his joke about his mother's name, which, if I remember right, was Gladyce Shapiro Epstein Levine). I forget what else he said. But a few days later I got a call from Harold Hayes, who had initially accepted the piece with what I thought to be enthusiasm, but now he asked if I had shown it to Jason. When I said I had, he said, with what I thought to be a note of irritation in his voice, "That explains it." Apparently he had run into Jason on the street (*Esquire*'s offices were a few blocks from Random House on Madison Avenue), and Jason, who was a mumbler, mumbled something like "I like Victor, but if you run that piece I'll sue."

Hayes explained why it was unprofessional and unwise to show a piece to its subject in advance of publication. After-the-fact libel suits were not a problem, since all articles were vetted in advance by *Esquire*'s lawyers and the magazine carried libel insurance; but a before-the-fact motion for an injunction could result in hundreds of thousands of copies not leaving the warehouse, costing millions of dollars.

There are few things more depressing to a freelance writer than to have his commissioned article turned down; but as I was soon to learn, from an economic point of view, rejection had its compensations.

Esquire paid the full fee for the piece even though it never ran. Then, a year or two later, *The New York Times Magazine* called to ask if I was interested in doing an essay on the New York intellectual community. I subsequently discovered that they had first called Calvin Trillin, whom I had interviewed for the Epstein profile (I had shown him a draft, too—was there anyone to whom I hadn't shown a draft?), and since he was otherwise occupied with *The New Yorker*, he recommended me.

When I first asked him what he knew about the New York intellectuals, Trillin had said, "Oh, you mean the College of Irvings." Say a little more, I said. "You know," he said, "Irving Howe, Irving Kristol, Irving Podhoretz, Irving Sontag, Irving Macdonald—those guys." Trillin should have done the piece himself.

I did a new round of interviews, and on Sunday, March 27, 1966, the *Times Magazine* published my "Notes on Cult; or, How to Join the Intellectual Establishment." My life was changed, but I'll concede that maybe that's because it was also my wedding day, and the rabbi (who incidentally was the New Haven radical civil libertarian Bob Goldburg, who took the train down from Connecticut to perform the honors) began the ceremony by saying he had read the *Times* on the way down from New Haven and "I'd like to welcome you to a different sort of establishment . . ."

I can't figure out who was a slower learner, *Esquire* or me. Despite my mistakes with my first article, and despite their not running it, over the next few months they came back with three ideas for a second one: following "Suzy," the high-society gossip columnist, on her rounds; covering the shooting of *Lilith*, directed by Robert Rossen and starring Jean Seberg; and eating out on $1,000 a night with only one guest (and a cap of $200 for wine). I had never read Suzy, so I didn't really understand the idea for that one; I had not yet come to appreciate the importance of *Lilith* director Robert Rossen, who had been a controversial resister and then an informer before HUAC (telling the committee, "We no longer have the luxury of individual morality"), and didn't know that Seberg was the object of an FBI surveillance and harassment campaign; and although I was tempted by the idea of eating out on $1,000 a night, I thought I had a better idea. How about a profile of W. H. "Ping" Ferry? I asked. Who? asked Byron Dobell. Dobell was Hayes's deputy and a *Monocle* admirer. He was credited with having turned the young Tom Wolfe's writer's block into a sensational article that launched his career, by asking Wolfe to send him a letter on what he had found. It became: "There goes (VAROOM! VAROOM!) that Kandy Kolored (THPHHHHHH) tangerine-flake streamlined baby (RAHGHHHH!) around the bend (BRUMMMMMMMMMMMMMMMMM) . . ."

I explained that Ferry, a deputy director of the Center for the Study of Democratic Institutions, was America's town crank. He had publicly quit the Democratic Party in protest over the Vietnam War, proposed the abolition of the stock exchange; his solution to the perils of the Cold War was a pact committing the President of the United States and the Premier of the Soviet Union to the personal slaughter of fifty children before going to war; he had suggested that only older people be drafted, because they had less life to lose; he favored showing executions on cable television to high-school students; and he had attacked America's most sacred cow, FBI director J. Edgar Hoover, as an inefficient "spy-swatter"; he— Byron made a stop sign, then raised his arms above his head and made quotation marks with his index fingers. "The Man Who Attacked J. Edgar Hoover!" he said.

I got the assignment. I did the piece. *Esquire* bought the piece. *Esquire* never got around to scheduling the piece. I liberated the piece. This time *The Atlantic Monthly* bought it and published it under the headline "The Happy Heretic."

This business of selling the same piece twice seemed to me to have a future. The tricky part was to avoid being paid a "kill fee" (traditionally one-third of the promised payment) if an article didn't work out. To get paid twice it had to be good enough to be accepted but not urgent or great enough to warrant immediate publication—at best, a delicate balance.

But the *Times Magazine* made that difficult. After the article about

New York intellectuals, they seemed to want to publish my articles as fast as I could write them. Only later did I learn that my batting average had less to do with me than with the *Times* system. Once one had passed the test by having an article published with positive feedback, the presumption against the writer shifted to a presumption in his favor. One could do no or little wrong.

Over the next six years, roughly between 1966 and 1972, I wrote sixteen articles for the *Times Magazine*. In 1970, five years after *Monocle* went out of business, and having written for the *Times* on subjects ranging from "The Harvards vs. the Yales" (Legal Division) to "Advertising Is an Art? A Science? A Business?" to "The Haunting of Robert Kennedy" on his presidential campaign, I went to work as an editor there. If at *Monocle* I learned unexpected lessons about the magazine business, at the *Times* I learned unexpected lessons about the relationship between news and opinion, fact and value, objectivity and ideology.

I say this less to brag than to confess. I suspect a canny teacher of journalism ethics or communications theory could find in each article I wrote for the *Times* what professors call a subject for discussion.

For example, although I had never taken a course in journalism ethics, I knew that somewhere it must be written, Thou shalt not set up thy subject. That's what Janet Malcolm was writing about many years later when she began *The Journalist and the Murderer*, a book about the journalist Joe McGinniss and his relationship with his subject, a former Green Beret convicted of killing his family, with these two remarkable sentences: "Every journalist who is not too stupid or too full of himself to notice what is going on knows what he does is morally indefensible. He is a kind of confidence man, preying on people's vanity, ignorance, or loneliness, gaining their trust and betraying them without remorse." I am too stupid or full of myself to agree with her fully, but she has a point.

It's not hard to set up one's subject, and it's not always easy to resist the temptation, even if one knows it's wrong. I may have failed the test when I wrote about Hubert Horatio Humphrey's 1968 campaign for the presidency of the United States. I followed the Vice President on a five-day pre-convention swing through Salina, Kansas, Salt Lake City, Los Angeles, and San Francisco. This was shortly after the murder of Bobby Kennedy in Los Angeles, and when the candidacy of Senator Eugene McCarthy was still a very live option.

My notes showed that in the course of his trip the loquacious Mr. Humphrey spoke of "the politics of hope, not fear," "the politics of the future, not the past," "the politics of public service," "the politics of commitment—not by word but by deed," "the politics of service rather than noise," "the politics of happiness," "the politics of tomorrow," "the politics of personal sacrifice," "the politics of self-involvement," "the politics of commitment, personal service, personal action." ("This is what I call the Volunteer Generation," he told an educational television interviewer.) But when we returned to Washington and I visited Humphrey in his Senate office, as I reported in the *Times Magazine*, "I asked him what he thought of the New Politics and he said, 'I think that the New Politics is just a phrase.'"

It made for a nice punch line, and indeed, he said it as I knew (or hoped) he would. But the truth is that what I asked him was "Do you think the so-called New Politics [which was said to have animated the late R.F.K.'s campaign as well as that of his rival for the nomination, Senator McCarthy] has any content, or is it just a phrase?" At the time I had mild compunctions about what I had done, but I persuaded myself that he deserved it. Now I'm not so sure.

Within weeks I was at the 1968 Democratic Convention—the one where Mayor Daley's thugs roughed up hundreds of antiwar protesters, where police-incited riots culminated in the famous trial of Abbie Hoffman, Bobby Seale, Jerry Rubin, and the rest of the Chicago Eight—with an assignment from the *Times Magazine* to cover the convention.

My way of doing it was to follow around Lawrence O'Brien, Humphrey's campaign manager. His convention consisted of alternating between work in a backroom office on the second floor of the amphitheater—from which he would periodically venture forth on a back-slapping, hand-shaking, kiss-blowing, elbow-locking, congratulations-receiving, ear-whispering, sound bite–providing tour of the floor—and private smoke-filled meetings in his suite on the twenty-fourth floor of the Conrad Hilton (the Vice President was on the twenty-fifth).

His desk at the convention center faced an adjoining "boiler room," which contained a long, green, felt-covered table at which regional delegate counters sat (four young women down each side and one at the head). They were equipped with telephones connected to the floor, TV monitors, delegation lists, and all the other paraphernalia needed in the pre–cell phone era to maintain informal floor contact while staying in touch with O'Brien.

The night of the nomination, the *Times*'s photographer caught O'Brien leaning against three stacked television sets in his command post at the convention hall. One of them showed the police, four miles away, tear-gassing and clubbing demonstrators in front of the Conrad Hilton Hotel, headquarters for the convention. One of them showed speakers from the podium. (District of Columbia delegate and *Monocle* shareholder Phil Stern was arguing, "You can break heads with billy clubs, but you can't destroy ideas with billy clubs.") And the third consisted of interviews on the floor. At the moment Richard Goodwin, one of J.F.K.'s people, who after Bobby Kennedy's assassination had defected to McCarthy, was holding forth. O'Brien was listening to the Goodwin interview and had tuned the sound off on the others.

It didn't occur to me until much later that O'Brien's entire convention—and that of the Democratic establishment—had turned the sound off on the interaction between the demonstrators and Mayor Daley's thugs in favor of listening to an insider interview on the horse race. As a result, he and many other members of the party's elite never really experienced the convention as it was seen by most of America.

At the time I had more important things to think about. Me. I had, after all, been covering a critical presidential convention for the country's paper of record. I had phoned in my story (in those pre–e-mail days one phoned one's story in to a recording machine), and the next morning I heard back that it would run in the following Sunday's *New York Times Magazine*. I was in a cab headed for the airport when the driver asked if I was a delegate and I told him no such luck.

What are you doing here, then? I told him with an appropriate air of self-importance that I was a journalist covering the convention.

What's your name? he said.

You wouldn't know it, I said with appropriate humility.

Tell me, he said. What's your name?

Really, you wouldn't know it, I said.
Don't be coy, he said. Tell me your name.
All right, I said. Victor Navasky.
"*Monocle!*" he said.
And it made my day, week, year.

3

THE VIEW FROM
WEST FORTY-THIRD STREET

It took a Chicago cabdriver to remind me that not everybody saw the *Times* the way those of us who worked there saw it. The *Times* tended to define the world in terms of itself rather than vice versa. Once I started writing for *The Times Book Review*, I was asked to write for the *Times Magazine*. And once I started appearing in the magazine, I got invited to lunch by the Arts & Leisure editor, who told me that he heard I had written a funny piece for the magazine and was I interested in writing for Arts & Leisure? And not long after I wrote a piece in Arts & Leisure, I ran into Abe Raskin on Martha's Vineyard, where we were subletting a two-week summer rental with another couple, and he told me that the Editorial Board was looking for someone to write light essays, and if I was interested I should write three 500-word essays on subjects of my own choosing and if they worked . . .

It became clear that success at the *Times* was the main credential for success at the *Times*. And why not?

As a freelance writer I had been spending twelve hours a day staring at my typewriter and getting three hours' worth of work done on my book. On the assumption that I could get my three hours of writing done before or after an eight-hour day, I took a job as "manuscript editor" on the *Times Magazine* in 1970, with the understanding that I would stay for at least two years and would write something like three articles a year. And when I went on their payroll I began to understand how *Times* assumptions affected what got published and how.

I loved going to work at the *Times*, even if it meant putting on a suit and tie. I loved going to the daily meeting, where you got to sit around with a dozen bright people and talk about the political and cultural events of the day. And I loved submitting ideas for subjects that other writers should write about even though initially only a small percentage—and not the most interesting ones—were getting through. And I loved sending cables asking for background memoranda or advice from *Times* bureau chiefs around the world, frequently the best-informed Western journalists in their region.

At first I naïvely thought my job was to commission articles on trends or movements or ideas ahead of everybody else, to help identify new issues and topics to put on the national agenda. But I soon discovered that if a subject had not already appeared in the daily *Times,* it was approached with great suspicion. Did it really exist? How, after all, could it be worthy of the in-depth background treatment that only the *Times Magazine* could provide if it had not even been noted in the daily? The News of the Week in Review was no help, since in truth that turned out to be the news-as-reported-in-*The-New-York-Times*-that-week-condensed-and-recycled. I didn't understand the real meaning of all this until my friend J. Anthony Lukas, then a staff writer for the magazine, identified what he called the Afghanistan principle. He formulated this principle while covering the 1969–70 trial of the so-called Chicago Eight. That was the trial where Judge Julius Hoffman brutally ordered the manacling of the black defendant Bobby Seale.

When Lukas filed his copy, which reported that Judge Hoffman had brutally ordered the manacling of the black defendant Bobby Seale, his editor told him he couldn't use the word "brutally." Why not? Because that would be editorializing in the news columns and this was supposed to be an objective job of reporting. Lukas said he didn't understand: When he had been reporting from Asia he had frequently filed stories with leads such as "Today, the Wali of Swat brutally put down the uprising of 2,000 peasants . . ." and nobody on the foreign desk complained. The Afghanistan Principle held that at *The New York Times,* at least, one's ability to tell the truth was inversely proportional to one's distance from West Forty-third Street.

At *Monocle* we joked in our 1960 pilot issue, "Every magazine is edited with a Typical Reader in mind; and *Monocle* is no exception. *Playboy*'s is the young man-about-town; *McCalls* is the family; *The*

New Yorker's is not the little old lady from Dubuque; the *Dubuque Monthly Garden News*'s is the little old lady from Dubuque; *Seventeen*'s is the teenage girl; and *Monocle*'s, we have discovered after exhaustive research, is Jack Kennedy." At the *Times* the ideal reader was what the law used to call "the reasonable man." It took me a while to understand that the definition of the reasonable man was the *Times*'s then-publisher, Arthur Sulzberger. I'm joking, but I'm serious. If a writer's *assumptions*, as distinguished from his conclusions, varied too much from the un-spoken consensus symbolized by the owner-publisher's middle-of-the-road, commonsense, responsible-citizen, League of Women Voters' understanding of how the world worked (or ought to work), then his article could be headed for trouble.

Example: One day it was decided at the daily editorial conference that the magazine should commission an article on the use of the word "fascism." The then-editor, Lewis Bergman, a brilliant man and won-derful editor, thought that term was being abused by a generation ig-norant of its true meaning.

Lewis was at heart—or rather, at mind—a European intellectual, sentenced to serve his time among colleagues whom Dwight Macdon-ald would have dismissed as mid-cult hacks. I never knew his story, but I know he had to have had one. He had a world-class sense of humor, dressed in two-tone shirts and high style, had contempt for phonies of all stripes but especially those ahead of him in the *Times* hierarchy, and even more so those on what he regarded as the fashionable left. His personal politics seemed to me to be those of the Congress for Cul-tural Freedom, frozen in the mid-1950s, when it was founded, i.e., he was a classic Cold War liberal. But he was not so liberal. And Lewis had a problem. As I have indicated, he was an engaged, sensitive edi-tor constantly pushing to make the magazine better, livelier, more dis-tinctive. He looked like a man in a perpetual state of high anxiety. And whatever his personal problems may have been, I always thought that his main professional problem came half from the clash between his personal values and the *Times*'s system, which gave him top editorial responsibility without top editorial authority, and half from the clash between his political values and his editorial sensibility (when they were in conflict, the latter usually carried the day).

But I should explain how the *Times* was organized in those days.

The daily paper was presided over by the Executive Editor. And the Sunday Department, which consisted of the Travel section, the News of the Week in Review, the Arts & Leisure section, the *Book Review*, and the magazine, was presided over by the Sunday editor. This division ended in 1976 with Max Frankel's promotion from Sunday editor to editor of the editorial page. Until that time the editorial page had been run, presumably to be on the safe side, by a member of the publisher's family, though to say that hardly does justice to John Oakes, a fiercely independent intellect and close to a First Amendment absolutist. His consistent defense of civil liberty during the dark days of McCarthyism was a rebuke to less steadfast confreres.

The Sunday editor was a nice man named Dan Schwarz, who had the mis/mixed fortune to have served much of his professional life under the legendary Sunday editor who had preceded him, Lester Markel. When I say legendary, I mean he was legendary the way Stalin was legendary, a micromanager and a tyrant who ran the Sunday Department according to a series of strict formulas. There was a joke about the typical *Times Magazine* article in Markel's day. It was called "The Five Stages of Economic Growth," and it was written by the establishment economist Barbara Ward, and she was required to revise it five times, and the *Times* ran all five versions.

By the time I got to the *Times Magazine*, Markel had retired, but some of his conventions lived on. At the daily editorial conference, Dan Schwarz, who saw himself as something of a reformer, made a show of consulting his subordinates in an orchestrated series of deferences—to rank, to seniority, to quality of presentation, to shadow (of the powers that be, men like executive editor Abe Rosenthal who were not in the room but who might be offended by this or that), occasionally even to merit. And Lewis Bergman, being no slouch in the bureaucratic studies department, had designed a series of ingenious strategies for getting around Dan and working his will.

The daily two-part editorial meeting ran for an hour and would usually be convened either at noon or at 2:30, you never knew which. Occasionally it would begin in the late morning, break for lunch at 1:00, and resume at 2:30. We were advised to make our luncheon appointments at 1:00. It took me months before I figured out that by their keeping us guessing as to the time of the meeting, we could never take more than an hour and a half for lunch.

During the first part of the meeting manuscripts already in house would be discussed. The Sunday editor would have a pile of them before him, each with a series of pages attached, known quaintly as barnacles, that recorded comments and recommendations of the commissioning editor; the comment on his comment from the articles editor; and if the articles editor disagreed with, or for one or another reason didn't trust the commissioning editor, he might seek second and third opinions, which could also become barnacles; and the pile would be topped by a blue sheet with Bergman's comments for Schwarz.

Since Schwarz was making 100 percent of the decisions with only at best 20 percent of his time—he had, after all, the entire Sunday Department to run—I came to suspect that he hadn't always done his homework, i.e., he hadn't read all the pieces under discussion, which was where Lewis had his edge. I arrived at this suspicion after I saw by chance one of Lewis's blue cover sheets to Schwarz, which said, "I agree with Mr. Navasky that the writer has not done his assignment." Had Mr. Schwartz bothered to read the barnacles he would have discovered that although Lewis had quoted me accurately, he had quoted only a part of what I had said. My note read: "The writer has not done his assignment. But what he has done is more interesting and challenging than what we asked for. Here is what I propose . . ."

Now, of course, it was always possible to speak up at meetings or, as I sometimes decided, wiser to send an after-the-fact memorandum with carbons to all concerned appealing a decision taken at the meeting, but that had to be the exception rather than the rule. At one meeting I argued in vain on behalf of three articles I had commissioned, only to see them all shot down. Tom Buckley, a staff writer, no doubt trying to be kind, volunteered, "Well, Navasky fights for his writers. You have to give him that." The truth was that under the prevailing system the magazine published only one of every three pieces it commissioned. I had the theory that if the editors spent as much time making sick pieces better as they did commissioning new ones, the magazine wouldn't suffer in quality, would save a little money on kill fees, and wouldn't feed the army of disgruntled freelancers out there. (There is no longer a Sunday Department and I'm told things have changed for the better.)

At one of my philosophic discussions with Lewis over a martini at the upstairs bar at Sardi's, where he could be found every day at 1:05 p.m., I asked him what he thought of magazines like *The Nation* and *National Review*, which were open about their politics rather than adhering to a formula which required the appearance of narrative neutrality. He said, "I have a revolutionary idea. How about a magazine that just tells the truth!?" None of that postmodernist nonsense for him.

Once or twice a year Dan would propose that we have lunch. At first I thought it was because he liked me, and then I thought he was pumping me. Then I realized it was because that was the way it was done. At our last lunch he asked me how I thought the editorial system at the magazine might be improved, and I told him that if I were he, I'd let Lewis Bergman make all the final decisions, that the daily meetings were frustrating because too many decisions were taken based on extracurricular considerations. The daily meetings were an innovation in the direction of democracy, he told me. I should have been there under Markel, who made all the decisions by himself. Well, okay, but that was then and now was now. Once, I asked Bergman why he didn't simply tell Dan that as the magazine's editor of record he should make all the editorial decisions. He looked at me, smiled, and asked only half plaintively, "What's my hole card?"

The way the system worked was this: If an editor had an idea for an article, he would submit it in writing to the Sunday editor, who would read out the ideas at the second half of the daily meeting. If the idea survived the shooting gallery (Didn't we already do that? Are you sure it is important enough for the magazine? What will Abe say?), there might be a discussion about who should write it. Or the articles editor—it was then Harvey Shapiro, who in his other life was the poet Harvey Shapiro—would send you a note asking you to nominate three or four possible writers. Eventually a writer would be approached, and you'd do your best to persuade him to write the piece.

Let me tell you how naïve I was. After about three months, Harvey Shapiro invited me to lunch. Since we had lunched regularly when I was freelancing, I assumed that was a belated carrying on of the old tradition. But no, he had another purpose, or should I say mission, in mind.

Harvey put on what I knew to be his article editor's voice, a half-tone louder and more assertive than his usual laid-back style, and said something like "You know, Vic, at the magazine it doesn't matter how good a writer you are, how nice a guy you are, or how smart you are about the pieces you read. Ultimately we judge our editors by how many pieces they get in the magazine."

Much later I figured out that my probation period was coming to an end and this was my evaluation lunch; under the contract with the Newspaper Guild, during the first thirteen weeks the paper could fire you at will, but once you survived your probation period, you were protected by the Guild contract, and if you stayed sober until noon, didn't disrobe in public, steal from the petty-cash box, or fly yourself to Las Vegas on the company expense account, you had a job for life.

I did a quick count of the number of pieces I had "gotten" into the magazine and found that the number was 0, *nada*, zilch.

"Why didn't you tell me?" I asked my former friend somewhat lamely.

I don't remember whether he dignified the question with an answer, but I gathered that I was such a nice guy they were going to give me a second chance. Translation: They would notify the Guild they were extending my probation period by three months. And over the next three months I changed my ways, and all of a sudden my ideas started going through and "my" articles were published in the magazine. When the probation period was over, I was again taken to lunch and told what a fine job I was doing.

Now, for the first time I reveal the secret of how I improved my batting average from 000.00 to something in the stratosphere of the eighth floor (where the Sunday Department was lodged).

Basically I had a two-pronged strategy. I had noticed that one of the main reasons for turning down a story idea was that it was deemed not really newsworthy, and the definition of news, for better or worse, had to do with whether or not the *Times* had published something about it. For example, once I proposed an article about wiretapping. At the meeting there was a disagreement on how newsworthy the practice was, and I was instructed to cable a member of the *Times*'s Washington bureau who covered the Justice Department to ask whether he thought wiretapping was a good subject for the magazine. This was a no-win situation: I was putting the reporter in question in a bind. If it was such a great idea for the magazine, why hadn't he written about it for the daily paper already? Conversely, if he had already done justice to the subject in the daily, why would the magazine want to duplicate his efforts? And finally, if he were unscrupulous he would tell you that by great coincidence he was working on just such a piece at that very moment and proceed to steal your idea for the daily.

Another editor on the magazine, who seemed to have better luck than I in getting his story ideas commissioned (who didn't?), occasionally used to attach a clipping from the daily paper that had inspired his idea. And so I changed my profligate ways and wrote down ideas as they occurred to me on a yellow legal pad, but didn't actually send them in until I found an article in the *Times* that I could clip as an accompaniment. This, of course, meant a delay—sometimes of days or weeks or months, but my acceptance-to-submissions ratio took a great leap forward. And as far as getting the article itself accepted after the green light had been given to the idea, I noticed that if a writer's work had already appeared in the magazine a couple of times, virtually all the statistics were reversed: i.e., from being one of the two-out-of-three commissioned articles that were turned down, the piece became the one out of three that was accepted.

So the second element in my strategy was to stop suggesting new writers, especially if I had had a vaguely creative, off-beat, or politically charged idea for an article. I had naïvely believed that I was supposed to bring to the magazine some new connections, having to do with my Rolodex of new writers. And I hadn't been entirely wrong. There was, at the start, a real openness to giving my first-time-writer nominees a shot. It was only after the articles came in that they were shot down. So now I included on my list of potential writers only tried-and-true *Times Magazine* regulars who had already survived the system.

The one exception was an irresistible fable submitted by Neil Postman, whose day job was N.Y.U. professor of education but who was also a longtime *Monocle* contributor. Neil's tale of how New York City's public-school students, if liberated from school, might find their education in the process of saving the city sprang from his longtime belief that it was "not written in any holy book that an education [only] must occur in a small room with chairs in it." His tale, which ran in the magazine on June 14, 1970, proved so irresistible to my *Times* superiors that five years later, on October 12, 1975, when the decline of civilized life in our cities had accelerated, for the first and only time in its history the *Times Magazine* ran the same article again, without changing a word, this time under the heading "A Case of Déjà Vu: A Fable Whose Time Has Come."

At my next evaluation lunch, if that's what it was, I was told what a fine job I was doing. Of course what I was doing was giving them precisely those ideas and writers for which they didn't need me. But that was their business. After about a year of my ideas sailing through and finding a home in the pages of the magazine, the presumption seemed to shift sufficiently in my favor for me to be able to suggest non-*Times* writers for *Times*-type ideas, and vice versa. Slowly I persuaded myself I was making a modest difference.

In 1970–72 the Vietnam War had inspired its own subsidiary culture wars throughout the academic and media communities, and the eighth floor of the *Times,* where the magazine was located, was no exception.

In the culture at large protest against the war ranged from marching in demonstrations and writing letters to editors to withholding taxes and "levitating" the Pentagon. At *The New York Times* a number of editors indicated their opposition by growing beards (in those days there were only a handful of female editors), and one editor on the *Book Review* announced that he would not cut his hair until the war was over, thereby showing solidarity with the long-haired, antiwar hippies whose culture had given rise to the Off Broadway hit *Hair.* Eventually the publisher issued a memorandum recommending that reporters not wear jeans to interviews.

I was not a tax withholder, I had no beard, I was not even a regular demonstrator. But whatever progressive politics meant, I had them. I was, I guess, what would be called a left-liberal, although I never thought of myself as all *that* left. I believed in civil rights and civil liberties, I favored racial integration, I thought responsibility for the international tensions of the Cold War was equally distributed between the United States and the U.S.S.R., and I opposed the Vietnam War.

Once, I chanced to hear my friend and bearded colleague Gerry Walker reporting back to a writer who had turned in an article having to do with war resisters that had run into some editorial resistance from the management. "They are trying to jerk you around," he said. "If I were you I would withdraw it." He seemed to be counseling a sort of preemptive grief avoidance.

"Are you really sure that's the right thing to do?" I asked him later, when we talked about this.

"Well," Gerry said, "they were jerking him around and I said so. What's wrong with that?"

Maybe nothing was, but it made me uneasy, so Goody Two-shoes said, "Well, I thought our job was to get pieces like that in the magazine, not keep them out."

Gerry replied, saying, "You have the idealism of inexperience. Maybe I have the cynicism of experience."

In the end I decided—and still believe—that we were both right. As the *Times* columnist Tom Wicker wrote in another connection, when you take on the establishment at the *Times*, or seem to be intruding on national security or otherwise proceed on unconventional assumptions, there is a tendency for the paper "to pull in its horns." A different and more demanding set of standards comes into play.

At the same time, there were any number of ways to get unconventional, independent, alternative, and even radical views in the magazine, and why not try? One way was to choose writers with political labels and ask them to make the case for or against them. It would have been easier to get Stokely Carmichael, a high-profile leader of the radical wing of the civil rights movement, to write "The Case for Black Power" than for a relatively unfamous journalist to argue for black power in an otherwise "balanced" piece about civil rights in the South. In *Times*-think, the notoriety of the writer puts the reader on notice that he should read with a caveat.

Another way to navigate the shoals of competing ideological assumptions was to adopt a strategy of transparency, i.e., set forth the various positions of A, B, and C (quoting their most eloquent or best-credentialed exponents) and then openly set forth the reasons and the evidence for believing that A, B, or C had the better of the argument. For me it all went back to *Monocle*'s line about every magazine's typical or ideal reader. When a writer wanted to challenge the ideal reader's assumptions, he had to send a signal that that was what he was doing. If I am right, and if at the time *Times* writers were expected to incorporate assumptions of the so-called reasonable man, that did not mean the reasonable man had to agree with the writer's conclusions. But it did seem to mean that the writer had to put him on notice as to his assumptions.

Whenever I think of this hypothetical reasonable man—so beloved by lawyers—I think of a moot-court argument I once witnessed at Yale Law School. A first-year student was arguing the defense in a censorship case. I think it involved the Swedish film *I Am Curious (Yellow)*, which the United States was trying to ban as pornographic. Counsel argued that even though parts of the movie might seem lewd, lascivious, and of only prurient interest, "a reasonable man would find that the work taken as a whole had redeeming social significance" and therefore should not be banned. At this point the judge, a third-year student (he went on to become the head of the ACLU in Illinois), asked, "Suppose, counsel, a reasonable man walked in on the middle of the movie?" And of course no one in those years thought to ask, What about a reasonable woman?

And so now we come back to the idea of an article on the use of the word "fascism." It was Lewis's idea, if I remember correctly, but I was asked to suggest some writers for it, and so I turned in my list. At the head of the list, which included a number of *Times* regulars, I put the name Phil Green. As it happened, Phil and I had taken an honors seminar in political theory at Swarthmore together, and he had written what I took to be a definitive paper on Fascism. By 1970 he was teaching political science at Smith College, where he was the leading democratic socialist on campus, but I thought it sufficient to mention that he was a member of Smith's government department. One credential, it seemed to me, was enough. Happy day, the powers that be okayed the proposal, and Phil wrote his article.

But when it came in, it contained not only a sophisticated description and analysis of the unique conjunction of elements that constituted Fascist thought but also Phil's conclusion that for some blacks living in the Deep South their experience was equivalent to life under Fascism, and "as of now, the evidence suggests, it may be that America is pioneering a new political system: of formal democracy for the many, and a kind of informal Fascism for the few."

Lewis had some questions. "Come on," he said to me. "He can't say that. Call him and tell him to save himself and us a half-dozen letters-to-the-editor pointing out that there are no concentration camps in the South. When was the last time a black was turned into a lampshade or a bar of soap? And also, what about the Black Panthers themselves? Aren't they racist and violent and nationalistic—aren't they fascistic? Will you call him, will you do that?"

Yes, I would, and I did. Phil understood, and he made what he thought were the appropriate adjustments, adding among other materials the following paragraph:

At this very moment to be an organizer of blacks is sometimes as dangerous as it was to be an organizer of workers in Italy in 1921: All across the country, after all, policemen are killing black men—and boys—with impunity, destroying their offices, confiscating their arms, arresting those who protest on trumped-up charges. All across the country, too, an armed mob has taken nascent shape; indeed, in many parts of the United States where the races confront each other uneasily across shifting residential boundaries, whites are probably much more heavily armed than the Italian and German Fascists were in the nineteen twenties.

And as far as Lewis's query about the Panthers being fascistic, Green wrote:

As for the often suggested equation between radical blacks and Fascists, that can surely only leave a bad taste in the mouth. The Black Panthers, for example, are lower class, self-proclaimed revolutionaries; precisely the kind of people who were the objects of Fascist terror. Indeed, in no case is the use of "Fascist" as an all-purpose derogatory for those one does not like as clear as it is in the case of the Panthers. It is not necessary to admire them to appreciate how erroneous is that usage any more than one had to admire the German Communists in order to appreciate that they were not Nazis.

... Even the occasional anti-Semitism of some Panthers— as distinguished from their perfectly legitimate anti-Zionism— is of the crude popular variety that has existed in almost every Christian nation for centuries and has nothing in common with the pathological and genocidal Nazi version. Whatever else one may think of the Panthers, therefore, and their calls to what they insist (with considerable historical justification) is self-defensive violence, they simply cannot be tarred with the Fascist brush.

The end result was that "Can It Happen Here, Is It Already Happening?" by Phil Green appeared in *The New York Times Sunday Magazine* of September 20, 1970, and close to one million readers had the chance to read it. But ironically, to achieve the appearance of a balanced perspective, Green spent so much space anticipating and dealing with Lewis's counterarguments that the article as it finally appeared was, ever so slightly, off balance.

Occasionally, very occasionally, an article got in the magazine that any serious student of *Times* politics, values, and bureaucracy would have assured you in advance had no chance whatsoever. My record on scoring controversial pieces was no better than most, but whatever the reason—perhaps my blindness to *Times* taboos—every once in a while I had a breakthrough (I was going to say break-in, because that's what it felt like), although now I can think of only one.

In 1970 I had read an article in *Harper's* by Joseph Epstein, then editor of the *American Scholar*, on his attitude toward gays, and it had disturbed me. The gay rights movement was barely under way. The phrase "come out of the closet," already coined by the feminist writer Kate Millett, was not yet in general circulation. I mentioned Epstein's article to my *Times* colleague Gerry Walker, thinking he would find it of interest, since his novel *Cruising*, about a homosexual killer and the latent homosexual cop who tracks him down, was on the brink of publication, and I told him he should read it. He said he would, and by the way, he was having lunch that day at the Chambertin, a little French restaurant on West Forty-sixth Street, with Merle Miller, whose former wife was a friend of mine, and whose work I admired, and would I care to join them?

Gerry and Merle were already there when I arrived. The Chambertin was named after a French wine, so I ordered a glass. "I hear you thought Epstein's article was great," said Merle. No, I said, I thought it was a powerful piece of writing, but I found it upsetting. Among other things, Epstein had written: "If I had the power to do so, I would wish homosexuality off the face of the earth. I would do so because I think it brings infinitely more pain than pleasure to those who are forced to live with it."

"Well," said Merle, "the portrait he paints of homosexual life is warped. It's not that way at all. I have many friends who are homosexual, all my closest friends are homosexual, in fact I'm a homosexual myself, and I can tell you his piece is full of shit." On further conversation it turned out that Merle had never so declared himself before in mixed company. "Look, goddamn it," he repeated, "I'm homosexual, and most of my best friends are Jewish homosexuals, and some of my best friends are black homosexuals, and I am sick and tired of reading and hearing such goddamn demeaning, degrading bullshit about me and my friends." It was clear that he had much to say on the matter. Why don't you write a piece for the magazine by way of an answer to Epstein? I asked. Gerry thought that was a capital idea, "but they'll never go for it." What do we have to lose by proposing it? I said. Whoa, said Merle. He wanted to think about it first. A few days later he told me he'd like to try it if they were interested. By this time it was a true tripartite project in which Gerry had more than his share of input. "But you propose it," he said. "Leave me out. They'll think I'm trying to promote my book."

And that's what we did. After one of the longer editorial meetings on record—What will he say? What if we have to turn it down? We are not a proselytizing magazine, will he proselytize? They are picketing *Harper's*, will they picket the *Times*? Can he be objective? (no kidding)—Dan said I could invite Merle to try it but should warn him that it was a first for the *Times* and might not work out.

I called Merle and gave him all the warnings. He agreed to the assignment, and though he certainly didn't proselytize, he didn't compromise either. His article brought in more than two thousand letters, some sort of record, and ended up as a book of its own, *On Being Different: What It Means to Be a Homosexual*. I guess it was a little ahead of the straight journalism curve.

Here is his coda, an implicit answer to Epstein: "Well, yes, I suppose. If I had been given a choice (but who is?), I would prefer to have been straight. But then, would I rather not have been me? Oh, I think not, not this morning anyway. It is a very clear day in late December, and the sun is shining on the pine trees outside my studio. The air is extraordinarily clear, and the sky is the color it gets only at this time of year, dark, almost navy blue. On such a day I would not change to be anyone else or anyplace else."

Not all the lessons I learned at the *Times* had to do with news content. If one is to understand the way big media work, one must also master the rules of their bureaucracy.

Working past 5:30 was, I discovered, frowned upon. This was because under the Guild contract, one was entitled to put in for overtime, which was really frowned upon. All employees were entitled to use the employees' cafeteria. All executives (including the editors) were entitled—with reservations—to dine at the slightly more expensive executive cafeteria (where, if memory serves, dessert and coffee were delivered to your table). And the upper echelons could reserve private dining rooms for special occasions.

Then there was the matter of expense accounts. Basically the system at the *Times* was a simple one. You were encouraged to take writers to lunch. That meant you were working. I must say, in my freelancing days I had always looked forward to having lunch with my editor. This was because he paid; but also because the lunch was more elegant than it would have been had I been on my own. And no editors took you to lunch unless they were interested in your writing. Then there were the martinis, the literary gossip, and finally there was the content, the ideas, the conversation. At least it got you out of the house.

As an editor paying for the lunch, the pleasures were only slightly different. Even though I was doing the signing, it was the *Times* that was paying, and the lunches were more elegant than if I ate in the *Times* cafeteria. I only took writers to lunch in whose work I was interested. Then there were the martinis and the possibility of intellectual exchange, the excitement of new ideas, advancing the story.

The *Times* policy regarding expense accounts was that if lunch cost $25 or under, you could get a same-day cash rebate upon presentation of your receipt at a second-floor cashier's window. If it cost more than $25, you had to get it signed and authorized by Lewis, and your cash refund would not arrive until a week later. Editors were not permitted to take each other to lunch.

Only once in my years at the *Times* did a writer take *me* to lunch. And that was the result of, shall we say, special circumstances.

The year was 1972, and the trial of Charles Manson was about to begin. The crime, involving the murder of a movie star, Sharon Tate, hippies, drugs, and a James Dean look-alike guru, was made for cable TV, though cable didn't exist yet. The tabloids could barely contain themselves. It was, in other words, precisely the sort of story that the *Times* instinctively played down, if it played it at all. This was partly a matter of taste, partly because the competition were better at covering it, and partly out of a sort of reverse news snobbism.

So the *Times Magazine* coverage of this trash news, if it was to happen at all, would have to have a veneer of dignity.

The story seemed to be worth telling. Who were these people? What did the Tate killings have to say about our country and our culture? I had an idea. Why not ask Truman Capote, author of *In Cold Blood,* the best-selling "non-fiction novel" about another sensational murder, to cover the trial?

And I even had what I thought was a bright business idea. Since the *Times* fee, then an unvarying $750, might not be enough to entice a man who had made millions from his nonfiction thriller, perhaps Times Books would want to publish a transcript of the trial? Surely an introduction by Capote (in the form of his article) would be worth $25,000. What could be more synergistic than that?

The editors laughed, knowing there was no way in the world that Capote would say yes, but told me I was free to ask. So the magazine sent a telegram to Capote's home in the Hamptons, and imagine our astonishment when he called the next day to say that although he had some legal problems that might interfere with his availability, he was interested.

This immediately sent tremors though the Sunday Department, as visions of Capote's expense account for wild all-night parties at the Hotel Bel-Air danced through Lewis's head. He told me we should offer to pay Capote's travel expenses, but that if they amounted to more than $500 a week, they would have to be cleared in advance with the *Times.* Another deal killer, I was sure. When I called Capote to give him the bad news about the *Times* expense policy, he giggled and said he wasn't doing this for the money. He was intrigued by the case. But he did have this little legal problem, and he wasn't sure it could be solved in time, since his lawyer, Alan Schwartz, who knew all the facts about the situation, was traveling in the Soviet Union.

Capote had taped some interviews for a television special with a Los Angeles–based prisoner on death row. The last time he was in L.A., the district attorney had asked him for a copy of the tapes in connection with a case he was prosecuting. Capote declined to turn them over, but he invited the D.A. to lunch at his Beverly Hills digs to explain why. "And would you believe it, the man no sooner waltzed in the door than he served me with a subpoena *duces tecum* demanding that I appear in court with the tapes. So I invited him in for a drink, arranged for a limousine to pick me up, and before he knew it, I was out the back door and on the next plane to New York. The nerve of that man. Anyway, it seems there is a bench warrant out for my arrest, and according to Alan, before I can set foot in California we have to clear up this little matter."

"Is that all it is?" I asked, relieved that he was not balking at the *Times*'s meager expense account. "Who is the judge? Let me give him a call and see if we can't work something out. There is no way they are going to put you in prison over this."

He gave me the name of the judge. I called him and explained the situation, told him that Capote's attorney was traveling in the Soviet Union and wouldn't be back until after the Manson trial began. Could anything be done?

"Just tell Mr. Capote that as soon as he arrives in L.A. County he should present himself in my court, and don't worry, I will do the right thing."

So I called Mr. Capote and told him we had worked something out and we were in business.

Almost. In those days until a trial was over court transcripts were, oddly, deemed to be the property of the court reporter who took them down. And court reporters were known to charge exorbitant fees for access to the daily transcripts, which Capote needed.

Normally, when you send a writer on a story, the next time you hear from him is on deadline day, when he calls and asks for an extension. But in the case of Capote I thought I'd hear from him when he arrived, if only to report on how things had gone. When he failed to call that day or the next, and his hotel told us he had yet to check in, I began to worry. The rich and famous are different from you and me.

On day three my secretary came running. "It's Truman Capote on the phone!" He was calling to thank me; he had spent the last night in jail, where the judge had put him for ignoring the bench warrant, personally explaining that that was the right thing to do. And then, after he was released, Capote found himself in a room smaller than his cell, where for a fee the court reporter permitted him to review the day's transcripts. "When I get back to New York, we had better have lunch," Capote warned ominously (or was it wearily?).

Lunch with Truman Capote, that's better than breakfast at Tiffany's, I thought. "This one is on the *Times*," I said generously.

"No, it isn't," said Capote. "If the *Times* is buying, we'll go to Nedicks. Meet me at Lafayette at 1:00 p.m. on Thursday."

I knew Lafayette to be a four-star, very expensive restaurant, and if I hadn't heard of it before, I knew about it by the time I arrived, because a few days earlier Gael Greene, the restaurant critic for *New York* magazine, wrote a scathing review of its snobby service staff, advising the hoi polloi to stay away.

I arrived five minutes before the appointed hour and I was shown to Capote's table. Ten or fifteen minutes later Mr. Capote made his entrance. As he came through the door, the maître d' removed his cape and handed it to the coat-check girl, and a waiter appeared with what I later learned was his standard drink, a Lillet vodka martini, in which a second waiter deposited a scorched piece of orange rind (my memory may be playing tricks on me, but I think I witnessed the scorching on the rind's way into the martini glass). Mr. Capote sat down, introduced himself, took a sip of his martini, smacked his lips, gave the restaurant a quick once-over, and said, "I don't know what that bitch was talking about, the service here seems perfectly fine to me."

The service was better than fine, but he never did turn in his article.

Just before I left the *Times* I began a monthly column on publishing (from the writer's vantage point) for *The New York Times Book Review* called "In Cold Print." I didn't see it that way at the time, but my experience with *Kennedy Justice* had constituted a short course in the politics of publishing which would serve me well as a publishing columnist.

First, the book was signed up by David Segal, a brilliant young editor at New American Library (NAL), who had recently arrived from McGraw-Hill, where he had had a falling-out with his two superiors, who lacked enthusiasm for his intellectual approach to publishing. Shortly after we signed our contract, it was announced that his two McGraw-Hill superiors had made a deal to join and take over NAL's trade-book department. "I feel like the Jews who fled Germany for France in 1941, just before the German invasion," said Segal. Then, a couple of years later, after Segal died an untimely death, on the old-fashioned theory that a writer ought to have some sort of personal rapport with his editor, Lynn Nesbit, my friend and agent, arranged for me to have lunch with Peter Rittner, the new NAL editor who had migrated from Macmillan, where he too had a reputation for brilliance. Rittner took me to an elegant lunch on the Upper East Side. He was a charming and exceedingly well-informed luncheon companion, willing to share his knowledgeable views on any number of subjects. But as we ordered our dessert it occurred to me that conspicuously absent from the impressive array of subjects he had covered were any comments on the fifty-page research report I had submitted, or indeed on the book in general, and I noticed that he was glancing at his watch, a sign that a more important appointment awaited him in his office. Fortified by the alcohol I had consumed in a brave but not quite successful attempt to keep up with my host, yet fearful that I was breaching some unwritten rule of publishing lunch etiquette, I tentatively asked if he had any thoughts he might wish to share about my book.

"Of course," said Peter (he had asked that I call him Peter). "I published Bill Shannon's book on Robert Kennedy," he said, "and it sold 20 to 25,000 copies. I see no reason why yours shouldn't do as well." And that was that. End of lunch and end of literary discussion. I have thought about this conversation over the years. On the one hand, I was disappointed at the failure of my fifty pages to engage my possible new editor intellectually. On the other hand, it turned out that Rittner's sales forecast was accurate.

At the time, however, I yearned for an editor I could talk to, and lucky for me, my friend Michael Meltsner, whose idea the book was in the first place, had run into Richard Kluger, recently arrived at Atheneum Press, and told him about my circumstance. Kluger had been a *Monocle* fan and I had written for him when he was editing *Book World,* which in those days appeared as an insert in the New York *Herald Tribune*, the *Chicago Tribune*, and *The Washington Post*. Shortly thereafter I received a note from Kluger telling me that he was not one of those hot-shot editors who specialized in luring writers away from their publishers, "but I'm trying to learn how to become one."

Atheneum bought out my contract, and with agent Lynn doing her stuff, I even made some money on the deal; Kluger was an attentive, enthusiastic, and creative editor, but publishing being what it is, just before *Kennedy Justice* was published in the spring of 1971, Kluger had his own falling out with Atheneum and feelings were so raw that Pat Knopf, who was running Atheneum, dispatched its young PR woman to inform me that if Kluger showed up at the publishing party (which Kluger had arranged to be held at the Watergate Hotel in Washington) he would be banned. Pat later explained to me that this was strictly an economic decision. He believed that if Dick were there it would provide fodder for publishing gossip columnists, who would write about the contretemps rather than the book. So Dick wasn't there and the publishing gossip columnists weren't either, and nobody wrote about anything.

In a further introduction to publishing economics, when I told Atheneum's PR person that I had arranged to have dinner with Kluger after the party, the hapless young woman informed me that that would be fine but that her instructions were that she was not allowed to pay for Kluger. (Now it can be told—as an accommodation to me, she allowed me to slip her a personal check for Kluger's portion of the meal, and he was none the wiser.)

The next morning I did my first television interview. It was on a local D.C. morning show where I arrived at 7 a.m. ready to be grilled on my seven years of research. The happy host had time for only one question, however: "Would you say the Kennedys were the Rover Boys of American politics?" (I wouldn't and I didn't.)

I also learned a thing or two about publishing PR when, in the course of my author's tour, I was told (yes, that young woman earned her salary and I'm happy to say that today she has her own agency) that while the trip to Philadelphia was still on, my appearance on the highly rated Donahue show had been canceled. The breaks of the game, I thought, until my new confidante somewhat sheepishly explained that the substitute Donahue guest was another Atheneum author. It seems that Atheneum had another candidate for the bestseller list, and when the Donahue people explained that while they were interested, they simply had no opening unless Atheneum was willing to replace author A (that's me) with author B (that's not me). Since by this time it was clear that author A's book was not destined for bestsellerdom, Atheneum made the market-indicated business decision. Had I not been so grateful for the learning experience, I might have found all this a little petty and depressing.

After *Kennedy Justice* was published in 1971, Richard Kluger, who by this time had his own publishing venture, Charterhouse, suggested that I ought to think about doing a book on the then still untouchable J. Edgar Hoover, whom I had already touched in *Kennedy Justice*. In fact, Hoover's FBI took up about half of that book, as the FBI accounted for 40 percent of the Justice Department's budget and at least that much of the drama of Kennedy's attorney generalship. What happened when the country's maximum Attorney General, the President's brother, with the President's full confidence, came up against the country's number-one bureaucrat, the keeper of the country's secret files?

But I had another leftover interest from *Kennedy Justice* which had to do with Bobby Kennedy's other nemesis, Jimmy Hoffa. After a number of false starts, the Justice Department finally put Hoffa away in 1964 for trying to fix a jury in a 1962 case. This had required the testimony of a federal informant in Hoffa's camp, Edward Grady Partin, who was let out of prison explicitly for the purpose of infiltrating his buddy's entourage. I knew all about Hoffa's evil doings, but something bothered me about convicting him on the word of a man who had a twenty-year criminal history that included convictions of breaking and entering, a bad conduct discharge from the Marines, indictments for rape, embezzlement, forgery, first-degree manslaughter, and the misuse of union funds, and who was let out of prison in the expectation that he might eavesdrop on otherwise privileged attorney-client conversations.

My interest in Partin got me thinking about informers (Hoover was always insistent that they be called informants, which sounds more honorable), which in turn led me to consider writing a nonfiction book on the history of the informer. As far as I could tell, no one had before. For many years I had been interested in the House Committee on Un-American Activities and their hunt for evidence of subversion in Hollywood. As you know, I had bumped into victims of the blacklist at the homes of high-school friends, in the Adirondacks resort where I worked while in college, and again in the stacks of my law school library. In

1965, I reviewed a memoir, *Inquisition in Eden*, by Alvah Bessie, along with Dalton Trumbo, a member of the Hollywood Ten. He wrote to complain about my observation that when he endorsed censorship of Fascist ideas he missed the free-speech lesson of his incarceration, and asked, "Why should I grant free speech to those who would exterminate me?" I bought him a complimentary membership in the ACLU.

But in 1972 when I read (and reviewed) Eric Bentley's collection of testimony from these hearings, *Thirty Years of Treason*, I was reminded that they were a veritable Olympics of informing. I was particularly struck by the irony of having men like the director Elia Kazan, the actor José Ferrer, the writer Budd Schulberg, and the choreographer Jerome Robbins tell the committee that they had left the Communist Party because they resented its clumsy attempts at thought control and censorship, and then not object to colloquies like the one Congressman Clyde Doyle inflicted on Robbins:

> MR. DOYLE: Again, I want to compliment you. You are in a wonderful place, through your art, your music, your talent, which God blessed you with, to perhaps be very vigorous and positive in promoting Americanism in contrast to Communism. Let me suggest to you that you use that great talent which God has blessed you to put into ballets in some way, to put into music in some way, that interpretation.
>
> MR. ROBBINS: Sir, all my works have been acclaimed for its [sic] American quality particularly.
>
> MR. DOYLE: I realize that, but let me urge you to even put more of that in it, where you can appropriately.

Exchanges like this, not to mention the testimony of Martin Berkeley, the screenwriter on *Lassie* and *Francis the Talking Mule*, who mentioned 162 names of Communist Party members, led me to consider the 1950s as the Golden Age of the Informer.

The most dramatic story centered on the great director Elia Kazan and the Pulitzer Prize–winning playwright Arthur Miller. By 1952, when Kazan testified before HUAC, he had directed Arthur Miller's *Death of a Salesman* and Tennessee Williams's *A Streetcar Named Desire*. He not only ended up naming names for HUAC but took out a full-page ad in the *Times* urging others to do likewise, arguing that the only way to fight totalitarian secrecy was with democratic openness.

Miller, on the other hand, having failed to talk Kazan out of naming names, put his own freedom on the line by refusing to name names for HUAC. Like the Hollywood Ten, who went to prison for contempt of Congress, he relied on the First Amendment's guarantee of free speech rather than the Fifth Amendment's protection against self-incrimination, which had kept many noncooperative witnesses out of prison. He and Kazan were going to collaborate on a movie about corruption on the waterfront, but when the producer asked him to change the bad guys from thugs to Communists, Miller dropped the project; and he went on to write *A View from the Bridge,* in which a series of tragic events is set off when an uncle informs on the illegal immigrant who is courting his niece. Shortly after that, Kazan won an Oscar for *On the Waterfront,* in which Terry Malloy (played by Marlon Brando) comes to maturity when he realizes it's his obligation to name names before the committee investigating corruption on the waterfront.

Miller and Kazan stopped talking to each other, and it was not until a few years later that they once again came together to collaborate, under the auspices of a new national theater at Lincoln Center. The occasion was *After the Fall,* Miller's autobiographical play, inspired in part by Marilyn Monroe, to whom he had been married and with whom Kazan had had a liaison. Kazan ended up directing a character who names names, based on himself, and after the play closed, he married the actress, Barbara Loden, who had played the Monroe-based character.

I am not a novelist, but this seemed to be a novel. And I saw four possible books, any one of which I thought would be worth reading: the history of the informer, the Miller-Kazan story, the story of the blacklist, or something of an amalgam of all of the above. I sent off an odd book proposal saying as much. Instead of proposing one of the books, I said I couldn't tell which it would be until I did the first part of my research. I felt like a swimmer headed for one of four islands, but uncertain which, only knowing that the first part of my journey would be the same, no matter which island I eventually chose. I was ready to plunge in right away, and following my precept about not leaving one job until I had another, I told my agent I could do this only if the advance on the book was the equivalent of two years of my annual salary at *The New York Times*, which was then just under $30,000.

Happily for me, some offers came in, and we were "in negotiation" with The Viking Press when I was summoned to Dan's (or was it Lewis's?) office. It seemed the editor of the Travel section, Bill Honan (with whom I had briefly overlapped on the magazine staff), had accepted a job with Charney and Veronis, the new owners of the old *Saturday Review of Literature*. These hot-shot magazine consultants had figured out that the way to make their fortune was to take the fine (if somewhat staid) old magazine, which had, under Norman Cousins, prospered and grown from being a review of literature into a literary journal with a civilized humanist-internationalist take on world affairs, and subdivide it into four separate *SR*s, each aimed at a distinct segment of the market that *Saturday Review* already served: national affairs, the arts, education, and the sciences. Anticipating the trend toward niche publishing, they would expand the audience for each subject, discover and cultivate specialized advertisers who could reach their audience more efficiently. What could be more fun and profitable than that? This left a vacancy at the *Times* Travel section. Would I, Dan asked, take on the job of travel editor?

Let's pause here to look a little more closely at *Saturday Review*, because its history turns out to be something of a parable of magazine publishing.

In the beginning there was the old *Literary Review* of Boston, founded in 1897 by Edwin Ruthven Lamson as a little five-cent monthly. Here is what a rival magazine, *Chap-Book*, had to say about it: "People who have been waiting for something that would lift them above the sordid reality of everyday existence—something sweet and pure and true—are advised by the *Review* that they need wait no longer: Mr. Lamson has arrived and begun to lift."

Twenty-seven years later, along came Henry Seidel Canby, who, with the help of $50,000 from Thomas Lamont, amalgamated the *Literary Review* (circulation then 10,000) with the book section of the *New York Post*, which he raided (taking its top editors, two of his former Yale students). In three months, on August 2, 1924, *voila!* there was the *Saturday Review of Literature*—funnier, broader, spiffier than the old *Literary Review*.

Norman Cousins, who in the 1960s led the magazine to its highest circulation by "connecting the world of books to the world of ideas" and making it "a bridge between artist and audience," wrote of the intervening years:

> All four editors . . . in its first half-century were militantly opposed to cynicism. All shared substantially the same values. All were deeply rooted on native grounds, with different centers of attraction. For Canby, it was the world of Thoreau, Emerson and Whitman. For Bernard De Voto, the early explorers of the American West. For George Stevens, the perception of America by Steinbeck and Cather. For me it was the kind of ideas ventilated in the Jefferson-Adams correspondence and much later, in the Holmes-Pollock letters.

By 1963 circulation was 339,000. It started as a literary review, then as the *Saturday Review of Literature*, added music, television, movies, and advertising. In 1952, it dropped the "of literature" and became *Saturday Review* or, more colloquially, *SR*. Cousins politicized it in a transpartisan way. He sold it, bought it back, and then the money men moved in to cash in on the brand he had created and destroyed it. In the case of *SR*, they hired Honan to oversee four monthly magazines, but through no fault of Honan's, it took not much more than a year before all four *SR*s were shut down and Honan returned to the *Times*, where he soon became culture editor.

I told Dan I was flattered by the offer, but I was in the last stages of negotiation on a book I wanted to write and couldn't accept. He then gave me what I took to be the Speech. "At the *Times,* the top executives have mandatory retirement at age sixty-five. Look around," he said—Lewis, the Op Ed–page editor, the News of the Week in Review editor, none of the top editors in the Sunday Department had more than five years to go. "At the *Times* we recruit from within. Right now you have one-half secretary working for you. At the Travel Section you'll have twenty-four people working for you. Not only that, but if you have a book you want to write about the Hollywood blacklist, you're the *travel* editor. So travel! And of course there's more money in it for you. Don't decide now. Ask yourself where you want to be ten years from now. Go home and talk to your wife about it."

I went home, talked to my wife about it, decided that ten years from now it would be nice to have Lewis's or Dan's, or for that matter, the publisher's job, but right now I wanted to write my book. *Times* policy at the time was not to allow book-writing leaves of absence, so I left for good.

The farewell party you are given when and if you leave the *Times*, I discovered shortly after I arrived, is directly proportional, in its venue, size, expense, and guest list, to your length of service and your place in the status hierarchy. Those higher than I in the hierarchy had farewells in view of the entire eighth floor, at Sardi's or more elegant restaurants and clubs; and for those at the very top, the publisher did the honors.

My favorite farewell was the goodbye party given for Jack Desmond, assistant Sunday editor under Dan Schwarz and editor of the News of the Week in Review, who had been at the *Times* for most of his career. He was known as a pro, a loyal *Times* man, and an old-fashioned rewrite man who could hold his share of martinis and then some. He had hoped that when Dan, who was a year or two older, stepped down under the mandatory retirement rules of the paper, the publisher would let him sit in the Sunday editor's chair for a year or so while Dan's true successor was chosen. Instead, the publisher chose Max Frankel (who went on to be editorial page editor and then executive editor). Jack was given a reasonably generous buyout, and that was that.

The sun was shining brightly as maybe fifty or sixty guests chatted amiably on the lawn of Dan's Scarsdale home. Elegant hors d'oeuvres were passed, and then the *Times* hierarchy spoke, one after another, including finally his boss, Dan Schwarz, and then the publisher. Encomium was piled on encomium, each more flowery than the last. It was clear by the time Jack was called upon to say a few words that he was beloved, appreciated, a journalist's journalist. Nobody could have asked for finer or warmer words of farewell.

Jack ceremoniously took his place at the podium, with dignity lifted his martini glass high, and said, "If I did such a great job, why did you fire me?"

It's the only goodbye—and I went to more than my share—that I will always remember. As for me, when I left after two and a half years, Lewis called me into his office, pulled out a bottle of Scotch, and, with a dozen friends and colleagues, wished me well and farewell.

Although my contract for *Naming Names* called for delivery of the book in two years, I didn't actually turn it in until seven years later. This sort of thing can give writers a bad name, so I must say a few words in my own defense. During this period I also wrote my "In Cold Print" column for *The Times Book Review*. I took time out to manage a campaign for the U.S. Senate. I continued my freelance writing and I taught book-related courses at various universities. For example, I taught a course in N.Y.U.'s Media Ecology program on the subject of film propaganda, where I showed movies from the 1930s and 1940s made by the people I was writing about.

And, of course, I continued to take freelance assignments that would enable my project. Thus early in 1973 I traveled (at the *Times Magazine*'s expense) to California to do a story on whatever happened to the Hollywood Ten. Assignments such as these did more than help me cover costs and advance my research. They complicated (and sometimes, therefore, slowed down but deepened) my book and simultaneously showed me how much I still had to learn about my craft.

Example: here you will have to excuse me if I get technical. Up to this point I had much preferred the pen to the tape recorder when interviewing. But since I was embarking on a project that involved historical players nearing the ends of their lives, it occurred to me that now was the time to start taping. The argument for taping is quite simply that it ends the argument. The offended subject can't claim, I didn't say that. He did, and you've got it on tape. (Yes, it's possible to doctor tapes, but I'm not talking about fraud. I'm talking about journalistic practice.)

Gabriel García Márquez, who when he is not writing his magical realist novels runs a journalism program in Cartagena de Indias, Colombia, has named the tape recorder as one of the guilty parties in much that is wrong with modern, speeded-up journalism.

Before it was invented, the job was done well with only three elements of work. The notebook, foolproof ethics and a pair of ears that we reporters used to listen to what the sources were telling us. The professional manual for the tape recorder has not yet been invented. Somebody needs to teach young reporters that the recorder is not a substitute for memory but an evolved version of the notebook, which served so well when the profession started.

His point is that the tape recorder listens and regurgitates, but it does not think, "it does not have a heart." In the end, for García Márquez, the literal version of the spoken words it captures "would never be as trustworthy as those kept by the journalist who pays attention to the real words of the interlocutor."

My more prosaic objection to taping is that it can freeze a conversation. It's like the gorilla in the room: It puts the subject on guard. And then, when the tape recorder is packed up and the subject and interviewer are saying good-bye at the door, the subject lets her guard down, is herself, reveals the key fact, talks in her own voice for the first time.

Also, when taking notes during an interview, the journalist writes down key phrases or sentences—what is important, what captures the speaker's voice. Tapes miss eye-rolls, body language, pregnant pauses, and commentary-by-emphasis. The rhythm of an interview with a tape recorder whirring is different from when the reporter waits to ask his next question until he has finished note-taking on the answer to the previous one. The pace speeds up with the tape. But even if it is working fine, the techno-incompetent like me is listening with only half his attention, the other half worried about the machinery. This can be a major distraction.

When I arrived with a tape recorder at my first interview with Albert Maltz, one of the surviving members of the Hollywood Ten, I said, "I hope you don't mind if I tape."

"Mind?" exclaimed Maltz. "Not only do I not mind. This is too important to history not to tape. I'm taping it myself," he said. So we both sat there taping each other taping each other. He then produced a typed statement that seemed to run about 500 words, which he told me he would give to me on condition that I use all of it. It was an attack on a fellow surviving member of the Hollywood Ten, Dalton Trumbo. A few years earlier, Trumbo had given a speech in which he had said that those who were too young to remember the blacklist should study it, but if they did, they should not look for heroes and villains because "none of us is without sin" and "there were only victims." Maltz had been mulling over Trumbo's speech for two years. For Trumbo to say that there were "only victims" was like saying there was no difference between the guard and the prisoner at the concentration camp, said Maltz.

But if they were all equally victims, why had the Hollywood Ten gone to prison? Much more was said, but after about an hour, Maltz looked up at me and said, "Why is your tape still running when mine is ready to be changed?" Since both were hour-long tapes, I said, "I guess one of our tape recorders is broken."

"Not mine," said the methodical Mr. Maltz, with confidence. (And I was only slightly humiliated when I had to call the next day and ask for a copy of his tape of our conversation, which he gladly and triumphantly provided.)

The following afternoon I arrived at Trumbo's household—just a block and a half away on the other side of St. Ives Drive, and made what I later decided was a tactical error. I showed Trumbo Maltz's statement shortly after we sat down, and we never got much beyond it. He couldn't get over it. "Do you mean to say Albert has been stewing over that for two and a half years?" he asked incredulously. "Let me see that thing again," he would say, picking up the paper and shaking his head. When I finally asked him what he thought about it, he took a few puffs on his famous cigarette holder, downed what remained of his highball, and said, "Fuck Albert Maltz."

Then, a few days later, when I was back in New York, my phone rang. It was Trumbo and he had a favor to ask. While he understood that I would want to run Maltz's statement, he thought it unseemly that he get into a public squabble with another member of the Hollywood Ten. "We were in our cups," he said, "and I said some personal things about Albert. We shouldn't be pissing on each other when it's the goddamn committee we should be talking about."

I told him the *Times* was a family magazine and wouldn't let me quote what he said anyway, so I would save his epithet for the book. In the article I would confine myself to quoting from Trumbo's observations on the issues Maltz had raised. This seemed okay by Trumbo and we said goodbye. In the end, I learned a little about how to reconcile the competing demands of compassion and justice, but much about who to ask what in which order, whether, when, and how to tape and transcribe, and the subjective nature of objectivity.*

My book, meanwhile, focused on the cooperative witnesses, the informers who named names. And it turned out that for the most part, informers are not too eager to talk about what they did. One might even say some of them stonewalled.

Take the case of Elia Kazan. I couldn't very well send him a letter saying, "Dear Mr. Kazan, I am writing a book on the informer and you are a key subject . . ." Instead, I wrote an informal letter telling him that I was not interested in refighting the battles of the 1950s (true); that the deeper I got into my subject, the more complicated I saw it was (true); that I was going out of my way to get the perspectives of cooperative witnesses, whom by the way no previous writer or researcher had talked to (true); that I had no idea where it would come out (half true); and that I hoped he would talk with me.

I also took a job at Wesleyan University in Middletown, Connecticut, teaching what they called a short course (because it met only six times) on the history of cooperative witnesses. (If this strikes you as a narrow subject, consider that those were the days when the university librarian taught a short course on "Irish revolutionary war songs.") Wesleyan, by the way, was where Kazan had deposited his papers, not yet open to the public. They were kept under lock and key in a special room on the top floor of Wesleyan's library. I briefly considered a break-and-enter job. After all, I rationalized, he had gotten a highly publicized mega-tax write-off for the donation of his papers, yet taxpayers were denied access until he had completed his memoirs. I even persuaded his graduate-student curator to escort me through the inner sanctum, but in the end I decided that unlike J. Edgar Hoover and Robert Kennedy,

---

*Maltz's attack on Trumbo would eventually spark a far-reaching, history-making Maltz-Trumbo correspondence—a mix of dialectical bile, Talmudic wisdom, moral argument, Hollywood gossip, and deep history. I heard about it from U.C.L.A. Professor Howard Suber, only after Trumbo died, but when I tried to get a copy from Maltz, he balked on the grounds that Trumbo was the better polemicist, that because Trumbo was dying of cancer, Maltz had withheld some of his best shots, and last but not least, he held the copyright on his own letters. Cleo Trumbo, Dalton's widow, had no such qualms. So ironically, in the end I was able to quote the quotable Trumbo and only paraphrase Maltz.

who were at the core of *Kennedy Justice* and, as such, appropriate targets for no-holds-barred investigative reporting, Kazan and Miller were of primarily symbolic importance and, as such, inappropriate subjects for such dirty tricks. Nevertheless, I did all I could to gain access to Kazan himself.

And when the writer Patricia Bosworth asked me if I wanted to sublet her rent-controlled one-room office on the fourth floor of 1545 Broadway, I snapped it up, because it was a bargain and it didn't hurt that Kazan's office was on the second floor.

I devised an equally Machiavellian full-court-press strategy to go after each of the informers, and before it was over, more than a dozen of them sat for my interviews. BUT THESE THINGS TAKE TIME.

And to help pay the bills, one year I became Ferris Visiting Professor of Journalism at Princeton, where I taught a course on politics and the press. One lesson I strove mightily to impart to my students was that in the world of magazines, article deadlines on timely subjects are sacred. In fact, I told them it would count against them if their papers were late. When one wisenheimer asked me how my book was coming along (at that point I was only three years late), I patiently explained my philosophy: Magazine articles have to be on time because magazine issues are planned around them; but a book, if it is any good, will outlive its author, so the challenge is to do it right. Besides, if a publisher pays an author for two years of his time and the author gives three or four or five, who is the publisher to complain?

I have no such sophistic theory to defend taking time out to manage (some would say mismanage) Ramsey Clark's 1974 campaign for the U.S. Senate other than that it was a once-in-a-lifetime opportunity—and the book was going to be late anyway. Clark, having left the Justice Department when Nixon was elected, had moved to New York and become chairman of the board of the ACLU. Since Ramsey announced at the outset that he was going to limit campaign contributions to $100 per person, and thereby anticipated by decades the campaign-finance-reform movement, a conventional campaign manager would be of little use to him. That's also why instead of bringing in a political fund-raiser with traditional big-money connections as our treasurer, I brought in a publisher, Paul Gottlieb, who was used to raising money (selling subscriptions) via direct mail in units of $100 or less.

One of the ethical issues bedeviling journalism has to do with the propriety of journalists shuffling back and forth between covering, let's say, the State and Defense Departments, and working for, let's say, the State and Defense Departments.

My own (self-serving) view is that this is more of a problem for establishment journalists who garb themselves in the accoutrements of objectivity than for opinion or advocacy journalists, who tend to wear their politics on their sleeve. Years later, when *The Washington Post*'s incomparable investigative reporter Walter Pincus addressed the graduating class at Columbia's Graduate School of Journalism, he told them that the eighteen-month experience he had running an investigation of foreign lobbyists for a four-senator subcommittee of Senator J. W. Fulbright's Foreign Relations Committee was "among the most rewarding" experiences in his professional life. He went on to recommend that all journalism students take one semester working (not in public relations) for a government agency. Or politics, I thought to myself.

Of course when I went to work for Ramsey I was fresh from the *Times* and did not yet know I was headed for *The Nation*. As I saw it at the time, it was a trade-off: I was sacrificing the appearance of objectivity for the chance to see politics from the inside. Also, a chance to work for a man and a cause in which I believed. I jumped at the chance.

After the Clark campaign (he won the Democratic primary and lost the general election to the incumbent liberal senator Jacob Javits, then the biggest Republican vote getter in the country), I became an (unscholarly) Visiting Scholar at the Russell Sage Foundation in 1975. One day I noticed an item in the paper about how *The Nation* might be for sale. When I was doing my research on the Hollywood blacklist, I read through all the magazines published in the late 1940s and 1950s, and I came to admire *The Nation* more than any other for its coverage of the cultural consequences and the constitutional implications of the domestic Cold War. I had also interviewed its former editor, Carey McWilliams, both about those years (Carey had helped to draft a brief on behalf of the Hollywood Ten and was the author of *Witch Hunt*, which anticipated—and pre-named!—the McCarthy decade to come) and about the reprint publishing business, for my column "In Cold Print" (Carey had sold more copies of his various books via reprinters like Greenwood Press than they had sold in their original editions, an untold story).

I thought of Carey the way I thought of Tom Emerson. It was not just that like Emerson he parted his hair down the middle (although in Carey's case it was a tribute to his iconoclastic culture hero, H. L. Mencken), but rather that they were both understated non-Communist rebel-radicals who regarded home-grown red-baiting as a greater problem than home-grown reds, and who were not above tough, intellectual infighting. When in the early 1950s Emerson and McWilliams signed the call for a civil liberties conference, the historian Arthur Schlesinger, Jr., in a column for the *New York Post*, wrote: "None of these gentlemen is a Communist, but none objects very much to Communism," and he called them "typhoid Marys of the left." McWilliams replied in the *New Statesman* that Schlesinger "speaks the language of McCarthyism with a Harvard accent." Carey had come to New York from California in 1950 to put together a special issue of *The Nation* called "How Free Is Free?" and stayed on for twenty-five years. In 1955, when he officially became editor, he recruited as publisher first George Kirstein (brother of the Lincoln Kirstein who ran the New York City Ballet), recently resigned as executive vice-president of the Health Insurance Plan of Greater New York; and, when Kirstein resigned after ten years, James J. Storrow, Jr., a General Motors heir in the microfilm and print technology business who had been turned onto progressive politics by *The Nation's* in-depth coverage of the case of Sacco and Vanzetti. (Storrow had served as publisher of *The Nation's* 335-page centennial issue, dated September 20, 1965.)

In 1975, Carey had retired, and Storrow, who had been in John F. Kennedy's class at Harvard, had persuaded another old Harvard classmate (a *Crimson* editor), Blair Clark, to take the editor's chair. Now, for health reasons, Storrow felt it was time to pass the torch, and for personal reasons, Clark was ready to step down.

At the time, I had a number of talented friends trying to decide what to do with their lives, and so I began suggesting to the more entrepreneurial of them that they consider buying and publishing *The Nation*. I proposed it to Paul Gottlieb, who had just left *American Heritage* magazine, where he had worked his way up to being president, but he was more interested in Abrams Publishing, which specialized in fine-art books, and which he shortly joined as president (many years later at my behest he became a modest *Nation* shareholder). I also spoke about it with my friend Larry Grauman, who for one shining moment had been an impressively entrepreneurial editor of *The Antioch Review*. He had a small trust fund and was doing a study of little magazines for the Twentieth Century Fund. Grauman met with Storrow, but he didn't follow up. I even mentioned it to "Ping" Ferry, who had invited me to lunch at his favorite club, the Century. Ping nodded, but he had more important matters to discuss—a party he was giving for himself a year hence to celebrate his seventieth birthday. He had in mind to invite thirty-two old friends (POFs he called them, Ping's Old Friends) to his favorite inn, The Masons Arms, in Devon, England, at his favorite time of year (September), at his expense. Would Annie and I come? When I accepted his invitation, little did I suspect that it would prove a giant step on my own road to *The Nation*.

And then there was Hamilton Fish, a mere twenty-three years old, who had run the fund-raising office of the Clark campaign. Why don't you do for *The Nation* what you did for Marcel Ophuls? I said to Ham. After the campaign was over, an item had appeared in *The New York Times* about Ophuls, the genius writer-director of *The Sorrow and the Pity*, the unforgettable documentary about French collaboration with the Nazis; Ophuls had been fired from his new film on the Nuremberg trials merely because it was a year or two behind schedule, still unfinished, and a couple of hours longer than it was supposed to be. Ham had called Ophuls and said in effect, "If I raise money to buy back the rights to your film, would you finish making it?" Ophuls had said yes, and after a long, messy, complicated, but ultimately successful negotiation, Ham pried the rights loose, raised the money, and the mercurial genius Ophuls finished *The Memory of Justice*.

My theory about Ham—which he vehemently denied—was that it was in his genes to run for Congress from the district in upstate New York which had been represented by one or another Hamilton Fish since before I was born. But that until that happened he should do— was doing—good works. His first good work had been a student get-out-the-vote campaign, which he co-sponsored when he was still an undergraduate at Harvard. His second was with the Clark campaign.

His third was the Ophuls film. And here was a chance to do a fourth. He could raise the money to secure the fortune of this irreplaceable, invaluable part of America's cultural heritage, recruit an editor and publisher to run it, and then move on to his next good work.

Ham was intrigued. He called Storrow, and not long thereafter came staggering back from what we later were to learn was James's specialty—a three-martini lunch at the Harvard Club—with a message. Yes, *The Nation* was for sale. Yes, Storrow was interested in Ham's interest. There was, however, an incipient buyer in the wings, so if Ham was serious, he would have to move fast.

Ham told me he was interested, but only on condition that I would agree to be the editor. I told Ham that that was flattering, but there was no way I could do it. First, I had this book to write, in which I had already invested three years of research; second, I had this family to support, in which I had already invested eight years of everything else; third, a magazine with *The Nation*'s economics could never afford to pay its editor a living wage; and besides, the *Times* had made noises about inviting me back and I had declined the honor. It just wasn't in the cards for me to go back into the magazine-editing business.

Suppose, Ham said, suppose you didn't have to start until you finished your book, suppose he raised enough money to match my old *Times* salary, and to carry *The Nation* for at least three years (and I could specify how much that would require), *and* suppose he gave me total editorial control?

How could I say no? I told him I would think about it, and I called Blair Clark. I knew him from Eugene McCarthy's campaign in 1968, which he had co-managed and I had covered for the *Times Magazine*, and I had written a review or two for him at *The Nation*. At lunch I told him of my conversation with Ham, and I told him that if he had any reservations about our idea, or if he had plans of his own to put together a group (as he had helped to do for *The New York Review of Books*, as one of its original founders and funders), then I would tell Ham that as far as I was concerned he should cease and desist. Blair, always gracious, said that he appreciated my sharing this news with him, that he had already heard about the lunch with Ham from Storrow, and that for personal reasons he was not available to take over the magazine, much as he cared for and about it. But, he added, "between us," the deal to pass *The Nation* on to another party as yet unnamed was virtually done.

Sure enough, a few months later, the front page of *The New York Times* announced that *The Nation* was being sold to Thomas Morgan, most recently editor of *The Village Voice* (and before that Mayor John Lindsay's press secretary), and his wife, Mary Rockefeller, of the Rockefeller Rockefellers. It was, Morgan told the *Times*, his lifelong dream to have his own magazine, and now "my dream has come true." Blair was to stay on for a year as editorial director.

And that, I thought, was that. The following fall I moved with my wife and family to Princeton, New Jersey, where I taught for a year. Then one morning the phone rang. It was Blair, who, as it happened, lived in Princeton. Could we have a drink later in the day? It was a matter, it seemed, of some urgency. Over a single martini he explained that despite the front-page story in the newspaper of record, the Morgan deal had never "closed." Not only that, but it was about to unravel, and the story would be out in a matter of days, and "if young Fish is still interested, now is the time for him to make his move."

The last time around, something like twenty-four groups had come forward expressing an interest in *The Nation*, and Storrow seemed to enjoy the process of entertaining them, even as he suffered failing health, including a recent operation for glaucoma. Blair's interest, on the other hand, was in not repeating the flirtations (his word), lest the future of the magazine remain too long in doubt. Among those who had already expressed an interest was an affluent ad man who wanted to install his son as an editor; another magazine editor who had organized a group of interested Texans; Irving Louis Horowitz, founder of *Transaction* magazine; the writer Milton Viorst and Ronald Goldfarb, an attorney who represented many Washington writers (both coincidentally old friends of mine); two New York–based journalists, and various others.

Blair Clark, meanwhile, had an odd but distinguished background. Heir to the Clark thread fortune, Harvard classmate and friend of John Kennedy, buddy of Ben Bradlee in Paris—where Blair collaborated briefly, to his later regret, with the CIA—he had been an associate publisher of the *New York Post*; vice president and general manager of CBS News, where he hired Walter Cronkite, America's eyes, ears, nose, and throat for the middle years of the twentieth century; he had even served a term at Marshall Field's progressive daily, *PM*.

Magazines are, for the most part, sold to the highest bidder. Not *The Nation*. Storrow had recently turned down a bid, for example, from a group headed by Alan Baron, former press secretary to the 1972 Democratic presidential candidate, George McGovern, because, despite *The Nation*'s affection for the senator and general agreement with his political orientation, the fastidious Storrow felt such a sale would betray *The Nation*'s credo, which promised in 1865 that the magazine "would not be the organ of any party, movement, or sect." Then, according to Blair, when Tom Morgan, without consulting Storrow, offered Baron a job as *The Nation*'s man in the nation's capital, at his own instigation Storrow undid the deal, which legally had not yet closed.

Blair later explained to me that he enjoyed informal veto power over Storrow's successor. Such an arrangement, it seemed to me, was an invitation to trouble-making, but it also seemed consistent with *The Nation*'s culture, where editorial considerations prevailed over economic ones. I took Blair's background briefing to be a vote of confidence in the Fish-Navasky effort to acquire the magazine.

The number-one candidate that Ham and I had for publisher was Alan Sagner, a real-estate developer who had been referred to us by Storrow when he called to inquire about purchasing the magazine. A longtime *Nation* supporter who had helped found the Fair Play for Cuba Committee, and had a career as a progressive political player, he was then acting as treasurer for New Jersey governor Byrne's re-election campaign. But when Byrne unexpectedly won a second term, he and Governor Mario Cuomo of New York asked Alan, who had served as head of New Jersey's Department of Transportation, to take over the Port Authority, which he did.

As 1977 drew to a close, Ham and I thought we had another ideal candidate for publisher, the highly energetic and sharp-minded Alan Meckler, who was publisher of a trade magazine which did for microfilm what *Publishers Weekly* did for books. I had met him in my *Monocle* days, when he and the great Columbia historian James Shenton had the idea that *Monocle* should publish faculty baseball cards. (The faculty picture would be on the front, and a list of key publications and other statistics on the back: "I'll trade you one Arthur Schlesinger for two Henry Steele Commagers," and so on.) The only question was whether to include the bubble gum. But when he forgot to show up at a key backers' session—we had rented a room at the Algonquin Hotel

for the occasion—and when a second publisher-candidate didn't pan
out, either, Ham decided by default that destiny had called, and I proposed that he be publisher himself.

Ham was back in business—although first he had to take a little
trip up the Nile on the Hollywood philanthropist Max Palevsky's yacht,
along with Lillian Hellman and other progressive notables—all candidates, I assured Ham, for participation in the syndicate he would have
to organize if the Fish-Navasky *Nation* were to be a reality.

I will not here go into the fund-raising saga that ensued, but I
should mention a September 1977 meeting in the august law offices of
Paul, Weiss, which had agreed to take Ham as a client. Adrian (Bill)
DeWind, the firm's senior tax partner and the progressive former head
of the New York Bar Association, had gotten to know Ham in the
course of the student get-out-the-vote campaign, and Joseph Eisman,
Paul Weiss's top tax man, was enthusiastic about the venture. The object of the meeting was to get James Storrow to agree to sign a legally
binding option to sell *The Nation* to our group. The issue at hand was
me. The Storrows scarcely knew me. Present for the occasion, in addition to James, his wife, Linda, and Blair, were DeWind, "Ping" Ferry
and his wife, Carol Bernstein Ferry. Also present were my old *Iron
Mountain* co-conspirator the novelist E. L. Doctorow, coming off the
success of his best-selling novel *Ragtime*; Alan Sagner, who had now
signed on as a potential investor and silent partner; and Ralph Nader,
who was passing through town and wanted to help.

In the course of the meeting, Doctorow eloquently described the
role and function of an editor so that only I met the job description.
And although James clearly would have preferred postponing the matter of editor selection until the end, it was agreed that I would write a
brief statement of my philosophy, and if it passed muster, Ham Fish
would have his option. Somewhere in there, *The Nation*'s longtime
Washington correspondent, Robert Sherrill, sent on one of his advocacy love-letter masterpieces to Storrow extolling me. (I don't remember whether he mentioned that a couple of years earlier I had extolled
his blockbuster of a book, *The Saturday Night Special*, in my *New York
Times Book Review* column, but what are friends for?)

The next day I sent James 3,000 words paying tribute to *The Nation*'s past and (a) saying that the most important contribution that I or

anyone else could make would be to maintain its astonishingly high standard of excellence, (b) describing what I had learned from my days at *The New York Times* and freelancing, and (c) setting forth my own worldview, which I said:

> consists of a simplistic, absolutist view of the First Amendment, after the fashion of Black-Douglas-Tom Emerson; on matters of race I am an unreconstructed integrationist although I think *The Nation* is an appropriate forum for black nationalist and other views to be put forth and tested; in the world arena I am afraid of multinationals, soft on old World Federalists and perhaps as a result of my years at Swarthmore College, a Quaker institution, I have a profound presumption in favor of disarmament over armament and am paranoid about nuclear weapons; I worry too much about automation and what the new technology has already done to our culture; I am a privacy freak and I believe all forms of electronic eavesdropping ought to be banned; I don't agree that the programs of the Great Society were tried and didn't work—indeed they may not work, but I don't think many of them were ever really given a fair chance; I have an enduring sympathy for socialist experiments, preferably decentralized, and keep looking for one that works. Which is quite different from presenting "both sides" of every issue. Occasionally, on an issue like "Should There Be a Palestinian State?" there is ample room for a symposium, but as a general proposition I sympathize with Heywood Broun when he said he was sick of *The Nation*'s "policy of fair play, and everybody must be heard whether or not he has anything to say. This isn't an amateur tennis match. It's a fight, and the well-being of masses of men and women depends upon the result . . . Even an open mind needs to pull down the window at certain times or it becomes less a mind than a cave of the winds." (Actually he said this apropos *The Nation*'s failure to endorse FDR's court-packing plan which he favored and I oppose, but I agree with the sentiment.)

The remainder of my letter included an inventory of the resources I would make a special effort to put at the disposal of *The Nation*: the

Freedom of Information Act, the research products of the burgeoning community of public interest and left, liberal, and radical think tanks and public-policy institutions; and the books published and represented by editors and agents with anticonglomerate sensibilities.

Should *The Nation* seek out the famous? Not for their names alone, but I might mention a number of well-known writers who I thought might be available to contribute if given the appropriate subject. Then I added:

> In the long run, of course, the success of *The Nation* does not depend on luring the famous into the magazine but on how many new, young writers *The Nation* can discover and nourish. Where is the new Nader, the next Dan Wakefield? There are many ways to make contact with the coming generation, not the least of which is a system of student interns. This might be done in association with journalism schools, as part of the field periods of schools like Bard, Antioch, Bennington or in conjunction with one of the foundations and institutes which are making a specialty of investigative journalism.

Finally I suggested some specific projects (one or two of which actually came to pass), and I talked about what I had not talked about:

> I have not talked about *The Nation* as a moral monitor, as evaluator of the evaluators. I have also not mentioned the possibilities for new graphics even within *The Nation*'s existing formula . . . And I have said nothing of the publisher-editor relationship, which I hope would be a precise replica of what has gone immediately before. But I hope I have given you a feeling for my feeling for *The Nation*. In a world of *Time, Newsweek,* Cronkite and Barbara Walters it seems to me indispensable that *The Nation* continue to perform its unique weekly services: To question the conventional wisdom, to be suspicious of all orthodoxies, to provide a home for dissent and dissenters, and, to be corny about it, to hold forth a vision of a better world.

The option basically gave Ham the rest of the year to raise $950,000, which included the purchase price of $125,000. Our projections, which we claimed were conservative, showed that we could reach and pass the break-even point with an investment of $500,000. But because we were nervous (and based on my *Monocle* experience I believed that no matter how "conservative" we were, projections always turned out to be optimistic), we set out to raise twice that. In the end, because that is what we thought we could raise, we compromised on the figure of $950,000. Since Paul, Weiss would eventually agree to take its $50,000 legal-services bill in new *Nation* stock and Doctorow advanced Ham $10,000 walking-around money, that left only $890,000 to go.

When I wasn't teaching, I spent my year at Princeton drafting and then circulating a prospectus, writing *Naming Names*, waking up Hamilton Fish with daily long-distance phone calls (he would explain why the money wasn't rolling in, I would suggest new fish for him to catch), meeting with Ham and prospective investors as needed, and soliciting and ignoring editorial and business advice from friends and neighbors.

Could we live up to the promise of our prospectus? The magazine prospectus, like a sonnet or a sestina, has a form, an internal logic of its own: a section on why the magazine is like no other ("America's oldest continuously published weekly"); a section on the "demand" for it (don't take this on faith, we'll test it); a spread sheet (showing us passing the break-even point in three to five years); a section on the competition (showing that it is no competition); a section on personnel (geniuses all); and a section on editorial hopes stated, of course, as plans ("We will make as well as report news").

One piece of business advice from a Princeton neighbor, Theodore Cross, the proprietor of *Business and Society Review* and a bevy of moneymaking newsletters, had to do with the part of our prospectus concerning the competition. Ted thought we should eliminate it: "Bear in mind that your most productive mailing lists will probably be the lists of your competition. (They scratch each other's backs.) Why alienate them, since the attack (and in some places it is truly an attack) does not advance the goals of your publishing prospectus?* I would simply

*The prospectus included a section contrasting *The Nation* and *The New Republic* in terms of their respective treatment of the 1961 invasion of the Bay of Pigs. *The Nation* had blown the whistle and *The New Republic* had killed a scheduled piece at the request of the Kennedy White House. See below, p. 173.

allude to the other magazines generally and put out that you are creating something entirely different, and state that purpose in the most compelling fashion possible."

As we saw it in 1978, the need for a magazine like *The Nation* was real, the prospectus was the place to say so, and to say it right we had to talk about the competition. Despite the well-publicized performance of the *Times* and *The Washington Post* in publishing the Pentagon Papers, and *The Washington Post* in helping to expose Watergate, the press (including those papers, not to mention the chains and the TV networks) seemed more homogenized than ever. It was organized around journalistic beats (some called it "building" journalism, because you had a Pentagon reporter, a White House reporter, a Justice Department reporter, etc.) rather than to address the profound economic and political changes which seemed so ripe for scrutiny. Although isolated reporters like Seymour Hersh had made inroads into the intelligence community, the incentives in the establishment press had to do with the exposure of yet another Mafioso. "Sacred cows are safer here than in India," our prospectus proclaimed.

We thought that the magazine community itself was lagging. Looking at the variety of opinion journals, we said we were struck by "the narrow range" in which they operated. There were the conservative journals like *National Review, American Opinion*, and *Human Events*. There were the neoconservative journals like *The Public Interest* and *Commentary*, which, although it specialized in Jewish affairs, had a legacy of Cold War assumptions of how the world worked (as did the less embattled, late-1970s *New Leader*). There were the general-interest magazines such as *Harper's, The Atlantic, The New Yorker*, and *Saturday Review*, which divided their space between culture and politics but had "no sense of urgency" about the national condition and whose leisurely publication schedules (with the exception of the weekly *New Yorker*, which in those last years of Mr. Shawn behaved as if time was of no consequence) seemed to preclude close coverage of the day-to-day decisions of the political and economic institutions which had come to dominate our lives. The newsweeklies such as *Time* and *Newsweek* and *U.S. News* "had become as much lifestyle as newsmagazines."

There were the special-interest or niche magazines like *Atlas, Co-*

lumbia Journalism Review, *Ms.*, *Foreign Affairs*, *Foreign Policy*, and *Mother Earth News*, each catering to its own constituency. *The New York Review of Books*, intellectually stimulating though it was, was basically a book review (or so we argued) and seemed more academic than it had been in the late 1960s with its antiwar essays by I. F. Stone and Noam Chomsky, and its New Left cultural critiques and analyses by such as Andy Kopkind and Tom Hayden. *The Village Voice*, a weekly paper, and *Rolling Stone* and *New Times*, biweeklies, all spoke vaguely from the left, but ultimately their contribution had primarily to do with culture, and avant-garde, hip-rock culture at that. *Commonweal* concerned itself with issues primarily of interest to liberal Catholics. *Washington Monthly* specialized in muckraking with a narrow, Washington focus. *The Progressive*, with its Madison, Wisconsin, base, its monthly schedule, and its populist perspective, was important but at a considerable distance from the vortex of the contemporary policy-making process and politics. And then there were the publications like *Mother Jones*, *Seven Days*, the socialist *In These Times*, and the undergrounds which we saw "as having in different degrees more or less given up on the political process, which they regarded as hopelessly square."

In other words, from our perspective, the left-liberal weekly franchise had been deeded by default to *The Nation* and *The New Republic*, which under Martin Peretz had already started to veer off in a neoliberal direction (and, especially in matters involving race and the Middle East, a neoconservative one). It was our contention that while there certainly was room for both, and while the concerns of these two venerable journals frequently overlapped, the differences which defined them underlined the need for a journal with *The Nation*'s particular heritage and mission.

Once James signed the option, he turned over a list of past *Nation* funders to Hamilton. At the top of the list was the name Corliss Lamont, the radical humanist, by then in his eighties. Lamont—who had run for the U.S. Senate as a candidate of the old American Labor Party, sued the CIA, and signed every petition for peace with the Soviet Union then extant—was an old antagonist of Ham's grandfather, the reactionary former member of Congress, now in his nineties.

One day young Hamilton called Corliss Lamont, who was out, so Ham left his name. Here is the conversation that ultimately took place when Lamont returned the call (as reported to and eventually from young Hamilton):

LAMONT: This is Lamont, returning your call.
FISH: Who?
LAMONT: Corliss Lamont.
FISH: Who?
LAMONT: CORLISS LAMONT.
FISH: The *COMMUNIST* CORLISS LAMONT? You want my grandson! [*Click.*]

A year or two after we went into business, Ham, who was the fifth Hamilton Fish but didn't put a number after his name because he thought it pretentious, came into my office with a letter in his hand. "What do you make of this?" he asked.

It was a letter from his grandfather enclosing a printed subscription solicitation signed "Hamilton Fish, publisher" and a note saying, "If you don't cease and desist sending Communist propaganda over my name, I shall be forced to take appropriate action."

I said I thought it meant if he did not add a number at the end of his name, he would be disinherited. Close readers of the *Nation* masthead will note that in the issue dated December 3, 1981, the number III sprouted at the end of Ham's name (by tradition one counts only the living).

Desperate as we were to find investors, occasionally it was necessary for us to turn down potential backers. Thus, for better or for worse, one day Ham called me at Princeton. He had met an unlikely character who was reported to be worth more than $100 million, smoked a big cigar, and had a big idea: why not combine *The Nation, The Progressive, The New Republic, Washington Monthly*, and *Mother Jones*, and that way instead of a half-dozen ineffectual liberal magazines, you would have one big effectual liberal magazine? I thought the idea was unrealistic, and I also thought it was a good, not a bad idea, to have variety on the liberal left, so I told Ham not to waste his time. Actually, the man with the big cigar and the big idea was eventually to play a significant role in *The Na-tion*'s history. I'll give you a hint. His first name was Arthur.

We also turned down Dorothy Schiff's offer to fund the entire mag-azine. She didn't like the idea of being just one limited silent partner among many (which she called "taxation without representation"). Why not let her fund the whole thing and be its publisher? Ham would be its associate publisher, and I would be her new Jimmy Wechsler. Uh-oh. Instead, what we agreed to, not without some trepidation, was that she would be our single largest shareholder (she put in $150,000) and I would consult with her every week.

As things worked out, Mrs. Schiff had a phobia about rickety eleva-tors, so after the first week she stopped coming by *The Nation* and asked if she sent her car would I mind coming down to her office at the old *Post* building for lunch (which turned out to be a tuna sandwich and a cup of coffee). I didn't mind. But after we ran an editorial calling Judge Simon Rifkind, senior partner at Paul, Weiss, and her personal friend, a "fixer," she stopped meeting. By her lights, if we were going into business with Paul, Weiss (they were, after all, shareholders), we had shown bad form in attacking one of the firm's most important partners.

On the other hand, my earlier Devon excursion with Ping Ferry and his hiking, sightseeing, and pub-crawling Old Friends turned out to pay some unexpected dividends. Ham and I were looking for twenty people to commit $50,000 each, and Ping and his wife, Carol, became the first to do so. Among their guests, Charles "Bud" Mandlestam went on to hire my brother-in-law-the-lawyer, and the firm ultimately be-came *The Nation*'s lawyers, and he, too, became a shareholder; David Hunter, who consulted to the rich and anonymous on their social-responsibility investments, including among his clients Phil Stern (re-member him from *Monocle* days, when he professed reluctance, then got with the program? he did the same for *The Nation*); Leslie Dunbar, leader of the Southern Regional Council during the civil rights strug-gles of the 1960s, who was in the process of retiring as president of the Field Foundation (as in Mrs. Marshall Field; small world, isn't it?), had no investment capital of his own, but agreed to head up the Nation In-stitute, our nonprofit arm. And then there was the courtly, formal—he alone appeared nightly in suit and tie at our modest country-inn dinner table—F. Palmer Weber. Palmer was to become our guru, our rabbi, our well-connected player, who not only signed on as a shareholder himself but was willing to inveigle if not manipulate his friends into joining him in his folly.

The late great F. Palmer Weber was a stockbroker with a Ph.D. in Hegelian dialectics. Weber invoked the Fifth Amendment in April 1953, when called before Senator William E. Jenner's subcommittee to investigate the administration of the Internal Security Act, where he was asked about Communist Party membership from 1934 to 1940. Weber had lots of friends on the Hill, where he had worked as a consulting economist to various congressional committees. He had also worked for the Political Action Committee of the CIO, and when Henry Wallace ran for President on the Progressive Party ticket in 1948, Palmer was national coordinator for the eleven Southern states. The Jenner Committee asked why he had lobbied against the Mundt-Nixon Bill, a proposed piece of legislation that would have made it a criminal offense to be a Communist Party member, and that would have required all so-called Communist-front organizations to register.

Mr. Weber—one of my all-time favorite congressional witnesses—said:

> You see, I am a Virginian, born and raised in Virginia, and my people fought for the Confederacy, and I grew up under Thomas Jefferson's shadow and I would rather die than take away any man's right to hold any opinion whatsoever that he chooses on the basis of his own reading and understanding. I wouldn't do it. I wouldn't consent to it and I would not penalize any man for his personal opinions.

Because he was blacklisted from further government employment, he was forced to go to work on Wall Street, where, applying Marxist analysis to the a, b, c's of production and consumption, he made fortunes for his old left cronies, many of whom had themselves been forced to go into business because of their unpopular politics (i.e., past membership in the Communist Party). Palmer imposed only one condition—the Mormons call it tithing: he insisted that each client put a percentage of what he made—say 10 percent—into one or another good, progressive cause. It has long been my belief that Palmer personally was responsible for the financing of the peace and civil rights movements of the 1960s and early 1970s. Lucky for us, in 1977 we became Palmer's cause of the moment.

We met for breakfast in the greasy-spoon coffee shop at the old Royalton Hotel before it was upgraded and became the favored hangout of Condé Nast and *New Yorker* editors. There Palmer Weber conducted a weekly seminar in magazine fund-raising, philosophy, history, and human engineering. His auditors included writers, editors, potential investors, and advertisers, and occasionally I would even invite a friend from another magazine to show them what they were missing.

To give you just an inkling of what we are dealing with here, Palmer did not limit his interventions on our behalf to his progressive friends like Studs Terkel, *numero uno* talk-show host and America's oral historian; or his clients like Corliss Lamont himself or Ralph Shikes and Sam Chafkin, political refugees whose success in private enterprise yielded investment capital which Palmer then helped them grow. It was not beneath Palmer to propose that we might go after the multimillionaire Pritzker family in Chicago because he had heard they were rumored to have Mafia connections and "The Mafia has a stake in the Bill of Rights—*The Nation* can help educate them on their stake in the constitutional protections." (We didn't go after them, because our connection to the Pritzkers was as elusive as their alleged connection to the mob.)

I learned so much at these seminars that I kept them going long after we had solved our cash problems and were well into the business of putting out a weekly magazine. Breakfast with Palmer became sort of an initiation rite, whether the subject was North Sea oil or Thomas Jefferson. Palmer would use forks, knives, and salt and pepper shakers to explain the dialectics of history, taking full advantage of the Royalton's greasy cutlery. He was, of course, the darling of the aging waitress—this courtly, Southern gentleman who overtipped her outrageously—and she called him "sweetheart."

As our year-end deadline approached, we had raised $650,000, but truth to tell, Blair had given up on our team's ability to come up with the necessary capital, and informed Storrow that he was quitting at the end of the year. Storrow turned elsewhere, but he kept on turning until he came to me. By that time we were pretty tight (good friends), and he invited me to the Players' Club for dinner.

"Victor, my boy," he said, sipping his Tanqueray (also my favorite at the time), "I want you to be editor of *The Nation*." I know that, I said, and we (by this time I was helping Ham virtually full-time) are doing the best we can. "No," James said, "I mean, I want you to be the editor starting next year. Blair, for family reasons, has to leave, and I'd like you to take over." He meant: whether or not Ham raises the money.

I told James I was flattered, but before he had even started his second martini, I said of course the only circumstance under which I could or would consider it would be if he would extend Ham's option, so that when and if Ham raised the rest of the money he could exercise it.

He said, "By all means." We agreed that this called for "another drink" later in the week. In between I spoke with Ham, then had lunch with Carey McWilliams at the Library, a modest restaurant near his home on the Upper West Side, where he was at work on his memoirs, brought him up to date on negotiations, and asked him what he thought. Carey was wise in the ways of the world, wiser in the ways of the Storrows, whom he called "charming children," and wisest in the ways of *The Nation*. He told me he thought it took about three years for an editor to put his stamp—his imprint—on a magazine.

In a change of venue, I made my way down to The Players club to see Storrow again, and I set forth my terms—if James would extend Ham's option and guarantee to finance publication of the magazine for three years, I would sign on, and even though my book still had a way to go, I would start, come January.

James agreed. This led me to a further proposal, to which Blair had said the Storrows would never agree. Here we were $300,000 short and our deadline looming. We asked for another meeting, which this time took place in the Storrow home at 25 East End Avenue. Present: Blair, James and Linda Storrow, Ham and me, and my brother-in-law the lawyer. A conversation along the following lines took place:

The magazine now loses $125,000 a year, so by signing me on as editor and guaranteeing three years of publication, you have already in effect committed more than $300,000 to the magazine over the next three years, right?

Right.

If you will make that commitment to Ham's syndicate, which is $300,000 short, he will have closed the deal, right?

Huh?

Moreover, we will not call on your $300,000 unless we run through the first $650,000. You yourself have assured us that the magazine loses only $125,000 a year.

And our prospectus calls for us passing the break-even point in year four. If your numbers are right, we will only have spent $500,000 by that time—right?

(Silence.)

What do you say?

Believe it or not—(Blair couldn't believe it)—Storrow said yes. And three years later, when we had to call in his $300,000, he raised lots of objections, but he was as good as his word. And to the extent that he made loud and negative noises even as he kept his (legally binding) promise, Linda Storrow, his wife and associate publisher and gracious lady, kept assuring us that it was all right, that we were doing a fine job, that all was well with the world.

The timetable was that Ham would start in November 1977 and learn the publishing ropes under Storrow, while I would go into hibernation in upstate New York, attempting to finish a draft of what became *Naming Names*, and I would start at *The Nation* in February 1978.

I tentatively lined up both a new literary editor, an editorial assistant, and a part-time assistant editor who would start when I did. I was fairly far down the road in conversations with my candidate for the critical literary post when I came to a stop sign in the form of the incumbent, Elizabeth Pochoda. Betsy, who had a Ph.D. in Renaissance literature, an addiction to pop culture, and a healthy lack of reverence for the received wisdom in every field, had been recommended to Blair Clark by the novelist Philip Roth, with whom she had gone to graduate school. I met with Betsy, listened to (and read her memorandum on) her ideas for the section, and called off my search for her successor. And as it turned out, I was also so impressed with a young part-timer, Kai Bird, whom Blair had recruited from Princeton, that I asked him to stay too, and gradually converted his job from part- to full-time. When I arrived, I brought with me only the superefficient Karen Wilcox as my assistant; years later, she went on to the Yale School of Management and a career as a public-interest headhunter.

While Blair was very good about calling me for writer suggestions, essentially he ran the magazine until I got there.

My first day at 333 Sixth Avenue, I took the rickety elevator, on which Carey had been famously mugged a few years earlier, and got off at the eighth floor, where Greta the receptionist, who doubled as telephone operator, sat putting in and pulling out plugs on her old-fashioned switchboard. Greta's protective style and thick German accent were legendary. Callers who innocently asked to speak to the editor would be met with a suspicious "Vot do you vant mit him?" (When my wife called, on the other hand, Greta would confidentially inform her, "He chest vent to lunch mit a putifool blonde.")

Greta gave me a big hello and ushered me into "Mr. McWilliams's office," which faced a courtyard, and included some bookcases in which there was a thesaurus and bound back issues of *The Nation*, and also a huge old-fashioned wooden desk that I was assured belonged to Mr. McWilliams. On it was an old-fashioned dictograph machine, and over the right-hand top drawer was a sliding board taped onto which were five numbered rejection forms, each one more encouraging than the last.

At the *Times* I used to sit in a great open space with more than one hundred other Sunday Department employees, directly in front and one seat to the left of my direct supervisor, Harvey Shapiro, the articles editor. When I had an idea or a thought or a question, I would turn to my right and ask Harvey. My first day at *The Nation*, seated at Carey's great old wooden desk (which someone had polished for the occasion), I had an idea. Reflexively, I turned around to my right, and there in *The Nation*'s unwashed window, embedded with chicken wire, I saw my own reflection.

4

LOOKING BACKWARD

As I sat there in Carey's squeaky old chair, wondering when the phone would start ringing, I leafed through bound volumes of *The Nation*, starting with Volume I, number one, July 6, 1865.

Imagine the courage it took to launch a magazine with this opening sentence: "The week was singularly barren of exciting events."

That was July 6, 1865. Now contrast that opening line with the immortal statement of William Lloyd Garrison's abolitionist paper, *The Liberator*, whose subscription list *The Nation* had inherited: "I will not equivocate—I will not excuse—I will not retreat a single inch."

It occurred to me (and that doppelgänger in my window) that if I was going to do my job right I would have to draw on both traditions—the disdain for sensationalism, trendiness, and hype, and the passionate commitment to crusade against injustice. To quote from one of my all-time favorite *Nation* editorials, dated June 18, 1908:

> There is no force so potent in politics as a moral issue. Politicians may scorn it, ambitious men may despise it or fight shy of it, newspapers may caricature or misrepresent it; but it has a way of confounding the plans of those who pride themselves on their astuteness and rendering powerless the most formidable . . . party or boss.

But even the impassioned Garrison, for whom truth was Truth ("Ours is the incendiary spirit of truth that burns up error"), and who believed in Harsh Language ("because truth is harsh"), along with God, abolition, and prophesy, also believed in free discussion and untrammeled inquiry (because slavery "could not stand up to free discussion"). "Slavery and freedom of the press," he said, "cannot exist together."

And just as Fish and I had explained to potential investors that our independent little company (what today's magazine mavens call a "stand-alone") was structured to protect editorial independence, Garrison had said that *The Liberator*'s independence was the guarantor of its role as an open forum. He would, he often said, accept advice on any subject but one: how to run his paper. In his valedictory he referred to *The Liberator* not as a propaganda sheet for his various causes but as "a weekly method of communicating with each other."

Garrison blessed *The Nation* as heir to *The Liberator*, but this dual legacy of emancipation for the slaves and an independent, free press as a means of agitation and discussion was not without its complications.

Even before the first issue, it was evident that the magazine's business structure needed adjustment. *The Nation*'s 1865 prospectus made clear that the new weekly was not going to serve any sect, party, or movement. It was going to be a conscience, a gadfly to "wage war upon the vices of . . . exaggeration and misrepresentation." The editorial formula—to have the best thinkers of the day apply reason, logic, criticism, *moral* criticism, to the key problems of the day—entailed a business structure that would insulate the editor from untoward interference. E. L. Godkin, the Anglo-Irish journalist who came to this country in 1856 and created *The Nation* a decade later, thought he had worked it all out. He raised $100,000 in capital and signed on the elite and most thoughtful of the then–literary establishment, including Henry Wadsworth Longfellow, James Russell Lowell, William James, Henry James, Henry Adams, and William Dean Howells.

Although I did know that the editor-publisher relationship which obtained at *The Nation* was not exactly the prototype for the editor-publisher relationship elsewhere, at first I didn't understand the significance of *The Nation*'s business history.

At most magazines the money men get their way at the expense of the literary men (and in those days they were almost all men). Not so at *The Nation*. I don't know how it was in 1865, but these days when money men set out to launch a new magazine, what they want is buzz, buzz, and more buzz. Yet despite *The Nation*'s buzzless lead, subscriptions started coming in at the rate of forty a day. There seemed to be no stopping it.

And then it was almost stopped. The money had a problem. The largest single contributor to Godkin's $100,000 capital was the Boston abolitionist George Luther Stearns, a lead-pipe manufacturer who had supplied John Brown with the weapons that were used at Harpers Ferry. A second significant source of money was a Philadelphia group headed up by James Miller McKim, one of the founders of the American Anti-Slavery Society. In keeping with the tradition of these journals, McKim was also looking for a job for his prospective son-in-law. Thus Wendell Phillips Garrison, the abolitionist's son, at the outset was made the magazine's literary editor and invented the system of sending books out to reviewers with credentials relevant to the subject matter. Other monies came from a Boston-based group affiliated with the Loyal Publication Society, which distributed broadsides free of charge to nearly a thousand editors on such subjects as Negro citizenship and financing the war.

Although Godkin's *Nation* endorsed the early Reconstruction program—the Freedmen's Bureau, the Civil Rights Bill of 1866, the Reconstruction Acts of 1867 and the Thirteenth, Fourteenth, and Fifteenth Amendments—Stearns and Co. had a problem. Godkin balked at proselytizing on behalf of the radical reconstructionists. He even qualified the magazine's support for freedmen voting when he proposed an education test for suffrage. It soon became clear, as the historian James MacPherson writes in *The Abolitionist Legacy*, that "Godkin did not conceive of *The Nation* as a champion of the freedmen but as an intellectual review of politics and the arts modeled on the English *Spectator*." On behalf of the other abolitionist backers and himself, Stearns complained, as did the radical reconstructionist Wendell Phillips, who told the Anti-Slavery Society in Boston, "Look at this new journal, *The Nation*, which undertakes to represent these Freedmen's Associations, and which all the subscribers of anti-slavery are advised to take instead of old anti-slavery journals. How uncertain its sound! How timid, vacillating, noncommittal is its policy! . . . Are you willing such a neutral should represent us?"

So much for Rush Limbaugh and other *Nation* detractors, who prefer to believe that from day one *The Nation* has followed one or another party line. It wasn't true then, and it isn't true now.

Godkin, for his part, had more mundane matters to worry about. From the start, the magazine was losing nearly $5,000 a month, and as he saw it, his nearest competitor, *The Round Table*, benefited by not having to concentrate primarily on the freedmen. "I am told," he wrote his Boston friend and *Nation* contributor Charles Eliot Norton, "they rely for success against us, on their freedom from any responsibility with regard to the Negro, and on being more sprightly." In another letter he remarked:

> When the editorship was offered me, I took it on the understanding, which was afterwards reduced to writing, that I was to be completely independent to any extent that an honorable man could be. Of course, I could not call myself an honorable man, if, having been converted to proslaveryism or secession, I failed instantly to resign. But it was never understood or hinted that I was to be inspired by, or was to edit the paper under the supervision of Major Stearns, or of anybody else . . . It was not to be a party paper. It was to devote a good deal of attention to the social and political condition of the blacks at the South, not as their organ, but as one of the great questions of the day. And it was to discuss this and all other questions in such a tone and style as to secure the attention of a class to which anti-slavery journals have never had access.

Godkin went on to say that he undertook to produce a paper not aimed at commercial success but rather one "whose influence on those who read it, and on the country's papers, would be enlightening, elevating, and refining." He was concerned that *The Nation* not degenerate into "a mere canting organ of the radical wing," and he argued that "too close identification with a factional or partisan cause was bad journalism as well as bad policy." When Stearns threatened to withdraw if Godkin didn't mend his ways, the financer Samuel G. Ward told Godkin that to make *The Nation*'s "assurance double sure," he would himself "take every share that had not been paid up," and he did so "on the spot." Whereupon, with the help of Frederick Law Olmsted, the architect of Central Park who had put Godkin in touch with the money men in the first place, Godkin arranged for a new corporate structure that prevented anyone from telling him what to do.

In other words, whereas at most magazines when an editor antagonizes his backers, either he shapes up or they fire him and get a new one, at *The Nation* Godkin in effect fired his backers and got new ones. Down through the years this precedent has more or less become a *Nation* tradition.

These days most people assume that *The Nation* has always been on the left. But the truth is that politically it has sometimes zigged and sometimes zagged. By the 1870s Godkin's *Nation* had concluded that Reconstruction was a failure because it had undertaken "the insane task of making the newly emancipated field hands led by barbers and barkeeps fancy they knew as much about government and were as capable of administrating it as whites." In the early days Godkin's *Nation* was pro–free trade (his backers were split on that, too) and anti-imperialist, but it looked upon socialism as something to be stopped. "John Stuart Mill was our prophet," he wrote, "and Grote and Bentham were our daily food." It accepted the late-nineteenth-century synthesis of classical economics, Spencerian science, and Protestant theology. By 1880 Godkin had even published an article on "The White Side of the Southern Question." His *Nation* attacked the trust and the railroad barons, but he was suspicious of labor, opposed giving women the vote, called the striking Pullman railroad workers "Debs' Desperadoes," and seemed oblivious to the fundamental changes wrought by the Industrial Revolution. His main preoccupation was by that time civic reform. Boss Tweed and his influence on New York politics replaced abolitionism as *The Nation*'s most covered subject. The *Springfield Republican* wrote that Godkin's *Nation* functions "as a sort of moral policeman of our society, our politics, and our art . . ." One wag dubbed *The Nation* the "Weekly Day of Judgment." In politics, Godkin became a neo-Mugwump, bolting from the Republican Party to support Grover Cleveland in the 1884 presidential campaign.

Yet, as William James wrote: "To my generation, Godkin was certainly the towering influence in all thought concerning public affairs, and indirectly his influence has certainly been more pervasive than that of any other writer of the generation, for he influenced other writers who never quoted him, and determined the whole current of discussion." Godkin's *Nation* is more quoted in the histories of the period than any other contemporary periodical.

I. F. Stone once noted, "Don't forget he took the name *The Nation* (rather than the more passive 'Union') from a Dublin weekly described as 'remarkable for its talent, for its seditious tendencies, and for the fire and spirit of its political poetry.'" But Godkin's legacy, made possible by radical reconstructionist backing, had less to do with radical or even liberal politics than with journalistic integrity and independence. And that meant either legally insulating the editor from interference by the money men or finding money men whose consciousness on these matters had already been raised.

In 1881, when the railroad magnate Henry Villard purchased the *New York Evening Post* and offered Godkin a job as associate editor, Godkin accepted only on condition that *The Nation* was part of the deal. At most publications, over time the takeoverer folds the takeoveree into its pages. Not so with *The Nation*. As it happened, Mrs. Henry Villard was a daughter of the abolitionist William Lloyd Garrison. Oswald Garrison Villard, the Villards' son (and later *Nation* editor and publisher), confides in his memoirs that his father "gave his majority stockholding to my mother and then trusteed it, giving complete power to three trustees" in order that no one should say that *The Nation* "was dominated by a Wall Street man and also to assure to the editors their complete independence." Godkin turned over *The Nation*'s daily editorial chores to Wendell Phillips Garrison, Mrs. Villard's brother. And Oswald Garrison Villard, who began writing for *The Nation* in 1894, became a *Nation* editorial writer and president of *The Nation* Company in 1908, but didn't take over as editor until 1918. Thus, from 1881 to 1918, *The Nation* was an insert in or a weekly supplement to the *New York Evening Post*, and like Rip Van Winkle, it went to sleep.

Under one editor, Paul Elmer More (1909–14), a Sanskrit scholar, *The Nation* even described itself as an "organ of thinking people, the exponent of sane progress, of wise *conservatism!*" [my italics]. But even in those years of confused political identity, the editors cherished the magazine's high standards, and its owners left it alone.

H. L. Mencken captured this interlude in the magazine's history best when he wrote in *The Baltimore Sun*:

> *The Nation*, since the passing of Godkin, had been gradually dying. It was, perhaps, the dullest publication of any sort ever printed in the world. Its content consisted on the one hand of

long editorials reprinted from the *Evening Post*, and on the other hand of appalling literary essays by such pundits as Paul Elmer More. [Oswald Garrison] Villard, when he took it over [in 1918] threw out the garbage and started printing the truth. The effect was instantaneous. Its circulation increased four or five-fold in a few months.

Indeed, circulation jumped from 7,200 in 1918 to 38,087 by 1920.

Villard was a believer in nonviolence, but he was the sort of militant pacifist who could write: "President McKinley ought to have been shot with his entire cabinet for putting us into an unnecessary war with Spain." He was a founder of the Anti-Imperialist League and of the NAACP. His *Nation* opposed conscription during the years of World War I (which Villard regarded as a war between rival imperial powers), and fought for the release of conscientious objectors. In the war's aftermath, in a famous and influential article, *The Nation* denounced "The Madness of Versailles," and the thousands of cancellations that came in the wake of *The Nation*'s antiwar stance were recouped only when the postmaster seized its September 14, 1918, issue as seditious. Ostensibly the government objected to an editorial by the senior editor Albert J. Nock criticizing President Wilson's appointment of AFL president Samuel Gompers to represent labor at an international conference in London (Gompers had "held labor in line" in deference to wartime patriotism); but the seizure could have as easily been motivated by Villard's own editorial denouncing the Justice Department for having arrested 75,000 citizens in two days to ascertain whether or not they were draft evaders. Villard put the advertising and circulation value of the seizure at over $100,000.

His *Nation* campaigned in 1916 for an executive pardon for the unjustly condemned labor organizer Tom Mooney, and in the 1920s for a new trial for the anarchists Sacco and Vanzetti. His 1927 editorial ("A Decent Respect for the Opinions of Mankind") helped to radicalize, among others, a young Bostonian named James J. Storrow, Jr. *The Nation* opposed the "theft" of the Panama Canal and the plan to annex Hawaii, and supported independence for the Philippines and self-determination for the Irish. But the editor-publisher relationship at *The Nation* was not always one of utopian tranquillity. Even when the editor and publisher were the same person, as was the case with Oswald Garrison Villard, there were inevitable tensions. One scholar has observed that had Villard—one part patrician, one part social reformer, by conviction a pacifist, by temperament a fighter—been less divided against himself, *The Nation* from 1918 to 1933 might have been more consistent, but it is difficult to believe it would have been as interesting.

As we have already seen, in the peculiar economics of *The Nation*, even owners have backers, and since these backers are not in it for money, they will periodically erupt over a matter of social policy. Thus it was that in 1918–19 Francis Neilson—a former Canadian M.P., the husband of a meatpacking heiress, and a longtime major patron of *The Nation*—came to feel that he had a call on its economics editorials. In addition to putting up $30,000 a year, Neilson was paying Nock's salary. Not coincidentally, both of them were single-taxers. When in November of 1919 Villard declined to endorse the single tax—a formula aimed at eliminating land speculation and promoting economic equality as the solution to the country's economic woes—Neilson withdrew his support and founded a new magazine, *The Freeman*, with Nock as its editor. The first issue appeared in the spring of 1920, and Villard welcomed it to the ranks of liberal journalism in an editorial to which Nock quickly replied, "You make your appeal to the liberals; we make ours to the radicals."

One of Villard's most successful innovations was a fortnightly sixteen-page International Relations Section, which would print original documents. It didn't really pay for itself, but as the then–managing editor Lewis Gannett recalled, "*The New York Times* and the other papers were killing off Lenin and Trotsky and crushing the Russian revolution three times a week," so *The Nation* felt it needed its own reports. It was, for example, the first to print the new Soviet constitution, among other scoops. Although at first he was a believer in the Soviet "experiment," by the early 1920s Villard had few illusions about the Bolsheviks, writing that "with all their desire for peace, justice, liberty, and equality for a nation of workers, [they] offer side by side with tremendous benefits, the methods of a Caesar, a Cromwell, a Franz Joseph, a Nicholas, a Mussolini." He came to regard Stalin and Hitler as rival dictators and thought Americans should butt out.

Under Villard, then, the editor-publisher relationship was really a matter of the great man coming to terms with himself. His willingness to support his editorial instincts with his pocketbook, albeit in the non-extravagant style that has become *The Nation*'s trademark, may be gathered from his January 5, 1928, wire to Carleton Beals: CAN YOU PROCEED IMMEDIATELY NICARAGUA FOR NATION SENDING EXCLUSIVE STORIES AMERICAN POLICY MARINE RULE POPULAR FEELING ETCETERA, REACHING SANDINO IF POSSIBLE. TRIP POSSIBLY OCCUPY A MONTH. CAN OFFER A HUNDRED A WEEK AND EXPENSES. WIRE COLLECT. His exclusive interview with Augusto Sandino, leader of the revolt against U.S. domination in that small country, and the series that grew out of it were reprinted worldwide (although not in Nicaragua). And reviewing *The Nation*'s lonely battle for justice in Haiti under U.S. Marine occupation in 1915–34, Villard wrote: "I look back upon these crusades on behalf of our Caribbean neighbors with unbounded satisfaction. They also seem to me to have justified all the time and money I put into *The Nation*."

In 1934 Maurice Wertheim, an investment banker and longtime generous and non-interfering patron, offered to buy *The Nation*—which he saw as a major link between the defunct Progressive Movement and the Depression era—for $50,000. Villard said no thanks. A year later, Villard was faced with a deficit, sons who had no interest in taking over, and estrangement from his editors over such matters as the extent of American involvement in the conflicts in Europe and Asia. The irrepressible radical Heywood Broun, who helped found the American Newspaper Guild from his *Nation* office, was moved to write in his weekly *Nation* column: "Oswald Garrison Villard is the product of an interesting experiment. His mother's grandfather was an abolitionist and his father a railroad magnate. As far as the researchers of science have gone, the rule seems to be that when you cross abolitionist blood with railroad stock you get a liberal." When Wertheim again offered to buy the magazine—this time for $25,000—Villard accepted, with the understanding that Freda Kirchwey would become the new editor and Villard would continue to write his weekly column, "Issues and Men."

Freda Kirchwey spent virtually her entire working life at *The Nation*. In 1918, a recent Barnard graduate (who had been voted "Most Famous in Future," "Best Looking," and "Most Militant"), she heard from a friend that there was an opening in *The Nation*'s new International Relations Section, and wrote to her economics professor Henry Raymond Mussey, a *Nation* editor, "If you think I'm the man [she said it, not me] for the job, will you put in a word for me?" She went on to become managing editor, literary editor, editor, and ultimately, like Villard, editor and publisher. Wertheim and Kirchwey were good friends, and the magazine received a dividend in the Depression years in the form of Maurice Wertheim's daughter Barbara (later Tuchman), who, still in her early twenties, reported for *The Nation* on the Spanish Civil War.

It was not long before *The Nation*'s peculiar tradition of publisher obeisance to editorial freedom asserted itself once again. Wertheim, it seemed, was becoming increasingly hostile to the New Deal in general and his brother-in-law, the eminent Secretary of the Treasury Henry Morgenthau, in particular. By early 1937 he was "fed up," his business partners had stopped talking to him, and his annual loss was up to $35,000. When *The Nation* came out in favor of F.D.R.'s proposal to increase the U.S. Supreme Court's membership from nine to twelve, as a means of ending the run of 5–4 decisions finding New Deal legislation unconstitutional, he blew his stack.

At most publications the *owner* would fire the old editor and get a new one. Not at *The Nation*. Wertheim, who was publicly committed to the ideal of editorial freedom, at first tried a modest end run by putting people like the journalist-academic Max Lerner on the payroll in the hopes that they would turn the magazine's progressive New Deal policy around, but when that didn't work—they supported it—he summoned Miss Kirchwey to his office and issued his ultimatum: either she would buy him out for $30,000 or he would sell to the highest bidder. She said she had only $15,000 and asked if she might have time to put together a syndicate. He said no, his Civic Aid Foundation would lend her the other $15,000. She took the loan and bought the magazine. (Before Wertheim died, he gave his three daughters one piece of advice: Never invest money in magazines. Yet two of them, Nan Werner and Jo Pomerance, ignored or overcame their father's warning and joined the consortium that Hamilton Fish and I put together to purchase *The Nation* in 1977.)

It was perhaps inevitable—given Oswald Villard's volatile temperament and his strong antiwar, pro-neutralist position—that he and Kirchwey would quarrel. In 1939, after the Soviet-German non-aggression pact, she started killing what she regarded as his more hysterical columns, including one which seemed to suggest that the movement in favor of American intervention in the European war was a Jewish plot. Eventually, Villard broke with *The Nation* over this issue, which was splitting the left-liberal community in the late 1930s. As Norman Thomas put it in "The Pacifist's Dilemma," there were two total evils in the world, war and Fascism, but it now began to seem to him (and to Freda Kirchwey too, not incidentally) that "resolute and effective opposition to fascism means war."

"I have never been able to work happily with men or women who are incapable of hot indignation at something or other," Villard wrote in his memoir. "To minimize every evil is to my mind to condone it and in time to destroy one's influence." Villard, ever faithful to his credo, did not go gently. On June 13, 1940, he wrote a letter to Freda Kirchwey:

> After reading your last two issues and particularly your coming out for universal military service, I want to notify you at once that I cannot continue to write for *The Nation* and I will wind up my connection of 46 years with a valedictory next week. It is, as you know, a complete and absolute break with all the traditions of *The Nation*, of which there is nothing left now but the name. Some day perhaps I shall have some explanation as to how Freda Kirchwey, a pacifist in the last war, keen to see through shams and hypocrisies, militant for the rights of minorities and the downtrodden, has now struck hands with all the forces of reaction against which *The Nation* has battled so strongly. There is now, of course, no reason for buying *The Nation* when one can read Walter Lippmann, Dorothy Thompson, *The New York Times*, or *The New York Herald Tribune* . . . You have, according to my beliefs, prostituted *The Nation*, and I hope honestly that it will die very soon or fall into other hands.

She was a leader on many issues—sexual freedom, birth control, democracy vs. Fascism and Nazism, the Spanish Civil War, collective security, refugees, McCarthyism and censorship, the peaceful use of atomic energy, and Zionism. (After World War II she went to Palestine as *The Nation*'s correspondent, and her visit to Ein Hashofed, a kib-butz founded by Americans, turned up forty *Nation* readers.)

After Villard's departure, Freda Kirchwey's *Nation* was deeply in-volved in the effort to rescue refugees from Nazi-dominated Europe, believed that a Jewish "homeland" was the best hope for democracy in the Middle East, and saw Jewish emigration to Palestine as a matter of "elementary justice." When the Nazi-Soviet pact was signed, she called it "menacing," and correctly predicted that "the long-range ambitions of Stalin and Hitler were bound to clash." Although in 1937 she had pub-lished criticism of the purge trials in the Soviet Union and the Spanish Loyalists' conduct of their cause, of the brutal Soviet invasion of Fin-land in 1939, she wrote: "The horrors that fascism wreaked in Spain are being repeated in the name of peace and socialism in Finland." Her general attitude was: "To my mind the effort to promote unity on the left will fail if it is predicated on a categorical declaration of faith in the virtues of the Soviet Union." Her biographer, Sara Alpern, concludes that she was a "moralist against fascism" but a relativist where the So-viet Union was concerned—probably a fair judgment.

Her fierce anti-Fascism, further fueled by the exigencies of war, led her to suspend *The Nation*'s traditional preference for First Amend-ment absolutism when she demanded within months of U.S. entry into World War II in December 1941 that the government "Curb the Fascist Press!" It was, she wrote, "a menace to freedom and an obsta-cle to winning the war." She resigned her membership in the American Civil Liberties Union. Yet after the war, as Carey McWilliams has writ-ten, "Nothing in its history does *The Nation* more credit than its res-olute refusal, under Freda Kirchwey's editorship, to join the cold war or to chorus in on the domestic witch hunt." She was an unrelenting critic of McCarthyism.

Because of its stance, the magazine's financial problems became more acute in postwar years. As a publisher without independent re-sources, Kirchwey depended on fund-raising to make up the annual deficit. In 1943 she had transferred title of ownership of *The Nation* to a nonprofit entity called Nation Associates, in which subscribers were asked to enroll as members at from ten to one hundred dollars a year. The Nation Associates supported the magazine and also ran confer-ences and conducted research. (For example, it commissioned twelve studies on the Middle East, some documenting collaboration between the Nazis and the Grand Mufti of Jerusalem.) But now, traditional cause "fund-raising" became almost impossible.

Kirchwey described *The Nation* during her tenure as a "propaganda journal"—not in the sense that it omitted inconvenient facts to make its points, but rather that it openly espoused many causes. Unlike the pacifistic Villard, she was not a particular champion of lost ones. Indeed, when the magazine described Henry Wallace's 1948 Progressive Party campaign as "Quixotic," J. W. Gitt, publisher of the *York Gazette and Daily* and longtime *Nation* supporter, wrote: "My God, woman, all my life I have been engaged in what some people have called 'Quixotic endeavors,' and if I may be pardoned for saying so, I fear that you have been too. At least I thought so."

Anti-Fascism was her overarching cause to the end, and it undoubtedly contributed to the mindset that led her to take an action which would come back to haunt her and her magazine. When Clement Greenberg, *The Nation*'s famous former art critic, sent a letter to *The Nation* accusing its foreign affairs editor, J. Alvarez del Vayo (who had been foreign minister of the Spanish Republic in 1936–39), of being an instrument of Stalin, Kirchwey, who either was or wasn't having an affair with her foreign affairs editor, had warned him, "If the letter is published or circulated anywhere, we will immediately bring suit for libel against you . . . [a periodical] has a public as well as a private duty not to spread untrue and malicious statements." And when Greenberg then arranged to have his letter published in the fiercely anti-Stalinist *New Leader* magazine in May 1951, Kirchwey sued *The New Leader*.

Kirchwey obviously didn't subscribe to *The Nation*'s current view that such suits, whether or not legally justified, constitute a de facto infringement on political speech, contribute to a generally chilling effect, and set a dangerous precedent. More pressing in her mind was del Vayo's refugee status in the United States, which made him vulnerable to deportation. She also calculated—wrongly, as it turned out—that the lawsuit would stop the endless debate about whether *The Nation* should have printed Greenberg's letter in the first place, which she considered a diversion from more urgent matters. On advice of counsel, other letters concerned with the del Vayo matter (including one from the embattled young historian Arthur Schlesinger, Jr., accusing the magazine of printing "wretched apologies for Soviet despotism") also went unpublished; and Robert Bendiner and Reinhold Niebuhr, contributing editors, asked to have their names removed from the magazine's masthead. *The Nation* ran an editorial explaining why it sued and published letters supporting and criticizing its stance, including one from my old Yale law professor Thomas Emerson, who said that although generally speaking he was in accord with del Vayo on matters political, he thought *The Nation* should have met Greenberg's attack "in the area of discussion rather than by bringing suit. Resort to the courts cut off further argument and, in effect, brought a breakdown in the rational exchange of ideas. I do not think *The Nation* should have been so quick to abandon the basic principle of full discussion to which its long and honorable existence has been devoted."

The dispute festered for four years, and the lawsuit was not dropped until Carey McWilliams accepted Kirchwey's invitation to replace her as editor, but only on condition that the case be abandoned. By 1955, in debt, exhausted, and confident that McWilliams was "the right man for the job," Kirchwey retired.

Not only was the case against *The New Leader* abandoned, but before turning the magazine over, Freda Kirchwey also abandoned another problematic project: a merger with, sellout to, or takeover of (take your choice) *The New Republic*.

When I first arrived at *The Nation* in 1978 and people asked what I did and I told them I worked at *The Nation,* as often as not the response would be "Oh, *The Nation* and *The New Republic*, I used to get those," as if they were joined at the hip. Nowadays only the 285 million Americans who don't read them aren't in on the secret that they have long since gone their separate political ways. Although both are still to the left of the far right, they differ in tendencies, emphasis, analyses, values, and perspectives on issues ranging from affirmative action, the meaning and status of the Cold War, Israel and the Palestinians, Iraq, feminism, and presidential politics.

Freda Kirchwey never wrote her memoirs, but curiously, Carey McWilliams says nothing about this episode in his autobiography, *The Education of Carey McWilliams* (1979), nor does Michael Straight, one-time editor and publisher of *The New Republic*, in his memoir, *Af-*

ter Long Silence (1983). Maybe they were embarrassed. But the paper trail is long, and if archives are to be believed, during the darker years of the Cold War, these fiercely independent journals seriously explored the possibility that they could solve their respective business problems and end their money-losing ways by doing what other magazines do in their circumstances: merge.

On paper it seemed to make sense. As W. D. Patterson, for *The Nation*, wrote in May 1949 to Michael Straight: "We regard the merger not only as a logical publishing step, but as a combined opportunity and responsibility to serve the future of liberal journalism in this country."

Encouraged by the young New York book publisher George Braziller, who also believed these venerable New York weeklies should merge, the lawyers for *The Nation* and *The New Republic* met for almost a year. Indeed, in preparation for their first meeting, in July 1948, Evans Clark, head of the Twentieth Century Fund and, not incidentally, husband of Freda Kirchwey, helped to put together an eleven-page background memorandum to serve as the basis for discussion. "*The New Republic* and *The Nation* are obviously the two outstanding organs of liberal opinion in the U.S.," it began. "By and large, their attitude and point of view—barring minor differences on specific issues—are very much the same. Ideologically and politically, there has been very little excuse for two separate publications." The memorandum went on to list the "cogent editorial and publishing arguments for consolidating these two magazines": that 1948–58 would be a decade of "challenge and opportunity for American liberalism," calling for intellectual leadership of the sort "a strong magazine" could provide; that the two united would be "far stronger than the sum of their separate strengths"; that, published separately, each magazine operates at a loss, whereas merged they could make ends meet; that "each of the present magazines is far too dependent on a single controlling individual."

They proposed a relatively simple business plan: To merge *The Nation*'s 40,000 circulation with *The New Republic*'s 47,000; discounting an estimated overlap in subscribers, they projected a starting circulation of 75,000 (60,000 subscribers, 15,000 newsstand sales) for the merged magazine. With a subscription price of $7 a year and a magazine that alternated between thirty-two and forty pages an issue and a $400 per-page advertising rate, they estimated they could sell an average of two and a half pages per issue—they'd be off and running. All that remained to be decided was the division of labor between Kirchwey and Straight, as well as some "details" like the location, format, and title of the merged magazine and a new contract with the Newspaper Guild. If they could announce the merger after the 1948 election but before January 1, 1949, they could build momentum in time for what they regarded as the peak direct-mail promotion period of January to March.

Actually, Michael Straight and *The New Republic* were just emerging from a traumatic ride on the readership roller coaster. In 1946, when Straight joined the magazine that his family had funded since its inception in 1914, its circulation was down around 20,000—too small, he thought, to survive in the postwar world. His plan was to invite former Vice President Henry A. Wallace, whom Harry Truman had just fired as Secretary of Commerce, to be the new editor. Wallace's critique of the Truman administration would be just the thing to drive up circulation.

Wallace accepted, Straight became publisher, poured hundreds of thousands of dollars into the mails, and within a year three things happened: *The New Republic*'s circulation shot up to 90,000 (although the advertising revenue expected to accompany the rise never materialized); Wallace resigned as editor and accepted the Progressive Party's nomination as candidate for the presidency of the United States, whereupon *The New Republic* canceled his weekly column and ended up supporting Truman (*The Nation*, believing a third party counterproductive but disheartened by Truman's cold warriorism, supported nobody); and *The New Republic* lost 50,000 Wallacite readers.

The lawyers met, the accountants met, the treasurers met, Kirchwey and Straight conferred, and memorandums moved back and forth; but by July 11, 1949, the deal was still undone, and Kirchwey told Straight that as a result of recent conversations with *The New Republic*'s editorial director, Bruce Bliven, and others, she had some "fundamental doubts." She feared that *New Republic* people favored the merger for the wrong reasons—as an economy measure rather than "as an opportunity to create a powerful liberal journal." They had what she dubbed a "storm cellar" psychology, and it worried her. For example, the latest projection of joint newsstand sales was only 8,000, which was "almost exactly the present level of *Nation* sales."

Despite word from Straight's attorney that "Mike is determined to make every effort to bring the merger off," Straight's ideas on how the new magazine would work were not Kirchwey's. Instead of Kirchwey running the editorial section and Straight the articles section, as had been discussed, Straight's new thought on August 29 was that Kirchwey could be in charge of articles.

Thus it probably came as no surprise that on September 9, back from vacation in the Springs on Long Island, Kirchwey wrote her friends at *The New Republic* to say that the deal was no deal.

"Perhaps at some later date we can start all over again on a different basis. Meanwhile, good luck to us both!"

End of round one.

Over the next two years both publications suffered financial and political stress. *The New Republic*'s woes were compounded by family problems. Michael Straight's brother, Whitney, and the family's legal advisers wanted him to shut down the magazine because of all the money it was losing, and in any event, he was put on notice that the annual $150,000 subsidy that the magazine realized from the family trust was in jeopardy. Moreover, *The New Republic* had lost its main advertiser, General Electric, as a result of the magazine's wartime exposé of that company's ties to the Krupp arms-dealing empire in Nazi Germany. In *After Long Silence*, Straight wrote that in December 1951, his attorney told him that *The New Republic* was "in worse financial shape than we had supposed"; he felt that "at best, we might keep it going until spring." On the theory that "it would be better to close down *The New Republic* in a dignified manner than to see it dishonor its own tradition" by being sold to an inappropriate buyer, Straight began work on what he thought would be his final editorial. But the staff, rallied by its Washington editor, Helen Fuller, offered to work without salary, and Straight decided to pay for the magazine out of his own savings while he hunted for "a friend who could keep it going."

Describing his search "for wealthy liberals who might take over," Straight mentions flying to Dallas to see Stanley Marcus, to Chicago to see Marshall Field, and to New York to see Averell Harriman, all to no avail. What he omits, however, is a call he made to Carey McWilliams, who by this time was de facto editorial director of *The Nation* under Freda Kirchwey in New York. Unaware of the prior round of negotiations, an intrigued McWilliams immediately told Kirchwey about the conversation.

But negotiations now hit another snag. Where was the new magazine to be located? In 1950 Straight had moved *The New Republic* and his family from New York to Washington, and on September 19, 1952, he told McWilliams that since D.C. was America's political center, it made sense for a political magazine to be published from there. McWilliams responded three days later that, as the political center, Washington "allows for very little perspective, which is the lifeblood of a political magazine. Outside of *The New Republic* I know of no publication of importance which is published from Washington." Moving *The New Republic* to D.C., he added, didn't seem to have changed or improved it, "apart, obviously, from the convenience of publishing the magazine in the city where you reside." By return mail, Straight offered *U.S. News* as an example of a political magazine published in the capital. Besides, he explained, he had moved to Washington because that's where he thought the center was, not vice versa.

Clearly, the magazines were separated conceptually as well as geographically, but nevertheless, on December 8, Straight set forth "the basic conditions under which I would undertake the merger of *The New Republic* and *The Nation*." These included that "there should be only one office and that should be in D.C." Straight added, "I have assumed that Freda would write a weekly signed editorial and I would write an unsigned editorial. I suppose that on articles some form of veto power would have to be established. (For example, while our editorials in the issue of December 8 were very much the same, I could not conscientiously publish the article appearing in *The Nation* by Claude Bourdet.)"

The differences between the parties were not easily bridged, and once again the project appeared stalled, when a letter arrived from across the seas. Enter Kingsley Martin, editor of the British weekly the *New Statesman*, which itself had merged with a British magazine also called *The Nation* (no relation). In a "confidential" letter to Kirchwey dated December 18, he said he was "not allowed to mention names" but "you can take it that I am not basing myself on rumor":

You don't need telling that Michael Straight has been spending fantastic sums of money on the N.R. What you may not know is that it is not going to be possible for him to continue to spend more, and that the paper is therefore privately "on the market" . . . I recall that the *Statesman* and *The Nation* both ran at a loss until they amalgamated, and it seems silly to suggest that the U.S. cannot support, without loss, one such newspaper.

. . . I think if you have a proposal of amalgamation, you may assume without question that Michael himself will not be an obstacle. I do not think he will continue on the paper in any case . . . I should be the appropriate post office for you to use if you have any comments or proposals to make.

Kirchwey cabled Martin: MOST GRATEFUL. ACCEPT SUGGESTIONS. AIRMAILING TERMS. She followed with a long letter detailing the elaborate on-and-off "months of intensive work" and the "blank wall" they had come up against—she believed that the $150,000 a year *The New Republic* received from a trust fund would be cut off in the event that *The New Republic* was transformed into *The Nation and New Republic*, the awkward proposed title of the merged magazine.

Kirchwey also wondered "whether there is an understandable reluctance on Mike's part to give up an institution founded by his father and in which there is a great deal of personal identification" or whether he harbored "subconscious resentment that we, who have never had any funds except those we could raise through circulation, advertising and gifts, have managed to survive, to increase our reputation." On January 7, 1953, Martin replied, "I am authorized to inform you that he has absolutely no legal power to attach any conditions or strings if you make an offer to buy the paper. I doubt if you now have any competitor in the field in spite of the rumors. You can be as tough as you like in bargaining without fear of losing the deal providing the financial offer is considered reasonable."

On January 15, Kirchwey told Straight that she had heard he was interested in selling, and she was as tough as she liked. Her alternative proposal: that *The Nation* would (1) pay $35,000 for the assets of *The New Republic* ($20,000 in cash and $15,000 in ten annual installments); (2) fulfill unexpired subscriptions; and (3) call the new publication *The Nation* and *New Republic*. Straight replied the next day:

Dear Freda:

Thanks for your letter of January 15. I don't know where you hear these rumors but I will be grateful if you will discourage them and not give them any further currency. Since there is no basis to them I will not comment in detail on your proposal. My very best regards,

Sincerely yours,
Michael Straight

End of round two—but a coda to come on May 8, 1953:

Dear Freda:

I obtained permission a while ago to let you know rather more fully what happened . . . I was told specifically by others who had lost money in the *N.R.* that the usual source of money was at an end, that M. would be compelled to accept a fair business offer, and that it was believed no other offer was in the wind. I later learned that he found another source of money, as you know, and without members of the family knowing, and was horrified at the very idea of any amalgamation with *The Nation* on the ground that Carey McWilliams's position on the paper meant that it must definitely be accounted part of the Communist front! Naturally this was told to me in confidence and it is not to be passed on. I felt you should know and that it was only fair you should understand what the obstacle proved to be. (Or was it only the excuse?)

Ever,
Kingsley

Well, the rebel-radical Carey McWilliams was, as anyone who knew him knew, neither a Communist nor a Communist front. Before he died, Straight told me he harbored no ill will against McWilliams, "although I may have looked up some files." Kingsley Martin's source turned out to be Whitney Straight, who resented the fact that as the older brother he hadn't been granted control of the family trust.

Michael, without telling the family until the deal was done, arranged to sell the magazine to Gilbert Harrison, his old friend from the

American Veterans Committee (where he had fought against what he regarded as a Communist takeover attempt), and Harrison's new wife, Nancy Blaine, heiress to the Chicago fortune of Anita McCormick Blaine. Harrison became editor when Straight stepped down in 1956. *The Nation* reorganized as a limited partnership; using Nation Associates as a nonprofit fund-raising vehicle, it hunkered down to fight its anti–Cold War battles.

It is now apparent that although *The Nation* and *The New Republic* may have shared the "same" politics in the late 1940s and 1950, they also had significant differences. In 1949 Arthur Schlesinger, Jr., wrote in *The Vital Center* that *The Nation* and *The New Republic* were journals of "the type of the progressive today . . . the fellow traveler of the fellow traveler." Yet *The Nation* was calling NATO "a new declaration of cold war" and saw the Atlantic Pact as a vote of no confidence in the United Nations, whereas *The New Republic* was becoming an enthusiast of Harry Truman's foreign policy. Both were foes of McCarthyism, of course; but where *The Nation* sounded a piercing alarm, Michael Straight, who four decades later was to write about his own ambiguous dealings with Soviet espionage agents, was more sanguine. "I know of no citizen branded traitor today because, yesterday, he practiced Americanism," he wrote in *The New Republic* in 1954.

Thereafter, the two magazines acquired new owners and editors and traveled down very different roads. *The New Republic* had a more benign view of the Kennedys than did *The Nation*. And consider our contrasting coverage of the Bay of Pigs. On the one hand it was *The Nation* that alerted the country, on November 19, 1960, to an impending invasion of the Bay of Pigs, for which it was ignored, vilified, and/or investigated at the time. And on the other, as Arthur Schlesinger, Jr., tells it in *A Thousand Days*, in early April 1961 Gilbert Harrison sent him galley proofs of a *New Republic* article slated for publication. It was, wrote Schlesinger, then on the White House staff, "a careful, accurate and devastating account of CIA activities among Cuban refugees in Florida." Schlesinger showed the article to the President, and at the President's request, *The New Republic* suppressed it. The invasion took place a few days later, on April 17.

By 1982, when *The Nation* denounced—and *The New Republic* defended—Israel's invasion of Lebanon, the idea that these old friends still shared a political project was no longer tenable. Commentators may differ about how far *The New Republic* has moved to the right or whether *The Nation* has become reflexively left. They may argue about whether the now Washington-based *New Republic* is too close to power to see it or the New York–based *Nation* is too far from power to understand it. But at a time when independent voices, not to mention dissenting, iconoclastic, and minority views, are few and fewer, perhaps there is one thing on which the editors, writers, staffs, owners, and readers of these two relics from the print age might agree—that we are all fortunate that the merger that didn't happen didn't happen.

In debt and exhausted, Kirchwey retired in 1955. Any traditional publisher-owner would then have found a successor publisher-owner who would have hired an editor. Not *The Nation*. Confident that McWilliams was a worthy successor, Kirchwey appointed him editor and he recruited his own publisher before he took the job—George Kirstein, a recently retired business executive with *Nation* politics, a modest family inheritance, and few illusions about *Nation* economics. "Without exception," McWilliams later wrote, "every publisher has regarded the responsibility as a public trust. Any publisher who thought of a magazine as a possible profit-making venture could not have been familiar with its history."

In the late 1940s and 1950s, even publications with vast fortunes behind them, such as Marshall Field's progressive daily *PM*, went down. *The Nation*, McWilliams wrote in his memoirs, "was lucky to stay alive." At one point its finances were so precarious that he had to arrange for the magazine to be printed at the plant of Aubrey Williams's *Southern Farmer* magazine in Alabama, where costs were lower and Williams was liberal in extending credit.

After ten years, Kirstein turned the publishership over to Storrow, a fifth-generation Harvard graduate, and incidentally a classmate of Blair Clark, former top executive at CBS-TV and the *New York Post* who would briefly succeed McWilliams as editor. Kirstein and McWilliams together had gotten to know Storrow when he worked on *The Nation*'s ambitious centennial issue. His wife, Linda Eder, became associate publisher.

During the Storrow-Eder years *The Nation* was probably the only magazine in the country to have two thoroughfares named after its publishing family—Storrow Drive in Boston, Massachusetts, and Eder

Road in Fishkill, New York. But holding McWilliams in awe, they kept their hands off the editorial side of the magazine. McWilliams served as editor until 1975, and the debt-free magazine that Storrow turned over to his successors was a tribute to McWilliams's editorial ingenuity. In the hardest of times he continued to put out a magazine that became mandatory reading for a beleaguered constituency. A jotting from McWilliams's notebook: "It is always a question of finding that reader for whom a publication like *The Nation* is a lantern in the dark. Once he learns of *The Nation* he is a likely reader for life."

McWilliams always insisted that he was not an innovator, that *The Nation* he ran from 1955 to 1975 was informed primarily by his study of Godkin's conception of a journal of opinion. It may well have been true that McWilliams hitched his own rebel-radical politics to Godkin's basic idea, but the magazine he produced had a character uniquely attuned to its time. For example, in an era of extreme xenophobia he discovered William Appleman Williams, who went on to become the most influential of Cold War revisionist historians. Indeed, there were few revisionist historians whose first work did not appear in *The Nation*—Walter La Feber, Gabriel Kolko, Barton Bernstein, H. Stuart Hughes, Howard Zinn, and many others appeared week after week. Under McWilliams, *The Nation* also sounded the alarm on American involvement in Vietnam—it ran sixty-six pieces on the subject between January 1, 1954, and June 1, 1966.

McWilliams emphasized that *The Nation* was not a news magazine, that its destiny and its strength had to do with ideas, with opinion journalism, with explaining the underlying meaning of the events on which others often reported in greater depth. Yet Leonard Downie, Jr., in his book *The New Muckrakers*, correctly credits McWilliams's *Nation* with "keeping the muckraking tradition alive in the decade from 1955 to 1965." It was not really *The Nation*'s beat, but the need and the opportunity were obvious, so *The Nation* kept the spotlight on the inquisitorial tactics of the U.S. Congress then. In the issue of May 23, 1953, it also ran one of the first significant articles (by Dr. Alton Oschner, of the Tulane Medical School, an acknowledged expert) linking cigarette smoking to cancer; on March 11, 1961, it published perhaps the first article about the right-wing John Birch Society to appear in a general-interest magazine. McWilliams understood that it was important to deal with taboo subjects simply because they were regarded as taboo. Fred Cook's issue-long exposés of the

FBI and the CIA helped end forever the sacred-cow status of those institutions. And *The Nation*'s 1961 special issue "Juggernaut: The Warfare State" put the military-industrial complex on the agenda in a way that other media found hard to ignore. Nobody ever accused McWilliams of putting out a humor magazine, but articles like Dalton Trumbo's exposé of the Hollywood blacklist and former FBI agent Jack Levine's on the Bureau's anguish over the fact that "through its dues-paying FBI contingent, it had become the largest single financial contributor to the coffers of the Communist Party," offered sardonic relief.

Something of a frustrated publisher, McWilliams would stay up late drafting what he called "Night Thoughts" on how to fund the magazine and build its subscriber base at the same time. Since *The Nation* lacked the resources to conduct expensive direct-mail campaigns, why not revive the idea of *Nation* dinners pioneered in New York in the late 1940s by Lillie Schulz, the gifted young organizer, only this time hold them around the country—at least twice a year, but eventually once a month—and build up the magazine's subscriber base that way? The dinners could feature speakers like the Rev. Martin Luther King, Jr. (who starting in 1955 and until his death in 1968 wrote an annual civil rights status report for *The Nation*). McWilliams believed that each dinner could attract at least a thousand people who would enroll as subscribers as part of their admission fee. Ten to twenty thousand new subscribers a year for a magazine with an average circulation of 30,000 in those years wouldn't be bad. But he and Storrow were still too busy dealing with the vestiges of McCarthy the ism—which persisted long after the Senate's censure of McCarthy the man in 1954—and figuring out how to meet next week's payroll, to implement these well-conceived schemes. Nevertheless, it was at a *Nation* conference in 1967 that Dr. King first came out against the Vietnam War.

Came 1975, and McWilliams began to feel that "I was writing a frenzied, never-ending serial on The Last Days of Richard Nixon with alternating notes on This Week in Vietnam." An era was coming to a close, he had books to write, and he told Storrow his time was up.

5

LOOKING LIKE
WHAT YOU ARE

I knew that as a journal of opinion or, as Carey called it, "critical" opinion, *The Nation*'s job was to explain the underlying meaning of the news.

I knew we should try to relate relevant articles in each week's issue to some more generally coherent political analysis (without imposing any ideological straitjacket on our writers).

I knew we should try to build for a better future.

I knew, as Bob Sherrill put it, if we ever published anything that could appear in *The New York Times Magazine* we would not be doing our job.

I knew that our job was to carry on a conversation with our readers, our constituents, our country.

I knew we should report news missing from the mainstream media.

I knew we had to make news as well as report it.

I knew I needed an editorial board who knew more than I knew.

I knew we should report at least some things from the bottom up.

I knew that philosophy and theory had a bad name in America; yet the times seemed incoherent, out of joint, in need of a "new synthesis," so I went out of my way to put a philosopher on our editorial board.

I knew we should be relevant, but I knew we had to say it better, that we needed a vocabulary appropriate to our mission.

I knew we had to be a place of thought, but also of action—we had a role in organizing the culture, even as we covered it.

I knew that we were in the business of questioning the official line.

I knew we needed an advertising policy.

And I knew, because Phil Green brought it to my attention in a memorandum I had requested in advance of arriving at the magazine, that "Americans impatient for change have often tended to take too seriously Marx's injunction that the point is not to interpret the world but to change it, thus ignoring the lesson of Marx's life which is that he spent a large part of his next forty years interpreting it—with one eye towards change, of course, but change based on understanding." I'm no fool; I put Phil on our editorial board, too.

I knew the magazine should look like what it was, which it already did.

I knew or thought I knew that while nothing I have said so far was inconsistent with *The Nation* as it was, changes would be required, and readers, especially readers of a 113-year-old magazine, were resistant to change.

The problem was merely how to apply what I "knew," especially since it meant ignoring as much advice as I took.

One of our potential investors, Jerome Grossman, who had founded MassPax, a Cambridge-based peace organization, had advised us to do two things and stop doing a third. First, we should put a subtitle on the magazine so that the masthead would read "*The Nation*: And How to Change It," and follow every article with a little paragraph telling the reader what action to take to ameliorate the outrage described in the article he had just finished reading. These seemed fine ideas, but not for *The Nation*. I suggested he take them to Ralph Nader, who was in the business of organizing social change.

Mr. Grossman's third idea was to drop book reviews. "Why book reviews? I boldly ask. Is it really possible to give adequate treatment to a serious work in the limited space you offer? Wouldn't a survey be in order to determine if your subscribers rely upon you for book reviews or even to determine whether they read your reviews? Do they subscribe to other magazines which treat books more thoroughly?"

I didn't need a survey to tell me that while I very much liked Mr. Grossman, I didn't like this third idea (and he didn't need a survey to tell him he didn't need to invest). I was more attracted to, though not enough to implement, E. L. Doctorow's half-serious proposal that we "keep the magazine more or less as it is, but move the important stuff—books and the arts—into the body of the magazine—and don't stop printing those articles about global warming or the dangers of nu-clear armament, but put that in smaller type in the back."

In the end (i.e., at the beginning)—ignoring Carey's warning that foolish new editors always want to change the look of the magazine to announce their presence, we did ask the design team of Milton Glaser and Walter Bernard to come up with a new design to announce our presence. I also hoped it would make the magazine more readable. The guidelines I gave Walter and Milton were:

1. No increased production costs (this was a necessity, and it also took into account Carey's wisdom that Godkin's low-production-costs formula helped to explain *The Nation's* survival).

2. The magazine should be self-designing (this would save us the cost of an art director, and spare the editors from having to argue with an art director and enable fast turnarounds).

3. Consider an all-type cover. They ingeniously devised such, with two columns divided by a billboard telling the reader what was inside.

4. "There should be a strong sense of continuity with the past." Milton and Walter discovered that the first *Nation* had had a big, fat period at the end of its name, which became our logo—as in *The Nation.*

5. The design should "reflect, capture, express" *The Nation's* fo-cus on the issues, its skepticism of the conventional wisdom, its combination of muckraking and analysis.

And finally, we asked that they devise a black-and-white format that would take advantage of the brilliant pen-and-ink artists, like Ed Sorel, Ed Koren, Bob Grossman, and David Levine, R. O. Blechman, Lou Myers, Isadore Seltzer, Randall Enos, Marshall Arisman, Seymour Chwast (*Monocle* alumni all), Sue Coe, Frances Jetter, and others who identified with *The Nation's* politics and would want to be part of our project.

Many years later, in 1996, when our fortunes had improved, Walter and Milton adjusted the design with a little color. At that time, *I.D.*, *International Design Magazine*, quoted Milton as saying: "The fear at *The*

Nation is that a serious, scholarly product could be trivialized by design. Even introducing color is using the tools of the enemy." (He was talking about me, not Katrina vanden Heuvel, who had succeeded me as editor. She was all for brightening things up.) *I.D.* also accurately reported a staff revolt over Milton's attempt to introduce a dotted rule. Glaser said, "It was as if that dotted rule were a stake through their eyes."

Why then, asked the reporter, did you get involved with these *Nation* people in the first place?

"It's only cranky people who would make a product like this," said Glaser, "because these are the only people who care about injustice in the world."

An unsigned editorial in the September 20, 1978, issue of *The Nation* explained: "Our decision to begin our stories at the beginning—on the cover—is at once a tribute to our heritage, an unspoken announcement that reading *The Nation* involves a degree of intellectual commitment, and it has the added advantage of increasing the amount of text we can print in the issue."

We also said that our continued use of butcher paper was a protest against Madison Avenue slickness, and because it went without saying that butcher paper was cheaper, we didn't say it.

Nor were we alone. At the same time that I joined *The Nation*, a number of other magazine projects on the liberal left were under way.

Tom Morgan had picked up his marbles, dusted himself off, and with his wife, Mary Rockefeller Morgan, began publishing a handsome biweekly called *Politicks*. James Weinstein, who had moved to Chicago, had launched his independent socialist weekly *In These Times*; and with the peace activist Dave Dellinger as their leader, a group of movement types organized a collective and announced *Seven Days*, whose aspiration was to be a sort of *Time* magazine of the left.

Politicks, which the smart money was betting on, was the first to go, though its center-liberal politics might have been expected to have the largest appeal. Its look was striking—a European-style oversized magazine like *Paris Match*, with lavish use of such artistic talents as Ed Sorel and Tomi Ungerer. The difference between *Politicks* and *The Nation* may be symbolized by our contrasting takes on Allen Weinstein's book about Alger Hiss, *Perjury*. *Politicks* seemed to accept Weinstein's findings and signed up an enterprising journalist, Philip Nobile, to get an exclusive advance interview with the author—which he did, or thought he did—that would contain all of the new "news" that Weinstein and his researchers claimed to bring to the table. *The Nation*, on the other hand, published what our executive editor, Robert Hatch, called in a cover line "an investigative review," by yours truly, which culminated in an early-morning showdown at Weinstein's front door. Don't worry, I'll have more to say about that in due course.

Politicks lasted six months and went out of business, Morgan told me, because all its projections—revenue, advertising, circulation— were off by 50 percent.

Given its good reception, why didn't Morgan go back and seek to refinance his baby? My own theory is that because he was married to a Rockefeller, Morgan didn't want it to appear to her or anyone else that he was presuming on her wealth. Had he been a better student of the long history of spousal support for journals of opinion, *Politicks* might still be alive. (On the other hand, down the road Morgan and his bride went their separate ways, so maybe not.)

Seven Days aspired to report each week's news from a radical-left perspective. It was run as a collective with the charismatic war resister Dave Dellinger as its spiritual leader. Ham complained that everyone to whom he went for money had already had their pockets picked by Dellinger. But *Seven Days* soon ran through more than Dellinger had raised, and *The Nation* inherited their subscription list, although of the 75,000 "subscribers," only 16,000 were paid up, and of these, only a small percentage converted to *The Nation*. Among *Seven Days's* gifts to the culture was a brilliant movie reviewer and culture editor, Peter Biskind.

The third musketeer, *In These Times*, celebrated its twenty-fifth anniversary in 2001. James Weinstein, a respected historian (and no relation to Allen), at one point laconically observed, "When I founded *In These Times* I thought I was going to be an editor, but I discovered that to keep it going I had to become a beggar." *In These Times* believed that its job, "to bring capitalism into politics," was "the great issue of our time," and, as Weinstein said in 1976, "to have a movement—be it populist, socialist, feminist, abolitionist—you need a press." As it stated in its opening editorial in the first issue on November 15, 1976: "This newspaper is committed to beginning the job and to seeing it through." Weinstein modeled it after *Appeal to Reason*, the socialist weekly that had supported Eugene V. Debs for President four times (including 1912, when he received 900,000 votes) and featured the writing of such rabble-rousers as Upton Sinclair and Mother Jones. (Members and supporters of Debs's Socialist Party had published some 325 English and foreign-language daily, weekly, and monthly newspapers and magazines, most of them privately owned and related to the 5,000 Socialist Party locals reaching more than 2 million subscribers.)

Perhaps it was because of his sense of history, or maybe it was because he was not married to a Rockefeller, but Jimmy Weinstein, who had some family money of his own, did what Morgan didn't—he kept on begging. His prospectus gave a prophetic assessment of why *ITT*'s impact on the world had fallen short. In the prospectus Weinstein acknowledged that "the prospects of a publication like ours ultimately depended not only on its quality, but also on the status of the left in the United States. If the left grew and prospered, I was confident that we would also grow rapidly. If on the other hand, the left stagnated, I knew we would have to scratch and claw our way through bad times. The left didn't grow and prosper. In fact, it didn't even stagnate. It floundered and shriveled, leaving us to paddle furiously against the tide just to keep from being swept into oblivion." Maybe he was right. But *The Nation*'s experience, as our bad joke had it, was that "if it's bad for the country, it's good for *The Nation*." Are these two insights compatible? I think so, for reasons we shall come to. At the time, we did our best to compete with the competition.

We put subscription forms on the back of our business cards, an idea we borrowed—stole, actually—from Whitney Ellsworth, publisher of *The New York Review of Books*. When *The New York Times* reported in February 1979 that in the wake of *The New Republic*'s shift "to the right," disaffected readers were moving to *The Nation*, owner-editor-in-chief Marty Peretz complained in a letter to the editor in the *Times*, "We have no feud with that magazine. Its readership is too tiny, its contents too reflexively gauchiste to trouble with." Our response? We took out a classified ad on the front page of the *Times*: "Martin Peretz, please come home. All is forgiven. *The Nation*—still unfashionably liberal after all these years . . ."

We sold subscriptions on the streets of New York's annual New York

Is Book Country fair. We piggybacked on a book publisher's exhibit at the annual American Booksellers Association convention. We moved our letters-to-the-editor page from the back near the classified ad section to the inside front cover, and invited our writers to answer critical letters in the same issue in which they were published (simultaneously announcing a presumption against publishing "puff" correspondence). I let Ham and my friend Earl Shorris, then head of "creative" (I love Madison Avenue's self-regarding vocabulary) at N. W. Ayer, persuade me to lend my name and mug to an ad for *TV Guide*. I was part of a national campaign that featured unlikely regional *TV Guide* readers of various degrees of celebrity. My staggeringly original contribution was to say, "It's a well-edited magazine, full of surprises."

I liked the way Earl used his position in the country's largest ad agency to aid the country's smaller magazines. He had helped found the Leadership Network, an ad consortium for "thought leader" magazines like *The New Republic*, *National Review*, *The New York Review of Books*, and *Commentary*. When *The Nation* application for membership in the consortium was vetoed (both *The New Republic* and *Commentary* objected, we were told), Earl, who was a sometime *Nation* contributor, seemed to go out of his way to help us.

No sooner did the *TV Guide* ad appear than I received a letter from a young *Saturday Review* editor named James Traub, now a contributing writer to *The New York Times Magazine*: "I know some ad people over at Vitalis who are searching around for celebrity endorsements, and I was wondering if I could give them your name. Seriously, though, I've been thinking about a 60-second spot for Ban Roll-On Deodorant which would show you fuming around the office with a voice-over saying, 'Vic Navasky, editor of *The Nation*, has more reasons than most for getting hot under the collar, not to mention the arms . . .'" and it went on from there. His arguable point: "I was more than a little nonplussed at the endorsement, as well as the sincere hard-hitting copy that accompanied it. I suppose that you did it with the hopes of gaining exposure for the magazine, since I know how important that is to you. I think that's a laudable objective, though I honestly don't know whether it's worth getting into step with Madison Avenue in order to achieve it."

Neither did I. But among the reasons I was not unhappy to do it was that *TV Guide* was then edited by a talented friend, Roger

Youman, with whom I had worked on the Swarthmore *Phoenix*. I liked that Roger had recruited our old political science professor and *Monocle* contributor John Roche (whose politics I no longer liked but whose humor was acerbic and whose prose was pungent); I liked that he had published an article or two by the quirky investigative journalist my friend Edward J. Epstein; and I thought it funny that he had persuaded big thinker Arnold Toynbee to do an occasional essay. Also, I counted on *TV Guide* to alert me to late-night movies made by my Hollywood reds and their nemeses.

Wouldn't you know, I received a call from the *New York Post*'s gossipy "Page Six" asking me what I had gotten paid for the ad (one whole dollar), and then, thinking to trip me up, asking me to cite two *TV Guide* articles I particularly liked. I told them there were too many to choose from, but I particularly liked the work of Arnold Toynbee, John Roche, and Edward J. Epstein. The puzzled reporter thanked me and hung up.

Here is what the December 13, 1979, *Wall Street Journal* had to say (in a front-page article by Stephen Grover):

> Since *The Nation* is a political publication with a weekly circulation of only 35,000 and since nonpolitical *TV Guide*'s weekly circulation of 20 million makes it the best-selling magazine in the U.S. today, the Navasky ads [which, he forgot to mention, took up a half page in *The Wall Street Journal*] were a bit unusual.
>
> But in the you-scratch-my-back-I'll-scratch-yours world of endorsement advertising, both publications stood to reap benefits. *TV Guide* got a recommendation from the editor of a publication whose influence far exceeds its circulation. And *The Nation* got its name and that of its newly named editor from coast to coast.

Also, our circulation was the beneficiary of something that we hadn't even conceived of in our Kobak projections: the ghoul factor—we picked up the subscription lists of dead magazines.

When *Civil Liberties Review*, a bimonthly journal, went under in June of 1979, its people came to us and told us that *The New Republic* had offered to fulfill their unexpired subscriptions and pay them some money to boot; but they preferred to turn their list over to us, if we would agree to fulfill their unexpired subscriptions. We would and we did, and 40 percent of their subscribers converted to *Nation* subscribers. We made the same sort of deal with *Foreign Policy Bulletin,* a West Coast–based newsletter, and as I mentioned, later in 1980, when Dave Dellinger's *Seven Days* went under, we were there to pick up some of its articles and some of its subscribers.

One of the reasons *Civil Liberties Review* had turned to us is that they saw us as a civil liberties review under another name. Aryeh Neier, who had recently retired as executive director of the American Civil Liberties Union, joined *The Nation's* editorial board in September 1978 and wrote regularly on civil liberties and human rights topics, including a controversial public letter the singer Joan Baez issued (and many opponents of the war in Vietnam signed) in 1979, criticizing Vietnam for human rights violations. Aryeh supported the signers and wrote a persuasive analysis of their critics. Starting in April 1978, we ran a six-part series on Skokie, Illinois, where neo-Nazi marchers were pitted against a city of Holocaust survivors; the philosopher Carl Cohen, our author, defended the ACLU's defense of the right of the Skokie skinheads to march. Frank Donner, an eloquent and frequent contributor to *Civil Liberties Review*, became a more frequent contributor to *The Nation*, as he had been under Carey McWilliams. He wrote about such subjects as the scapegoating of alleged terrorists, the strange odyssey of Lyndon LaRouche, and the smearing of the nuclear-freeze movement. And we reported on and supported the Freedom of Information Act against the Justice Department's attempt to undermine it. We recruited former CIA agent Frank Snepp to write about the CIA's lawsuit to enjoin publication of his memoirs. We joined a suit against the FBI's preemptive destruction of files.

Someone (okay, it was me) once counted the number of words in *Time* magazine and then counted the number of words in *The Nation*. *Time* looks a lot fatter, but that's because of the ads. The week I counted, *Time* had 33,000 words and *The Nation* had 30,000. Now count the number of full-time editorial employees on the masthead. Not counting stringers or international edition staff or secretaries or columnists, *Time* had roughly 125 and *The Nation* had exactly 12. Does this mean that *Nation* word people work ten times as hard as *Time* word people? I wouldn't be surprised. (Just kidding, just kidding.) But it does mean that while weekly news magazines like *Time* and *Newsweek* are primarily staff-written, a magazine like *The Nation* depends for its opinion and interpretation primarily on a stable of outside contributors, freelancers, and scholars. Editors prefer to think of themselves as indispensable, and it is true that while it took a Carleton Beals to go into the jungles of Nicaragua and track down Sandino, it took an Oswald Garrison Villard to send him there; that if Philip Bernstein's groundbreaking 1942 *Nation* series on the slaughter of European Jews was a tribute to his doggedness as an investigative reporter, it was also a testament to Freda Kirchwey's commitment and determination to alert the world community to the "vastness and ghastliness of the Jewish tragedy in Europe"; and that even before there was such a term as an "investigative reporter," Fred Cook's remarkable series of exposés owe as much to Carey McWilliams's determination to take on "the idols of the tribe" and his skill at motivating his writers as to Fred's ability to analyze, organize, process, and distill the essence from masses of material. Having said that, I have to tell you that after my first year at *The Nation*, a well-meaning friend with alarm in his voice asked what would happen to *The Nation* if I disappeared or got sick or died? I thought about that, and I'm only slightly embarrassed to tell you my answer: For at least a year *The Nation* would continue to come out as it always has. The main difference would be that it would lag (even more) behind the news. This is because as a result of *The Nation*'s having been around for more than a hundred years with its clear political and cultural identity, the manuscripts keep pouring in. No matter where or what or how obscure the subject—be it the Balkans, the psychology of torture, genocide, nuclear fission—rest assured there are scores of scholars who have been toiling away on it for years in obscurity, and when their subject comes into the news, a fair percentage of them will reduce a 500-page dissertation into a ten-page manuscript, give it a news peg, and put it in an envelope with a self-addressed, stamped return envelope. On receipt our executive editor, be it Bob Hatch or Dick Lingeman, who replaced him, was there to work his magic.

And of course the back of the magazine would be unaffected.

Carey McWilliams had once observed that the editor of *The Nation* was a "captive" of its traditions, and no tradition was more firmly ensconced than the independence of its literary editor. (A tradition, by the way, that turned out to be a major convenience when confronted by the hordes of friends, contributors, and shareholders, each of whose books seemed to its author a natural for a *Nation* review.) In this respect it was not unlike its British counterpart, the *New Statesman*—during the Cold War, both magazines ran back-of-the-book reviews and essays questioning front-of-the-book assumptions.

Another thing we did was to conscript some new writers and even a columnist or two for the front of the magazine, while keeping the great Group Theatre director and *Nation* drama critic Harold Clurman and other culture critics in place in the back. This provided continuity even as we gained infusions of new blood. The first new columnist was Kansas City's gift to American letters, Calvin Trillin, although to sign him up I had to agree to his two humiliating conditions: that he could make fun of the editor and that there would be a "no diddling clause" (i.e., editors were not to change a comma without his permission).

At the lunch at which we first discussed the possibility of his writing an every-third-week, 1,000-word column for *The Nation*, Calvin Trillin asked what he would be paid for this privilege, and I said we were thinking of something in the high two figures. It was my line, and this guy parlayed it into a coast-to-coast one-man stand-up comedy routine. True, when he appears on television, he rarely fails to mention *The Nation*. But then again, what does he say about it?

Once, many years ago, my then ninety-year-old father heard that Calvin Trillin was going to be on *The Tonight Show* to talk about his new book of *Nation* columns, *Uncivil Liberties*, and the next morning he called to tell me he had seen the show.

Is he supposed to be a friend of yours? my father asked. Why do you ask? I asked. My father replied, So why does he call you "the wily and parsimonious Victor S. Navasky"? Well, I explained, it's a joke going back to the days when he wrote for *Monocle*. I know, said my father. Trillin also said his strongest memory of *Monocle* was "receiving a bill from Navasky for a piece of mine the magazine had published along with a note explaining that the office expenses for processing the piece exceeded what he had intended to pay me for it."

And when Johnny Carson asked Trillin to describe *The Nation* in one word, my father asked, Did he have to say "pinko"?

My father had a point. I didn't tell him it was probably preferable to

Trillin's more extended description: "I would describe it as a pinko magazine printed on very cheap paper. It's probably the only magazine in the country if you make a Xerox of it, the Xerox looks a lot better than the original."

I will say this about Trillin. We got our money's worth. Or at least we did until he stopped writing prose and instead gave us a weekly verse. For old times' sake we kept him at his old rate, which by that time was up from $65 to $100, not a penny more, not a penny less. That meant when he turned in one of his famous three-word poems, he might have been among the highest paid poets in America. Consider his poem on the O. J. Simpson case:

O.J.
Oy Vey.

Of course it helps to have a Trillin as part of the mix in a serious journal of critical opinion. This is true even if—maybe because—his targets included the left as well as the right and the center. He was an equal-opportunity offender.

As part of his assault on the stereotypical *Nation* mentality, he even invented a character called Harold the Committed, who suggested that one of Trillin's daughters dress up for Halloween "as the dangers posed to our society by the military-industrial complex." And in a column titled "Pinkos at Rest," he wondered why *The Nation* published only every other week in July and August "even though the oppression of the down-trodden goes on every day." He claimed I couldn't be reached for comment because I was on Martha's Vineyard (untrue, I was in Hillsdale, New York), "a place where renowned writers of a progressive bent use their gifts to compose No Trespassing signs." He innocently inquired why employees in health-food stores always looked so unhealthy. He launched a campaign to change the national Thanksgiving dish from turkey to spaghetti carbonara. He proposed a presidential commission to investigate why stewardesses who sold drinks on airplanes never had any change. He supported legislation that would eliminate the word "whom" from the English language on the grounds that it makes everybody who says it sound like a butler.

———

For the pages of *The Nation* itself we couldn't afford to import overseas talent, but we could try something else. So on July 23, 1980, I wrote to Bruce Page, then editor of the *New Statesman* with a modest proposal: the first international editors' exchange in history. But the background to this began soon after I got to *The Nation*.

I had first met Christopher Hitchens through his elegant *New Statesman* pieces on the Middle East, but also, it seemed, everywhere else. If he was traveling the world anyway, why not write an occasional article for us? I asked via old-fashioned snail mail. And he did, to everyone's satisfaction. And then one day around 5:00 p.m. a dimpled, five-o'clock–shadowed face peered through my half-open door surrounded by a haze of smoke. "Drink?" asked the deep, richly accented baritone voice that accompanied all of the above. If it is possible in one word to convey an upper-class sensibility attached to a heart ostentatiously identified with the toiling masses, Christopher Hitchens, whom I had been looking forward to meeting, succeeded.

We repaired with some comrades, as he liked to call all who partook of his charismatic company, to the Lion's Head, our local pub, where we indeed had a drink or three, and this was the beginning of a twenty-five-year adventure which I hope was as rewarding for him as it was for the magazine, despite (and sometimes because of) the occasional political collision.

By the time I wrote to Page, Christopher had contributed four timely articles in which only his English spelling had to be changed, and Kai Bird, his editor, who had been working eighteen-hour days while commuting from Princeton, where his wife was studying international economics, was ripe for a new assignment. So my idea was that we exchange one *Nation* editor (Kai) for one *New Statesman* editor (Christopher) for a period of three to six months, commencing January 1981; that Hitchens stay on the *New Statesman* payroll and Bird stay on our payroll for the duration of the exchange, thus obviating the need to deal with guilds, unions, border patrols, green cards, immigration authorities, and bureaucracies; and that during this period Hitchens and Bird take on, to the best of their abilities, each other's obligations, rights, and duties for their respective journals.

In my letter to Page, I took the precaution of listing the potential perils of such an undertaking: "What happens if one or the other of the exchangees defaults, defects, alienates, or otherwise finds the new environment unorganized, the new responsibilities overwhelming, boring or whatever. What happens if in your/my judgment X can't do Y's job? My feelings about that," I wrote, "are that if they are willing to take the risk, we ought to be." I proposed we might envision the exchange as a three-month experiment with the mutual option to renew for a second three months, contingent on the agreement of all four parties. I was sure there were 1,001 obstacles (insurance, carfare, living space, the fact that Kai was then primarily an editor whereas Chris seemed primarily a writer, not to mention unfamiliarity with the other country's writers, culture, etc.), but it seemed to me that the accident of two relatively footloose transatlantic peers with their extraordinary talent and apparent adaptability made it possible. What did Page think? If it is a wild, crazy, or otherwise impractical idea, "have no hesitation in telling me to go away," I wrote. Finally, because I had the advantage of having met, liked, and published Hitchens, whereas to Page, Kai was an unknown quantity, I added by way of assurance that "Kai is well-read, well-informed, something of an expert on the Middle East, a gifted editor, and a pleasure to work with (come to think of it, probably much more of a pleasure than Hitchens, who strikes me as a trouble-maker). He also is frugal, cheerful, thrifty, brave, and loyal." Bruce said yes.

Christopher demonstrated that it was possible to down his share of lunchtime martinis, supplemented by however many glasses of red wine, return to the office, and in fifteen to twenty minutes write an elegant 250-word unsigned editorial to space, not one word of which had to be altered.

In March 1981 we renewed the three-month experiment for a second three months, by the end of which it was apparent that Christopher was ready to defect to *The Nation*. Our first idea was to have him apprentice himself to Palmer Weber and do a Marxist-covers–Wall Street series of articles. Christopher was not averse (in fact, he liked the idea, especially if the apprenticeship came with a Wall Street salary), but he kept telling us that economics was not his forte, and so eventually he ended up writing a biweekly "Minority Report" column from Washington.

Although he wrote some of his best (i.e., my favorite) pieces for other publications—I include among these his essay on discovering that his mother and, therefore, he were Jewish, for *Grand Street*, where he memorably wrote: "I was glad to see that I was glad"; and his essay in defense of drinking and smoking for the *London Review of Books* ("On Fags and Booze")—and although we had our later differences over what I regarded as his obsession with President Bill Clinton's alleged public and private derelictions and the nexus between them; over his willingness to testify before the House Judiciary Committee as to private conversations with his friend the then White House aide Sidney Blumenthal, concerning what Sidney had or hadn't said about Monica Lewinsky being a stalker (I wrote an editorial about that); and over President Bush's so-called war on terrorism and invasion of Iraq, which Christopher supported before, during, and after, I much regretted his resignation in the fall of 2002 over *The Nation*'s position on what he regarded as one of the great moral issues of the day, the Iraq War.

His last column appeared in the October 14, 2002, issue. In its parting paragraph he wrote:

> This is something more than a disagreement of emphasis or tactics. When I began work for *The Nation* over two decades ago, Victor Navasky described the magazine as a debating ground between liberals and radicals, which was, I thought, well judged. In the past few weeks, though, I have come to realize that the magazine itself takes a side in this argument, and is becoming the voice and the echo chamber of those who truly believe that John Ashcroft is a greater menace than Osama bin Laden. (I too am resolutely opposed to secret imprisonment and terror-hysteria, but not in the same way as I am opposed to those who initiated the aggression, and who are planning future ones.) In these circumstances it seems to me false to continue the association, which is why I have decided to make this "Minority Report" my last one.

I (we) didn't and don't recognize my (our) position in his summary of it. I thought that was too bad. His "Minority Report" had been well named, and *The Nation* benefited from having literate, informed, and original second, third, and fourth guessings of Christopher's sort in its pages. In the early days, it seemed to me, Christopher would have welcomed the argument. In the end, he chose to walk out on it.

Andrew Kopkind had moved from *Time* to *The New Republic* (where with James Ridgeway he invented a new kind of cultural reportage) to *May Day* (later called *Hard Times*, a radical newsletter he founded with Ridgeway and Bob Sherrill), to a commune in Vermont (where he seemed to stop writing), to various Boston alternative papers and a hip radio program (where he miraculously seemed to overcome his stutter every time he went on the air), to the short-lived biweekly *New Times* to *The Village Voice*, when he moved back to New York with his partner, John Scagliotti, who went on to become general manager of Pacifica's WBAI and eventually the Emmy-winning producer of *In The Life* on PBS. In 1982, we hired Andy to cover the culture wars, but over the years he served as our movie critic, covered presidential politics, and, as often as not, wrote at least one unsigned editorial a week.

We met at Shelly's, a greasy spoon next to *The Nation*'s Thirteenth Street office in late 1982. I had known Andy Kopkind since *Monocle* days and been trying to get him to write for *The Nation* ever since I got there. Now he seemed ready to sign on. He had just written an article for *The Village Voice* on the gayification of Columbus Avenue, and I said to him, "You had me until you got to the part about Pershings having gay hamburgers."

"You don't know what they put in them!" said Andy, whose laughter at his own jokes always invited you along.

When I started to talk about *Nation* politics, Andy interrupted. "Spare me," he said. "It's not about politics. It's about watching Dan Rather or Brokaw or Jennings or whoever and thinking, That's not the way it is. That's not the way it is at all. We should say that and say why and say the way it is."

Some months later, not long after *Three Days of the Condor* had opened, the movie starring Robert Redford as a CIA agent on the run, one of *The Nation*'s best-informed, occasionally paranoid (sometimes with reason), more radical academic writers got word that a consortium of universities, including his own, was about to sign a secret research agreement with the Pentagon. He was willing to be an anonymous source, but we were not permitted to call him at his office or at home, as he was persuaded that the powers that be had tapped his phones. Nor were we to call him from our office phone, which, he assured me, was also probably tapped. We told him (from a pay phone) that we were putting Kopkind, whose work he knew and respected, on the case, and they arranged to meet in an appropriate outdoor setting on his campus. A few days later the phone rang and it was Andy. "This is Condor," he said. "May I come in now?" (The story, by the way, checked out.)

Andy's style was as distinctive as his radical politics. Yet a part of him preferred to write the unsigned *Nation* editorials because that was where the magazine set forth its policy. He would call in, ostensibly to get his assignment, although he usually knew just what he wanted to write about and the line he thought we should take. What, he would ask, was the subject of the week? If I didn't come up with the one he had in mind, he would diplomatically make certain that I thought of his subject before too long. Depending on what it was, he'd ask, What is our line? Or, if he suspected I was politically retrograde, which was often the case, he would educate me in advance with an esoteric, very funny, not quite contemptuous story about some third-party jerk who believed exactly as I had not yet told him I did, and then ask me what I thought. If I expressed an idea about which Andy had a modest reservation, he would pause, enthusiastically agree, and then restate it in a way that reflected his sophisticated, unique, and radical, updated 1960s politics.

Or if he thought the conversation wasn't going anywhere, he would say, "Why don't I try to write something and we'll see how it comes out?" Without a hint of sarcasm he would add, "Is that all, boss?" He liked to call me boss.

Andy never wrote anything I didn't want to publish. He was too good a writer. That was his problem, and sometimes mine too. When he wrote something that went beyond where I thought *The Nation* was ready to go in its unsigned editorials, I would suggest that it appear with his byline. That was our compromise.

I never could tell—still can't—whether our readers are as sensitive to the different meanings we assign to signed and unsigned editorials as we are. Signed means it's one person's opinion (although if it appears in the editorial section it also means that it's within *The Nation*'s zone of values, but it may also mean that it was a short piece written close to deadline and that was the only place where it fit in). Unsigned means that *The Nation* endorses it as *The Nation*'s position.

The British weekly *The Economist*, which on the surface seems to go out of its way to speak in a moderate, distinctive voice, publishes no signed articles, yet since its inception in 1843 it has thought of itself as a "journal of opinion," whereas *Time* and *Newsweek*, which used to be unsigned, now have articles with multiple bylines, but insist that their journalism is objective, unbiased, "fair and balanced," to quote the slogan of Fox News, which, of course, too often is unfair, biased, and unbalanced, at least in my opinion.

The debate goes back to the early 1800s, when *The Edinburgh Review*'s founding editor opted for anonymity, presuming that anonymity signified authority. His critics believed that the anonymity worked only because the *Review*'s editors were united in their Whig assumptions (that slavery was bad, Catholics should be emancipated, the poor deserved an education, and so forth). But even in those days anonymity had its limits. Neil Berry, in his history of those years, *Articles of Faith* (2002), has written that "the new era with its flux and skepticism called for 'signature' for personal argument and responsibility. It seemed to be more democratic. Signed reviews were less oracular, less obscurantist." The arguments haven't changed much in two hundred years. An unhappy contributor to *The Edinburgh Review* was ambivalent: "It was true that anonymity made possible the monstrous charlatanry of the 'editorial we.' Equally it enabled a vain editor (like [Francis] Jeffrey [editor of *Edinburgh Review* from 1802 to 1829]) to rewrite reviewers' copy with impunity. Yet on the other hand the reviewer who has signed his name was apt to turn into a mere performer, a crowd pleaser who wrote only what was expected of him."

In Andy's case the dispute would have been moot, since his style was his signature. When he died in 1994, *The Independent* in London (which quoted his line about how "Congress declared war on poverty in 1964 and has been trying to withdraw from battle ever since") called him "the most important radical journalist of his generation . . . and also the most entertaining." It was altogether fitting and proper (Andy would have liked it) that his obituarist was Don Guttenplan, a former *Nation* intern and colleague.

We also reached backward in time and re-enlisted some old-timers, not least the legendary I. F. (Izzy) Stone. I had introduced myself to Izzy Stone, whom I recognized in 1953 by his Coke-bottle glasses and the hearing aid he was said to turn on and off strategically, when I spotted him going through the card catalogue at the Library of Congress during my college semester in Washington. He told me about the newsletter he was about to launch.

I had read him in *PM* and its successor, *The New York Star*, and also in the *Daily Compass*. And I had always read *I. F. Stone's Weekly*, which he had written and published on his own from 1953 to 1971. For years people asked me who my role models were and for years I told them I didn't like the term, but if I had one, Izzy would be he. As Murray Kempton (another one) once wrote (in his introduction to *In a Time of Torment*):

> The argument could be made that the average issue of *I. F. Stone's Weekly* is more illuminating than the average Sunday edition of *The New York Times*, let alone its inferiors; yet I do not think such an argument really renders Mr. Stone his due . . . The special qualities of Mr. Stone's work are larger than those we expect even in the best journalism; he is employed in the higher criticism.
>
> He travels alone and is in no way alienated. His spirit is absolutely open; his method is monastic. He has kept intact the strongest opinions without developing the smallest visible prejudice. He is a romantic, untempted by whatever particular romance happens to be fashionable.

As early as 1942, Izzy had prophetically written about the Holocaust for *The Nation*, calling it "a murder of a people so appalling . . . that men would shudder at its horrors for centuries to come." But Freda Kirchwey had fired him as Washington editor in 1945, when he forgot to notify her that he had signed on with *PM* to become the first journalist to travel with the Jewish underground. Now my goal was to get Izzy back writing for *The Nation*, or at a minimum mentoring our young Washington editors.

When I returned from my Washington semester, I had heard Izzy give an inspiring speech at Swarthmore (where his son Jeremy was a freshman). Izzy explained how he always refused to attend off-the-record briefings and then scooped those who were there but who were precluded by the ground rules from reporting what they had heard. Izzy would debrief them and then check out what they had been told. So when the literary agent Timothy Seldes told me he was having his uncle, the crusading foreign correspondent George Seldes, then in his nineties, to dinner, and Izzy and Esther Stone were coming in from Washington and would I join them, I jumped at the chance. I knew that Izzy had modeled his own newsletter after Seldes's *In Fact*. I wouldn't miss it.

Despite his poor eyesight, Izzy saw what others missed even though it was in plain sight. Seldes had been more of an old-fashioned, blunderbuss muckraker, while Izzy, whose project was to synthesize Jefferson and Marx, was more of an investigative reader, working from the public record. But they both operated outside the conventional wisdom. They were guerrilla journalists, idealists whose weapons were facts, and, in Izzy's case, ideas as they showed themselves in the great forces and fundamental struggles that shaped our history.

Walking down from Seldes's apartment in the East Nineties to the Tudor Hotel on Forty-third Street, where Izzy liked to stay when he was in New York, Izzy said he had an idea that he thought might be appropriate to his energy level. He would write a weekly paragraph, maybe 150 words, under the heading "Izzy Says . . ." Every week he had at least one thing to say, he said. We asked David Levine to come up with a design for this, and he provided the perfect logo: Izzy holding a life-sized pen the way a medieval warrior might carry his spear.

Sure enough, the next week Izzy sent in a 150-word item on Reagan's Defense Department. A few hours later, though, he called again. The story was bigger than he thought, it seemed; he'd gone to the press building and read the wire reports. He had another 200 words. Our layout people remade the page. Here we were on press day when Izzy called again. "I think we have something of a scoop," he said gleefully, and proceeded to dictate his "final" addition.

Over the next few weeks *Nation* readers were treated to a number of "Izzy Says . . . ," at least one "Stonegram," and a few "I. F. Stone Reports." Our young staff members, increasingly impatient with Izzy's cheerful but last-minute modus operandi, looked skeptical when I told them how grateful they would be in the future for having had the privilege to have worked with this legendary maverick.

Then one day Izzy called to say apologetically that he had better stop. "I'm an old war horse," he said, "and once I get started I can't stop. I have to go down and read the wires. I have to follow up. Let's go back to the old system, and I'll just do occasional pieces as they occur." And he did.

We hired I. F. Stone's brother Mark to publicize our new format, and although the press release got the address of Automation House wrong (Dorothy Schiff had arranged through her friendship with the labor arbitrator Theodore Kheel for us to hold the press conference there), it yielded a front-page story in *The Wall Street Journal*, which quoted me as saying that my goal for the magazine was to have the best writers in the country lined up around the block wanting to write for us.

Harold Clurman called in high dudgeon. "The story is fine," he said, "except for one thing." So what are you complaining about? "You already have the best writer in the country," he said. "Me!"

And as our prospectus foolishly promised, before the first year was out we had indeed made some news. A year's worth of White House Cabinet minutes (March 14, 1977–March 13, 1978) came into our possession. The fact that they contained not one iota of "news" didn't stop us. Instead of trumpeting the non-news in the minutes, we trumpeted the big news *of* the minutes, and signed up four commentators to meditate on them—Robert Sherrill, our White House correspondent (the only White House correspondent who was permanently banned from the White House: his propensity to punch those whom he suspected of doing him dirt led to his being denied security clearance); Kurt Vonnegut, the mischievous novelist; Marcus Raskin, who had been a member of the special staff of the National Security Council in the Kennedy administration and now co-directed the Institute for Policy Studies, a progressive think tank; and Marcel Ophuls, documentarian *extraordinaire*. The minutes revealed that the Cabinet members spent much of their weekly meeting remarking on their own and each other's press clips and media coverage; as Vonnegut noted, "What could a Cabinet meeting be, after all, given our society and form of government, other than an adult version of Show and Tell?" So the acquisition of the non-newsworthy minutes made news across the country, especially among those journalists whose works were the subject of Cabinet conversation. I saw this as a sad comment on the state of the profession. *Time* magazine, for example, on October 9, 1978, devoted a page to what it called "without doubt a weighty scoop." *The Washington Post* did an editorial on "those boring minutes," comparing them with the racy secret transcripts of the Nixon administration. Even though "the chief surprise of the minutes is that they contain no surprise," America's Pollyannaish press found them reassuring. As *Time* put it: "The minutes provide an overall sense of an Administration providing orderly and dedicated, if not exactly brilliant, care taking—an image that may explain why no one at the White House seemed very upset that the minutes had been made public."

What did it say about *The Nation*'s much-vaunted muckracking apparatus, not to mention the nation's press, that our most covered story of the year was a nonstory?

I have already said a little bit about why, despite *The Nation*'s 113 years of money-losing (as of 1978), neither Fish nor I was enthusiastic about reorganizing our relatively radical weekly journal of dissent into a nonprofit. But there is more to say.

Although our political sympathies were with the socialists, I continued to believe that a for-profit business environment would, ultimately, be good for business. And I didn't agree with Buckley that a little magazine could never make money. Besides, we liked our business plan, which could not have been more lucid. Based on our study and analysis, with a hefty assist from Jim Kobak and the software program he had taught me to use, we thought the economics confronting us were a no-brainer. In 1977, it cost the magazine $10 (including production and mailing costs) to service each subscriber with forty-seven issues. *The Nation* was charging $21 per subscription, which meant that the magazine was "making" $11 per subscriber, out of which general overhead and editorial costs had to be paid. Jim Storrow had told us that *The Nation* had approximately 25,000 subscribers and was losing between $120,000 and $150,000 a year. This meant, we naïvely believed, other things being equal (as they never are), that *The Nation*'s deficit would disappear if we received a windfall of only 15,000 or more subscribers. Our plan called for an initial test mailing of 100,000 subscription solicitations, to be followed by four mailings of 500,000 each over the next two years. The estimate assumed a modest net 1.5 percent return on these mailings (based on past mailing history). According to Kobak's projections, within three years *The Nation* could reach a circulation of 60,000, which would put it in the black. Or would it?

But we weren't all that naïve. Although we didn't know that 7,000 of *The Nation's* 25,000 subscriptions had expired by the time we arrived, we knew the history of Buckley's failed prediction for *National Review*. We knew that *The New Republic* lost money. We knew that according to various historians of *The Nation* it had lost money in every one but three years, though none could tell us which three. We knew that every journal of opinion in history had lost money. Why, then, to repeat myself (and themselves) did we not file to become a nonprofit? That way, at least the investors could get a charitable deduction for their money, our mailing costs would be much lower, and we would be eligible for foundation grants.

My slightly complicated answer had originated in an experience I had had in 1968, ten years before I knew I was going to have anything to do with *The Nation* other than read it. In the course of my research for *Kennedy Justice* I had discovered that all the Attorney General's speeches, press releases, and "opinions" were stored on the shelves of a little room off the main Public Information Office (across the hall from the Attorney General's fifth-floor office), which contained as furniture only a desk and a chair. Since it was empty and since I had taken the trouble to make a friend of the director of Public Information, when I asked if I might use the office I was told yes; its previous occupant, an attorney in the civil rights division, had completed her research and it was temporarily available.

This was a generous gesture, a great favor, and an implicit statement of trust. Who needed a reporter in an alcove where he was in a position to watch official traffic and, if unscrupulous, eavesdrop on who knows what official business?

Naturally the first thing I did when I sat down at the desk was to open the drawer, where I discovered some leftover confidential memorandums. As I saw it, I had four choices: I could pocket the memorandums, I could read the memorandums, I could turn them over to the Public Information director unread, or I could not read them, say nothing, and leave them in the desk. I decided on the fourth option, but I did read them just in case. And I am glad I did. One of them was a memorandum from the Civil Rights Division to the IRS which listed some segregationist and white hate groups that enjoyed nonprofit status. Weren't the activities of these organizations in violation of the Equal Protection Clause of the Fourteenth Amendment to the Constitution? And if so, why not challenge their nonprofit status and put them out of business? This is in fact what happened.

I was all for putting unconstitutional segregationist organizations out of business, but even at the time I worried about the potential for abuse of IRS discretion by selective harassment of political critics. I even had qualms about the way the Revenue Service in 1930 had gone after Al Capone for tax evasion rather than for his "real" crimes, and I wondered whether it would be such a wise idea to convert the tax status of America's oldest weekly magazine into one that made it a potential hostage to the administration. (By the time Reagan was President, that administration was, in truth, our weekly target.) Especially since when the IRS took away your nonprofit status, they also went after you for past taxes not paid, interest, and penalty payments. For example, when *Ms.* magazine first went nonprofit, in 1978, they estimated that their postal savings alone would be $600,000 per annum. Let's say after five years the IRS successfully challenged this status. They would lose their annual $600,000 saving, the IRS could and probably would demand back payments for monies owed the government (5 times $600,000 equals $3,000,000), plus interest plus penalties payments. And that doesn't include lawyers' fees. In the guise of protecting national security they might, in other words, do to an impoverished progressive journal what the Kennedy and Johnson administrations had done to the segregationists.

This fear was more than theoretical. Technically what we are talking about here is a provision of the revenue code known after its numbers and letters as "501(c)(3)." In 1985 I borrowed an idea I had found in a memorandum in the files of Carey McWilliams and convened a conference on the role of the journal of opinion, held at Carey's old alma mater, the University of Southern California. It was at that conference that we were able to explore systematically what I apparently already understood intuitively—the case against converting the unprofitable *Nation* into a nonprofit institution. One of the livelier panels dealt with the question of ownership, and one of the livelier panelists was Cynthia Kling-Jones, who had worked on *Channels*, a nonprofit magazine about television, and then was publisher of *Nuclear Times*, which was organized as a nonprofit by some well-wishers in and around the Rockefeller Foundation and was about, well, life in the nuclear age.

As Cynthia put it, because of 501(c)(3) "if you are a political publication, you check your first amendment rights at the door." (She also explained that foundations had no respect for magazine business cycles. The magazines *knew* they would be getting their subvention but never knew when, which doesn't help when you have printers and writers to pay. "Also, these foundations still work on the Old Boy network principle and you'd better have an Old Boy working for you in order to see anybody.")

Perhaps as a result of listening to their lawyers and doing their best to please the foundations, neither *Channels* nor *Nuclear Times* ever had their tax-exempt status challenged. But perhaps such caution had its effect on the editorial material, and perhaps it helps explain why both those estimable periodicals are no longer with us.

Ironically, *Mother Jones*, whose tax-exempt status was challenged by the IRS, is still in business. As Deirdre English, its then-editor, observed at the conference, "You could say that for a magazine like *Mother Jones*, if you are in the for-profit world you will be censored by corporations, and if you work in the nonprofit world you'll be censored by government."

Mother Jones, thanks to its enterprising young publisher, Richard Parker, was one of the first magazines in the country to take advantage of 501(c)(3). When they started in 1976, they didn't foresee IRS problems, because their focus was on investigating corporations rather than trying to influence the government. That changed when the IRS did indeed start investigating them. The *Mother Jones* case is worth looking at in some detail (a) because *Mother Jones* prevailed, and so periodicals that have and wish to retain tax-exempt status can and should study how it did; (b) because it illustrates the dangers, risks, perils, and costs that can come with tax exemption; and (c) because it had consequences for other publications.

For example, the late Erwin Knoll, longtime editor of *The Progressive*, explained in 1985 that among the various reasons it switched to nonprofit status was *Mother Jones*'s eventual victory over the IRS. *The Progressive*'s operating deficit had been about $250,000 a year, about 20 percent of the budget. As Erwin saw it, he could raise about $200,000 of that in small contributions from subscribers, which is basically the way the magazine had stayed alive for decades. But about $50,000 a year came from foundations or from a few rich contributors for whom tax deductibility was a factor. "We managed to devise all kinds of ingenious laundering mechanisms," said the ever feisty Knoll. "But I think we were spending as much energy laundering money as the Mafia does in order to receive these tax deduction funds, and we thought our time and attention could be better spent.

"Then, after *Mother Jones*'s triumph over the IRS, we looked at the IRS requirements and found that it had been many years since our magazine endorsed a candidate (as a rule the American system doesn't serve up candidates we feel like endorsing). And we don't do that much lobbying for legislation, because we think it's more important for us to talk to our readers than to talk to members of Congress. Finally, there is now so much overt, blatant political activity by organizations on the right that have tax deductible status that we would welcome the chance to fight the IRS on this issue."

But there was a darker side. The regulations on which the IRS made its judgments were disturbingly vague and ambiguous. Trying to decipher the three-volume, small-print IRS code with its rulings, explanations, interpretations, voidings, and superseding was more complicated than trying to decode *Finnegans Wake*. As Dennis Caniff put it in *Quill* in April 1985, "The government's tax collector has in effect become an arbiter of editorial content of non-profits."

I thought it poetically apropos that the main previous IRS ruling concerning a magazine's nonprofit status had also involved a publication named after a mother, *Big Mama Rag*, a Denver-based free paper. Its charter said its purpose was to create a channel of communication for women on issues of concern to women. The IRS said its main concern was to promote lesbianism. Judge John Sirica, of Watergate fame, took away its status as an "educational" institution because, he said, under IRS regulations, it's okay to advocate a particular position, but you have to present "a sufficiently full and fair exposition of the pertinent facts" to permit the public to form its own opinion. He didn't think *Big Mama Rag* met the test. Luckily for *Big Mama* in the short run, Judge Sirica was overruled by Judge Abner Mikva;

nevertheless *Big Mama Rag* went out of business a few months thereafter.

After *Big Mama*, the IRS challenged the tax-exempt status of a
newsletter called *Attack!* And out of that came a "four-step methodology" test for determining who was and who wasn't entitled to nonprofit
status. The problem was that the Court of Appeals only partially endorsed their so-called methodology. It was enough to drive the editors
of *Mother Jones* and its lawyers into a twelve-step program.

Here is a rough chronology of what happened to them. In 1980 the
IRS began what everybody assumed was a routine audit of the Foundation for National Progress, *Mother Jones*'s tax-exempt parent, which
also ran a business school for nonprofits and served as an informal conduit for other projects.

Then came the election of Ronald Reagan and the rise of the radical right. Richard Viguerie, publisher of *Conservative Digest* and the
right wing's direct-mail guru, wrote an article proclaiming: "Defunding
the left should be a principal priority of the Reagan Administration." In
March 1981 the IRS told *Mother Jones* that it had tentatively decided to
revoke its parent organization's tax-exempt status, and in August 1982
the Northern California office of the IRS ruled that *Mother Jones* was
a commercial rather than an educational enterprise. The tax ruling
would cost them an estimated $200,000 a year on lost postal savings,
$100,000 lost in donations, and they had already spent $150,000 on
legal fees.

At first this seemed like something of a joke. How could *Mother
Jones* be termed commercial when it differed from such other nonprofit magazines as *National Geographic* and *Smithsonian*, which were
not being investigated by the IRS, mainly in that its negative stories
consistently alienated (and the magazine lost) its biggest advertisers—
alcohol, tobacco, and automobiles. By January 1983 *Mother Jones*
shared with its readers the conclusion of its legal counsel: that the
Reagan administration "proposes to end the threat that *Mother Jones*
poses by putting *Mother Jones* out of business."

On September 27, 1983, they got some good news. The IRS National Appeals Office overruled the Northern California office and
held that the magazine's primary purpose was educational, but it
left standing the lower tax court's decision that proceeds from adver-

tising and rental of the subscription list were "unrelated taxable income."

In November, in an Advice Memorandum, the IRS acknowledged that, as the magazine had argued three and a half years earlier, the articles *Mother Jones* had published indeed had resulted in cancellation of ads. But it declined to enumerate a predictable, definitive rule regarding nonprofit publications, and stamped on the documents that upheld *Mother Jones*'s nonprofit status these words: "This document may not be used or cited as a legal precedent."

Given the semi-chaos created by the combination of the "four-step methodology" (two of whose steps were in doubt), the vagueness of the distinction the IRS tried to make between commercial and educational publications, the lack of a definitive predictable rule regarding who was or who wasn't and isn't nonprofit (as distinguished from nonprofitable), and the vast discretion that tax bureaucrats enjoyed to function as editors with fingers in the political wind, it's no wonder that the nonprofit community found itself in a tizzy.

Father Brian Wallace, in a signed editorial in *Today's Catholic* titled "Nuts!" asked, "How in this land of Freedom has the IRS been able to gather the power necessary to restrict the content of a newspaper?" The IRS may not have been able to issue meaningful guidelines, but that didn't stop the Catholic Press Association (CPA) from issuing its own guidelines on how to avoid IRS ire, which led one of its members to denounce it for "counseling cowardice." All of which prompted a *Christian Century* editorial observing: "While we must always worry about a government agency's encroachment on religious freedom, we would have to point out to Father Wallace that his First Amendment press freedom is already compromised by the fact that he accepts a nonprofit status under federal tax law guidelines." The underlying conundrum: Should the nonprofit press have to sacrifice its advocacy rights for the privilege of tax exemption?

At least one member of Congress tried to press the IRS for explicit criteria that would help magazines know just where the elusive line was, and finally one S. A. Winborne of the IRS replied: "If a magazine takes a controversial position . . . and insists on espousing that position but does not in any way use an educational methodology such as presenting enough information that a reasonable person could make a reasonable position being espoused . . . that could possibly call into question the exemption of that magazine . . ."

Is everything clear now?

Whether or not everything was clear, *Mother Jones* was shortly in the clear. As they put it in an editorial headed "Never Mind" in December 1983, the IRS accepted *Mother Jones*'s 1980 point about its main business being to expose and thereby alienate profit-making corporations, not to become one. And, as might have been predicted while *Mother Jones* was happy to have won back its tax-exempt status, a year later, like Father Wallace, it was back complaining about the muzzle that this status imposed on the magazine. Deidre English wrote in her "Backstage" column for November 1984 that the rules proscribing candidate endorsement and promotion of legislation constituted "a little chill, and amounted to an unconstitutional form of censorship against the tax-exempt." Among the "things we are not allowed to do": "We're not even allowed to state whether we're for Reagan or Mondale . . ." Perhaps she called it only a "little" chill because not even she could claim with a straight face that *Mother Jones*'s readers didn't know which candidate *Mother Jones* would favor. But, she added, "censorship is still censorship and should be ruled unconstitutional."

Although *Mother Jones* survived its ordeal, it is now a bimonthly. As a magazine that does its best to make weekly trouble, and has already attracted more than its share of IRS audits, we preferred not to take the nonprofit chance.

During the first year of Reagan's presidency *The Nation* organized a Writers Congress at New York's Roosevelt Hotel that drew so many writers protesting the administration's crackdown on the creative spirit (4,000) that the fire marshal complained and we had to open a second front across town at the West Forty-fourth Street headquarters of 1199, the union of hospital and health workers. (And speaking of unions, the National Writers Union was born at that congress—and whose apartment house do you think it threatened to picket when negotiations over their first magazine contract broke down? Right again.)

To lure registrants across town, we conscripted Studs Terkel and Calvin Trillin to conduct a daylong public conversation with visiting littérateurs. And not long after, one of the fledgling cable channels put *The Bud and Studs Show* on the air for something like twenty-six weeks.

All this public activity and more is something that journals of opinion are particularly well equipped to encourage, given their cause-oriented nature. It was therefore no surprise to us that the most resonant events we organized involved other publications. A debate on whether Julius and Ethel Rosenberg had been framed,* co-sponsored by *The New Republic* and *The Nation*, filled New York's Town Hall with living history. Among those present, in addition to various Rosenberg relatives, were Arthur Schlesinger, Jr., Irving Howe, and Professor Irwin Corey, the ancient, double-talking, stand-up comic who bills himself as "the world's leading authority." He took advantage of the question period to consternate all concerned.

A series of debates with *National Review* followed on subjects ranging from affirmative action to capital punishment to government funding of the arts (the latter held at the Berkshire Theater Festival in Stockbridge, Massachusetts). We like to think they exposed audiences young and old to presumptions at odds with, and often more radical than, those prevailing in the center-mainstream media, but at some level we must have also realized that they were a form of entertainment. The proof: When searching for a moderator acceptable to both *National Review* and *The Nation* we settled on the neoconservative former mayor of New York City, Ed Koch. We issued the invitation, and

---

*Walter and Miriam Schneir (authors of *Invitation to an Inquest*), for *The Nation*, took the affirmative. Ronald Radosh and Joyce Milton (authors of *The Rosenberg File*), for *The New Republic*, argued for the negative. Twenty-two years later, on July 11, 1995, the National Security Agency released forty-nine decoded Soviet intelligence messages, with two thousand more to come. Based on these but also on their own research in Prague and Moscow, including interviews with two men accused of having participated in the Rosenberg spy ring, the Schneirs concluded that Julius had indeed run a non-atomic espionage spy ring and that Ethel was probably not a member but was used as a "lever" in an unsuccessful attempt to pry a confession from Julius. They reported these findings in the August 14/21, 1995, *Nation*, adding "We know that our account will be painful news for many people, as it is for us. But the duty of a writer is to tell the truth. Admittedly, in the swamp of fin de siècle disillusion, that is a pitifully slim reed. Nevertheless, we still cling to it."

he accepted. I had known Koch in his more carefree early days as the left-liberal lawyer for *The Village Voice* and leading figure of the Village Independent Democrats. He took me aside and said, "I can see why *National Review* would want me, but why you? As you know, I'm opposed to *The Nation's* position on capital punishment and affirmative action." I knew Ed would lean over backward to be fair, and I assured him, "It is because of the stature you will bring to the proceedings." He nodded sagely, and as a moderator he was boffo.

We also received a grant, courtesy of Ping Ferry's old friend David Hunter, which paid for a series of lunchtime lectures at City University of New York's graduate center in midtown where we introduced speakers mostly from other countries: E. P. Thompson, the radical British social historian and founder of the Campaign for Nuclear Disarmament; Meron Benvenisti, the iconoclastic former deputy mayor of Jerusalem; Michael Manley, the socialist Prime Minister of Jamaica; Jacobo Timerman, the outspoken dissident Argentine newspaper editor and publisher fresh from torture in Argentine prison. They had in common only that their perspectives were unfamiliar to American audiences. The specially invited guests, who ran the gamut from scholars to journalists to talk-show bookers to moochers (never underestimate the value of a free lunch) seemed to appreciate the non—as distinguished from un—American perspectives. A number of the speakers, like Thompson and Manley, ended up as regular contributors to *The Nation's* pages; others, like Timerman, we got to know in other ways.

The spring of 1981, when I had been at *The Nation* for three years, saw the publication of his powerful memoir *Prisoner Without a Name, Cell Without a Number*. The Argentine journalist Timerman had been "disappeared," imprisoned, and tortured during the 1970s by the military junta in Buenos Aires, and his memoir vividly evoked that experience. Although some members of the organized Jewish community took exception to his argument that the mass "disappearances" were tinged with anti-Semitism, he and his book (with a huge assist from his human-rights-activist publisher, Random House's Robert Bernstein) were widely celebrated.

I thought he should expand on the underlying meaning of his story for *The Nation*, and I was looking forward to meeting him one evening at a small dinner party in his honor. Then I opened my *New York Times* and there on the Op Ed page was an article by a CBS television producer headlined "Torture? On TV?" In it the producer of *CBS Reports*, Eric F. Salzman, claimed that when he met with Timerman to ask what he wanted to discuss on his program, Timerman told him to forget about the questions: he wanted to be tortured.

> Mr. Timerman looks at me, I say nothing. Is he testing to see if I will do anything for a program that will generate controversy and pull a large rating? I stare and listen for clues to see if the man is mad.
>
> "It is not very difficult," he continues. "I will not die, don't worry. Do you know how it is done? The subject is tied down and his body wet with water. Electrodes are applied. The apparatus allows more or less energy to pass." He moves his thumb and forefinger as if twisting a dial—"So, the body twitches and jumps. The subject howls or his flesh is burned or he may die. But it is controllable, you see. A doctor would make sure I don't die. There can be a problem of shock to the heart." He rubs his chest, making a small circle. "But it can be massaged. There can be a problem of exploding something but I have survived. I would survive. In half an hour it is over. Can you arrange this?"

Salzman wrote that he was struck silent as Timerman went on to say that there were excellent torture doctors in abundance—in Argentina, El Salvador, Iran, Cuba, Brazil, the Soviet Union.

"If you volunteer to be tortured," Salzman told him, "you will trivialize the evil of torture. People will call it a publicity stunt."

The TV interview went on as scheduled, and there was no torture.

So that night I met Timerman at the home of a liberal labor lawyer. We were introduced, and I asked him, What's the story on the Op Ed story?

In his heavily accented English, he told me, "They want me in twenty minutes to explain what I've already written in hundreds of pages. How do you explain to the American people what is torture in twenty minutes? So I said you want to explain what it is to be tortured? Torture me on television."

At dinner the toasts were plentiful and much wine was consumed while Timerman explained to us that the Argentine government said it couldn't account for the thousands of people who were disappeared, and the State Department had lists of thousands of names but declined to release them.

After dinner and after after-dinner drinks, as he was leaving, Timerman put his arm around my shoulder and said, "So tell me, Veektor, what is so terrible if I am tortured on television?"

Salzman hadn't been able to figure out whether or not Timerman was serious, and at some level neither could I. But his point was profoundly serious. How, given the media glut, do you break through and communicate the terrible truth?

A few years later, I witnessed another writer facing a similar conundrum (albeit with no torture involved). J. Kirkpatrick Sale, whom we had signed on as a contributing editor to *The Nation* specializing in radical environmental, green, spiritual, and other issues (what some called New Age but Kirk liked to think of as "cutting edge"), was explaining the Luddites, the subject of his new book, to an audience at Town Hall. He was one of two dozen speakers brought together by the *Utne Reader* to speak about alternative perspectives on the events of the day/week/year. What entranced Kirk about the Luddites, who had asked what was called in their time "the machinery question," was less their resistance to new technologies than the forceful way in which they raised the question and demanded a voice for those affected by the answers.

Kirk's way of making his point at Town Hall was to end his brief talk by picking up—with no advance warning—a sledgehammer and smashing a computer screen, scattering shards of glass, wires, and other technological paraphernalia all over the stage. Word of his action spread, and some months later, when a reporter from *Wired* magazine asked him about it, he said:

It was astonishing how good it made me feel! I cannot explain it to you. I was on stage in New York's Town Hall with an audience of 1,500 people. I was behind a lectern, and in front of the lectern was this computer. And I gave a very short, minute-and-a-half description of what was wrong with the technosphere, and how it was destroying the biosphere. And then I walked over and I got this very powerful sledgehammer and smashed the screen with one blow and smashed the keyboard with another blow. It felt wonderful. The sound it made, the spewing of the undoubtedly poisonous insides into the spotlight, the dust that hung in the air—some of the audience applauded. I bowed and returned to my chair.

What had he accomplished? "It was a statement. At other forums I attempt to discuss the importance of understanding new technologies and what they are doing to us. But at that moment, when I had only four minutes to talk, I thought this was a statement better than anything else I could possibly say."

And indeed, how can one break through the mass-media fog, the miasma of platitudes, clichés, stereotypes, and untested assumptions that the increasingly conglomerated communications combines share? This is the question that bedevils all small magazines and all others who challenge the national complacency. Those of us in the opinion-journalism business are occupationally dedicated to the proposition that it can be done through critical reasoning, careful analysis, moral argument. But Timerman and Sale remind us that sweet reason alone may not always be enough.

The first time I heard of Ralph Schoenman was in April 1978, when he threatened to sue *The Nation*. Our reviewer had given a bad notice to his wife Joan Mellen's book, *Big Bad Wolves: Masculinity in American Film*, and since our literary editor and Mellen were (in his view, not our literary editor's) "rivals" in Temple University's Department of English Literature and somebody's tenure was at stake, according to Ralph it was a put-up job. It wasn't, and they didn't sue. But during this contretemps I learned a little about Ralph's background. He had been the executive director of the (Bertrand) Russell International War Crimes Tribunal, which in the 1970s had held hearings in connection with the Vietnam War and other events in Southeast Asia. He also had something of a reputation in Trotskyist circles, and he was, I was assured, a Trot (at that point I wasn't sure whether it was a good or a bad thing to have been one).

The next time I heard from Ralph was in August 1981, on the cusp of the Solidarity rebellion in Poland against the Soviet-dominated regime headed by General Jaruselski. It was important, he said, that the left show solidarity with Solidarity, and he had an idea: *The Nation* should rent Town Hall and invite a dozen high-visibility people to have their public say on the issue of freedom in Eastern Europe. We could fill the hall, he would do the work. What did we say?

Since I and my colleagues thought there were better reasons for objecting to General Jaruselski's crushing of the democratic movement in Poland than the Cold War rhetoric offered in the United States by President Reagan and General Haig and in Great Britain by Prime Minister Margaret Thatcher, I thought it was a good idea to come together to condemn the martial-law regime in Warsaw, so I said yes. And so did Susan Sontag, E. L. Doctorow, Daniel Singer, Kurt Vonnegut, and a host of other human-rights and left luminaries. The night before the big night I found myself in Doctorow's kitchen in his New Rochelle home (not unlike the house that opens *Ragtime*), where two Polish dissidents were teaching Pete Seeger the songs of Solidarity in preparation for the sing-along portion the next evening.

The event itself was stirring. A secondary purpose of the meeting was to transcend the hand-wringing platitudes of the Reagan administration and to create some distance from the manifestly hypocritical policy of "Let Poland be Poland." This duality was most eloquently expressed by the Mexican novelist-diplomat Carlos Fuentes, who sent a long a message of support culminating in the admonition: "Let Poland be Poland, but let El Salvador be El Salvador."

At Town Hall there was much talk of "Fascism with a human face." But for much of the audience the most striking statement of the night was Susan Sontag's. The part that attracted all the attention wasn't included in her prepared remarks. She said, "Imagine, if you will, someone who read only *The Reader's Digest* between 1950 and 1970, and someone in the same period who read only *The Nation* or the *New Statesman*. Which reader would have been better informed about the realities of Communism? The answer, I think, should give us pause. Can it be that our enemies are right?"

My own view was and is that *The Nation* had it precisely right about the domestic politics of the Cold War, while *The Reader's Digest* was basically an apologist for the worst aspects of McCarthyism. Internationally *The Nation* was indeed slower than the *Digest* to comprehend the internal corruption and repression of Stalin's Russia, but on balance it was a much more perceptive analyst and interpreter of the dynamics of the Cold War, especially the Cold War in Africa, Latin America, and southern Asia.

Anyway, after confessing that when as a college student in 1953 she had first read portions of Czeslaw Milosz's passionate exposé of life under Communism, *The Captive Mind*, she thought of it as an instrument of Cold War propaganda, Sontag reported that twenty-seven years later, in 1980, on the eve of her first visit to Poland, "I took down my old copy of *The Captive Mind* and thought: But it's all true . . . that Milosz had, if anything, underestimated the disgrace of the Communist regime installed by force in his country." How was it possible, she asked, that she and many others on the left could have been so suspicious of what Milosz and "the rest of the exiles" had been telling us?

Sontag's answer was that the politics of many people on the democratic left, herself included, "has been governed by the wish not to give comfort to reactionary forces. With that consideration in mind, people on the left wittingly or unwittingly have told a lot of lies. We were unwilling to identify ourselves as anti-Communists because that was the slogan of the right, the ideology of the Cold War and, in particular, the justification of America's support of Fascist dictatorships in Latin America and of the American war on Vietnam." She challenged this view by arguing that the principal lesson to be learned from the events in Poland "is the failure of Communism, the utter villainy of the Communist system."

Harper's assigned Walter Goodman, a neoconservative *New York Times* man, to do research on *The Nation* and the *Digest*, and what he found was what he expected to find: "*The Nation* may have been more enlightening than *The Reader's Digest*, in general, but when it came to 'the realities of Communism' *Digest* readers were more accurately served." I had known and had cordial political disagreements with Walter over the years. In fact, soon after I arrived at *The Nation*, we published his amusing account of his brief engagement with the CIA, so his conclusions didn't surprise me.

The issue that Susan raised was joined in *The Nation* itself, which followed its reprint of her speech with commentaries from a half-dozen writers to which she replied. For example, Philip Green wrote:

> I don't know which émigrés Sontag could find only in the anti-democratic *Reader's Digest*. I do know, though, that she could have learned many other "truths" from that magazine, such as that "International Communism," China not excepted, is a monolithic conspiracy directed from Moscow; that she herself was not an opponent of the Vietnam War but rather an agent of the Kremlin; and all the other formulations of the "professional anti-Communists." At least the émigrés and dissidents *The Nation* has published over the years and whose books it has reviewed, frequently and often favorably, are democrats. Contrarily, American or Russian, the right is anti-democratic. Its truths, such as they are, are always encapsulated in a larger lie. If Susan Sontag really needed to learn from the right, that was her problem, not ours.

Most persuasive to me was the response of Aryeh Neier. It seemed to me then, and it does now, that he met Sontag on her own ground, and he defined the point where I like to think *The Nation* itself came out, and still does. (To get there, given the range of views we published, extending from Diana Trilling to Andy Kopkind, took some doing.)

> As Sontag is well aware, mainstream anti-Communism is not concerned with promoting liberty, far from it. Rather, it has been a pretext for suppressing liberty at home through loyalty investigations, political purges, surveillance and dirty tricks, and for doing worse abroad through the bombardment of Vietnam and Cambodia, the "destabilization" of Chile and the arming of murderers in El Salvador. The atrocities committed by anti-Communists do not mitigate in the slightest the evils of Communism. Nor do they excuse those among us who have been apologists for Communist oppression. But they do explain the reluctance of many on the left to shout "me too" when main-

stream anti-Communists proclaim the evils of godless Communism.

Although Sontag's speech was momentarily divisive ("She hijacked my rally," lamented Schoenman), much of the audience left Town Hall humming that golden oldie of the old left, "Solidarity Forever," but also the songs of the new Solidarity rebellion.

6

THE LEGAL LANDSCAPE

When I came to *The Nation* I knew that one of the ways that Ham and I would try to make ends meet was to improve on the ad situation. The ad guy, who worked half-time, a nice man named Martin Fleer, told me he earned $18,000 a year. When I asked him how much advertising he had sold the previous year, he said, "Sixteen thousand—but I also do public relations."* Luckily for me, under prevailing journalistic ethics as I interpreted them, ideally the editor would have nothing to do with ad sales; it was not my department. (This formulation reminded me of a routine Richard C. Neuweiler used to do about Wernher von Braun, the German rocket scientist who came to the West after the war. When asked about the rockets he had built for Hitler that landed on London, he would say, "I had nothing to do with it. That was the 'down' department. My department was 'up.' 'Up,' that was my department.")

Certainly a clear separation of editorial and advertising departments was true at the *Times*. It had not been true at *Monocle*, but then at *Monocle* I had been editor and publisher, and we still didn't sell many ads.

Richard Beebe, our ad guy, thought it was unethical to talk about readership numbers as opposed to paid circulation numbers, because we had done no independent research to document what our actual readership numbers were. (On most magazines the assumption is that

*By 2004 *The Nation* billed more than $1 million in ads.

for every paid subscriber there are at least three readers.) At *The Nation*, however, because such a high percentage of our subscribers were libraries, I knew things to be different.

I always thought that by studying the practices institutionalized by Carey McWilliams, and at *The New Yorker* by Harold Ross and William Shawn, I would know all there was to be known about the relationship that ought to prevail between advertising and editorial.

1. Avoid the ad trap. As Carey McWilliams used to explain it, mass magazines are caught up in a self-defeating process for which they themselves are largely responsible:

> The mass magazines must have circulation in order to get advertising and the more vicious the competition for the advertiser's dollar, the more circulation it must have. Getting circulation is expensive. Maintaining circulation is expensive. In effect it has almost reached the point where the mass magazine is willing to pay the reader for the privilege of adding his name to the list. With the advent of television they saw the competition growing even more fierce. As the giants battle it out for top circulation position, their editorial sights are lowered. They must aim at the common denominator of interest and this denominator is becoming very common indeed. Sharp controversy is avoided. Certain subject matter is taboo.

2. Avoid ad people. Under Harold Ross and William Shawn, *The New Yorker* made an art form out of banishing ad types from the editorial floor. Shawn even tried not to ride down in the same elevator with them, or anyone else, for that matter. Years later, in 1986, when Arthur Carter bought *The Nation*, the document sealing the deal referred explicitly to "*The New Yorker*" model, of separating state (business/advertising) and church (editorial). Theodore H. White's novel *The View from the Fortieth Floor*, said to be inspired by the rise and fall of *Collier's* magazine, is in effect a dramatization of these theses. "The bigger they are, the harder they fall" was the conventional wisdom of the 1960s when not only *Collier's* but *Life*, *Look*, and the *The Saturday Evening Post* went under.

Also, even if one was careful not to build up false, bloated circulation figures, advertiser loyalty to a journal of opinion would be at best a transient thing. At the appearance of a single unflattering word they would cancel out from under you, and they did, regularly, at any number of magazines as well as at *The Nation*. That is one of the reasons that whereas mass magazines, sold primarily on newsstands, count on advertising for half or more of their revenue, the journal of opinion counts primarily on its subscribers. Advertising, in *The Nation's* case, brings in no more than 10 percent of its revenue.

Carey pointed out that the strength of Godkin's original low-budget formula was that no advertiser could dangerously jeopardize the magazine's future by precipitous withdrawal of promised ads. James Storrow liked to brag that Bell Telephone had canceled its advertisements after a *Nation* article lambasting the telephone company. One could understand why *The Nation*, rather than a more advertising-affluent publication, was one of the first magazines to blow the whistle on the relationship between tobacco and cancer, when you knew that in the world of glossy magazines, for years cigarette manufacturers in effect paid for the full-color front covers by taking out repeated ads on the back cover.*

So I still can't figure out why I didn't follow my own advice and instincts when, in the spring of 1979, our new and aggressive saleswoman, Susan Heitler, asked if I would do her a favor. She had scheduled a luncheon with Erwin Glickes, then editorial director of Basic Books, a subdivision of Harper & Row, and he had asked if I would join them. The lunch was at the Minetta Tavern, only a couple of blocks away. "The whole thing won't take more than an hour and a half," she told me. Erwin was an old friend from the days when I wrote about publishing for *The New York Times Book Review*, and so instead of saying no, I said (to myself), Why not?

The day before our luncheon I found out why not, but I get ahead of myself. I did her the favor. It did take only an hour and a half. And to this day I don't know whether had I skipped the lunch we might have avoided the lawsuit that came in its aftermath, the appeals all the way to the Supreme Court (whose opinion reshaped the law of the land for the worse), and the hundreds of thousands of dollars of "free

---

*The cost of the added colors would be included in the price of the ads, since back and front are printed on the same press at the same time.

publicity" that came with it. It also caused a series of ancillary conflicts for *The Nation* which collectively illustrate the vulnerability of small publications.

I felt awkward about taking my leave of Erwin and Susan before the coffee was served, but I had to get back to the office to see a friend who had called the day before. My friend had asked me if I was interested in getting an advance look at the galleys of former President Gerald Ford's forthcoming memoirs, to be published by Harper & Row. (Coincidences happen!) Not really, I had said, why do you ask? Because the publisher is keeping them top secret until pub date, he said, so they must have some news value. Then absolutely, I had said. And I arranged to get a twenty-four-hour look. He would drop the manuscript off after lunch the next day; I promised to read it overnight, make no copies, and return it.

I quickly discovered that Ford's memoirs were difficult to read overnight because for the most part they put you to sleep. But there was one part of one chapter, where Ford wrote about his decision to pardon Richard Nixon, that seemed to me not only newsworthy but important because on its surface it appeared deceptive.

Ford described an episode on August 11, 1974, a week before Richard Nixon resigned, when General Haig took Vice President Ford for a walk in the Rose Garden and told him that the "smoking gun" tapes had been found which established Nixon's complicity in the Watergate cover-up, and that they had to get Nixon, who was going bonkers, out of the White House. There were, Haig explained, five ways to do that. The first four were impractical, but the fifth was possible: if Ford promised subsequently to extend a presidential pardon to him, Haig thought that perhaps the President could be persuaded to resign. Ford then asked Haig if it was possible to pardon an individual before he had been indicted. Haig said yes, adding that White House counsel had checked this detail out. The way Ford told it, the conversation was all very innocent.

Ford then went home, said nothing to his wife, Betty, and went to bed. But the next morning when he mentioned this conversation to his press aide, Bob Hartmann, Hartmann asked him what his response had been to Haig. Ford said he had said nothing. Hartmann said, "Silence implies assent." Then, when Ford consulted another aide, Jack Marsh, he also asked, "And what did you say?" And when Ford said he had said nothing, Marsh looked alarmed and said in that context mention of a pardon was a "time bomb. "

According to Ford, he then telephoned General Haig and read him the following statement over the phone: "I want you to understand that I have no intention of recommending what the President should do about resigning or not resigning and that nothing we talked about yesterday afternoon should be given any consideration in whatever decision the President may wish to make."

Well, I read this section of Ford's memoir and made a phone call of my own to my brother-in-law the lawyer. It seemed to me that not only did we have a chance to make news, but by scooping Ford with his own version of what happened, strip him of his gloss of innocence. We had a chance at publishing an important story about a very significant deal that smelled very much like a fix, possibly even an obstruction of justice. The carefully prepared statement that Vice President Ford read over the phone seemed to me to have the purpose of making a formal record of deniability rather than clarifying a conversation.

My brother-in-law the lawyer reminded me that under the doctrine of Fair Use of copyrighted material, we could quote only a minimal number of words from the book. This was fine by me, because nobody, least of all me, was interested in appropriating Ford's literary style. (It was Trevor Armbrister, his ghostwriter's style, anyway.)

I quickly wrote an article of around 2,256 words, fewer than 500 of which were quoted words from the 110,000-word-long book, most of those from documents that I believed were in the public domain, such as the note Ford said he read to Haig. And in truth I quoted the other words only because I didn't want to be accused of distorting Ford's own account for partisan purposes. I left out the gossip, such as the fact that Betty got jealous whenever Gerry kissed a starlet as part of his ceremonial duties, but I did report on some news tidbits—such as that he had considered appointing Edward Bennett Williams head of the CIA and that it was Nixon himself who gave him the idea of naming Rockefeller as Veep. I also self-indulgently included a direct quotation from a passage about how he learned at the Yale Law School from Myres MacDougall that sometimes it "was important to put social policy considerations ahead of the law." I considered it newsworthy that the President of the United States misunderstood what he had been taught at Yale.

We had a researcher call Harper & Row to see if they had any serialization plans for the book and ask some routine questions (what was the print order?), and she was told that *Time* and *The Reader's Digest* were each running a portion. A print order of about 50,000 was expected. We put these facts in my article and sent it to our lawyer, who read it and said that he thought we were within the Fair Use limit set by the copyright law, asked whether I thought they might sue, and I said no, I don't think they'll sue. Good Old Erwin, I pointed out, is a friend of mine.

Also, I had a belief that the public, rather than public figures, should own the news about public figures; that while it was proper for President Ford to copyright and make a profit from his memoirs, the inflated price—Ford and Betty got $1 million for their book contracts—came from the news value in the memoirs, which is not copyrightable; that the President, Henry Kissinger, or anyone else who wrote books about their public service had no inherent right to make millions of dollars from their use of secret public papers having to do with public business and accumulated while on the public payroll and withheld from the rest of us for profit. I or any other citizen should have equal access to public documents created on President Ford's watch. So we published the article.

Soon I received a call from Herbert Mitgang of *The New York Times*, asking if I had a comment on the telegram that Harper & Row had sent to us requesting that we cease and desist "excerpting" the Ford memoirs. This of course was not what we had done. And we had received no such telegram. So I couldn't comment except to say what I have already said.

When we finally did receive the telegram, it threatened a lawsuit. And some months later, Harper & Row sued. They asked for $12,500, which they said was the amount of money *Time* didn't pay them for its planned excerpt. In later discovery proceedings, we found out that under the terms of the contract, Ford had agreed not to talk about any of the news in his book prior to publication. If any news came out, the contract was to be renegotiated. We also discovered that after our article appeared, *Time* offered to publish a week early, but after a quick conference Harper & Row said no, and *Time* then canceled its publication plans. Harper & Row's chief executive officer, Brooks Thomas, said they wanted to make a test case of this under the new copyright law. In a debate with him before PEN's Freedom to Write Committee, I said it might be a test case to *them*, but to us it felt like harassment. (PEN voted unanimously to support *The Nation*.)

I spent the next few weeks attempting to arrange for legal representation. After three meetings and a lot of paperwork, and perhaps aided by the fact that our editorial board included Aryeh Neier, the ACLU agreed to take us on, and my old law-school classmate Floyd Abrams, now perhaps the leading First Amendment lawyer in the country, also agreed to represent us on a pro bono basis. We considered this poetic justice, because it was indeed a test case. Where did the First Amendment right to report the news stop and the protection of literary property start?

We assumed that Harper & Row had picked us rather than *The Washington Post* or *The New York Times*, both of which had quoted as much or more than we had from forthcoming newsworthy books by former administration officials, because it thought our defense would be less formidable. But before the case was over, PEN, the writers' organization, and any number of newspapers and periodicals, not least *The New York Times* and *The New York Review of Books* had filed amicus briefs on our behalf, arguing that in a case like this, First Amendment considerations should prevail. On the other side, the Association of American Publishers' Freedom to Read Committee (then chaired by the chairman of Harper & Row) seemed to feel that justice lay with Harper & Row. The Authors Guild, on whose board I sat, declined on advice of its counsel, Irwin Karp, to take a position. (I recused myself from the discussion.) Since one of the guild's primary missions is to protect the writer's property rights, this was understandable; but since its deeper mission is to protect the writer's freedom to write, I found this disappointing. All of this only begins to hint at the cascade of conflicts-of-interest that followed. They show what can happen to business-as-usual at a small magazine when it goes to court.

Conflict #1: During this period a dispute arose between the ACLU and other groups on how to oppose proposed legislation that made it a crime, among other things, to publish the names of intelligence agents even if they were already on the public record—the so-called names of agent bill. More radical civil libertarians argued (and we agreed with them) that the legislation was unconstitutional and should be opposed per se. The ACLU took the position that since two versions of the bill were before Congress and one was bound to pass, it had an obligation to work for the less draconian measure. This was precisely the sort of issue on which our readers look to us for comment and guidance. With perhaps hundreds of thousands of dollars of free legal work at stake, one might think that if ever there was an occasion for sinning by omission, this was it. But as it happened, I wrote and we published our editorial explaining our opposition to both versions of the bill; this was bitterly resented by the ACLU, which also resented an article we ran by a dissident board member who argued that the ACLU should never deal with non-union suppliers. Luckily for us, the ACLU really does believe in free speech, and it not only continued to provide legal support for the magazine throughout the litigation but also took a second *Nation* case. (We were sued for libel by Othal Brand, the litigious sheriff in McAllen, Texas, whom we had described as discriminating against Chicanos in his administration of the voter registration laws, because he did discriminate against Chicanos in his administration of the voter registration laws. With the ACLU's help, we won a summary judgment on the ground that Brand's suit was barred by the free press clauses in the Texas and U.S. constitutions.)

Depositions, discovery, and preparing materials for interrogations in the Harper & Row case took hundreds of hours. They wanted to prove that we had printed the Ford story as part of a nefarious plot to increase circulation. I was deposed three times by a battery of high-priced attorneys, which caused our pro bono attorney to estimate that before the case was over, Harper & Row might spend as much as $250,000 to collect their $12,500. How would that measure against the cost in lost time and investigative articles and other work not undertaken?

Conflict #2: We prepared for trial, and the case was assigned to Judge Richard Owen, a Nixon appointee with a reputation as a strict protectionist. After many postponements the case went to trial, and we introduced four volunteer expert witnesses to testify on the issue of what news is. Our contention was that the only quotations from Ford's book that we had used were newsworthy, news wasn't copyrightable, and they were well within the fair use permitted by the law. The Pulitzer Prize–winning writer David Halberstam, the presidential biographer

Richard Reeves, the book publisher Richard Seaver, and Ed Murrow's old producer Fred Friendly, by then teaching ethics at Columbia University's Graduate School of Journalism, all testified that what *The Nation* had published was newsworthy. The other side put on no one to refute them.

Three out of our four witnesses were having books published that year. As it happens, *The Nation* runs a notoriously independent book review department, frequently ignoring or panning the books of our shareholders, staff, and contributors, but I put to you the hypothetical predicament of an editor faced with the question of whether to publish a negative review of a book by a writer whom we are trying to persuade to come to court, at great personal inconvenience and for no fee, testify on our behalf.

Conflict #3: The trial was at one point, and for various reasons, recessed, and during the recess *The Nation* happened to sponsor its Town Hall meeting featuring Susan Sontag's attack on us. As a courtesy we asked Ms. Sontag's permission to reprint her remarks, which she gave. Her enthusiasm was partly prompted by the fact that an alternative-press paper, the *Soho Weekly News*, believing (correctly, I believe) that her remarks were in the public domain, had printed her speech without her permission, and incensed, she sued them for copyright infringement. Her *Soho Weekly* case and ours were distinguishable on any one of a number of grounds, and *The Nation*'s position was that as a matter of policy and law, and of common sense and public relations, she should not have sued. And whom was the Sontag case assigned to? Judge Owen. Floyd Abrams made it clear that he was the last lawyer in the country who would tell a client not to print something, but in this situation he wanted to see what we wrote about Sontag before it was published. "And you're not, I hope, going to say anything about the court?" Censorship? No. But we got the message.

Conflict #4: Remember that when one of Calvin Trillin's stipulations for writing a humor column for *The Nation* was that he would be allowed to make fun of the editor, I had said, sure, we all have our civil liberties priorities.

I did not expect, however, in the midst of court proceedings before a hostile and obviously humor-impaired judge, against lawyers ready to wrench the slightest phrase from our promotional mailings wildly out of context, that Trillin would proceed to write not one but two columns referring to "sticky fingers" Navasky.

Shortly after the proceedings commenced, another publishing insider leaked to us a copy of Richard Nixon's forthcoming book, *The Real War*, which fortunately or otherwise, depending on your perspective, contained no news whatsoever. I decided to give it to Trillin to "preview." He called it "Navasky's second offense," and wrote that I was a "recidivist" who remained "at large."

> Naturally, I have no desire to see Navasky put away for eight-to-twenty simply because he is a two-time loser who seems to defy every effort at rehabilitation . . . If the men in blue ever did put the collar on Navasky, I suppose parsimony would be his first line of defense: considering what he is accustomed to paying writers, he could claim, stealing practically any manuscript would be no more than petty theft. At Navasky's rates, according to my calculations, Nixon's book is worth $137.50.

Conflict #5: In May the final briefs were filed, but Judge Owen had yet to render his verdict. In the meantime, however, he had rendered his verdict in another, more important case, which was Alger Hiss's petition for a writ of *coram nobis* to set aside the original verdict in his case. Hiss argued that his conviction should be overturned because new evidence, secured under the Freedom of Information Act, showed that the government had interfered with his defense in a way that deprived him of a fair trial.

After four years of mulling over Hiss's claim, Judge Owen said no, he found it unwarranted. Virtually no press attention was given to Judge Owen's highly technical opinion—a paragraph or two in the *Times*, and not much anywhere else.

A few weeks later William A. Reuben, who had been writing about and studying the Hiss case for thirty-five years, told *The Nation* that he could document more than one hundred factual errors in Judge Owen's opinion. Not arguments, but factual errors. To publish such a study would require a considerable amount of space, and the probability was that if *The Nation* didn't do it, no magazine would. If the article was what it was billed to be and we published it, it might influence

Hiss's appeal against Judge Owen's ruling and perhaps make history. Our other thought was that the judgment against us in the Harper & Row case could cause real harm to *The Nation* at the very time when Ham Fish was trying to raise capital to offset the annual deficit.

What would you do? The Nation Institute published Reuben's analysis as a monograph, which unfortunately didn't come off the press until a few days after Hiss's appeal had been turned down.

Conflict #6: Judge Owen decided against us, we appealed, and our case was heard before a court of appeals headed by Judge Irving Kaufman. Judge Kaufman had presided in 1951 over the trial of Julius and Ethel Rosenberg for conspiring to commit espionage on behalf of the Soviet Union. They were convicted, and after blaming them for the death of 50,000 Americans in Korea, he sentenced them to death by electrocution.

Documents obtained under the FOIA by Marshall Perlin, the attorney for the Rosenberg children, indicate that for the next thirty years Judge Kaufman continued to be obsessed by the Rosenberg case, and he was extremely sensitive to criticism about his performance in it. Every time criticism appeared in print he was in touch either with the editor to publish a rebuttal or with the FBI to discredit the criticizer.

You already know about *The Nation/New Republic* Town Hall debate on the question "Were the Rosenbergs framed?" And you already know that in *The Nation*'s corner were Walter and Miriam Schneir arguing the affirmative. What you don't know is that the widely advertised debate occurred when our appeal was before the Second Circuit. To make matters worse, I was committed to writing and publishing a review of these books that would come out before the Town Hall event, which was after Judge Kaufman heard oral argument in our case but before he rendered his decision.

If Judge Kaufman happened to see newspaper accounts of the Town Hall debate, he would have discovered that the only matter on which all four debaters and both magazines agreed was that his death sentence was an act of Cold War hysteria and that Kaufman's added opinion blaming the Rosenbergs for the death of 50,000 Americans in Korea would go down in history in the annals of hysterical infamy.

To his credit, Judge Kaufman ruled in *The Nation*'s favor in a decision that was both a ringing affirmation of the First Amendment and a statement that *The Nation* had operated within the law anyway, so any clash between copyright law and the First Amendment need not be reached.

Harper & Row appealed to the Supreme Court, which then ruled against us, insisting that *The Nation* had infringed Ford's copyright. So there you have it. A Nixon appointee ruled against us, F.D.R.'s appointee Kaufman ruled for us, and Reagan's appointee Sandra Day O'Connor wrote the final 6–3 opinion.

And in the end Floyd Abrams's firm, Cahill Gordon, which had compiled expenses in the six figures, after billing us forgave the debt.

We lost, in what I, doing my best to be objective, thought was a bad decision. Writing for the Court, O'Connor incorrectly assumed that because *The Nation* "attempted no independent commentary, research or criticism"—because my article was composed entirely "of quotes, paraphrases and facts drawn exclusively from the manuscript"—the news we hoped to make was the same news President Ford had hoped to make with his book. Hence her observation: "Like its competitor newsweekly, it [*The Nation*] was free to bid for the right of abstracting excerpts." In fact, *Time* is a newsweekly and we are no competitor of it but a journal of opinion, and as journalism professors incessantly point out to their first-year students, the same facts can be mobilized—with or without editorializing—to make vastly different points. From Harper & Row's point of view, the nub of the news contained in Ford's book was his account of his innocent decision to pardon Richard M. Nixon. From our point of view, it was the opposite, and by removing his interpretation but letting the facts and his statements speak for themselves, we had in effect made a serious accusation.

And why would we, a liberal-left magazine, want to *pay* for a Republican President's self-serving account which we regarded as deceptive? And why would any politician in the business of resuscitating his reputation (Ford was being prominently mentioned as a possible Republican nominee for President when his book came out) want to respond to a bid from a magazine out to question the truth of his study?

It seemed to me, as I noted in a *Times* Op Ed article I wrote at the time, that what made the case troubling for the country, as distinguished from *The Nation*, was that

> The Court's limited understanding of the nature of news blinded
> it to the fact that it made its own news judgment, or rather mis-

judgment. It has confused Mr. Ford's news-of-his-innocence with *The Nation's* news-of-his-guilt—both based on his own words and information. Justice O'Connor writes that "courts should be chary of deciding what is and what is not news," yet she handed down a decision that did just that. It also permits public officials to prevent unpleasant news about them from being released until it suits their financial and political needs.

Worst of all, the Court said that while its ruling is not intended to bar the press from independently reporting the news in important books before publication day, [under the court's ruling] the question of how many words is permissible (500 words used to be the rule of thumb) will be decided on a case by case basis. That means that unless Congress takes remedial action, the courts will be meddling in the news business for the foreseeable future.

I saw this whole thing as a textbook case proving my old mentor Fred Rodell right: he believed to his dying day that the law was not "a brooding omnipresence in the sky" (Harvard) but "what the judge had for breakfast" (Yale), i.e., that judges made more law than they found.

While the case was in the courts, Harper & Row's CEO, Brooks Thomas, who insisted that Harper & Row (at great expense) bring the case, told the press they were doing it as a matter of principle, that he didn't expect more than "a few folding chairs and paper clips." In the event, they won something like $12,500, half of which they took out in advertising in *The Nation*. Like Villard after the postmaster seized *The Nation* in 1919, we believed that we got hundreds of thousands of dollars of free publicity, but as the folksinger Lee Hayes said about being blacklisted, If it weren't for the honor of the thing I'd just as soon it never happened.

The moral for me was that Ross and Shawn were right after all: the editor had best not make ad calls. He's got enough to do without spending lunchtime with the space rep and potential advertisers. This is especially the case for the editor of a journal of opinion, for which advertising is less important than it is for virtually any other sort of magazine. And this is the case even though the struggle for space is always and everywhere a constant source of tension between the ad department and editorial. It becomes a problem only on those rare occasions when the ad person has actually sold a full-page ad for a particular issue and the editor has additional timely copy. The choices are to add extra pages, which costs money; condense the story, but let's say you've already done that; bump a page until next week, but let's say it's a special issue, geared to a specific event like an upcoming election. At *The Nation* our natural inclination would be to bump the ad.

The difference between a journal of opinion like ours and, say, a mass magazine is that the latter expects to make profits from advertising, whereas a journal of opinion doesn't, mostly because advertisers are not too eager to advertise in a magazine that regularly attacks their products. Was it a coincidence that a small-circulation magazine, with no automobile advertising to speak of, published Ralph Nader's exposé of unsafe cars, while mega-magazines, like the old *Life, Look, The Saturday Evening Post,* and *Collier's*, with vast editorial budgets were silent on the issue?

Before I became a magazine mogul, like most editorial people I regarded advertising with a mixture of bemusement and contempt. Now I'm not so sure. Consider the fallout from two ads that *The Progressive* magazine accepted. One was in 1984 from a group representing trade unionists and it was headed "We're the Tobacco Industry, Too." It pictured three tobacco workers—a black man, a white woman, and a middle-aged white guy—and complained that their good union jobs were threatened by "well-meaning people who haven't stopped to consider how their actions might affect others." And a few months later there was an ad from Feminists for Life, a group that opposes abortion. Knoll's position, with which I sympathized, was that "people who subscribe to *The Progressive* are mature, responsible, intelligent human beings who can be exposed to points of view we find wrong or downright obnoxious without being led down the primrose path to perdition."

The tobacco workers' ad drew subscription cancellations and a barrage of letters taking political exception, not to the ads themselves, but to their appearance in *The Progressive*: "You have prostituted your magazine, compromised your integrity, and shaken the faith of your readers." The Feminists for Life ad also drew more than its share of invective, but in addition, June Makela, executive director of a New York–based advocacy group, the Funding Exchange, wrote, saying that her organization "of course" had decided not to renew their subscription but in addition would cut *The Progressive* from their list of grantees. They urged other progressive foundations to do likewise. Knoll thought the Funding Exchange was guilty of "intellectual intolerance" and "censorship." "We will do our best to get along without your subscription and without your financial help, because [although] we prize both of them, they don't mean nearly as much to us as our integrity and our commitment to freedom of thought." First Amendment absolutists are my favorite kind of absolutist, but even some First Amendment absolutists make an exception when it comes to tobacco.

Here, a confession of sorts is in order. Along with Marvin Kitman and the artist-designer Paul Davis, I was one of three founding and only members of an investment syndicate that called itself the Cosa Nostra Syndicate, a.k.a. the Yellow Hand Society. We invented this in 1964, shortly after the Surgeon General's report linking cigarette smoking to cancer came out. Our investment theory was that people want to destroy rather than improve themselves, and since *Monocle* wasn't around anymore to publish our theory, we decided to put our money where our theory was, which we did by purchasing one share of R. J. Reynolds tobacco stock for $27. Some months later, when the president of R. J. Reynolds announced that the company was donating $300,000 to something called the Tobacco Institute of America, which would investigate the relationship of cigarette smoking to cancer, our president, Paul Davis, fired off an outraged letter: "If we wanted to fight cancer, we would have given our money to the American Cancer Society. Our goal is to make money off of people's propensity to destroy themselves." Besides, Davis pointed out, "the Surgeon General has already answered the question, and unless our company's money is going toward buying subsidiary rights to the S.G.'s report, this seems like a waste of shareholder money."

Believe it or not, the president responded to the Cosa Nostra Syndicate with a letter patiently explaining that because the Tobacco Institute of America was independent of the Surgeon General, its research results might well contradict the Surgeon General's findings.

Over the years our share of stock doubled or tripled in value, but unfortunately, when we tried to unload it, there were new stock exchange rules in place prohibiting the sale of stock by unregistered syndicates. (The Cosa Nostra Syndicate's assets were limited to its single share, so we had no money left over for registration.) It wasn't until the late 1990s, when Reynolds, going through one of its periodic consolidations, had to buy out all its fugitive shareholders that we were able to sell our share. The price: $727, an ill-gotten gain of more than 2,500 percent.

Anyway, in the 1960s and 1970s I was insensitive enough to the ethical issue about accepting automobile or tobacco ads that when in 1975 MORE, the counter-establishment magazine of press criticism founded by my friends Richard Pollak and J. Anthony Lukas, ran a full-page Marlboro ad in its December issue, I thought hurray for MORE, at last it's getting some of the advertising it deserves. I had no illusions about the dangers of tobacco, but I was sure that between the incorruptible editors of MORE and its highly sophisticated and well-informed readers, they could handle it.

Then in February 1976 I read an article in the *Washington Monthly* by James Fallows that made me think again. By taking tobacco advertising, Fallows argued, MORE had "demeaned itself as certainly as if it had sold that space to a gang rape club or a Mafia recruiter." By Fallows's lights, since magazines are not public utilities (or doctors, one might add), they have no obligation to take advertisers at random. As a matter of fact, he wrote, "when a publisher decides to present a product to his readers, he puts his name behind that product, at least to the extent of saying that it is worthy of readers' consideration." He suggested that to sell tobacco advertising was to have sold out, and he recommended that employees at places like *The New York Times* and *The Washington Post*, which routinely took such ads, should threaten to quit if they did not cease and desist.

Charles Peters, proprietor of the *Washington Monthly*, made it clear at a 1985 conference we co-sponsored with the University of Southern California on the role of the journal of opinion that the one kind of advertising his *Washington Monthly* would never take was cigarette advertising. "We feel that we know cigarettes are harmful, at least to a good many of the people who smoke them. We especially dislike the kind of cigarette advertising that makes smoking seem glamorous," said Peters, who started smoking when he was eighteen and for twenty-five years went through three packs a day.

But Michael Kinsley, a Peters protegé, didn't agree: "The correct position for a magazine that can get cigarette advertising is if you're a rich magazine and you can afford the luxury of refusing cigarette advertising, that's great, but that if you need the ad revenue and can get it, you ought to take it and not be influenced by it."

And even Peters conceded that he made an exception when dealing with political ideas. "If the Tobacco Institute came with an ad telling Congress what to do, I think I would have to run that—with great pain I think my obligation is not to deny somebody free speech in the realm of ideas. When I think I have a perfect right to censor them is when they're proposing a product that's going to kill people."

At *The Nation* there were no complaints about cigarette advertisements, because there were none. We did, however, receive a good share of protests over an ad for Blackglama mink coats featuring Lillian Hellman, and we received skeptical mail asking about the propriety of a magazine on the left accepting an ad from the National Right to Work Committee. And so when we ran a devastating assault by Bob Sherrill on *The New York Times* for "renting its cranium" (his way of characterizing Mobil Oil's weekly ads on the *Times* Op Ed page), I decided it was time to take action. Much as I had mocked *Saturday Review*'s advertising-acceptability criteria (when they turned down a *Monocle* ad for a fallout shelter parody because "We don't take ads for fallout shelters"), in close consultation with Aryeh Neier, we found ourselves devising some of our own.

Here's what we wrote:

Although the relationship of the First Amendment to commercial advertising is complex, we start with a strong presumption against banning advertisers because we disapprove of, or even abhor, their political or social views. But we reserve (and exercise) the right to attack them in our editorial columns.

We accept [advertising] not to further the views of *The Nation* but to help pay the costs of publishing. We start, therefore, with the presumption that we will accept advertising even if the views expressed are repugnant to those of the editors. The only limits are those that grow out of our interest in assuring that the advertising does not impede our use of the editorial columns in *The Nation* to say what we want. Examples of advertising we might reject are those where the typography and layout simulate our editorial format and, thereby, deceive readers; or advertisements that are lurid and typographically ugly or that distort the appearance of *The Nation* by their size, frequency or placement; or that are patently fraudulent, illegal, or libelous in their claims and language. Blatantly misleading ads or ads purveying harmful products will fall into a gray area of discretion, but as a general principle we assume our readers will have sufficient knowledge to judge for themselves the merits of commonly known products (such as cigarettes).

In imposing such limits, we will refrain from making judgments based on our opinions of the particular views expressed in an advertisement. If the purpose of the advertisement is to sell a product or service rather than to express a view, we will allow ourselves greater rein in making judgments about suitability. This reflects our view that commerce is less sacrosanct than political speech.

When we open our pages to political advertising that may be repugnant to the editors, we are furthering our editorial commitment to freedom of speech. Again, our obligation to accept anything in our pages does not derive from principles which must be applied to a public forum. Nor does it rise to the level of obligation that should be felt by a newspaper of general circulation or a television station which either by itself, or with a few others like it, enjoys a monopoly on communication with the general public in a particular community. Our obligation is of a lesser, but still important order: to use space in which we refrain from expressing editorial policy in a way that reflects our editorial commitment to diversity in expression of opinion.

In advance of publication I sent it around for comment. Norman Cousins, who had wrestled with these matters for the old *Saturday Review*, wrote: "*The Nation*'s editorial on its advertising policy represents to my mind the best articulated statement on the matter it has been my good fortune to read in forty years of magazine experience. It is soundly conceived and beautifully stated." On the other hand, William Bernbach, one of the smartest, most creative and admired ad men of his day, had, shall we say, reservations:

I don't quite understand why you would reject ads that are lurid or typographically ugly that can only do aesthetic damage and accept ads that are blatantly misleading or purvey harmful products and are therefore capable of doing physical damage. This, it seems to me, is a lovely sanctimonious example of the self-deluding rationalization process the mind uses to make the stay-alive instinct respectable. Rarely have I seen this process in purer form than in your words. We assume that our readers will have sufficient knowledge to judge for themselves the merits of commonly known products such as cigarettes. For God's sake tell it as it is. If we don't have advertising we will die. If we die we can't get our thoughts to our audience. We will take advertising that keeps us alive. We will not take advertising that can destroy us.

Over the years, this policy has resulted in our accepting ads from an organization called FLAME (an acronym for Facts and Logic About the Middle East), which any number of our readers deemed to be racist in their assumptions and rhetoric about "Arab terrorists"; Fox News, which bills itself as "fair and balanced," yet is anything but; the government campaign "for a drug-free America," which our magazine has pointed out time and again is misguided, ineffective, inhumane, and costly (which led one irate reader to ask, "What next? A Vatican-sponsored appeal to teenagers to 'just say no' to sex?"); Holocaust deniers (which we subsequently canceled); and any number of other abhorrent, degraded, and socially myopic individuals and institutions. (One wag wrote: "I think you're on to something. Why not assist nutty organizations in squandering their money? By accepting their ad dollars *The Nation* can do its small part to bankrupt neo-Nazis, white supremacists, the NRA, SDI fans, anti-choicers, the possibilities seem endless. I congratulate you on your devilishly subversive ad policy.")

Other magazines run advertisements for the revenue they bring in. At *The Nation* it began to seem as if we were running ads to vindicate the First Amendment principle of the thing (even though the First Amendment didn't apply), despite the hundreds of canceled subscriptions they cost us and hours (it felt like weeks) responding to irate calls, letters (including a few demanding that I resign), and e-mails, and occasionally even visiting delegations. And don't ask about the time our classified manager took some ads for "romance" tours. But let me tell you something about e-mail. Once in response to a particularly offensive FLAME ad, I was inundated with protesting e-mail. It was only when I noticed that many of them used identical language that I began to understand the potential (and limitations) of e-mail as an instrument of protest. I would still defend our advertising philosophy and guidelines, but despite the occasional postcard from First Amendment absolutist Nat Hentoff cheering us on for sticking to principle, life would be a lot easier if some freelance philosopher (maybe the pragmatist Richard Rorty, who always demonstrates the dangers of enunciating grand principles) would definitively prove that our policy is misconceived. That way we could, like some of our high-principled peers, at last, once again turn down advertising with a clear conscience.

Before I arrived at *The Nation*, I made one request. I had heard that a young Smith College scholar named Allen Weinstein had completed his study of the Alger Hiss case and concluded that Hiss was indeed guilty of perjury. The title of his forthcoming book was *Perjury*. I asked Elizabeth Pochoda, *The Nation*'s literary editor, to arrange for me to receive advance galleys of *Perjury*, because I was interested in the book for a number of reasons. The Hiss case had always seemed to me the quintessential Cold War episode. Technically the issue was whether the former high-ranking State Department official Alger Hiss was lying in 1948, when he denied Whittaker Chambers's charge that he was a member of the Communist Party and a spy; but to me the Hiss case symbolically had come to stand for more than the innocence or guilt of one man. As Chambers himself had written in his best-selling 1952 memoir, *Witness*, "The case stands for the whole [Communist] penetration of government." Senator Joseph McCarthy, Richard Nixon, and others had seized on the Hiss case to tarnish the entire New Deal, and Nixon had used it to jump-start his career.

I was then still in the midst of writing my book on the Hollywood blacklist, concerned with issues of the same sort. As I saw it, the Hiss case, along with the trial in 1949 of leaders of the Communist Party for "conspiring to teach and advocate the overthrow of the government by force and violence," and the case against the Rosenbergs in 1951 had done much to create the context of what I was writing about.

Also, the Hiss case was especially significant for *The Nation*. Every subscription list, the German theorist Jürgen Habermas has written, is a political organization. And a magazine, especially a journal of opinion, in times of political trouble can preform a rallying function and let people know they are not alone. If I considered one of the great strengths of the Kirchwey-McWilliams *Nation* that it resisted and fought against many of the myths of the domestic Cold War, others would say, and have said, that one of its weaknesses—sins—was that it didn't understand the evils of Stalinism. We can have that argument later; but if you believed, as I did, that *The Nation* had been essentially right in insisting that there was no internal "red menace" that justified the curtailing of civil liberties in the United States, then a new book that settled the Hiss case once and for all—either way—was an event of particular significance. This was also true, by the way, for ADA liberals like Arthur Schlesinger, Jr., Jimmy Wechsler, and Joseph Rauh—all vocal critics of McCarthy and McCarthyism, even as they decried the evils of the Soviet Union—who in varying degrees accepted the notion that American Communism represented a clear and present danger to the republic. Also, by the late 1950s *The Nation* as much as any other magazine in the country was perceived as a Hiss defender, although it was not quite the ideological monolith many of its critics claimed it to be. The democratic socialist and critic Irving Howe had written in his 1952 *Nation* review of Chambers's *Witness*, "That Whittaker Chambers told the truth and Alger Hiss did not seems to me highly probable.")

In early 1957 Carey McWilliams had asked Fred Cook, the old *World Telegram* reporter and four-time winner of the Newspaper Guild Award for investigative journalism to take a look at the Hiss case. Impressed by the documents Chambers had produced, Cook at first told McWilliams, "I wouldn't touch it with a ten-foot pole," and added, "I think Hiss is guilty as hell." McWilliams prevailed upon him to look at the record, promising to print what he wrote, and as Cook reports in his memoir, *Maverick*, "I was shocked at what I saw." He concluded that the FBI had forged the typewriter that had served as a silent witness confirming Chambers's testimony against Hiss. (An FBI expert testified that copies of the State Department documents Chambers claimed to have received from Hiss had been typed on that typewriter.) In late 1957 *The Nation* devoted an entire issue to the case, later published in a book, *The Unfinished Story of Alger Hiss,* by Fred Cook.

Unlike general interest magazines, Sunday supplements, or daily papers, the journal of opinion does not believe in the business of variety for variety's sake, or what my Swarthmore philosophy professor Monroe Beardsley dismissed as "the principle of elegant variation." When called for, *The Nation* not merely gave its writers ample space to make their case but in true crusader fashion never invoked the but-we-already-did-that excuse for nonpublication of follow-up pieces; to the contrary, follow-up was regarded as a virtue, the weekly venue being what gives the journal of opinion its comparative advantage. Our coverage of Allen Weinstein's book on Hiss was a case in point.

Weinstein had a semi-history with *The Nation.* When he started research on his book, he received a grant from the Rabinowitz Foundation, on whose board Carey McWilliams sat, and McWilliams had written in *The Nation* approvingly of an FOIA lawsuit in which Weinstein was a co-plaintiff.

While I assumed that the establishment media would pay attention to a book by a credentialed scholar that purported definitively to establish Alger Hiss's guilt, I believed it was part of *The Nation*'s mission to cover the matter in special depth. (And I knew that *National Review* would do the same.) Because of their complexity, the issues raised in the Hiss-Chambers affair didn't easily lend themselves to TV talk shows or panel discussions; they needed to be considered in forums where claims of evidence might be studied, modified, rejected, or accepted. The journal of critical opinion was the ideal venue, it seemed to me, for this undertaking.

My own view on the Hiss case (in contradistinction to my view on the Rosenbergs, where I was an agnostic) was more of an impression than a view. I was not persuaded by Fred Cook's argument, because it required me to believe that the FBI would fabricate a typewriter (probably with the knowledge of members of the administration and the Congress) and I was not that much of a conspiracy theorist. My impression that Hiss was not guilty came primarily from a combination of my having known Hiss slightly ever since he graduated from prison ("Forty-four months in the federal penitentiary," he used to say, "was a good corrective to three years at Harvard Law School") and my believing that Hiss's accuser was not to be trusted. Books like Matthew Josephson's *Infidel in the Temple: A Memoir of the Nineteen-Thirties* had convinced me that Chambers lacked the capacity to distinguish fantasy from reality. In 1933 Chambers had assured Josephson: "There'll be barricades by the end of the week in Union Square." There weren't and still aren't. Nevertheless, I also believed that when Hiss told HUAC that he had never known anyone "by the name of Whittaker Chambers," and when he later inspected Chambers's teeth before he would identify him as a man he had known under the pseudonym of "George Crosley," he was playing some sort of snobbish game, confident that this ne'er-do-well "deadbeat," as he later put it, could never bring him down with his false charges. He was, after all, one of Justice Felix Frankfurter's "hot dogs," who had clerked for the greatest of them all, Justice Oliver Wendell Holmes, Jr.

When the Weinstein galleys arrived, I plunged right in, and I must say I found the book impressive. First, there was the narrative arc of his own tale—the truth-seeking scholar who started out like many left-liberal academics coming of age during the Cold War believing in Hiss's innocence.

Victor Rabinowitz, son of the man after whom the Rabinowitz Foundation was named, had represented Hiss in his petition to have his conviction reversed, which Hiss lost; and in his Freedom of Information Act suit to get tens of thousands of documents relating to the case released, which he won—at least partially (an estimated 45,000 out of who knows how many more were released, as were the famous cans of 35-millimeter film which Nixon had waved on December 14, 1948, to the world as he called them evidence of "the most serious of treasonable activities in the history of America"). But Weinstein had a half-dozen new sources who, it seemed to me, if he had quoted them accurately and in context, bolstered Chambers's story and by extension perhaps fatally wounded the case for Hiss's innocence. I was prepared to revise my own view of the case, which also meant—since ultimately, no matter how much participatory democracy he is able to engender, the editor calls the shots—that *The Nation* was also ready to reassess its historic position. That, incidentally, is more or less what happened with Walter and Miriam Schneir, who over the years proposed the thesis that Julius and Ethel Rosenberg had been framed. I have already mentioned that as a result of their subsequent research, after many interviews and after the Venona decrypts had been released and the Schneirs had had the opportunity to check them out, they concluded that Julius at least had been guilty of low-level espionage, after all. Although they didn't retract their findings that there was no single secret of the atomic bomb to steal, that the FBI had improperly used Ethel as a lever to get at Julius, that the death penalty imposed on both of them was grotesquely inappropriate, that the FBI and its agents had improper behind-the-scenes *ex parte* contacts and conversations with Judge Irving Kaufman, which, had they been known at the time, would probably have rendered his verdict and death sentence reversible, they conceded that Julius had been a spy and published same in *The Nation*.

Nevertheless, I read the proofs of Weinstein's book with mounting suspicion and irritation. The proofs included no source notes, making it impossible to tell where much of the critical new data came from. I immediately requested a copy of the notes, but these did not arrive until quite close to the book's publication date—too late for most reviewers to consider them but after plenty of initial favorable publicity had appeared. As *Time* put it in a three-page pre-publication feature: "Weinstein turned up previously undisclosed evidence that inexorably led him to his unqualified verdict: 'the jurors made no mistake in finding Alger Hiss guilty as charged.'"

Also, although the tone and posture of Weinstein's narrative implied unbiased scholarship, his presentation of some of the most critical material seemed slanted in such a way as to make it difficult for readers to draw their own conclusions. Then there was the fact that the army of reviewers who saw this book as "the final nail in Alger Hiss's coffin"— including such eminences as the critic Alfred Kazin ("After this book it is impossible to imagine anything new in this case except an admission by Alger Hiss that he has been lying for forty years"), the conservative columnist George Will ("The myth of Hiss's innocence suffers the death of a thousand cuts, delicate deconstruction by a scholar's scalpel"), and liberals such as Arthur Schlesinger, Jr., Jimmy Wechsler, the scholar-journalist Garry Wills, Merle Miller in *The Washington Post*—were already on record as believing in Hiss's guilt.

Furthermore, I had a personal reason for irritation, which I hoped would not influence my judgment, although it did raise my suspicion. A couple of years earlier I had been shown a copy of Weinstein's letter to the Justice Department requesting access to material on the Rosenberg case, in which he assured the Attorney General that, unlike some other writers (whom he proceeded to name, yours truly among them), he believed the Rosenbergs guilty. But at the time I had written nothing about my views on the Rosenbergs' innocence or guilt, and in fact, I was undecided.

Finally, I was put off by the image Weinstein was presenting in his advance publicity as a truth-seeking scholar who had traveled 125,000 miles, pored over hundreds of thousands of pages of hearings and trial records, gone through interview after interview, archive after archive, and reluctantly been forced by the weight of the evidence to reverse his initial belief in Hiss's innocence. I had read all Weinstein's previous writings on the case: a paper delivered at the American Historical Association in 1969, a book and articles in *The American Scholar* (1971), *Commentary* (1970), *Esquire* (1975), *The New York Times* (1976), and *The New York Review of Books* (1976). And even though he told the editor of the *Daily Hampshire Gazette* (Northampton, Massachusetts) in a front-page interview that in 1974 he had co-authored a high-school textbook "which concluded that Hiss was innocent," on inspection neither the chapter in question nor any of his other writings did more than raise some questions about Chambers's reliability.

I resolved to conduct an elementary source check with some of Weinstein's more spectacular interview finds to see whether they had been quoted accurately and in context, and to examine some of the documents he cited. With the help of *The Nation*'s staff and network, I located and wrote to seven of his key sources and secured copies of documents from various archives. I also contacted Alger Hiss's brother Donald; this was because when Philip Nobile in a pre-publication interview for *Politicks* magazine asked Weinstein, "Would you say you made any discovery that clinches the case against Hiss?" he had zeroed in on Donald Hiss, by then a senior law partner in Covington & Burling, the prestigious Washington law firm, and what he called "the real Woodstock cover-up." It was unclear from the text of *Perjury* just what Donald Hiss had and hadn't told Weinstein.

Six out of the seven sources responded that they had been mis-
quoted, quoted out of context, misrepresented, misconstrued, or misunderstood. Although their denials did not prove that Alger Hiss was
innocent, their collective contribution seemed to me to bear directly
on the issue on which the case against Hiss turned—Chambers's credibility. Of course, it is not uncommon for a subject to disown even the
most accurate verbatim reportage once he sees what he said in cold
print, especially when it is used in a way that might compromise or embarrass a cause or a friend. What was distinctive about the six responses, however, was that they revealed a pattern. In five of the six
cases, the sources freely conceded that part of what they were quoted
as saying was true, but part was not, and the latter turned out to have
been contained in Whittaker Chambers's *Witness*, in his testimony, or
in FBI interviews with Chambers. I had to conclude that in a number
of instances Weinstein had transposed *Witness* from the first to the
third person, and that much more of *Perjury* than one might deduce
from the text or source notes drew on Chambers himself. Here I'll
mention only three of them. First, Ella Winter, who interested me not
least because she had been married to Lincoln Steffens in the 1930s.
Weinstein wrote that Chambers had "previously tried and failed to recruit her for the underground" and that she "corroborated Chambers's
role as an underground courier." But Ms. Winter wrote me that
"Chambers never 'tried to recruit me for underground work' or even for
the CP," and she added that "I never had any idea that Chambers was
an underground courier."

Second, Sam Krieger, who had recruited Chambers into the Party
in the first place. Weinstein described Krieger as "an important Communist organizer during the Gastonia textile strike of 1929" who "fled
to the Soviet Union . . . after being jailed by local authorities." When
Krieger wrote me denying that he had told Weinstein any of these
things, Weinstein called it "a non-denial denial" and said he had corroborated Krieger's identity through third-party sources. Krieger, who
resented being confused with a fugitive from a murder rap, sued Weinstein for libel. He also sued *Perjury*'s publisher and *The New Republic*, where Weinstein had chosen (and *TNR* permitted him) to reply to
my piece, "because a scholar can choose his 'forum' and also, presumably, because under *The Nation*'s ground rules the original *Nation*

writer (that's me) would get the last word in the same issue as the objecting letter, while in *The New Republic* (whose baffled readers were confronted with a detailed reply to an article they hadn't read) Weinstein's response would stand alone.

And third there was Chambers's one-time friend, business associate, and literary agent, Maxim Lieber. Weinstein quotes Lieber as saying about *Witness* that "most of it—as I know the incidents—is true." But when I talked to Lieber, who freely admitted to having been in the Party but denied knowledge of any espionage, he told me and gave me a letter which said, among other things, "I never read *Witness*— Weinstein is quoting me out of context." (He asked if he could borrow the office copy.)

Frequently there was one note cited at the end of a paragraph, listing half a dozen sources, leaving the reader unable to discern which fact or quotation came from which source. If I was right, I had identified a narrative method that gave us Chambers's version of events, sometimes in his own voice, sometimes in Weinstein's voice, and sometimes imputed to other characters in the drama—without ever making clear which was which, leaving the reader with no way of knowing. This, I argued in my review, added up to a psychological structure that lent Chambers a perhaps undeserved credibility—Chambers, it seemed to me, was being used to corroborate Chambers—in ways that were invisible to the reader. And I reproduced the documentation I had assembled.

The argument between Weinstein and *The Nation* migrated into a disagreement reproduced in *The New York Times*, *Newsweek*, on the *Today* show, and elsewhere. And it spilled into *The New Republic*, when *TNR*'s editors agreed to publish his letter disputing my charges in their letters pages. Ultimately, of course, it became an argument between Weinstein and history.

Two other things happened. Weinstein criticized me for not having contacted him before publishing my critique. What kind of an investigative reporter was I not to check with the subject? At the time I didn't see it that way. As I wrote in *The Nation*: "Because I bothered to check out his sources I was somehow obliged unlike other reviewers—to get in touch with him . . . If the book can't survive minimal fact-checking then no amount of *ex parte* communications from the author can save it." Although I still believe I was right, I now can see the arguments for contacting him prior to publication.

Nevertheless, on the *Today* show, on the radio, and everywhere else Weinstein announced that I should have called him, that his tapes and other documents would prove "the recanters" wrong, and he invited "Navasky and Alger Hiss and anyone else they care to bring along" to hear his tapes and inspect his files. So I telephoned him to take him up on his offer. After preliminary negotiations rivaling the Arab-Israeli peace talks, it was agreed that I and two associates (Bob Sherrill and Phil Pochoda, then working with his wife, Elizabeth, on our literary section, who later went on to a distinguished career in academic publishing) would inspect his materials on a Sunday between 10 a.m. and 1 p.m. When we arrived, we were met at the door by the then Mrs. Weinstein, who told us that her husband had sent a telegram the previous evening (which I didn't get until the next day) canceling the meeting. The telegram stated, "ALL MY FILES WILL BE DEPOSITED LATER THIS YEAR AT THE TRUMAN LIBRARY." The relevant files were not deposited that year or, as of this writing, any other year.

The other thing that happened was Krieger's lawsuit. He won a cash settlement (amount undisclosed, *New York* magazine put it in the low five figures), a retraction published in *The New Republic*, in which Weinstein said that his "statements about Sam Krieger were erroneous," and Knopf agreed to insert erratum slips in all extant copies of the book.

Six months after Weinstein's reply in *The New Republic*, I received a note from Donald Hiss. For more than a year he had been legally blind and so was just now catching up on his reading. Weinstein had claimed in his *New Republic* "reply" that he had discussed the search for the typewriter with Donald Hiss. Although Donald realized "full well" that due to the lapse of time it was too late for a letter to the editor on this point, he wanted me to know "categorically and unequivocally" that any such discussion never took place. "I report that his statement to the contrary in the above-mentioned *New Republic* article is a damned lie."

In 1997 an updated *Perjury* was published, ostensibly citing new information from Soviet archives bolstering Weinstein's original case—the so-called Venona documents, decrypted cables said to implicate hundreds of Americans who cooperated with Soviet espionage. In the new edition, he reprinted the disputed material, making no mention of the fact that five of six key sources had contested his claim that they corroborated Chambers's story. He did refer to the sixth, Sam Krieger, and his lawsuit in a "Note on Documentation" as follows: "A lawsuit apparently encouraged by supporters of Alger Hiss against the author, his publisher and *The New Republic* magazine—subsequently settled without trial—made it advisable to maintain the files accumulated through personal research . . ." I spoke with Krieger at the time (to decline his invitation to join his lawsuit and advise him against bringing it). Believe me, he needed no encouragement. This time around, not just Weinstein but a new generation of those we may call counter-revisionists, like their predecessors, cited Weinstein as having once again put "the final nail in the Hiss coffin." And although one or two reviewers who agreed with Weinstein about Hiss's guilt criticized his failure to document his sources, for the most part, like Weinstein, they neglected to mention the problems with his sources. In addition, they seemed by my perhaps dim lights to indulge in the dubious practice of mentioning new incriminating Hiss evidence but omitting new exculpatory Hiss evidence. I pointed this out in what some might say was an interminable July 16, 2001, essay in *The Nation*.

Those who would reconvict Hiss cite one *Venona* document which on its surface is arguably incriminatory (it mentions an agent code-named ALES who went from the Yalta conference to Moscow, as did Hiss) but neglect to cite another which on its surface is arguably exculpatory (it mentions Hiss by name, and in the world of Venona, real agents are mentioned only by their code names). They also cite the memoirs of ex-KGB agent Oleg Gordievsky, who wrote in his 1991 memoir, *KGB: The Inside Story*, that Hiss had been an agent (although he wasn't with the KGB during the period in question) but neglect to cite retired general Vitaly Platov, who wrote in his 1996 memoir, *Operation Snow*, that Hiss was innocent (and who oversaw Soviet operations in the United States during the period in question). And it does not occur to them to mention another retired officer, General Julius Kobyakov, who actually did research on the Hiss case and in 2003 wrote on the H-diplo Web site, "I am ready to eat my hat if someone proves the contrary."*

Then, in the spring of 2003, I found myself on the witness stand in London. Once again, in the most peripheral way, the Hiss case may be said to have been on trial. Alexander Vassiliev, Weinstein's KGB co-author of *The Haunted Wood*, a book based largely on former Soviet archives, was suing Frank Cass, the London-based publisher of the small journal *Intelligence and National Security*. They had published an article by the Hiss defender John Lowenthal, which argued, among other things, that *The Haunted Wood* had misrepresented alleged new evidence from the KGB archives to Hiss's disadvantage. I had been subpoenaed because Vassiliev had contacted me about my review of Weinstein's new edition of *Perjury*, and at that time he was talking of suing Weinstein, who he claimed had, among other derelictions, sub- stituted Hiss's name in brackets for the code name without consulting him. He wanted someone to recommend an American attorney, which I declined to do (I do not believe authors should sue other authors, es- pecially in highly charged political cases). The jury found unanimously against the plaintiff. And of course the decision went unreported in all the places which consider the Hiss case and coffin closed.

Above and beyond the Hiss case, writing about espionage obviously has special problems. The sorts of evidence we routinely demand in every other realm (with the possible exceptions of writings about the Mafia, theology, and certain aspects of supply-side economics) are nei- ther provided nor expected in what we might call espio-lit. Critical documentation is unavailable because it's classified or top secret or has been shredded or "cannot be produced for reasons of national security." Yet paradoxically, the vocabulary in espio-lit ("traitor," "treason," "atom

---

*General Julius Kobyakov had been the lead researcher for General Dmitri Volko- gonov, the military historian who, in October 1992, in a response to a request from John Lowanthal, Hiss's friend and lawyer, for any information on Hiss's alleged spying ac- tivities, had written, "On his and your request, I carefully studied many documents from the archives and intelligence services of the USSR as well as various information provided for me by the archive staff. On the basis of a very careful analysis of all the information available, I can inform you that Alger Hiss was never an agent of the in- telligence services of the Soviet Union." Subsequently, under pressure from American counter-revisionists, General Volkogonov conceded that documents might have been shredded and that he and his team had never inspected GRU files, but he never changed his "personal opinion as a historian."

spy") is significantly more vivid, incendiary, and accusatory than that found in most other modes of discourse.

In the winter of 2003 a new book called *In Denial* by Harvey Klehr and John Earl Haynes emerged, listing me among those who were "in denial" on the matter of Cold War espionage. I soon found myself with Haynes on National Public Radio, where I, of course, denied I was in denial. Perhaps I am wrong about the Hiss case. But I am certain I am right that the mystifications surrounding the subject of espionage, compounded by the emotional legacy of the Cold War, has interfered with a reasoned assessment of the evidence.

I always get a big laugh when people dismiss *The Nation* (or any journal of opinion) by saying that it "preaches to the choir" or is dogmatic or ideological or follows a party line. Barely a week has gone by in my years at *The Nation* when I have not had to answer a letter, a phone call, or, in more recent years, e-mail from an unharmonious dissident member of the so-called choir. And rather than march in lockstep, our contributors and staffers have disagreed, argued, feuded, and debated, among themselves and in our pages, on matters of principle, practicality, politics, policy, and morality.

On presidential politics, Micah Sifry, a Nader supporter in 2000, incurred the wrath of the Greens when he reported on Green schisms in 2004. More generally, not a presidential election goes by without an eruption between those charged with "lesser evilism" versus those charged with "political purism." The right, or even the mainstream, may not distinguish between the liberalism of the ACLU and, say, that of the more radical Center for Constitutional Rights, but in the early 1980s, debates over such issues as whether working with the CIA to create a legislative charter for it was a pragmatic way to make the intelligence agency more accountable or was, by definition, selling out, grew so fierce that *The Nation* invented a special running head, "In the Family," to cover disputes among members of *The Nation*'s extended family. Debate and disagreement over the assassination of President Kennedy spilled over from our pages to a 1992 Town Hall event (featuring Norman Mailer, Nora Ephron, Oliver Stone, Edward J. Epstein, Max Holland, and others) about Oliver Stone's movie *JFK*. It was sufficiently acrimonious to require an official onstage parliamentarian, the attorney Leon Friedman (who was himself the author of a one-act play, *The Trial of Lee Harvey Oswald*). Pounding his mallet, Leon enforced Robert's Rules of Order, settled factual disputes, and provided instant reference to the voluminous assassinationology literature assembled for the occasion. Then there was the week Carlin Romano, a literary critic with a law degree, began an essay review of *Only Words* by Catharine MacKinnon, the radical feminist law professor who had written that pornography was the equivalent of rape, with these words: "Suppose I decide to rape Catharine MacKinnon before reviewing her book. Because I'm uncertain whether she understands the difference between being raped and being exposed to pornography, I consider it required research for my critique of her manifesto that pornography equals rape and should be banned . . ." He chickened out, he said, because "people simply won't understand." Many staff members and readers didn't, and thought that his speculation was not funny, that it didn't belong in, cast a stain on, our magazine.

Alex Cockburn's column "Beat the Devil," whose title is taken from the cult film of 1954 based on his father Claud's novel, is a staggering rebuke to those who think of *The Nation* as monochromatic. When Cockburn mentions "Big Vic" in his "Beat the Devil" column, I smile in anticipation, because I know in the guise of an attack he will merely be wafting an underhanded ball of cotton in my direction for some imagined sin of political incorrectness. But when I spy a "Navasky," I know that in the guise of dissent against the powers that be, Cockburn will be making an unreasonable assault on a position I don't hold, an action I hadn't really taken, or a motive I don't have—almost but not quite as outrageous as his polemical vicious put-downs of some of the better writers, thinkers, and social activists of our time—among them Paul Berman, our former theater critic; the novelist-poet-essayist Cynthia Ozick; Bernie Sanders, the socialist congressman; Christopher Hitchens (write your own description); and other worthies such as Michael Klare, peace scholar, activist, and *Nation* defense correspondent; Michael Massing; Aryeh Neier; Susan Sontag; Todd Gitlin; *Nation* columnists Eric Alterman (often), Katha Pollitt (rarely)—in fact, so many distinguished public intellectuals, journalists, writers, and activists of the liberal left, right, and center that it would be more manageable to make a list of the exempt (starting with his late father and the rest of his talented family).

If I were better organized, I would have developed two form letters for responding to (a) those who tell me Cockburn is the only reason they keep getting the magazine (and threatening to defect should we fire him for his latest dereliction), and (b) those who demand that Cockburn be fired forthwith.

Here, for both pro- and anti-Cockburn contingents and anyone else who is interested, are the unwritten ground rules for *Nation* columnists:

1. In exchange for their turning in timely copy at regular pre-agreed-upon intervals they can more or less write about what they want when they want.

2. They all enjoy the same "no diddling" privileges accorded to Trillin.

3. The columns are fact-checked.

4. They are subjected to readings for libel.

5. Each columnist has an editor who raises questions of taste, clarity, overlaps with other material in the magazine, and so forth.

6. Columnists are expected not to violate house rules, such as commenting on material in the same issue in which their column appears (to which they are privy by virtue of our running an open office and their having on-site loyalists).

7. There is a presumption—yes, occasionally honored in the breach—that columnists will not use valuable space to launch personal attacks on fellow writers. (Ah, but what is "personal"?)

8. If there is a disagreement between the columnist and the columnist's editor, it will be resolved by the editor of the magazine.

9. Editors with questions about whether a columnist has fairly interpreted, summarized, or quoted from a document or speech may raise them—but in close cases, it will often be the columnist's call, since after all, the columnist's name goes on the column.

10. The bet is that over time readers learn to distinguish the prejudices, biases, idiosyncrasies, and occasional distortions of their most or least favorite columnists.

I will pass over the feuds. Pollitt vs. Hitchens (not really a feud but a short-term difference over the life and death of a fetus); Cockburn vs. Hitchens (said to be a front for the old battle of Stalinists vs. Trots, but in fact deeper, shallower, pettier, more entertaining, and wider-ranging than that); Cockburn vs. Alterman (over the merits of social democrats like Paul Berman, or Irving Howe, and much else); Cockburn vs. that demon researcher of the right, Chip Berlet, the Klan-watcher for the Center for Urban Renewal, Dan Levitas, and others. And I will also pass over the resignations from our editorial board: of the gifted sociologist Alan Wolfe, who on returning from a Fulbright in Sweden felt more comfortable publishing in the pages of *The New Republic*; Robert Lekachman, the economist and scourge of Reaganism, whose spouse gave him a very hard time about his appearing in the same magazine with some of our more radical commentators on Middle East politics. ("A name on the masthead, however small, should signify general approval of the journal's tone and content on major issues," Lekachman told me, on the occasion of removing it), and my old Swarthmore advisor Sidney Morgenbesser, the philosopher's philosopher. I will always regret that we did not take up Sid's idea, in the early 1980s, for a Town Hall debate on the question "Is Reagan a Moral Disaster?" For a while gay-rights activists felt their cause got too little attention in our pages (a complaint that more or less ended with the arrival of Andrew Kopkind), although pieces like Darrell Yates Rist's, who argued in "AIDS as Apocalypse: The Deadly Costs of an Obsession" that the gay community's "panicky faith that all of us are doomed" was undermining the struggle for gay rights, earned the magazine new enemies, gay and straight.

Then there was a special issue in 1989 called "Scapegoating the Black Family," conceived, written, and guest-edited by black women, with a special assist from historian Jewell Handy Gresham's white husband, Robert Nemiroff, who was the widower of Lorraine Hansberry, the gifted playwright of *Raisin in the Sun*. The issue was special because it was conceived as a response to *Nation* friend Bill Moyers's highly praised television special on the black family, which from the point of view of Gresham and Co. was, like the 1965 Moynihan Report, misinformed and damaging to the African-American image and community.

My own reading of the Moynihan Report—I hadn't seen but had

read about Moyers's program—was always ambivalent. On the one hand, I was persuaded by Herb Gutman's analysis of it as in part being an instance of blaming the victim; on the other hand, I believed that the condemnations of Moynihan, and now Moyers, were in part an instance of blaming the messenger. Yes, the African-American response to slavery, Jim Crow, lynching, poverty, the poll tax, and race hatred had amazingly included racial solidarity, a spirited struggle on behalf of civil rights, and much hard-earned wisdom, but surely it was not wrong to observe that four centuries of oppression and discrimination had taken their toll.

There is, by the way, a built-in difficulty with the guest editor: Who has the final say? At *The Nation* the normal bottom line is that the writer has the final say about the words that appear under her name, but the magazine has the final say about whether the words appear at all. With a guest editor a strong presumption exists on behalf of the guest editor's choices and decisions, but the magazine reserves the right—be it for legal, political, aesthetic, or space reasons—to veto, such rights not to be arbitrarily exercised if at all. When there are not one but three guest editors, one of whom has the personality and force of an Old Testament prophet, and when the guest editors are black and the magazine's staff is overwhelmingly white (so how could it presume to make final judgments on what went into a magazine billed under the rubric of black women's take on the black family), a wiser editor than I might have anticipated more than the usual contestation over how to fit eighty pages worth of articles into a sixty-page magazine. The issue was controversial not only within *The Nation's* extended family. The guest editors and *The Nation* editors had their differences, the guest editors had a falling-out among themselves (one quit *in medias res*), and reverberations continued in our letters pages down through the years, although the issue did win a nomination in the "Best Single-Topic Issue" category for a National Magazine Award, and I for one am glad we published it.

As I wrote Chip Berlet on May 2, 1993, when he threatened a lawsuit against a Cockburn column which he considered libelous, "Believe it or not, I always regret the intramural disputes that break out in *The Nation's* pages, since it seems to me there are better and more critical uses for our space, which is always in such short supply." On the theory that the worst venue for airing such differences was the courts, since dialogue usually ceases when court action is threatened, I invited him to write a letter to the editor. He answered privately, "I find your suggestion that I write a letter to the editor to be [either] subtle humor or an insulting attempt on your part to abdicate your responsibility as an editor . . ."

Backstage, the members of the so-called choir are even more out of harmony. Here is but one typical instance. A product of progressive education, I am more persuaded than ever that teaching people to think for themselves, inciting their intellectual curiosity, imbuing them with the love of learning is more important than, say, spelling. Maybe I'm wrong. I know there's a middle ground. So sometime in the late 1980s I get my weekly love letter from Old Dirt Road, where Bob Sherrill lives in Tallahassee, and he gives me what-for. It's his combination of elementary education and his continuing seminar on why I should let the editor (me) be the editor:

> I think anybody who wants schools to stress the elitist practice of "thinking" rather than the basics is simply willing to drive the underclass further under. I don't think that's what you want, but it certainly seems to be what the writer of that editorial wants. And if you don't want it, what is it doing on the front page—or anywhere else—in *The Nation*? THE EDITOR OF *THE NATION* IS *THE NATION*. I've said that a thousand times (that's an understatement) to you, but because you are too fucking soft for your own good, or the good of the magazine, you prefer to turn the policy making over to a bunch of elitist nitwits. That's the second time I've used the word elitist. If I had the time, I would write it a million times. Perhaps it would then sink in.

I don't know if Bob was right about my being too soft. (See, that's a softy statement right there. Maybe he's right.) I know that part of the editor's job is to impose his own views on the magazine, but part of it is to open subjects for debate. And another part is to orchestrate, to Socratize (how's that for an elitist vulgarism?) the ideas of others, and occasionally to bow to an internal consensus that he doesn't (may not yet) share. But he has to know on which occasion. On this occasion, Bob was "wrong" to imagine that elitist-me didn't agree with the editorial he called elitist. Though why advocating thinking makes me an elitist eludes me.

Once a protest gets under way, it's hard—for reasons that have partly to do with what became known as political correctness, partly to do with gender wars, and partly a simple matter of political sociology— to resist the stampede, what Harold Rosenberg once called "the herd of independent minds." But I learned that this was especially true in a journal that goes out of its way to present itself as a temple of words when it is confronted with the power of the visual arts.

One day in February 1984, David Levine called me. David is known to his fellow artists as one of the great realist painters, and is known in the media community as the genius responsible for the witty but wicked cross-hatched pen-and-ink caricatures that since its outset have helped to define the look of *The New York Review of Books*.

This was around the time of the Kissinger Commission Report on the Caribbean Basin, and he had done a caricature of Henry Kissinger on assignment for *The New York Review of Books*, to accompany an essay by James Chace on the Kissinger Report. But Bob Silvers, of *The New York Review*, felt it was "too strong" to go with Chace's meditative essay, and said they would publish it later. David was not so sure about that, and anyway wanted it published now. The cartoon, he told me, showed Kissinger on top and the world in the form of a naked woman on bottom. She had a globe where her head should have been, the Caribbean basin for a face, and they had an American flag for a blanket. Were we interested? David, I said, it will get me in all sorts of trouble with my staff, but send it over. Why will it get you in trouble with your staff? he asked. I don't know, I said, but I know it will.

The cartoon arrived an hour later. It was, as expected, a brilliant caricature, but it was more than that. Kissinger in bed and on top had on these thick-lensed horn-rimmed glasses and a look on his face that mingled evil and ecstasy as he did his dirty business with the world-woman under the cover of the American flag. I called David and told him we were putting it through. Two hours later a petition arrived on my desk, signed by two-thirds of the people in the office. Many of the signatures were followed by little comments. "Sexist!" one had written. "Why isn't he doing it to a Third World man?" asked another.

I called an officewide meeting. At the outset I told everyone it was important to keep three things in mind: First, I took the staff concern seriously, but there would be no vote at its end—you can't decide a question of political aesthetics by majority vote. Second, this work had been offered to us on a take-it-or-leave-it basis, so while anyone was free to say what he or she pleased, suggestions about changing the drawing would have no operative effect. ("Why doesn't he put Kissinger on the bottom?" one petitioner had proposed.) Third, I already had told Levine that we intended to use his drawing; the magazine could always reverse itself, but to do so might have lateral consequences, since it would have about it, fairly or not, the odor of censorship. I didn't add— I thought it might sound elitist—that here was a rare opportunity to publish the work of America's most brilliant and distinguished caricaturist.

The most articulate staff objection to Levine's drawing was that *The Nation* was supposed to fight against stereotypes, and this cartoon reinforced the stereotype of sex as something wrong and dirty, and something an active male does to a passive female. My favorite moment came when Christopher Hitchens, who had written a column about the Kissinger Commission, said he thought that the Kissinger character was ravaging the woman; it wasn't an act of sex but an act of rape, a comment on the American empire's abuse of power. One of our younger women staff members responded, "But if you look at the woman's hand, it seems to be gripping the mattress in what could be the grip of passion." The white-suited Christopher, who enjoyed posing as the office roué, leaned over and, gripping the young woman's hand, said, "Trust me, my dear, it is not the grip of passion." The sometimes tense discussion lasted for a couple of hours, and at my suggestion we invited David Levine to join the fun a few days later when it was resumed.

David pointed out that as a cartoonist he deals in stereotypes— which poses a problem when one is rendering, for example, members of a minority race: How do you make a visual comment on racism without falling into its trap? Nevertheless, the cartoonist's job is to play off of stereotypes that a majority of readers and viewers will recognize. And of course, David being David, he said all the wrong things. When asked why the man had to be on top, for example, he replied, "I'm just showing what normal people do." After he had spent two hours on the griddle, I asked him whether he was sorry he came. Levine said he had been doing this sort of work for twenty-five years and had never had such a serious a discussion of his work, and for that he was grateful. He had gotten some new insights into the problematics of cartooning. But, he added, "if I had it to do over again, I wouldn't change a line."

Six years later, the American Studies and Art History Departments of Columbia University decided to mount an art show to commemorate *The Nation*'s 125th anniversary, and the curator—having surveyed the work of thousands of candidates, including Louis Lozowick, Ben Shahn, Rockwell Kent, George Grosz, and other luminaries—in ignorance of the dispute, chose Levine's Kissinger as one of its pieces to be exhibited. And when the exhibit moved to the José Luis Sert Gallery at Harvard, they put it on the catalogue cover.

Another episode involved words as well as pictures. Starting in 1978, the year I did, Ed Sorel, America's Daumier, began contributing his devastating, often mordant commentaries—sometimes caricatures, other times cartoons and comic strips—to *The Nation*, and for a while he did a monthly visual "column." Then, in 1988, Sorel submitted a Feiffer-style panel about Frances Lear, the divorced wife of the television producer Norman Lear, who had just announced she was starting a new magazine, *Lear's: For the woman who wasn't born yesterday*. She told the press that she hoped to be a role model for other older women.

Sorel's cartoon panel showed an increasingly exuberant and disheveled Frances Lear explaining her venture, her expression moving from wild-eyed to cross-eyed. Panel One: "Oh! I'm so excited! My magazine for women over 40 is out at last!" Panel Two: "MEN said that a woman with no experience couldn't do it." Panel Three: "But I didn't choose to play by *their* rules. I just went ahead and did it." Panel Four: "I hope my success will inspire other women to dare to be great." Panel Five: "All a woman needs is vision, determination . . ." (here she is counting on her fingers). Panel Six: "a very rich husband who'll give her $112 million for a divorce . . . then she can break all the rules she wants" (here she is dancing as the dollar bills rain down).

After sending Ed's cartoon off to production, I dictated a letter to Frances, who was a friend and whose ex-husband was a shareholder in *The Nation*, to the effect that I hoped that she, as a fledgling publisher, would understand that our publishing this cartoon was nothing personal. I told Dennis Selby, my assistant, to get the note hand-delivered ASAP, because I expected that in two hours there would be a visit to my office. (Later Dennis pointed out I was wrong, it had taken only an hour and a half.) This time the staff members (with some brave exceptions) summed up their objection to Sorel's work in a letter to the editor. Because of a family emergency, I had to leave the office just as the debate was winding down. In my absence the staff letter appeared in the same issue as Ed's cartoon, rather than the following week, our normal procedure. I thought this breach of editorial decorum unfortunate, since some readers would see the cartoon through the lens of the dissenting letter rather than experience it unfiltered. Under the heading *Enter Sexism Vindictive* the letter read: "Readers should know that Edward Sorel's cartoon . . . appears despite the strong protest of thirty-four staff members. We are outraged that sexism is still a respectable prejudice, especially in a left magazine." The following week these letters appeared:

Lear on Sorel, New York City
   I am thrilled with the words in the lower right-hand box on page 293 in the March 5 *Nation* [see "Enter Sexism, Vindictive" and Edward Sorel, "Enter Queen Lear, Triumphant"], and I send everyone my gratitude for being right-on. I wonder about Sorel. I fail to see why he failed to see my still-steamy good looks.
                                                                    Frances Lear, Triumphant

Leery, New York City
   What has made the left so traditionally condescending to its artists? Edward Sorel is one of the great cartoonists and caricaturists of this century. Whether one agrees with his every cartoon or not, it seems to me that after thirty years of work on a level that is simply extraordinary, he shouldn't have to pass an ideological means test to get in *The Nation*'s pages. That thirty-four staff members tried to suppress Sorel when they disagreed with him reveals a contempt for the right of free expression that is not only shortsighted but, as Sorel's colleagues well know, predictable.
                                                                    Jules Feiffer

The magazine was deluged with letters, only one of which Sorel chose to answer. When the illustrator Lisa Blackshear raised the question of how Sorel reconciled his progressive political beliefs with his work for the Manufacturers Hanover bank, he replied, "I've never tried to justify working for banks to my politically correct friends any more than I've tried to justify working for *The Nation* to my accountant."

In this case it was the words more than the pictures that caused the upset, but I doubt that the words alone would have moved the thirty-four people to attempt again what seemed to me prior restraint on one of our own. Images, even in plain old black-and-white, are much more powerful, troubling, provocative, and threatening—if that's not too strong a word for it—than words. Why is this? It can't be because people, especially the young, don't read anymore. That may well be true for the community at large, but it certainly isn't true at *The Nation*, a bastion of word-people. Whatever the deep psychological reason, one of the surface sources of provocation is the simple fact that a caricature is almost by definition unfair. It is a misrepresentation, an exaggeration for effect, a parody. And when it appears as part of a cartoon that makes a cutting comment of its own, either directly, as against Frances Lear, or symbolically, as in Levine's condemnation of Kissinger's and America's support of El Salvador's death squads, there is no way for the disconcerted reader-spectator-viewer to answer it. I guess one can always cancel one's subscription, but surely a letter to the editor doesn't do the job. The only real way to answer it might be with a counter-cartoon, but then there is no such thing as a cartoon to the editor.

Take your choice. The *Sturm und Drang* surrounding the Levine and Sorel cartoons are either evidence that the editor is a sexist or evidence of the editor's failure to inculcate in his colleagues a proper respect for the free exchange of ideas. I like to think it's the latter, but either way it is the editor's fault. Such shows of solidarity against the editor are good for morale, I suppose, although not for the editor's. My wife, Annie, thought it was less a sign of disrespect than of affection that at one office Christmas party the donkey on which the tail was to be pinned was a photo of the editor taken from behind. My rule is never to take such things personally, so I can't even tell you the names of those (including my loyal secretary) who signed the Sorel letter. I did, however, happen

to notice that one name that was not on the list (and I think it was no
coincidence) was that of Eric Etheridge, the former *Nation* intern who
in 1982 instituted *The Nation*'s fact-checking system, using interns as
fact checkers, which means that since then we have trained a new
cadre of fact checkers every three or four months.

Some people think that magazines like *The Nation* and journals of
opinion generally are careless with and have even been known to slant
the facts. And any postmodernist will tell you there are facts and there
are facts, or that there are only contingent facts. I have always thought
that *because The Nation* is a journal of opinion, *because* it is open about
its political and cultural values and commitments, it is all the more essential that it get the facts right. The fact checker is the hidden hero of
magazine journalism, saving magazines from lawsuits, writers from
world-class embarrassment, and readers from misinformation. Naturally,
some writers resent fact checkers as censors without portfolio.

Before 1982, it had been my experience that fact-checking procedures varied from magazine to magazine. When I worked at *The New
York Times Magazine*, it had no fact checkers, while *Time*, on the other
hand, has always had fact checkers, who famously put a dot over each
word in a *Time* story to indicate that it has passed muster. Since *Time* in
the days of Henry Luce was known for slanting the news, at first I didn't
take fact checking seriously. That's why when in 1978 we were queried
about the authenticity of a spurious quotation from H. L. Mencken that
found its way into Calvin Trillin's humor column, which he called "remarkably prescient" and claimed was making the rounds of "Washington
egghead circles," I was able to assure skeptics that it "had been subjected
to *The Nation*'s normal fact-checking process." It was early in the second
year of the Carter administration, and the President's beer-guzzling
brother, Billy, had caused some embarrassment, and his proselytizing sister, Ruth, had raised some curiosity, while his daughter, Amy, seemed
sort of lost; Trillin purported to have discovered an old Mencken essay
where the Baltimore sage had written:

> Someday we will have a President from the deserts of the Deep
> South [and the President's brother will] gather his loutish com-
> panions on the porch of the White House to swill beer from
> the bottle and snigger over whispered barnyard jokes about the

darkies. The President's cousin, LaVerne, will travel the Hallelujah circuit as one of Mrs. McPherson's soldiers in Christ, praying for the conversion of some Northern Sodom's most Satanic pornographer as she waves his work—well thumbed—for all the yokels to gasp and the President's daughter will regard these events with her box camera.

A number of newspapers reprinted this "quotation." Others, in an effort to authenticate it, contacted Mencken scholars, including Theo Lippman, Jr., of *The Baltimore Sun*, who telephoned Trillin to ask where the quotation came from. Trillin later wrote: "When I told [him] that I had seen the quotation typed on a piece of paper rather than printed in a book or magazine, he asked if the piece of paper had been in a typewriter at the time." Trillin added, "Nobody challenged the quotation on substantive grounds. No one claimed that Mencken at his most hyperbolic Southern-baiting could not have predicted Carter almost precisely."

Of course, Trillin's "Mencken" remark refused to die, even after a *Los Angeles Times* reporter, Jeff Prugh, got the BBC's expert on Americana, Alistair Cooke, who had edited *The Vintage Mencken*, to conclude that the passage was a "mischievous parody." The tip-off was the use of the word "pornographer," which, Cooke informed the *Times*, was little used in the 1920s.

"Then, as so often happens in America these days," Trillin reported some months later, "the truth began to emerge through the efforts of an accountant." Don Harvey, an accountant in Chicago, wrote Trillin to say that "pornographer" not only was used in the 1920s but had been used by Mencken himself in 1920 in a *New Republic* article entitled "Star Spangled Men." If Trillin did not have access to back numbers of *The New Republic*, he could find the same essay reprinted in *The Vintage Mencken*, edited by Alistair Cooke.

Pedants like Trillin may fault Alistair Cooke for not knowing what's in a book that he himself edited. That's because they begin with the faulty assumption that experts know what they are talking about. They ought to read a little book called *The Experts Speak: The Definitive Compendium of Authoritative Misinformation*, a compendium of so-called experts in every field who were wrong. As it happens, the author-editors of this volume are Christopher Cerf and one Victor Navasky, the very same. As far as we are aware—and we are, you should excuse the expression, experts on the matter—*The Experts Speak*, which was first published in 1984, is the first and only collection of unadulterated, fully authenticated, footnoted expertise, all of which is false.

> "Stocks have reached what looks like a permanently high plateau."
> > —Irving Fisher, professor of economics at Yale University,
> > days before the great stock market crash of 1929

> "There is no reason for any individual to have a computer in their home."
> > —President of Digital Equipment Corporation, 1977

> "The sound of a flute will cure epilepsy, and sciatica gout."
> > —Theophrastus, Greek philosopher, c. 370–285 B.C.

> "Heavier-than-air flying machines are impossible."
> > —Lord Kelvin, British mathematician, physicist and
> > President of the British Royal Society, c. 1895

In our introduction we made our position clear: "We do not claim that all experts everywhere are always wrong. We are ready to concede that the experts are occasionally right. As a matter of fact, some of our colleagues have argued persuasively that the experts are right as much as half the time. Moreover, the fact that our own scientifically selected random sample has yet to turn up an expert who is right in and of itself proves nothing."

And above and beyond the Cerf-Navasky Institute of Expertology's critique of the experts, I had my own reservations about mainstream journalism's cult of the expert—the idea that the way to guarantee so-called objectivity was to quote experts "on both sides."

So when I received a call from a lawyer in California early in 1982 asking me if I would consider being an expert witness in the largest libel trial in history, I considered it an insult, and I said I'd consider it. (I had had a heads-up from my nephew Jordan Weiss, a tax lawyer, who had mentioned my name to a lawyer friend working for *Penthouse*'s California firm.)

The trial in L.A. County Superior Court in Compton, a low-income suburb of Los Angeles, involved a lawsuit brought by the owners of a resort called Rancho La Costa in San Diego, California, against *Penthouse* magazine, notorious for its dirtier-than-*Playboy* pictures of nude females doing lewd things; but also known among freelance writers as a high-paying market for serious investigative journalism which nobody read.

Two then-little-known but later famous and award-winning journalists, Jeff Gerth and Lowell Bergman, had in 1972 published in *Penthouse* an exposé of the La Costa resort in Southern California, charging among other things that it was a mob hangout, built and controlled by friends of the mob. Gerth had worked as Seymour Hersh's sidekick and went on to a job at *The New York Times*, where he won a Pulitzer Prize, and Bergman became a crusading anti-tobacco CBS-TV producer and was played by Al Pacino in the 1999 movie about his work (*The Insider*). He too went on to win a Pulitzer.

The proprietors of La Costa included Allard Roen, a partner in several Las Vegas resort casinos who had earlier pleaded guilty to stock fraud; and Moe Dalitz, who had been identified in the 1950s by the Special Committee on Organized Crime in Interstate Commerce chaired by Senator Estes Kefauver as a racketeer and longtime associate of organized-crime figures; also Mervyn Adelson and Irwin Molasky, of Lorimar Studios. They considered this description of their resort as mob-connected to be defamatory and sued for $630 million, which came to roughly $100,000 a word, the biggest libel award ever asked for in an American court.

The issue on which I was asked to testify had to do with whether *Penthouse*'s fact-checking procedures were consistent with contemporary practices in the magazine trade.

As it was explained to me, Bergman and Gerth had turned in their article, they were asked for a rewrite, which they provided, and the article was then "lawyered," during which *Penthouse*'s lawyers asked for backup materials regarding their description of La Costa as "mob-connected." They provided clippings from scores of papers, ranging from Hank Greenspun's *Las Vegas Sun*, famed for its chronicling of mob life, to the *Los Angeles Times* and *The New York Times,* and they also cited countless interviews with anonymous law-enforcement people. The lawyers did not insist that they reveal the identity of these sources.

Under the law of libel, if the subject is a "public figure," then in order for the alleged defamation to be actionable, the perpetrator had to be guilty of "reckless and malicious" intent. Because Dalitz and Roen were deemed to be public figures, eventually they dropped out as plaintiffs when it was decided that they could not prove malice. But the case persisted. Did *Penthouse*'s failure to insist that its writers disclose their sources qualify as "reckless and malicious" conduct on *Penthouse*'s part?

The case seemed to me an important one. As a member of the ACLU and on the board of PEN and the Authors Guild, I believed as a general proposition that libel suits against writers went against the spirit of the First Amendment. And an afternoon in court would not be burdensome. Besides, I had other things to do in California and my nephew and his family to see.

Norman Roy Grutman, *Penthouse*'s flamboyant and voluble counsel, told me that he had great admiration for me. In fact, he laid it on so thick that I began to be suspicious. Even I didn't have that much admiration for me. The way he explained it, I would first have to go over the files of the case—to look at the evidence, as it were. Second, they would have to "prepare" me as a witness. This is a sensitive business, because in prepping a witness, lawyers are not allowed to dictate what the witness should say, but they are allowed to tell you what you will be asked and make sure you've done your homework. Coaching was not allowed. I thought I heard a wink, if one can hear winks over the telephone.

Once on the stand, I would have to be "qualified," which apparently was not easy. Despite all the long-distance admiration, I was not their first choice as expert witness. A dean of a national journalism school had failed to qualify, presumably because he had not actually been in the magazine business (as had I). When and if "qualified," I would then be asked various hypotheticals and answer to the best of my ability.

There remained only the matter of the fee, which at first was of little interest to me. *The Nation*'s expert witnesses in the Harper & Row case had been volunteers who were not paid a penny. But as I learned more and more about the *Penthouse* case, the fee loomed larger and larger. First, it was not merely "an afternoon's work." There was travel

time between New York and California; there was the however many
days it would take me to go through and master the files; then I was to
return to New York and wait until summoned, when I would return a
couple of days in advance of my appearance, during which time I
would be "prepped."

I was ambivalent about the fee for a number of reasons, the main
one being that I did not in any way, shape, or form want to besmirch
the name of *The Nation* (GREEDY NATION EDITOR DEMANDS TOP
DOLLAR); on the other hand, this was demanding more time than I had
bargained for. It was the largest libel trial in history; witnesses, counsel,
and others were being shuttled back and forth between both coasts
first class; and my nephew kept reminding me that I didn't want to be
exploited. When Norman Roy Grutman asked me what my rate was, I
told him I didn't have one, and anyway was not sure I wanted a fee for
myself, perhaps it could be paid to the Nation Institute, our public
charity. I would think about it. Think hard, he said, you will earn your
money. And we want to pay you at the going rate—don't worry about it.

Out of curiosity as much as anything else, I called my nephew to
ask about the going rate. You can charge a per diem rate for when
you're on the road, he said—these could run to something like $1,500
a day—or you can charge an hourly rate. Then he paused and added,
If I were you, I would tell them whatever Jimmy "The Weasel" Fratianno is getting is good enough for you. Jimmy the Weasel was a former hit man turned government informant who was going to testify
about mob meetings he had attended at La Costa and how the Team-
sters Union pension fund was used like a bank to finance legitimate
and illegitimate projects. *Penthouse* and Grutman were counting on
this member of the federal witness protection program.

So of course I called Grutman back and told him money was not
my concern, I wanted my fee to go to the Nation Institute, but whatever was good enough for Jimmy the Weasel was good enough for me.
If you can hear a gulp over 3,000 miles I heard a gulp. Grutman explained that when he said he would pay the going rate, he meant the
top of the going rate, but Fratianno, whose criminal career involved
gambling, bribery, and many murders, could explain how the mobsters
worked and had his own over-the-top arrangement, and, well, let's just
leave it at that. Which I did.

When I first met Norman Roy Grutman, I saw an overweight, dapper lawyer immersed in his case, an odd combination of peacock, family man (his bejeweled wife, Jewel, was co-counsel and shared his practice with him), brilliant lawyer, and pompous ass, as if he had been sent over from Central Casting. (After the jury left the courtroom at the end of the trial, the TV producer and movie mogul Mervyn Adelson said to him, "Mr. Grutman, if Lorimar ever does a movie about a fat scumbag lawyer, would you play the part?") He told me my prep would be easy and we would do it later in the day. Later in the day proved impossible, so he said we could do it that night at dinner.

But what with one thing and another, my prep was postponed until the morning I was to appear. By that time I had learned that the judge and Grutman didn't exactly get along. In fact, Grutman believed that Judge Kenneth W. Gale was in the mob's pocket, and he had retained a private detective to look into his past. In 1971, then practicing law in Las Vegas (where he also represented one of the city's notorious union racketeers), the judge interceded with a parole officer on Fratianno's behalf and therefore probably should have recused himself from the *Penthouse* case. He was the only appointee on the bench whose page, in the book containing the pictures and legal biographies of every judge in California, was blank. He was rumored at the age of forty-one to have "purchased" his first wife, age fifteen, in Salt Lake City, where he owned a go-go bar, and he apparently picked up his second wife during eight mysterious years he spent in the Soviet Union. Oh yes, he was missing his right ring finger.

The Grutmans and I never did run through my testimony. At breakfast he and Jewel told me just to make clear what I had told them— that the *New York Times Magazine* and *The Nation*, among others, did what *Penthouse* did in those years.

When I finally got to the witness box, during a break in the testimony Judge Gale leaned over to me and asked where I or my family was from. "With a patronymic like that," he observed, "you're probably from the Soviet Union." I told him my family came from Kovna, and he asked if I had been there. I told him it had been closed to Westerners, and he told me it was now visitable and I should go.

During the lunch break I told Grutman of our conversation. "I think he likes me," I said.

"Are you Jewish?" Grutman asked.

"Yes," I said.

"He doesn't like you."

Earlier I had sat in on the testimony of Moe Dalitz. Now in his eighties, Dalitz had the appearance of a kind old uncle. He would say things like "I started out in the laundry business and then I was lucky enough to be given my own cabaret. And after a few years I was fortunate enough to have stars like Sophie Tucker. I was privileged to sit with her as she sipped her favorite martinis."

"But, Mr. Dalitz—that was in the 1920s, so that was during Prohibition, wasn't it?"

"You could say that."

By the time I was on the stand, it seemed as if the Grutmans had been working 24–7 for months. Everybody was high-strung, not least the judge. And no matter what any witness said, one of the plaintiffs' lawyers would jump up and make one of four objections: "Already asked and answered," "Irrelevant and immaterial," "Hearsay," and I forget the fourth, unless it was "Your honor already ruled on that." Judge Gale, when faced with an objection of this sort, would put his hands together to make a steeple (except for the missing finger) as he pondered how to rule, and then invariably, he would rule against Grutman.

The opposing counsel included the famous lawyer Louis Nizer, now with failing hearing and fading eyesight, who put himself within earshot of the jury, and from the witness stand I, too, could hear him talking loudly either to co-counsel or to himself. Whenever Grutman made a point, he would mumble just loud enough for the jury to hear but soft enough for Judge Gale to miss. "But that's not true." "Oh, he's lying."

When it was my turn, I was asked to describe the fact-checking process as it worked in the early 1970s. I began to respond, "Well, it varied from magazine to magazine . . ." All four plaintiff lawyers jumped up and started waving their right arms to be recognized, shouting that because I had "admitted" that there was no such thing as a standard I had disqualified myself as a witness. How could I testify on whether *Penthouse* had met a standard that I claimed didn't exist?

Clearly I had blown it. Jimmy the Weasel never would have made such a blunder. Then again, he had a better rate than I did. I felt awful for Grutman, for Bergman and Gerth (who by this time had mysteriously settled themselves out of the case), for the First Amendment, for the Nation Institute. I had let them all down.

Comes now Norman Ray Grutman to the rescue. But he is not having a good day. Five times his question to me is shot down before I have a chance to answer.

"Already asked and answered."

"Sustained."

In exasperation Grutman finally asked Judge Gale whether the problem with his question was one of form or of content. Judge Gale said it was a matter of form. "Well then, would your honor assist counsel in formulating the question in a way that would please the court?"

"That's your job, counsel, not mine."

A frustrated Grutman tried again to get me to undo the damage I had done. I thought I could see a tremor, or maybe that was simply from lack of sleep or too much coffee. He was at the lectern with a sheaf of papers in his hand. He looked at me and said, "Mr. Navasky, can you say to a *medical* certainty . . ."

I assumed he meant "to a reasonable certainty," and so I paused, not quite sure what to do.

He caught himself and began again: "Mr. Navasky, can you say to a *medical* certainty . . ." He shook his head, laughed nervously and began again: "Mr. Navasky, can you say to a *medical* certainty . . ."

Then, like a mouthpiece in a B picture, he took his sheaf of papers and in exasperation threw them upward. As they came wafting down, he turned and stomped out of court, shaking his head and making his getaway before Judge Gale could cite him for contempt for a third time. I sat in the witness box feeling naked, as the three unblind Mafiosi stared from the front row and the four-fingered judge made notes.

Like Jimmy Stewart in an early Frank Capra movie, Grutman's youthful assistant then rose, picked up the papers, reassembled them, went to the lectern, said something like "If I may pick up where counsel left off . . . ," substituted the word "reasonable" for "medical," and got Grutman's question in over an objection from the other side. In the end, *Penthouse* and the First Amendment triumphed, but not before more suits and countersuits, including at least one against the judge. And one fine day the Nation Institute received a check for $12,500.

I have already mentioned that in 1985, borrowing an old Carey McWilliams idea, we convened a conference appropriately enough at his alma matter, the University of Southern California, to consider the role of the journal of critical opinion.

What I have not yet mentioned is that even before we arrived in Los Angeles our own Alex Cockburn had attacked the conference from the left:

> Among the magazines participating are *National Review*, *The American Spectator*, *The New Republic*, *The New Criterion* and *Transaction*, *Social Science* and *Modern Society*. I'm glad the rights of these horrible journals are guaranteed under the First Amendment, but I don't think "they keep the mainstream honest." To the contrary, these are exactly the magazines that have helped corrupt the mass media and instruct them in the art of telling lies. These magazines have not widened debate, they have narrowed it to leather-lunged condoning of reaction, both in politics and culture.

At the conference Hilton Kramer, among others, attacked us from the right. "I mean, to put it bluntly, the reader of *The New Criterion* isn't interested in *In These Times* . . . It's a different readership, it's a different level, it's a different curiosity, it's a different orientation, it's a different public." To add to the insult, Hilton added, "I think it is also quite unrealistic not to recognize that the conference has been by and large a conference of journals of the left. I'm very pleased to be here, [but] what you're talking about is a kind of cooperation for circulating the ideas of the left."

The next day, to complete the circle, the conference was attacked from the center as the reporter from the *L.A. Times* accurately reported that the conference's formal agenda was typically ignored. "Instead of talking about the role of the journal of opinion, for example, participants argued about Israel, priggery, minority representation and the supposed Marxist domination of academia." Joseph Epstein, editor of *The American Scholar*, claimed that Marxists are so much in demand in American universities that in one case, a college was so intent on hiring a Marxist scholar that "if he'd had a dog, they would have offered the dog a job."

Meanwhile, Robert Chrisman, the militant and articulate editor of *The Black Scholar*, attacked us for not having more black writers. Then, when Jeff Escoffier, the entrepreneurial editor of *Socialist Review*, called to ask if he might publish my opening remarks, I thought maybe it had been worth it, after all—at least the democratic socialists understood the value of the project—only to discover that they would provide a convenient punching bag for *Socialist Review*'s associate editor Ilene Philipson, when they appeared in *Socialist Review*'s fifteenth anniversary issue later in the year. (*Socialist Review* went out of business before its next anniversary.)

Ms. Philipson, it turns out, is a student of the iron fist, but somewhere along the way they forgot to tell her about the velvet glove. She attacked the fundamental assumptions around which the conference was organized: "The premise for holding this conference was that . . . in the face of an accelerated 'massification' of the media, left-and-right-wing journals must realize that their interests will be better served by binding together in some fashion against a common enemy. They must not allow political differences to force them to go it alone in an industry dominated by electronics, bullied by corporations, and compromised by myths of objectivity."

(I couldn't have put it better myself, but boy, was I wrong. Or so said Ilene.)

> Navasky fears that "concentration of media power will limit the number of voices that are heard." But this concentration does not impinge equally on left and right wing periodicals. Small publications whose interests and visions of the world are consonant with those of the corporate-controlled mass media stand to lose less than those journals critical of corporations and their control and influence. As the concentration of media power limits the number of voices heard, it is the left and not the right that is in greatest jeopardy of being muted.

(She had me there, although if one's interest was, say, improving distribution, might the left not fare better by enlisting the right in a campaign to persuade superstores to carry both?)

Her indictment continued: "While Navasky recognizes that journals of opinion are 'perpetually on the brink of bankruptcy' this conference underlined how much more this is a problem for the left than for the right." (She had me there, too, as the editors of *Marxist Perspectives*, *Working Papers*, *WIN*, all defunct, would attest— the editor of *democracy*, also defunct, could not so attest, as its patron, Max Palevsky, a lefty himself, had pulled the plug for reasons of boredom.)

Next, she questioned my idea that the right and left should "work together to promote our common interests," at most in the form of a trade association, at least in agreeing to meet next year: "Navasky seems to base this suggestion on the idea that having an opinion per se is more important than the content of the opinion." (Not really, but of course that's only her opinion.)

According to her, I seem to believe that the right and the left could work together despite what are often fundamentally opposing views of the world, of human nature, morality, culture, and the role of journals of opinion. In so doing, I trivialize these by implicitly suggesting that mutual concern over making our voices heard "outweighs essential political, epistemological, and moral disagreements." And her final point: "Navasky suggests that 'perhaps it is in the interests of one to defend the interests of all in extending our space.'" Yes! Whereas she believes that in this period of right ascendancy, it is absolutely not in the left's interest to expand the space of the right. "Conservatives and those to their political right can take care of themselves . . ."

So much for my brilliant idea. She, they, were certainly correct about the left and the right not being able to work together. And I'm sure I was wrong in my growing suspicion that the far left and the near left might not be able to work together either. But for reasons that I hope will become clear, I haven't given up hope. In my rejoinder to Ms. Philipson in *Socialist Review*, I closed by saying that if we had it to do over, I'd have the business people discuss their bread-and-butter issues in seclusion and let the editors provide their circuses for the audience. But churl that I am, I did not resist adding, "None of this means, of course, that the left can't have its own caucus or association or whatever it wants to call it. So now let's get down to the serious business of whom we want to exclude from 'the left trade association' in future conferences."

Nobody can say I don't learn from experience.

After almost ten years in the editor's chair at least three things were clear. First, I needed a new chair. Carey's old chair squeaked, and what with the oil shortage, it might pay to get a new one. (Actually I did that when we moved offices.)

Second, the left was accident-prone, too often wounding itself in unnecessary sectarian culture wars. But third and most important, the mainstream media were out to marginalize us. Why they should want to do that, since we were already on the margins, I am still trying to figure out. But the means they employed is what interests me. They called *The Nation* many things, among them: liberal, stridently liberal, bleeding heart, progressive, leftist, left-wing, far left, hardcore left, radical, Marxist, Marxist-Leninist, Stalinist, anti-Semitic, Zionist, and much, much more. But the real zinger, the mother of all charges, was to denounce us as ideological.

The way I saw it, these charges were insidious, because they implied that somehow we were tainted, impure, untrustworthy, in contrast to publications like *The New York Times*, the newsweeklies, or the network news operations, which prefer to describe themselves as objective.

Before I'm finished, I'll deal with our old friend objectivity. I'll also deal with pseudo-objectivity, the false garb of neutral colors and moderate tones which so-called objectivity usually wears. (All right. If you can't wait, turn to page 408.)

But here I want to say something about the charge that *The Nation*, or the journal of opinion as a matter of definition, is ideological. I plead guilty. I am a practicing ideologist publishing an ideological magazine. Yet, it seems to me that although the term "ideological" is often used pejoratively to connote an overly rigid value system, we are all equally ideological. The difference between mainstream and more embattled periodicals has to do with (a) the content of the ideology, (b) our respective willingness or unwillingness to admit it, and (c) our ability to see it, not with who has it.

Ideology is simply a body of beliefs or doctrines. It is just that the mainstream media have the ideology of the center. To denounce journals like *The Nation* or our opposite number, *National Review*, as ideological confuses the issue because of the invidious variety of ways in

which the word "ideological" is bandied about. As a card-carrying ideologist, let me begin to count the ways:

Sometimes it is used as a synonym for a publication's place at either
end of the spectrum. Sometimes it is used to mean distorting the
news. Sometimes it is used to signify suppression or omission of inconvenient information. Sometimes it is used to mean predictable, or
to suggest that we are preaching to the already convinced.

Sometimes it has reference to tone. Sometimes it is used to mean
simplistic—or what we bleeding hearts might call idealistic.

As one disentangles—I have taken a pledge never to deconstruct—
this inventory of ideological uses of the term "ideological," it becomes
evident that frequently the charge of ideology functions as a smoke-
screen.

For example, if *The Nation* leaves out inconvenient facts or distorts
or invents facts (I thought that was the province of the new journalism
rather that the old left), then that is bad journalism and ought to be
identified as such, assigned a dart in the *Columbia Journalism Review*,
and pinioned by the press critics. But that should be true whether the
bad journalism appears in *The Nation*, the *Times*, or *The Wall Street
Journal*.

Let me put it this way. If *The Nation* has the ideology of the liberal
left and *National Review* has the ideology of the conservative right,
then *The New York Times*, *The Washington Post*, the newsweeklies, and
the networks have the ideology of the center, and it is part of the ideology of the center to deny that it has an ideology. So it seemed something of a non sequitur to call a magazine like *The Nation* ideological
and to suggest that it is exceptional or less reliable by virtue of that fact
alone. For example, the mainstream media give equal time to the Democrats and the Republicans, whereas *The Nation* sees part of its role
as serving as a forum for the debate between the radicals and the liberals. The editorial writers of *The New York Times* focus on Congress,
the editors of the openly Marxist *Monthly Review* focus on banks. In
the mainstream media, economics and politics are presented as if they
have nothing to do with each other. You don't read stories, as you might
in, say, an independent socialist journal like *In These Times*, on the relation of the capitalist system to pollution or the homeless, on the role
of multinational corporations in shaping American interventionist pol-

icy abroad. You do read stories based on what "official sources" say. In the United States, mainstream journalists like to call themselves objective, because for papers like *The New York Times*, or the newsweeklies or the television networks, official sources define the news. But does that really make them less ideological than journals of opinion?

At various times, various press observers have taken their own shot at defining the values that comprise the ideology of the center, although they didn't call it that. Jack Newfield, the late advocacy journalist, once wrote in an essay on what he called "Personal Journalism":

> Among these unspoken, but organic, values are belief in welfare capitalism, God, the West, Puritanism, the Law, the family, property, the two-party system, and perhaps most crucially, in the notion that violence is only defensible when employed by the State. I can't think of any White House correspondent, or network television analyst, who doesn't share these values. And at the same time, who doesn't insist he is totally objective.
>
> And it is these assumptions—or prejudices—that prevent publishers and editors from understanding, or even being open to, any new reality that might be an alternative to those assumptions. Potential alternatives are buried deep inside the black liberation movement, the white new left, the counterculture of rock music, long hair, underground newspapers and drugs, as well as in the nonwhite revolutionary movements in the third world. And it is these threatening and unfamiliar social movements that the mass media most systematically misrepresent. And it is their sympathizers who are excluded from positions of real power within media hierarchies.

The sociologist Herbert Gans, in his book *Deciding What's News: A Study of CBS Evening News, NBC Nightly News, Newsweek and Time*, tells us that there are eight clusters of what he calls "enduring values" that underlie the news brought to us by the mainstream news organizations he has studied. He lists these as: ethnocentrism, altruistic democracy, responsible capitalism, small-town pastoralism, individualism, moderatism, social order, and national leadership. He explicitly leaves out others because they are taken for granted, such as the desirability of economic prosperity; the undesirability of war; the virtues of family, love, and friendship; and the ugliness of hate and prejudice.

Michael Parenti, author of *Inventing Reality: The Politics of the Mass Media*, has reported that when A. R. Rosenthal was executive editor of the *Times*, he killed copy to "pull the paper back to the center." By Parenti's lights, "The center was a place on the spectrum not far from where the White House, the State Department, the Pentagon, and the giant corporations stood."

Anyway, it was with thoughts such as these in mind that with the help of a group of *Nation* interns I took a stab at defining the ideology of the center myself. Our theory was that the self-described newspaper of record, *The New York Times*, is at the center of the ideology of the center,* so we decided to do a case study of the ideology of *The New York Times* by way of its Editors' Notes, those episodic morsels of self-criticism which occasionally appear on page 2 right after the correction box.

We assembled all of the Editors' Notes since they began, and did our best to extract a working list of their explicit rules. We got about two dozen, which included: "*Times* policy requires anyone attacked in the news columns to be given a chance to reply." "The *Times* practice is to present the view of both sides of the controversy." "The *Times* has a policy of omitting racial, religious, or ethnic identification unless they're shown to be pertinent to the news." "The *Times* does not knowingly assign a book review to anyone who is an adversary of the author." "*Times* policy is to correct errors promptly." "*Times* practice is to reconcile its news reports with what it said previously." "The *Times* policy is to seek comments from subjects of its news articles." "The *Times* has a rule against anonymous pejoratives." "The paper policy is to avoid . . . opinionated wording in its news columns, and to omit personal criticism by sources who insist on anonymity." Then we conducted a search to see whether the rules were applied evenly across the board. Our preliminary findings resulted in a series of hypotheses:

---

*Others contended that the *Times* is better described as "liberal" rather than centrist. Call me ideological, but I don't see it that way. Either way, the experiment stands. If they are right, it merely means that instead of identifying the ideology of the center, we have identified the ideology of the center-liberal. Big deal.

That these rules don't apply to prisoners, that they don't apply to foreigners, that they don't apply to Communists, that they don't apply to terrorists, that they don't apply to children, that they don't apply to Jesse Jackson or Al Sharpton, or poor people generally, especially poor people of color. So ultimately, our hope is to tease out from all of the above the value assumptions at the *Times*, the ideology of the paper, i.e., of the center, or the liberal-center, as the case may be. (By the time we finish, maybe we'll discover which.)

7

A GLOBAL VISION

Beyond matters ideological, I had a much less abstract concern. When I arrived at *The Nation*, I thought it was important that we run at least one international or foreign policy piece per issue. But soon I found we were doing special issues like "The Question of Intervention: Under what circumstances if any is it permissible for one country to intervene in the affairs of another?"; "Myths about the Middle East"; and E. P. Thompson's issue-long "Letter to America" on the antinuclear movement. Even our nonspecial issues devoted more and more space to "foreign" affairs, international relations, globalization, call it what you will. This business of covering the planet with no budget for staff correspondents abroad was a killer. When we wanted to send Andy Kopkind to the former Soviet Union or South Africa, it was possible to call someone like David Hunter or Cora Weiss at the Rubin Foundation and get his travel paid for. But such ad hoc arrangements went only so far. Also there were transnational corporate behemoths that surrounded themselves with a praetorian guard of high-priced lawyers and PR people whose principal job seemed to be to keep their clients out of the papers. Maybe now was the time to try to do something about that.

By the middle of the 1980s, Arthur Carter, the man who had originally wanted to amalgamate all the left-liberal journals, re-emerged. This time he had James Goodale running interference. Over lunch Goodale, whom I had known when he was general counsel to *The New York Times*, explained that he lived next door to Arthur in Connecticut, that Arthur had told him about his conversation with Ham Fish some

years before, that watching the magazine under our stewardship he
had abandoned his ideas about a mega-mini-merger. But he wanted in.
He had no editorial designs. All he had was money, a townhouse in the
East Sixties with 10,000 vacant square feet, and a desire to recapture
the dream of his youth (he had worked on the business side of the student paper at Brown as an undergraduate). He didn't even want to be
publisher of *The Nation*, at least not so long as Ham was willing to
serve. No strings. Were we interested enough to at least talk about it?

On December 20, 1985, after many months of interminable meetings, we went into business together. One reason the "negotiation"
with Arthur took so long was that he had no previous history with either *The Nation* or left-wing philanthropy. Remember that when Ham
had first asked him about his politics he had replied, "Registered opportunist. Heh heh." And although he was ready and willing to sign all
sorts of pledges guaranteeing editorial independence, what guarantee
did we have that this mysterious self-made multimillionaire maverick
would be as good as his word? The thirty-three-page agreement, with
twenty-four exhibits, schedules, and attachments, that we all signed
said, among other things, "Seller and buyer desire to preserve the character and tradition of *The Nation* magazine . . . As stated in its original
prospectus in 1865, viz: '*The Nation* will not be the organ of any party,
sect, or body. It will, on the contrary, make an earnest effort to bring to
the discussion of political and social questions a really critical spirit,
and to wage war upon the vices of violence, exaggeration, and misrepresentation by which so much of the political writing of the day is
marred . . .'"

The real innovation was a three-year "trial marriage," during which
Arthur agreed to put up a minimum ($500,000 per annum)—and while
either party could walk out if the arrangement was not working, just in
case, we had a three-person team of mediators ready to step in: *The Nation's* nominee, Ramsey Clark; Arthur Liman, a partner in the firm Paul,
Weiss, Rifkind, who went on to serve as chief counsel in the Senate's investigation of the Iran-Contra affair (Arthur's nominee); and Thomas
Winship (our joint nominee), recently retired editor of *The Boston
Globe*. (Winship later became a small shareholder in *The Nation*.) The
agreement spelled out in quasi-legalese the principle that editorial independence and sound business practice were interwoven.

Arthur Carter was the latest in an impressively short line of proprietors who held (or went along with) the peculiar belief that the owner's job is to protect the principle of editorial independence rather than to make money or to visit his/her own views on the publication. Still, we had three or four concerns. Would he try to slick us up? Would he honor his pledge to protect our editorial independence? Would he try to protect his powerful friends? As it turned out, not only did he not want to Madison Avenue-ize *The Nation*'s look, he seemed to regard its newsprint feel as a landmark-protection project. He even raised the possibility of reverting to *The Nation*'s original 1865 small-type black-and-white format with an all-print cover. His most problematic encounter with the staff had to do with his wanting to turn down a classified ad because he thought it would sully the pages of the magazine. The ad was for a "penis poster" that purported to display penises in all their protean lengths and variety throughout the animal kingdom. Our advertising manager, a young Irishman with a thick brogue, favored the ad for its funkiness (and the commissions he earned from its placement). After a showdown meeting with much shouting, Arthur told Eamonn Fitzgerald to do what he wanted, Eamonn told Arthur he didn't want to antagonize his employer, and a compromise was worked out.

No sooner did Arthur come to *The Nation* than *Vanity Fair* came to Arthur. They wanted to publish a profile of him, and the writer, Michael Shnayerson, saw Arthur as a Gatsby figure whom he couldn't figure out. I was in England trying to conscript the *New Statesman* into joining a new international consortium of progressive periodicals when Schnayerson tracked me down by overseas long-distance with an urgent message to call back collect. One of my first projects after Arthur's arrival at *The Nation* was to try to put together an international network of magazines to do investigations on subjects that crossed national boundaries. Shnayerson had virtually finished his profile but had one more question. Arthur had told him of his hopes for increasing *The Nation*'s circulation. How high? Schnayerson had asked him. Very high, Arthur told him.

"A hundred thousand?"

Arthur said yes.

"Hundreds of thousands?"

Arthur said yes.

"A million?" Arthur said yes, but over time.

Did I think he was serious, Schnayerson wanted to know. I hope so, I told him.

One concern we had about Arthur had to do with whether he would, like Mrs. Schiff, take the position that his establishment friends were or ought to be off limits. We needn't have worried. Nothing made Arthur happier than when his high-flying buddies got their comeuppance in our pages. "What did you expect?" he would tell them. "It's *The Nation.*"

Many years before, in only my second week at *The Nation*, the copy chief, a marvelous woman named Marion Hess who, it seemed, had been at *The Nation* forever, had told me in some distress that her young part-time assistant had put in for overtime because she had worked extra hours, which she was technically within her rights to do under the terms of the magazine's contract with the Newspaper Guild. But Marion viewed the situation with alarm. It had never happened before. I told the staff that we intended to treat them as fairly as possible, and when and if the magazine's finances turned around, they would be justly rewarded. But my personal plan was to work sixty or eighty hours a week, to stay until midnight if required. If everybody put in time-and-a-half for overtime, we would go bankrupt.

It had been explained to me that when the radical journalist Heywood Broun helped to organize the Newspaper Guild in 1933 he had an office at *The Nation*, and he put *The Nation* in the Guild. I had assumed that membership in the Guild was mainly symbolic. What I didn't appreciate until our first round of negotiations, conducted by Ham, was that there were firm, even fierce Guild rules that were far from merely symbolic. When Ham explained what we could and couldn't afford, the Guild responded, "We've heard that before," treating him/us, as Ham said, as if we were *The New York Times*. The difference was that the *Times* cried poor when they weren't and Ham cried poor because we were.

Our circulation had gone up, but our losses hadn't gone down. We brought in some bright new young people, but I neglected to take into account that they had very good eyesight, especially the young women, and could read the small print in the contract promising a thirty-five-hour week and time-and-a-half for overtime.

Then, when the *Vanity Fair* profile was published in September 1986, it contained the information that Arthur was worth more than $100 million. The hardworking staff of *The Nation* was able to read that, too. Came negotiation time, it was very hard to explain to them why the magazine couldn't give them what they asked for. Never mind that Arthur's *Nation* was losing well over $500,000 a year; with his improvements the magazine initially seemed to be losing twice that. Things were not made easier by Arthur's negotiating style, which was to start from ground zero. "We are losing hundreds of thousands of dollars. How can they expect to get a raise?" I had to explain to Arthur that the staff in recent years had gotten raises when the publisher was the relatively impoverished Fish consortium, so they might not appreciate a hundred-million-dollar man breaking that precedent.

Every Thursday Arthur would drive down to *The Nation* office. (Ham pointed out to me that for the first five weeks, each time it was in a different car.) Ham and he and I would then go for lunch, usually at Il Mulino, a high-end Italian restaurant on West Third Street in the Village. The owner would always give us the same table. (Once, our table was taken and the next week the lunch moved to Da Umberto, a higher-end Italian restaurant a little farther uptown.) Arthur would survey and mull over the menu, and then after a Crystal on the rocks, he would order. "A little pasta, al dente." And then we would go down the business agenda.

We did a modest makeover of *The Nation*'s design, increased the weight of the paper stock, and Arthur chose a slightly creamier color. We rented another floor in our building, and Arthur arranged with the landlord, whom he knew from the real-estate wars, to build an internal staircase connecting the two floors. Later, wielding both a carrot (he would personally guarantee our lease) and a stick (he threatened to break the lease if the price was not right), he persuaded his erstwhile friend the landlord to lower our rent. We increased the size of our mailings. When Andy Kopkind (who had attended the London School of Economics) interviewed him for an editorial about the state of the economy, and he read what Andy wrote, he joined the legions of Kopkind fans. Maybe most important, Arthur passed what I have come to think of as the Vidal test.

The occasion was *The Nation*'s special 120th anniversary issue, dated March 3, 1986. To mark it, we invited observers from countries around the world to give us their impressions of how perceptions abroad of the United States had changed over the previous generation. They included Margaret Atwood from Canada (she wrote about what it was like growing up with one's nose pressed against the "one way mirror" of the United States), Carlos Fuentes from Mexico (he described the United States as "a democracy inside but an empire outside; Dr. Jekyll at home, Mr. Hyde in Latin America"); Benazir Bhutto from Pakistan; Willy Brandt from Germany; Margaret Papandreou from Greece; Yevgeny Yevtushenko from Russia; and Gore Vidal from Ravello, Italy, where he was then spending half his time. We encouraged our contributors to be personal, idiosyncratic, and anecdotal. Vidal chose to cast his comments on America's imperial life as a response to articles that the *Commentary* editor Norman Podhoretz and his wife, Midge Decter, had written attacking an earlier article of Vidal's.

Letters started pouring in, some of them public, some of them private. Some from strangers, and some written in the highest dudgeon from "friends." Some of them orchestrated. In reading the mountain of mail, I respected letters taking exception to Vidal's argument, I expected (and received) letters objecting to *The Nation*'s having published his essay, and I suspected letters impugning the motives of *The Nation*'s editor (and later discovered that in a couple of cases these were intended for blind-carbon lists of invisible readers). Even so, I was not prepared for the night when on my way home I picked up a copy of the *New York Post*, still an evening newspaper, with a column in it by Norman Podhoretz about a self-hating Jew who edited an anti-Semitic magazine.

It wasn't until I got to the next paragraph, curious to read about this despicable character, when I realized he was talking about me. *Moi?* My mother kept kosher and wouldn't allow so much as an evergreen in the house.

I guess he was upset that Gore had referred to "that wonderful, wacky couple, Norman Podhoretz and his wife Midge Decter," as "the Lunts of the right wing (Israeli fifth column division)," and had commented that in their old age, they were "more and more like refugees from a Woody Allen film: *The Purple Prose of West End Avenue*." He had quoted "Poddy" as saying, "To me, the Civil War is as remote and as irrelevant as the War of the Roses," and had extrapolated from that that "his first loyalty would always be to Israel."

As I saw it, Gore's contribution to our anniversary issue and Pod-horetz's column were the second round, coming after an earlier Vidal ar-ticle in *The Nation*, "Some Jews and the Gays," itself a caustic response to several anti-gay articles in *Commentary*, including one by Midge Decter called "The Boys on the Beach." Vidal's message had been: As mi-norities under attack, Jews and gays should make common cause against the common enemy: bigotry. Vidal, of course, did not put it so gently:

> Decter says that once faggots have "ensconced" themselves in certain professions or arts, "they themselves have engaged in a good deal of discriminatory practices against others. There are businesses and professions [which ones? She is congenitally short of data] in which it is less than easy for a straight, unless he makes the requisite gesture of propitiation to the homosex-ual in power, to get ahead." This, of course, was Hitler's original line about the Jews: They had taken over German medicine, teaching, law, journalism. Ruthlessly, they kept out gentiles; lecherously, they demanded sexual favors.

In my view Gore was and is an equal-opportunity offender, and the question was whether it was all right or automatically in bad taste for a gentile to make jokes about Jews and Jewish culture. To my mind, anti-Semitism—although its specter hovered over the proceedings—had nothing to do with it.

Irving Howe, a Peace Now supporter who reminded me in a cordial note that he found *Commentary*'s politics "detestable," wrote to say that Vidal's reference to Israel as Podhoretz's "country" was "utterly ap-palling," because it was reminiscent of the most vulgar sentiments against American Jews for having a "double loyalty." Yes, Irving was conceding, there is an excess in polemics, but "even in excess there ought to be a limit."

What did I have to say in my defense?

First, I want to quote from a letter I received from my friend the novelist Anne Roiphe. "I know you say you were only dancing to the First Amendment," she wrote, but she didn't think we would have printed an article that said, for example, "that Asians were wily."

Now here is my defense. Actually we did print such an article by, of all people, Gore Vidal. In fact, it was an earlier one on the American empire that Norman and Midge had separately attacked, and to which his new, 120th anniversary article was a riposte. In it he had argued that the United States and the U.S.S.R. ("the white race," as he put it) should get together to resist the impending hi-tech invasion by Japan (the wily Asians). One can take his yellow-peril argument literally, in which case it is racism, or one can take it as his way of commenting on the folly of the Cold War culture, as if to say, "If the only way I can persuade you two foolish superpowers to cease and desist from the arms race, which is depleting the resources of the planet it threatens to blow up, is to appeal to you in terms of your greed and racist stereotypes, then so be it."

To me it was the latter. And the question was not about free speech. It was about ironic speech. Gore Vidal is a satirist, an ironist, a man from Iron Mountain. By the same token, when he suggested that Jewish neoconservatives like "Poddy" should register as foreign agents for the state of Israel, either one could take his arguments literally, in which case they were anti-Semitic, or one could take them as his ironic way of commenting on the folly of Jewish intellectuals making alliances with the Moral Majority (who were the real anti-Semites).

This was all very ironic to me, because my political awakening had begun with two events: watching (and cheering) when Branch Rickey hired Jackie Robinson to play for the Brooklyn Dodgers, the first African-American in major league baseball; and my being hired as a "volunteer" (at $2.50 an hour)—my first real job—to pass out a contribution basket at Ben Hecht's play *A Flag Is Born*, which opened in 1946, the year after my bar mitzvah. The play begins in a cemetery of massacred European Jews. Using heavily symbolic characters, this long one-acter ends with a young man (played by a twenty-two-year-old Marlon Brando) making a flag from a prayer shawl and joining the anti-British underground in Palestine. Hecht had assembled an extraordinary team—Luther Adler was director, Kurt Weill wrote the music, Quentin Reynolds was the narrator, Paul Muni led the cast. We "volunteers" were instructed to arrive by 10:15. If you were on time, as you entered the theater, you heard Paul Muni saying, "The UN will put it on the agenda!" followed by mad, cackling laughter, suggesting that "putting it on the agenda" was a way of putting it off.

After curtain calls Luther Adler would come out, talk about the millions of Jews who had been massacred in Europe and the need for a Jewish homeland. He would explain that donations deposited in the baskets which we volunteers were passing up and down the aisles would be used—under the auspices of the American League for a Free Palestine—to help liberate Palestine from the British. In theory, as a fellow volunteer explained to me one night, this meant that the money would go to the Haganah, the Zionist organization whose main program was to encourage Jewish immigration—legal and illegal—to Palestine, but in fact the money would *really* go to the Irgun Zvai Leumi, which was in the business of engaging in acts of terrorism against the British. Indeed, the following year, in May 1947, Hecht used his own proceeds from the play to pay for an ad in the New York *Herald Tribune* congratulating the Irgun on blowing up British trains, robbing British banks, killing British tommies.

Little did I know that at the same time, *The Nation*'s Freda Kirchwey was lobbying for Israel behind the scenes at the United Nations.

The Arabs who lived in Palestine were missing from the consciousness raised by *A Flag Is Born*, and it wasn't until many years later that I came to understand and identify with their plight. As we put it in a special issue of *The Nation* on Myths about the Middle East, published not long after I arrived, "The logic of competing nationalist movements argues for territorial compromise."

Nor did I consider myself "self-hating." In fact, as my friends and enemies would have told him, if I had a flaw—and I had many—it ran in the other, i.e., self-regarding, direction.

As far as *The Nation* and the Jews went, well, it was a slightly more complicated matter, but only slightly. As Max Frankel asked in his November 14, 2001, *New York Times Magazine* article "Turning Away from the Holocaust," why wasn't the annihilation of six million Jews—the Nazi war within the war—front-page news in *The New York Times*? "Why, then, were the terrifying tales almost hidden in the back pages?" He contrasted *Times* noncoverage with "a few publications—papers like the *Post* (then liberal) and *PM* in New York and magazines like *The Nation* and *The New Republic*—[which] showed more conspicuous concern."

In 1946–47, Kirchwey traveled to the Middle East, where she talked with and listened to Arab leaders, but her diary tells us that her "mind was already made up: she was committed to a homeland for the Jews." She also was courted by Jewish Agency people. In the pages of the magazine, she wrote of the plight of 100,000 Jewish refugees from Europe with no place to go. She thought the British were "openly encouraging an Arab revolt." She thought—hoped—a democratic Jewish state would create stability in the Middle East. During the war *The Nation* had consistently advocated a Jewish home in Palestine: it was Palestine or Death. Kirchwey fought for a Jewish homeland with speeches, specially commissioned studies, and *Nation* articles. Twelve Nation Associate studies were submitted to the U.S. government and to the United Nations between 1942 and 1954, documenting collaboration between Nazis and Muhammad Amin Al-Husayni, mufti of Jerusalem and head of the Arab Higher Committee; and documenting the way Nazi money had financed the mufti's riots against Jewish Palestine as early as 1936. (In 1943 the Nazis had declared to the mufti "that the destruction of the so-called Jewish homeland in Palestine is an immutable part of the policy of the Greater German Reich.") The consensus among those who followed these matters, like the historian Abram Leon Sachar, was that the *Nation* documentation of the pro-Axis record of the Arab states "provided the Zionists with their most telling argument against the white [British] paper [which would have established a primarily Arab, independent Palestine]."

Under my editorship *The Nation* has published much that is harshly critical of Israel, particularly its policy with regard to the West Bank settlements. This has led critics to call the magazine anti-Israel. As I wrote to Barbara Tuchman, I didn't see it that way. On August 23, 1982, Tuchman, with whom I served on the Authors Guild Council, sent me a private letter complaining about a *Nation* editorial urging the Israelis to negotiate with Arafat. It began, "*The Nation* has been anti-Israel since long before your day . . ."

I took umbrage at Tuchman's letter and replied:

I think your use of the term "anti-Israel" contributes to the current confusion (and also to the current language pollution) by automatically stigmatizing as "anti" all those who believe that Israel's long-range interest and security are undermined by Israeli policies which exacerbate the conflict between Palestinian nationalism and Israeli nationalism.

By way of analogy, I don't consider those who wrote and protested against American involvement in Vietnam as anti-American.

I added that while I probably had no more use for Arafat than she did, "I think you are wrong if you think there are no internal politics to the PLO."

I said a lot more, but it is certainly true that after the war of 1967, with the rise of the Israeli nationalist right, the invasion of Lebanon and the two intifadas, *Nation* writers, including Vidal and the Palestinian intellectual Edward Said, among others, have piled on, and much of the time I have agreed with them. Nevertheless, when writing or assigning unsigned editorials on the Middle East, I did my best to honor the impulse that gave birth to the Jewish state and led Freda Kirchwey to the firm conviction in 1947 that the Jews could teach "a lesson in cooperative democracy planning . . . a lesson not for the Jewish people alone but for the world." Would that she had been a better prophet.

Israeli Peace Nowniks like the novelist Amos Oz, the journalist Hillel Schenker, the scholar Shlomo Avnieri, the radical former MP Uri Avnery, and satirical prophets like the dovish Israeli Op Ed columnist Amos Kenan have long been at the center of the *Nation* mix. In 2004 Roane Carey, a senior editor and specialist on the Middle East, set out to co-edit with Adam Shatz a special issue on the Middle East. As preparation he reread "Myths About the Middle East," first published almost thirty years earlier under its theme of the tragic confrontation of two national movements. "It still applies, we could run it today," he said. Still, it must be conceded that over time *The Nation* has done no better in prescribing for the Middle East than the parties themselves.

But back to Vidal. Another Vidal-related letter I received came disguised as an embossed invitation to lunch at the home of Bob Guccione and Kathy Keaton, owner and editor of *Penthouse* (which after many appeals had won their case and seemed to be riding high).

Since the *Penthouse* home was not a penthouse but, rather, an elegant East Side townhouse famous for its world-class art collection, I was only too happy to accept. Not since 1952, when Swarthmore College's president John Nason had summoned me and my *Phoenix* co-editor Bill Waterfield to his office to discuss an April Fools' Day ruse in excruciatingly poor taste—Waterfield and I rotated issue responsibility, and the April Fools' Day issue had been on my watch—did I approach a meeting with such curiosity and trepidation. I arrived at the appointed hour and was met by a lady I took to be Guccione's curator, who suggested that I might want to take a brief tour of the $200 million art collection before lunch. I paid my respects to Renoir, Degas, and Picasso, and fifteen minutes later was ushered into the dining room, where drink orders were solicited and I was joined by Guccione, Ms. Keaton, and four gentlemen, who turned out to be his circulation, marketing, advertising, and PR executives. We had barely consumed the *amuse gueules* when Bob told me how much they admired our 120th anniversary issue and all the press it had received. Then Bob asked me how much it cost to get Gore Vidal to write his essay. When I told him we had paid each contributor to that issue $25 and Gore got the same $25 that everyone else got, he almost choked on his Château Margaux and told me he had offered Vidal $50,000 to write an article for *Penthouse* and Vidal declined. He then proceeded to pass out Cuban cigars and brandy and to muse about how perhaps he might be interested in buying *The Nation*. Indeed, he said, he had been thinking about it for some time.

The fact is that people like Vidal (well, Vidal—there are no people "like" Vidal) write for *The Nation because* it is independent, and would never write for someone like *Penthouse*'s publisher at *Nation* prices. I tried to explain that to Gooch, but I'm not sure he accepted or understood it. On the other hand, when I told him that we had recently sold the magazine to Arthur Carter and I had first-refusal rights should Arthur ever want to sell it again, he seemed to understand. We shook hands all around and agreed to stay in touch.

What had Arthur Carter thought of this whole brouhaha? Just before our anniversary issue went in the mail, I had told him about Vidal's piece. I suspected that Vidal's anti-Zionist politics, combined with his personal assault on "Poddy," as he called Norman Podhoretz, would spawn the unwarranted charges of anti-Semitism which it did in fact elicit, and I had no idea how Arthur would take it. Not to worry, he said over lunch; he was more interested in talking about Zionism and what it really meant today.

At the time I had no idea that Podhoretz, with whom I had had cordial relations in the past, would mount a campaign against *The Nation*

because of this article. He had Marian Magid, his associate editor at
Commentary, write to thirty people on our masthead asking them
whether they had seen fit to protest it, and he described it as "the most
blatantly anti-Semitic outburst to appear in an American periodical
since the Second World War." Here, it seemed to me, was the ultimate
Arthur test: A number of close members of the *Nation* family themselves had objected to our publishing Gore's article, and many of
Arthur's friends and business associates were members of—indeed,
helped to constitute—the organized Jewish establishment.

At lunch the following week Arthur was all smiles and good cheer.
"Guess who called me yesterday," he said. It was Kenneth Bialkin,
head of the Anti-Defamation League, a close friend of Arthur's (and
someone I had known in my *Monocle* days, when he was Lionel Pincus's lawyer). "You want to know what I told him when he started to
complain? I told him, What do you think we are? It's *The Nation*, not
the Jewish Federation newsletter."

One project that would never have happened without Arthur's injection of capital (even though in the end a number of foundations put up
some money to help make it happen) was InterNation, our attempt to
promote investigative journalism on transnational subjects. But money
works in strange ways, and in this case I believe that knowing that
Arthur was there gave us the psychological confidence to go forward.

If I do say so myself (and I do), the theory was beautiful. And remember, this was before the Web, before the fax even. InterNation
would have three parts: a worldwide network of progressive investigative journalists who would collaborate with each other; an international body of cooperating progressive publications, which would
simultaneously publish investigative articles on subjects that by their
nature crossed national boundaries; and a series of annual conferences
around the world to jump-start, inspire, and discuss possible subjects
and articles and work out kinks in the network. The idea was that by
publishing and promoting each article in many countries, we might
simultaneously make worldwide news. That way, our press releases
could begin: "Today, *The Nation* magazine in New York, the *New*

Statesman in London, *Sydsvenska Dagbladet* in Malmo, Sweden, *Information* in Copenhagen, *Vrej Nederlander* in Amsterdam, *Il Manifesto* in Rome, jointly charged . . ."

We would each pay our traditionally modest fees. But from the writer's vantage point they might collectively be immodest (with an ample pooled pot for expenses). The perspective would be global, although each magazine would add its own local news peg and adjust the story to its own country's culture. And each international conference would be held in partnership with one of the overseas magazines. *The Nation* would raise the money to get people to come, and the host-partner would house, feed, and cover costs while they were there.

Even before our consortium was up and limping, it had some curious lateral consequences. With the Hitchens-Bird exchange behind us, we looked forward to fortifying our transatlantic relationship with the *Statesman* through InterNation. Early in 1986, amid fanfare about a new era being ushered in (why are eras always "ushered" in, can't they get there on their own?), I met John Lloyd, who had quit the *Financial Times*, where he was a rising star, to take over the *New Statesman*, which he was committed to revive. He was, he told me in his Scots accent, interested in InterNation—I was on my initial InterNation foray—but he let me know that as the *Statesman*'s new editor, he had two frustrations. One was financial. What else was new? He lacked the resources to bribe the British journalists he coveted to write for him. The other was political: Those he thought of as the "loony left" were giving him a hard time about his wanting the paper to be more "respectable" than it had been under our friend Bruce Page, when it was known primarily for its investigative coups. This was a moment when nuclear disarmament and anti-NATO sentiment were in the air, and those on Lloyd's left saw his vision for the paper as too centrist, too courteous, too close to that of his former employer.

Lloyd for his part believed that the *New Statesman* had a historic opportunity to engage mainstream political issues from a left perspective and position, but he had little patience for those he regarded as unilateralists, utopians, and purists. When I told him that some parallel divisions split the progressive community in the United States, he was interested, but when I added that I also believed that in the United States the further left the magazine moved the better it would be for circulation (not that I would ever stoop to such cynical tactics), Lloyd found that hard to believe.*

When I returned to the States, I mentioned Lloyd's financial complaints and asked Arthur if he would be interested in doing for them what he did for us. Arthur was interested. Visions of a left-mini-international publishing empire danced in my head when I told John the good news, that Arthur Carter might be willing to put up a nice chunk of change with the understanding that he would guarantee the publication's editorial independence. Was Lloyd interested? "Am I interested?" Lloyd asked. "I'm jumping out of my chair," he said, "and worried only that my head will hit the ceiling."

He mentioned the matter to Phillip Whitehead, the former Labour MP and now *New Statesman* publisher, who thought enough of the idea to call a few minutes later: As it happened, he was going to be in the United States the following week to discuss a television series with WGBH in Boston (in his other life he was a documentary film producer), and perhaps we could arrange a meeting.

The deal didn't happen, but the meeting did, and Whitehead dined out on it for the next ten years.

The meeting was scheduled for 4:00 p.m. at Arthur's home in Roxbury. He had to be in Connecticut then because a handmade piano carved from blond wood imported from Italy was to be delivered that afternoon, and Arthur, who had been something of a musical prodigy as a child, needed to check it out. Phillip's plane was to land in Hartford, a forty-minute ride away. Ham Fish and I drove up from New York and arrived a half hour ahead of time to discuss our strategy with Arthur. It boiled down to this: Let's hear what Whitehead has to say, no commitment. Shortly after we arrived, a horrendous show of thunder and lightning performed for our benefit in Arthur's driveway, and then torrents of rain came and continued well past 4:00 and then 4:30. No

---

*My theory was that there were a series of hard-core single-interest constituencies— radical feminists, gay-rights activists, black nationalists, nuclear disarmament unilateralists, various academic postmodernists, Marxists, and such who had as much contempt for liberals as they did for conservatives, and a weekly magazine which incorporated their sometimes parochial, sometimes conspiratorial worldviews would do very well; it was not, however, *The Nation,* with its long-running debate/argument/ conversation between the radicals and the liberals.

piano, no Whitehead, no word. At 5:15 a limo appeared through the wet. Ever the gentleman, Arthur got out his umbrella and welcomed the right honorable former MP. There was only a moment's embarrassment when it turned out that Arthur was welcoming Whitehead's distinguished limousine driver, who, to tell the truth, looked more distinguished than the disheveled and very wet former MP, of whom, it was once said, he trimmed nothing, not even his beard. Once inside, dried out, nursing a cup of hot tea prepared by Arthur's Guatemalan housekeeper, Phillip had barely launched into his pitch when the doorbell rang and out of the fog emerged a truck with many wet movers and a dry, well-covered, exquisite piano. I guess when you get a hand-crafted piano delivered direct from Italy you test it before you accept delivery. That at least is what Arthur did as he sat himself down on the imported stool and proceeded to play a ten-minute medley of Mozart, Haydn, and Schubert, stroking the keys with style, panache, and many flourishes for his wide-eyed and appreciative audience.

Down to business. As Whitehead explained it, the *New Statesman*, whose circulation had plunged from a high of 90,000 or more under the editorship of Kingsley Martin in the 1950s to its current 23,000, was cash-short, although things were not exactly desperate, since it could always sell its debt-free Great Turnstyle building.

Nevertheless, if John Lloyd was to remake the magazine as he hoped, it needed a healthy injection of capital. The problem was that as a result of a takeover attempts in the 1950s by a property developer friend of Aneurin Bevan, the left-wing Labour leader, a maze of interlocking subsidiary companies had been superimposed on the already ornate corporate structure dreamed up in 1913 by the *New Statesman*'s Fabian founders Beatrice and Sidney Webb (with an assist from George Bernard Shaw, who had talked them into putting up the money). To protect Staggers and Naggers, as *N.S.* was quaintly known, from political predators, there were now something like four separate but overlapping companies, each with three classes of shareholders. And then five so-called E (for editorial) shareholders constituted a sort of democratic-socialist-humanist palace guard. No substantial editorial change (including dismissal of the editor) could be undertaken without their unanimous approval.

But, Phillip said, all was not hopeless. Since Carter had no editorial designs on the paper, he needn't worry about the E's, and besides, Lloyd was as good an editor as one could get. If Arthur were willing to meet with key trustees and others, with Phillip vouching for him and paving the way, he "might be permitted" to buy into the trust and "perhaps own as much as one-third of the second-class stock." Arthur listened respectfully, taking it all in, and then said, "Let me give you some advice. Don't sell your building. If you'd like, I'd be prepared to lend you what you need with the building as security." Phillip returned to London, where the idea of going into hock to a rich, eccentric American had little appeal. John Lloyd, however, did attend our first InterNation conference in May 1987.

Our partner was a Dutch Weekly, *Vrej Nederlander*. Forty-five reporters, editors, and television producers from all over had signed on to discuss ways we might work together to muckrake transnational subjects (acid rain, international police agencies, nuclear weapons, multinational corporations, the banking community, organized crime). Who better to keynote the first InterNation conference than the great maverick journalist I. F. Stone?

I called to ask Izzy if he would consider coming to Amsterdam for the first ever InterNation conference of investigative journalists.

Izzy was interested. As a matter of fact, he said he and Esther had taken their honeymoon in Amsterdam, and so he had an additional, romantic motive for wanting to take the trip.

Hamilton Fish was slightly concerned about the cost of bringing along Esther, but I explained to Ham, as Izzy had explained to me, that he went nowhere without Esther, and besides, it would be a great—historic—occasion if Izzy were really to join us, as well as guaranteeing the success and gravitas of our conference. As it turned out, Izzy made it clear that he understood that no fee would be involved (a good thing, since, as Ham unnecessarily pointed out, we had no fee in our budget). Our budget was so tight that we had arranged with a nonscheduled charter airline for budget round-trip tickets at $400 per person, the only hitch being that they couldn't guarantee that the plane would leave when it was supposed to leave. At the other end, our friends at *Vrej Nederlander* had found a modest hotel on the outskirts of Amsterdam that agreed to give us all a fantastically low rate. (We would commute to the conference center by a chartered bus.)

A couple of days later, Ham stuck his head in my office to say we had a problem. Izzy and Esther, it seemed, were not fliers. Part of the attraction of the conference was that it would give them a chance to do what they always did when they went to Europe—take the *Queen Elizabeth II*. Don't worry, Izzy explained, we're happy to travel tourist class. He put Ham in touch with a travel agent in Jacksonville, Florida, who always took care of them and even knew which cabin they favored.

A few days after that, Ham stuck his head in the door again. I said, "Don't tell me," but he did. The *QE2* was going to dock in Southampton a few days prior to the conference and Izzy couldn't have been more pleased. "At our age," he explained, "we need a couple of days to get our land legs, and we have this little hotel in London which makes a nice base."

Ham was not surprised when, a few days later, his phone rang yet again. "You know, Hamilton, I'm a romantic," Izzy confided, and he explained that on their honeymoon he and Esther had stayed "at a small pensione on the canal which ran through the center of town, not very expensive, and if you could just locate that . . ." and we did.

It was not even a problem, two days later, when Izzy called to say that by happy coincidence, one of his children, her family and in-laws were going to be in Europe at the same time, and if they too could stay in a cottage by the canal . . .

Also, Izzy had an idea. There was a famous cathedral in Amsterdam which operated as a sort of agora and public forum. If we could arrange for him to speak—he had done so many years ago and seemed to have something of a following in Amsterdam—he would be pleased to donate his fee to help the defray the costs of the conference.

So we arranged, close to a thousand Dutch men and women showed up to hear Izzy speak, and forty journalists from all over Europe came to the conference. From the opening session Izzy peppered panelists with questions, anecdotes, and observations from the audience. His own keynote speech was truly inspirational, and at a farewell session at a local bar, as we consumed caviar and vodka, he raised a toast: "Comes the revolution, we will all eat like this."

The actual conference lived up to the theory in the sense that a loose network was forged, ideas were exchanged, and articles were born which later appeared in a number of periodicals whose editors were in attendance.

But for me another by-product was an insight I gained into our keynote speaker, the great Izzy. Back in 1954, when Izzy had spoken at Swarthmore, he billed the undergraduate organization which had invited him for a round-trip Washington, D.C.–Philadelphia club-car ticket. At the time this seemed to me something of an extravagance for a journalist so identified with the dispossessed. (And it never occurred to me that he asked for no fee.)

It was, then, part of Izzy's charm that he never accepted the idea that in order to be a heretic, a maverick, a solo practitioner, it was necessary to be a martyr or a monk. He once said, "I have so much fun I ought to be arrested." As Peter Osnos, who had worked briefly for Izzy at the start of his own more traditional distinguished journalistic and publishing career, pointed out, it was not only on *The Nation*'s ticket that he danced his way across the Atlantic. He and Esther used to go out dancing twice a week. More significantly, his insistence on his perks had less to do with hedonism than a sense of dignity, of self-confidence, of earned entitlement. He wasn't about to let a priggish journalistic establishment marginalize him. He once said, "You may just think that I'm a red Jew son-of-a-bitch, but I'm keeping Thomas Jefferson alive." He embodied the romantic idea of one man pitted against the system.

In the end I understood the social significance of Izzy's upscale travel preferences. For some years the Washington establishment had tried to treat Izzy as a pariah, but he never let them. He was entitled to his entitlements, and I admired him even the more for it.

The second InterNation conference in 1988 was the beneficiary of Stuart Weir, who replaced John Lloyd as *The New Statesman*'s editor. Lloyd returned to the *Financial Times* where he went on to cover Gorbachev's Soviet Union, presumably having despaired at dealing with the *Statesman*'s finances and its restless radical contingent. But Weir, fresh from the *New Socialist*, where he had made his own waves, was an InterNation enthusiast, and the second InterNation conference was the result. This one focused on the ways broadcast and print journalists might cooperate on international investigative projects. We raised the travel money, and the *New Statesman* arranged to house and feed seventy-five writers, editors, producers, and broadcast presenters at Royal Holloway College just outside London. Seymour Hersh gave the keynote.

Our third conference in 1992 was held in Russia at the Moscow State University School of Journalism, tri-sponsored *by Nezavisimaya Gazeta, Ogonyok,* and *Sovsherno Sekretna.* Two hundred fifty print and broadcast journalists, foundation executives, and Russian officials (including the deputy chief archivist) were in attendance, and Carl Bernstein gave the keynote. (For me the highlight was the opening banquet, when after many vodka toasts, the double-talking Professor Irwin Corey, who had crashed our Town Hall debate, walked in the door. It turned out that the "Professor," now well into his eighties, had paid his own way to Moscow and decided to invite himself to the opening-night festivities. As the MC, I immediately informed one and all that we were honored to have an unexpected guest, "the world's leading authority," and invited the professor to say a few words, which he proceeded, in his inimitable way, to do. My only regret is that we didn't have a videotape of the gradually growing consternation on the faces of the simultaneous translators as Irwin went into his pitch and one by one their puzzled auditors removed their earplugs.)

Although InterNation gave birth to important stories on a range of subjects including international monopolies (such as the cement cartel), corruption in connection with the Olympics, the dumping of nuclear waste in the Third World, and much more, the process of putting together the network had its own rewards. It provided, for example, a continuing and sometimes startling education on the culture of journalism itself. Consider what happened when I contacted my old Army buddy Lynn Noah (I told you we'd meet him again) and his favorite philosopher, Confucius. In 1990 my son Bruno was studying Japanese poetry on a Mombusho fellowship in Nagoya, Japan, and I thought I'd take the occasion of a visit there to make a side trip in search of Asian and South Asian journalists who might want to be part of our project. I called the State Department to see if Lynn Noah was still in Asia. As luck would have it, he was back in Washington. "You know," he said, "you should let the USIA book all your appointments."

"But, Lynn," I said, "we attack the USIA regularly in *The Nation.*

Just this week we ran a very strong editorial denouncing the USIA's
establishment of Radio Martí, whose main purpose seemed to be to
beam anti-Castro propaganda to Cuba. Why would they want to set up
appointments for me, and why would I want them to?"

"Well," he explained, "it is their job to handle the problems of visiting dignitaries, and that's what you are." (Which, I wondered, but
didn't ask: a problem or a visiting dignitary?) "Besides, when you're
traveling, it takes a day to get into a country and a day to get out. You
don't speak the language. You don't know how to work the phones. You
don't want to waste time setting up appointments. The USIA can set
up all your appointments for you."

This made superficial sense, but since I was not traveling under
government auspices, it didn't seem right to have the government setting up appointments for me.

"Why don't we compromise?" Lynn suggested. "You give me the
itinerary, where you will be staying when. I'll let them know you are
coming, and if you want to take advantage of their auspices, you can do
so. If not, not." That seemed reasonable, so I agreed. Well, sort of.

In Thailand the USIA officer organized a breakfast, to which he invited something like sixteen English-speaking Thai journalists representing a variety of Thai-based publications, including one called *The
Nation*, which had taken its name from where else? The first question
was put to me by a radical young freelance Thai journalist who had in-
terned in the United States with *Mother Jones*: "If you're so independent, why are you appearing at a breakfast at the house of the USIA
representative?" I explained the circumstances of my auspices, but I
took his point. In fact, my presence was a boon to the USIA, inasmuch
as our editorial attacking Radio Martí and the USIA itself had been
published, so my presence gave the USIA the chance to cite *The Nation* as an example of what pluralism and the free press were all about.

I learned something else, too. As a briefing for my breakfast, the local office in Bangkok shared with me a thick mimeographed dossier
that included the name of every significant journalist in Thailand (including Americans and Europeans), with a paragraph or two on each,
containing what appeared to me to be a quite sophisticated political
profile, including the journalist's sympathies, an assessment of the reliability of his reporting, whether he could/should be trusted, etc. I

hadn't realized that American diplomats kept track of the press so systematically. I suppose the real question is whether it is appropriate for civil servants of a democracy to collect and keep such dossiers—not to mention to ask about the uses to which they are put. I didn't like the idea of it, but at worst it was a venial sin, and I for one was glad to have the educational benefit of it.

The most astonishing journalistic discovery I made in the course of my trek to Asia had nothing to do with the USIA. It had to do with Korea's white envelope system. While visiting Seoul I was asked to address the foreign correspondents' press club, the president of which, a correspondent with the *Far Eastern Economic Review* named Mark Clifford, had gotten his start as a *Nation* intern. He thought the local press would be interested in a talk from me about McCarthyism and how it related, if at all, to the repression in South Korea, which had ignited massive student demonstrations that were then a feature of Seoul's political landscape.

I gave my talk, and a few desultory questions followed. Then I had a question for my audience. I had heard from various American correspondents in Japan of what was called the cartel system, whereby only members of a given press cartel were permitted to cover a given ministry. To cover the Ministry of Foreign Affairs you had to be a member of the Foreign Affairs cartel, and if you weren't, you weren't admitted to press conferences held by the Foreign Minister. It was considered bad form to scoop a fellow cartel member. They were supposed to help each other. This system, it seemed to me, was not calculated to encourage entrepreneurial journalism. And in Korea it was apparently the same, only more so. It was known as the white envelope system, because at the end of each month members in good standing of the various clubs would be handed sealed white envelopes holding cash money! It had been explained to me that this was a heritage from the days when the members of the press were in fact publicists for the various government agencies. As the press gradually became more independent, they went off the official payroll, but the practice of thanking them for the publicity lived on. What, I asked the dozen Korean journalists present, did they think about this system?

Decorum had reigned until that point, and we had talked in English, but a heated argument now ensued in Korean among virtually

all the journalists. Only after tempers simmered down was I able to extract a rough paraphrase of what had transpired. Indeed, there were
deep differences among them, but the differences were not quite what
I expected. I had thought that some of the local journalists might be offended by the white envelopes, but no, the real argument was not over
whether there should be these payments but rather over whether the
tips should be pooled, so that those not lucky enough to be cartel
members could share in the booty. Only one elderly gentleman showed
contempt for the lot of them. He turned out to be a publisher, and it
was his position that most Korean working journalists were lazy louts
who didn't deserve the tips in the first place.

As one who believes that a main function of the press vis-à-vis the
government and other institutions of power should be to act as watch-
dog, the people's surrogate, I did some research when I got home, and
here is what I found out. As David E. Halvorsen put it in a 1992 paper
for the East West Institute:

> The cumulative effect of the press club system is to dull the
> knife of aggressive journalism. The government has a captive
> club conventionally tranquilized by tradition. The club mem-
> bers value friendship above individual achievement. This virtu-
> ally assures that government pronouncements have a smooth
> journey to the editor's desk. A press club member is not going to
> walk down the corridor to a private phone and start checking
> out the veracity or motives of a government press release.

On the other hand, the desk editor who receives an article has the responsibility to see that it is more fully developed. The problem is that he
is usually older and, having been schooled under the repressive years of
previous regimes, as often as not ends up censoring himself. Who needs
government censorship when self-censorship will do the job?

And then there is Confucius, who long ago made the historical case
for accepting gifts. It turns out that the practice of reciprocity and mutual help (called *nip'ung yangsok*), is a venerated system from the time
when Korea was predominantly a rural society where villages and farm-
ers would help each other. As Korean society moves from an agrarian
system with Confucian values (family, filial piety, and community) to

an urban system with so-called Western values, one wonders how long the white envelope will survive. In this perspective, the ideas of Confucius, who believed that one's ancestors never really die because their blood lives on in their descendants, have yet to make the transition to a culture that regards small gifts and courtesies as "freebies," bribes, and conflicts of interest.

Another problem is that the small gift is no longer so small. Indeed, the year after I visited Seoul, various press scandals involving hundreds of thousands of dollars became public. I say "became public" rather than "hit the press," because part of the scandal was that the mainstream press was paid off not to write about them.

Of course, Koreans are not the only ones with this heritage. In *The Autobiography of Lincoln Steffens*, Steffens tells the story of the evening when Captain Schmittberger, "an honest policeman," was pacing his first night beat near Broadway and Thirty-fourth Street, then a neighborhood rife with houses of prostitution. When a "girl ran down the steps . . . pressed a ten-dollar bill into his hand and darted back into the house," Schmittberger was baffled, and he showed an old cop the money, telling him what happened. "'Sure,' said the veteran, 'that's what the Cap put you on that fat job for: to make a little on the side.'"

When Schmittberger, who had qualms, tried to turn the money back to the captain, he jumped down his throat.

> "What did I take him for? And where did I get my nerve? I was scared. I thought the old cop had put a joke on me to get me in bad with the captain, till all of a sudden he cooled down and said that he didn't take chickenfeed. I and the likes of me might take it and keep it."
>
> A look of bewilderment—the original expression that he showed the captain, I guess—recurred on Schmittberger's face as he drew for me the conclusion he evidently drew then: "It was the tip, the size of it, that made him mad."

Although InterNation took me to Asia and scores of *Nation*-connected journalists to conferences in Europe and Eastern Europe and yielded a number of stories of international consequence, it also had reverberations closer to home. Or, to be more precise, in the dining room of Arthur Carter's second home in Roxbury, Connecticut.

George Black, our foreign affairs editor, who eventually left to work for Human Rights Watch, had been in touch with Martin Edwin Anderson, an AP reporter covering Latin America. George had told Anderson about InterNation, and now he thought he had a story: An eleven-years-after-the-fact account of a June 10, 1976, meeting in Santiago, Chile, between then–Secretary of State Henry Kissinger and Argentina's then–Foreign Minister Cesar Augusto Guzzetti, just three months after a junta of generals had seized power in Buenos Aires. Both men were attending the Sixth General Assembly of the Organization of American States, whose agenda, ironically, was dominated by issues of human rights. According to the records of the Center for Legal and Social Studies, Argentina's foremost human rights group, by the time Kissinger and Guzzetti met, 1,022 people had been disappeared forever by the new Argentinean military government. (At least another 7,938 met the same fate afterward.)

The result of the meeting was a memorandum written by an assistant secretary of state, and unearthed by Anderson, which reported that the thousands of Argentineans who were subsequently "disappeared" might otherwise have been saved, except that Kissinger made it clear that the clamor about human rights abuses would not affect U.S.-Argentine relations; this military junta continued its murderous practices. Had Kissinger sent a different signal, Anderson wrote, thousands of deaths might have been avoided.

Under a cover line saying "An InterNation Story," *The Nation* published "Kissinger and the 'Dirty War'" on October 31, 1987. It did not have that much play in the States, but we were told it was front-page news in Argentina. And given the way weekly journalism works, that was that. The next week's deadlines were already upon us.

A few months later, Annie and I were invited to a small but high-powered dinner at Arthur Carter's country home in Roxbury, Connecticut. We were told in advance that the guests would include James and Toni Goodale; Arthur and Ellen Liman; John Brademas, former congressman for Indiana who was now president of New York University (on whose board Arthur Carter sat); and oh yes, Arthur's country neighbors Henry and Nancy Kissinger.

I had never met Kissinger before and couldn't help thinking of one of Bud Trillin's more cutting columns, "Dinner at the de la Rentas." (It was published not long after a *New York Times Magazine* article on the high-society Oscar de la Rentas, whose dinners always seemed to include one representative celebrity from each category: one novel-ist, one foundation president, one actor, etc.) In Bud's fantasy dinner a potential invitation to the Kissingers was not extended because, as one de la Renta reminded the other, "we've already got one war criminal."

Anyway, when Arthur introduced me to Dr. K. as "editor of *The Na-tion*," he politely shook my hand and then asked a question. "Tell me, Mr. Navasky," he said in his famous guttural tones, "how is it that a short article in a obscure journal such as yours about a conversation that was supposed to have taken place years ago about something that did or didn't happen in Argentina resulted in sixty people holding plac-ards denouncing me a few months ago at the airport when I got off a plane in Copenhagen?"

This was the first I had heard of it. I guess we have readers in Den-mark, I told him. I don't think I told him that one of those readers was Peter Wivel, editor of a Copenhagen weekly, *Information*, a paper founded by the Resistance during World War II; he had attended the original InterNation conference in Amsterdam and its successor meet-ings, and he had picked up Anderson's story, giving it a new lead pegged to Kissinger's Copenhagen visit.

Dr. Kissinger said he barely remembered the meeting with the Ar-gentine Foreign Minister and disputed the accuracy of the account. I told him he should have taken Anderson's phone call at the time, for at a minimum his denial would have found its way into the article. He suggested I write him a letter, and he promised to set me straight. I wrote him the following week. A few months later, in February 1988, he sent me a letter he had received from William Rogers, Assistant Secre-tary of State for Latin America during the period. Rogers dismissed An-derson's account as "quadruple hearsay," but since he himself wasn't at the meeting (his dismissal was quintuple hearsay, by my count), I found his letter unpersuasive. One point he made seemed worth pondering, though—the idea that any outsider, even Henry K., could have stanched the flow of blood by a word to the Foreign Minister in the summer of 1976 might flatter the national ego but vastly misreads the American capacity to control events 4,000 miles away. On that ground alone, he rejected Anderson's conclusion that Kissinger bore some sort of moral responsibility for the killings.

Years later, when I sat down to reread Rogers's letter in the course of preparing these words, I was feeling somewhat chastised. Then I opened my *New York Times* News of the Week in Review for December 28, 2003. It included a boxed feature summarizing some government documents newly declassified thanks to the National Security Archive, a private nonprofit group in Washington (whose executive director had attended InterNation's Moscow conference). The documents dealt mostly with Kissinger and human rights abuses in Chile, but the last paragraphs included an item about Argentina:

> Mr. Kissinger decided that the doctrine he had defined for Chile should also be applied to Argentina. Meeting with the Argentine Foreign Minister, Adm. Cesar Augusto Guzzetti, in New York on October 7, 1976, he made it clear that the clamor about human rights abuses would not affect relations, a response that Robert Hill, the American Ambassador to Argentina, later said in a cable had left Admiral Guzzetti "euphoric."

It quoted Kissinger as telling Guzzetti: "Look, our basic attitude is that we would like you to succeed. I have an old-fashioned view that friends ought to be supported. What is not understood in the United States is that you have a civil war. We read about human rights problems, but not the content. The quicker you succeed the better."

Okay, I said to myself. Two views. Then on August 26, 2004, I again opened my *New York Times* only to discover that the National Security Archive had retrieved yet another document, this one a thirteen-page memorandum on an hour-long meeting between Mr. K. and Admiral Guzzetti, on June 10, 1976, in Santiago, Chile. The reporter, Diana Jean Schemo, wrote that in the meeting Kissinger "raised no protest against human rights violations that were the start of Argentina's 'dirty war,' according to a newly declassified document from the United States government archives." Carlos Osorio, director of the Archive's Southern Cone Documentation Project for Paraguay, Uruguay, and Argentina, added that "the memorandum of the conversation explains why the Argentine generals believed the secretary extended a carte blanche for the dirty war." Kissinger was unavailable for comment (traveling again), but in an interview the next day William Rogers said that at the time Argentina was "virtually ungovernable" and that to interpret what

Kissinger said "as a green light for human rights violations doesn't stand the test of history."

Ultimately InterNation faded partly because of the difficulty of (pre-fax and pre-e-mail) international communication, partly because of the office politics on the home front—from the perspective of those who didn't get to go, it looked like something of a boondoggle—and partly because when Arthur turned *The Nation* over to me, I had to stop raising money for projects like InterNation (which had won support from the MacArthur and Schulman Foundations and various of George Soros's European funds and The Marshall Fund), and turn my attention to raising money for *The Nation*. Undoubtedly there were other cultural, political, and economic factors. But I did not know that in the late 1980s, when with Arthur's encouragement I embarked on my short tour of key editors in Europe, almost all of whom signed on.

Nevertheless, while it was up and running, InterNation put us in contact with an international brigade of talented journalists and made possible a series of stories and a worldwide network of venues for them which proved of some value even after InterNation was no more; and it provided an international kaleidoscope of perspectives. I remember sitting late one night in a bar down the street from the Hotel National in Moscow with three Soviet television journalists, one a member of the Communist Party. The other two said they were awaiting private ownership of Russian television with great anticipation, "so that we can have TV programs like Bill Moyers and the *MacNeil-Lehrer Newshour*." I didn't have the heart to tell them that these gentlemen were all made possible by state-owned public television, but I told them anyway.

The *New Statesman*, ignoring Arthur's advice, sold the Old Turnstyle building. And three years after Phillip Whitehead's historic Roxbury, Connecticut, visit, it was back on the street looking for financial support. Stuart Weir, having braved the sectarian wars at *New Socialist*, a Labour-affiliated paper, came to the *New Statesman* with a capacious plan to open it up to new constituencies.

The *New Statesman* and the American *Nation* had much in common. Until Weir's recent and colorful makeover, they were both weeklies printed on butcher paper. They were both on the left. They were both staunchly opposed to imperial adventures. They both refused to play Cold War politics, although it was commonly said of both the *New Statesman* under Kingsley Martin and *The Nation* under Kirchwey that like a pantomime horse, "the front half knoweth not what the back half doeth—and vice versa." They were both in sympathy with the antinuclear movement. And we had already collaborated on the first international editors' exchange in magazine history. We had also co-sponsored the 1988 InterNation conference on international investigative journalism just outside London, which was launched with a press conference in support of the *New Statesman*'s campaign for Charter 88, a belated British equivalent to our own Bill of Rights.

So when in June 1990 Stuart Weir, by then the *New Statesman*'s outgoing editor, called, told me that under the terms of their charter the "chapel" got to name one of the five (lifetime) E shareholders and my name had been proposed, and would I be willing to serve? I said yes. I wanted to be of help, and I admired the other E's: the thoughtful, progressive journalist and author Neal Ascherson; the radical barrister Helena Kennedy, feminist, writer, and TV playwright; the Labour statesman Benjamin Whitaker; and Margaret Hodge, an articulate Labour MP. I had long been curious about what happened at board of directors meetings (the closest I had gotten was that I was on the board of my alma mater, Swarthmore College, where by tradition no decision is put to a vote but, rather, reflects the sense of the meeting in the Quaker style). I was ready for the big time. Plus, to be Labour's man on the board, who could ask for anything more? Last but not least, I wanted to know more about the E-shareholder arrangement itself. This was partly intellectual curiosity. I had a more than passing interest in the cluster of questions that the arrangement was designed to answer: What is the ideal editor-publisher relationship? How do you secure editorial freedom and independence and yet provide for accountability? *The Economist* had three independent trustees (from the House of Lords, no less) with veto power over the appointment of the editor. Were the E's the functional equivalent at the *New Statesman*?

As Marjorie Scardino, the American CEO of *The Economist*'s parent company, explained to me, "The way it worked in practice was that the trustees never got involved, because the fact of the trustees was it-self a guarantee that an inappropriate editor would never be selected."

And partly my interest was closer to home. The "trial marriage" of Arthur Carter and *The Nation* by and large was working. We seemed to work well together. He had passed the Gore Vidal test with flying col-ors. And although he let me know which writers he admired most and least, and his style was sometimes the despair of those on the business side (at one point he proposed subjecting all new hires to a battery of psychological tests), he was scrupulous about honoring his no-editorial-interference undertaking. Norman Lear, a longtime *Nation* supporter, observed that any man who was willing to cover $500,000 a year in losses and not try to put his editorial imprint on the magazine was "a saint." Arthur was far from a saint, but I had learned a lot from him.

I was disappointed that the *New Statesman* deal didn't work out, but as Arthur saw it, to make it work, he would have had to have some-one in London to oversee the business end on his behalf and he was not ready to do that. When shortly thereafter Charles Peters of the *Washington Monthly* asked me whether I thought Arthur might be in-terested in a *Nation*-type arrangement for the *Washington Monthly* and Arthur said yes, I told him I was reluctant to raise my friend Charley's hopes unless he was serious. If his years on Wall Street had taught him nothing else, Arthur said, he knew deals don't happen unless you enter negotiations with maximum enthusiasm. "There will be plenty of time for problems to come up later." This seemed to me to be wise.

Nevertheless, Arthur's passion now seemed engaged by *The New York Observer*, where he was an activist publisher. And some months later, after Arthur had taken out a small ad in *The New York Times* to celebrate *The Nation's* passing *The New Republic* in circulation, *The Village Voice* had an article quoting Marty Peretz telling a *TNR* editor-ial meeting that Arthur had asked him over breakfast if *he* wanted to buy *The Nation*. This made some of our staff wonder, but it didn't make me worry. Arthur had told me he was going to attempt to make peace with Peretz, who reportedly had blackballed *The Nation* from membership in an ad sales consortium of "thought leader" magazines; and I knew that legally I had retained first refusal rights should Arthur ever want to sell. Still, I did wonder when I learned that Arthur had talked to the attorney of a friend about her possible interest in acquir-ing *The Nation*. Was he trying to send me a message?

Stuart Weir's letter about the (lifetime) appointment to the *New Statesman* as an E spelled out the expectations. E's were "charged with protecting the editorial integrity of the magazine," had the right to attend board meetings, and had individual veto power over such matters as the dismissal and/or appointment of the editor. There was also a clause that I didn't pay much attention to at the time but later was to prove pivotal. The E's, wrote Weir, were "designed to make sure that the magazine's integrity can be protected in the event of share deals, sale and so on."

I said yes to Stuart more for what I hoped to learn than what I expected I would be able to contribute in the way of wisdom. As it turned out, five years later, under the terms of this clause, in my capacity as an E shareholder I was called upon to grant consent to the *New Statesman*'s liquidation at the same time that as a result of Arthur's wake-up call, I took on the financial responsibility for *The Nation*. But I get ahead of myself.

The *New Statesman*, I soon learned, had gone through virtually every capitalist business model available to the small-circulation socialist magazine—takeovers, mergers, nonprofit, for-profit, and, after John Lloyd resigned and his successors could not make a go of it, employee ownership—all in the interest of avoiding a sole proprietor. And right from the start, one way the *New Statesman* survived was by swallowing its competitors. In 1931 it had gobbled up a British magazine called *The Nation* (no relation), which itself was the successor to *The Speaker*, a classy weekly journal founded in 1890 to support Gladstone and Irish Home Rule. That *Nation*, which started in 1907, had been edited by a famous liberal novelist of the day, Hugh Massingham, and it incorporated yet another journal, *The Athenaeum*, in 1921, when John Maynard Keynes hijacked it for what one historian called "his own version of secular salvation."

Keynes's heart was with that (British) *Nation*. Although its circulation was only 6,000–7,000 compared to *New Statesman*'s 10,000 (and *The Spectator*'s 18,000), it was said to be the most influential of the British weeklies. When Keynes couldn't persuade T. S. Eliot to leave Lloyd's Bank for the literary editorship, he hired Leonard Woolf instead. And when the editorship of the *Statesman* opened up, it was Keynes who in 1930 persuaded Kingsley Martin to take the job (after satisfying himself on Martin's politics) by arranging to merge it with

The Nation. Keynes may have been too clever by half. What was announced as a merger really turned out to be more of a takeover, and eventually even the name *The Nation* was dropped from the masthead. Along the way the new entity absorbed another periodical, *The Weekend Review*, which never made it onto the masthead at all.

History had repeated itself in 1988, when the *Statesman* merged with *New Society*, a biweekly founded in 1968 that covered issues of social policy. At the time Phillip Whitehead, chairman of the board, declared that the merger would combine the best features of both magazines and bring the joint circulation up to 40,000. The "relaunch," as they called it, cost £100,000. The new publication was called *New Statesman/New Society*, but at the time Paul Barker, the disaffected editor of *New Society*, said, "As far as I'm concerned *New Society* died in 1988." Six months later, sales were down to 32,000, and not long thereafter *New Society* disappeared from the masthead. So much for the takeover model. The *Statesman* didn't suffer, but as with many other small-magazine mergers, two money losers never seemed to add up to a moneymaker.

No sooner was I installed as an E shareholder than I was informed that a cash crisis loomed and two possible white knights were in the wings. One, Derek Coombs, seemed to be the frontrunner. Although fifteen years previously he had served as a Conservative MP, he had made his fortune helping poor people who didn't otherwise qualify for credit to build their own businesses, and now claimed to have abandoned his right-wing past and wanted nothing more than to help the *New Statesman* over its financial crisis. The other was a couple named Jeffrey. Philip, the husband, was in the consulting business and was involved with the Labour Party. But the Jeffreys seemed to want a say in running the business, whereas Coombs was ready to delegate; also, the Jeffreys proposed to make a loan, whereas Coombs was offering hard cash. Could I possibly come to London to meet Mr. Coombs, who was obviously everybody's favorite? I could and did, in July 1993. He was a likable chap who said all the right things. But when I emerged from our tea and met with Pat Coyne, the *New Statesman*'s business manager, I said, "He seems nice enough and he said all the right things. But am I not supposed to be concerned that my first act as an E shareholder is to vote to install as the new owner of the U.K.'s oldest English-language socialist weekly a Tory usurer?" I also told my fellow E's I had additional reservations.

First, I thought the £500,000 plus legal costs that Coombs was proposing was insufficient to accomplish what he/we wanted for the magazine. (When I had raised this with Coombs, he had said more money was there if needed, but management must practice fiscal restraint.) Second, I was uncomfortable in principle with a provision that permitted the editor to be removed in the event that revenue fell more than 10 percent below the agreed-on targets for three consecutive issues. Tying the editor to short-run financial performance was a bad idea. I conceded that had I been under such constraints at *The Nation*, I might have been out after my first three weeks.

A couple of months later, Pat Coyne reported to the Board:

> Both Coombs and the Jeffreys raise the spectre of the sole proprietor, something that has often haunted the left. Partly this is a combination of paranoia and lack of self-confidence, but an element of it is based in reality. Maxwell and Murdoch are enough to give anyone the willies. Ultimately, the question becomes again one of judgement. Proprietors could go ape, firing everyone in sight, insisting on mad editorials and selling out to even worse villains. All we can do is minimize the possibility. Ironically, Coombs seems to be bound much more tightly than the Jeffreys, especially if he takes the 49% option. He would be in a minority of the Board and would have the E shareholders to convince if he wanted to change things drastically.

With one thing and another, the Coombs bid didn't work out. For one brief moment in the early 1990s, with the help of a loan from the Jeffreys, the *New Statesman* staff reached into their own pockets, lowered their salaries, and bought the magazine for themselves while they looked for a new macro-shareholder; it entered a brief period of worker control, "the worker-owner model." In very short order, with Duncan Campbell, the foremost investigative journalist in Britain, in charge, it actually started to break even. Under Duncan, who had never in his life met a payroll, the staff took drastic pay cuts that the chapel would have resisted under traditional ownership, the size of each issue was reduced, and circulation plunged, which meant a lower printing bill.

Then on January 29, 1993, the New Statesman published "The Curious Case of John Major's Mistress," with a cover caricature of Prime Minister John Major and his caterer, Clare Lattimer. Everyone in the British tabloid press had been printing blind items about the Prime Minister's having a mysterious mistress, but nobody had bothered to check whether the rumors were true; the New Statesman had, and had concluded that the rumors appeared to lack substance! Major, who was flying from India at the time and didn't read the article, was told he should be offended by the cover cartoon, and indeed he was offended by the cover line. He sued. As The Economist put it in July, John Major sued "a down-at-heel left-wing weekly" for an article which said "he was not sleeping with his cook." On June 6, five months later, he abandoned his case in return for £1,000, his legal costs, but not before he almost put the Statesman out of business. Because of a curious quirk in U.K. libel law, the case cost the Statesman £250,000, and it had already been on the financial ropes.

Along with the New Statesman, Major had also sued its printers, distributors, and main retail outlets. He and his caterer quickly settled their libel suits against these latter defendants for an amount rumored to be in the neighborhood of £100,000. But the New Statesman, which lacked (prohibitively expensive) libel insurance, had, as is the U.K. custom, indemnified its distributors et al. against libel suits, and hence it was in a six-figure hole. (That's pounds, not dollars.) Facing possible bankruptcy, the worker-owned New Statesman accepted the Jeffreys' offer to put up some money and convert their loan into a 49 percent ownership interest as the first step toward refinancing the magazine by a broadly based "left-wing consortium"

A week or two later, John Major also sued a second magazine, Scallywag, which had printed its own version of the Lattimer story. Consider Scallywag. Its masthead said it was "published by the gifted, the inebriated and insane . . . Any part of it may be stolen and reproduced, provided the interested party buys the editor a pint." The suit cost Scallywag next to nothing, because it distributed next to no copies, indemnified nobody, and had nothing in the bank. Six weeks after the writs arrived, an ad appeared in the Financial Times: "Become Famous

Instantly. Buy the controlling 70% interest in the magazine *Scallywag*, currently being sued by John Major for libel. Good potential for expansion and profits. £50,000 for quick sale."

Too bad the stately *Statesman* couldn't follow *Scallywag*'s example. Instead, it was in bed, as it were, with the Jeffreys. Not quite a benevolent philanthropist, Philip Jeffrey was a quirky fellow. He had first been brought into the *New Statesman* picture by a friend of his daughter, the magazine's latest editor, Stephen Platt, who came to the *New Statesman* as part of the *New Society* merger. And Platt, whose decision it was to publish the story about Major and his non-mistress, was rapidly losing the confidence of his staff, not to mention my fellow E shareholders. Jeffrey's solution was to keep Platt and fire the E's, who for him represented authority without responsibility. He added, "If you don't do it my way I'll put Staggers in bankruptcy. Once it is in receivership, either I'll buy it back or you will assume responsibility when a Murdoch or Maxwell outbids me." This attitude did not endear him to the E's, who promptly voted not to accept his offer.

Over lunch I unsuccessfully urged Jeffrey to relent, and the E's were again offended, this time with me. I believed bankruptcy could terminate the magazine, but by then they considered him precisely the sort of proprietor they and I had been recruited to prevent. Indeed, he was constantly flying off to Japan or Australia and sending faxes telling the staff to shape up or "get on your bikes," and proposing that the Board meet with him at The Nag's Head opposite the Covent Garden station, rather than in the offices, where indeed the atmosphere might have been hostile.

But I had qualms about a bankruptcy, because it meant the staff (which had nominated me as an E in the first place) would go unpaid. As Jenny Shramenko, the associate publisher, put it in a personal plea to me, "The magazine is in free fall right now and once in the hands of the receiver no-one has any say over its future except company law." Eventually, however, along with the other E's, I voted to veto Jeffrey's plan to move the magazine to a new company and a clean balance sheet with no more pesky E's, and thus we allowed him to put the magazine into bankruptcy. (Neal Ascherson called it "death with honor.") The magazine missed a few issues. Although there were rumors that *The Guardian*, the respected left-wing British daily, and others were going to pick it up, in the end one Geoffrey Robinson bailed it out. In advance he called the E's to ask permission and said he would reinstall them (he didn't, at least not me). Then he joined Tony Blair's Cabinet as Paymaster General and put his interest in the magazine in trust. The new editor, Ian Hargreaves, described his new employer as "a distinguished businessman," but the investigative journalist Tom Bowers found that he was anything but. Bowers's research provoked an investigation by a parliamentary committee, Robinson resigned his Cabinet post and was officially censured. Nevertheless, under the editorship first of Hargreaves and then Peter Willey, the *New Statesman* seems to have made a modest comeback.

So despite its dubious proprietor the *New Statesman* survives. Coombs, by the way, went on to fund a quite respectable fortnightly, *Prospect*, whose politics are social-democratic and which bills itself informally as "*Encounter* without the CIA." It is only slightly marred by the occasional Coombs essay, which appears in its pages without meeting its otherwise admirable standards. But in retrospect I can see I was wrong to try to interest Arthur in the *Statesman* (he never would have stayed the course), I was wrong to try to keep Jeffrey from putting it into bankruptcy, I was wrong to believe that its new owner-publisher would restore the trustees to their trusteeship, and I was wrong to let InterNation, an idea ahead of its time, lapse, since the transnational media conglomerate against which InterNation aspired to be a modest counterforce was swiftly coming to dominate the global media marketplace.

By the late 1980s independent journals like *The Nation* in the United States or the *Statesman* in the United Kingdom were regarded as an endangered species; the age of the stand-alone is over, magazine consultants would solemnly (and expensively) assure their clients. Certainly we were surrounded by a sea of mergers, takeovers, acquisitions, consolidations. Although the problem of media concentration was rarely covered in big media, this was not exactly news.

In 1983 the media critic Ben Bagdikian wrote a book, *The Media Monopoly*, in which he documented the fact that "by the 1980s, the majority of all major American media—newspapers, magazines, radio, television, books, and movies—were controlled by fifty giant corporations." These corporations, he contended, "were interlocked in common financial interest with other massive corporate entities and with a few dominant international banks." At the time, the United States had an impressive array of mass communications. There were 1,700 daily newspapers, 11,000 magazines, 9,000 radio and 10,000 television stations, 2,500 book publishers, and 7 movie studios. If each had its own owner, that would have made for 25,000 different owners. But such was not the case. "Today fifty corporations own most of the output of daily newspapers and most of the sales and audience in magazines, broadcasting, books and movies. The fifty men and women who head these corporations would fit in a large room. They constitute a new Print Ministry of Information and Culture."

The book was quickly dated. When a second edition was published, the number of dominating corporations was down from fifty to twenty-seven. And so in 1989 *The Nation* asked Bagdikian to update his report. In a special issue dated June 6, 1989, he projected that by the end of the century the number would be down to six. (By the end of the century, Bagdikian's book was in its fifth edition, and depending on how you count it, the number was indeed down to six.)

AOL-Time Warner was first on Bagdikian's 1989 *Nation* list of media corporations then dominating the commercial race to reach hundreds of millions of minds in what Marshall McLuhan called the "global village," a world knit together and transformed by television and other marvels of the electronic age. Unlike McLuhan, who predicted that an information network would envelop the planet, spreading democracy and leading to general cosmic consciousness," Bagdikian was concerned that these mammoth companies would dominate, control, and homogenize the world's mass media. He was careful to observe that the rankings of the giants changes, sometimes week by week.

He argued that the newly powerful communications conglomerates had a shared ideology that came with the territory and that they used their unprecedented monopoly power to propagate four insidious myths: that government spending is "out of control"; that corporate taxes are rising "at a crushing rate"; that the graduated income tax "unfairly strikes the wealthy"; that unions have caused "a drop in American productivity." Above and beyond all that, he noted, "The gravest loss is in the self-serving censorship of political and social ideas, in news, magazine articles, books, broadcasting, and the movies"—sometimes subtle, sometimes not even conscious, and therefore most insidious.

Bagdikian, I thought, should know. Even before *Media Monopoly* was published, his publisher, the independent Beacon Press, received a threatening letter from the chief executive of Simon & Schuster (then owned by Gulf & Western) demanding to see a copy of the manuscript. It seems that in the course of his research, Mark Dowie, the *Mother Jones* investigative reporter who broke the story about the Ford Motor Company knowingly producing dangerous gas tanks in its Pinto cars, had told Bagdikian a story of his own: When he proposed a book on the history of this type of corporate decision-making to Nan Talese, then a top Simon & Schuster editor, she expressed enthusiasm. And when he asked what she thought of the title *Corporate Murder*, she asked, "Is Gulf and Western one of the corporations?" They weren't, they didn't bid on the book (Nan reported back that S&S's president, Richard Snyder, was vehemently opposed, "because, among other reasons, it made corporations look bad"); but S&S's attorneys did move to have the offending story removed from *Media Monopoly*, an effort they abandoned when it ran into a public-relations storm. (Mark later served as InterNation's director.)

If you can't beat them, join them, I always say. That, plus my exposure to Bagdikian-think, is undoubtedly what led me, early in 1989, to attempt to enter the takeover game on *The Nation*'s behalf. Time, Inc. had reportedly opened merger negotiations with Warner, but the business press was filled with stories about Gulf & Western's plans for a hostile takeover of *Time*. Despite their scary content, I liked reading such stories if only for their colorful vocabulary. The takeover world, you see, has a language of its own, complete with white knights, poison pills, and "highly confident" letters. The fact that I was having my own difficulties putting together a modest consortium of financially challenged for-the-most-part socialist journals did not for a moment stop us from joining the capitalist fray. With the assistance of Richard Lingeman, I crafted our own takeover offer:

J. Richard Munro
Chairman of the Board
Time, Inc.

Dear Mr. Munro:
    Don't swallow that poison pill. After many days of bad news, here is what I hope you will regard as glad tidings: A white

knight is coming to your rescue. *The Nation* is ready to take over Time, Inc.

Unlike the $10.7 billion hostile bid by Paramount Communications Inc., né Gulf & Western, which you correctly characterized as "Engulf and Devour," please be assured that there is nothing whatsoever hostile about our tender offer. As a matter of fact, it is so tender that we believe you and your colleagues will prefer it even to the sweet little $19 billion stock swap you have cooked up for yourself and fellow board members with Warner Communications Inc.

After conversation with our bankers, we are highly confident that we can do better than Paramount's $175 per share offer. Like other potential suitors, our plan is to pledge the assets of Time, Inc. as collateral on the loan we take out to buy you so cash will be no problem for us. Our negotiators will be the same people who persuaded columnist Calvin Trillin (who got his start as a *Time* reporter) to write for *The Nation* for a salary "in the high two figures." And as an added bonus, we are considering throwing in first refusal rights on our China policy, which has stood the test of time better than Henry Luce's.

Although the arbitrageurs don't seem to regard *The Nation* as a major player in the merger game, we were emboldened to make this offer by the example of money-losing Pan Am's bid to take over money-making Northwest Airlines. As you know, Pan Am's tax-loss credits made the deal plausible. As you may not be aware, however, *The Nation* has lost money for 125 years, which our research department informs us is a record among for-profit enterprises. Our tax-loss carry-forward is staggering.

We also think you will be happy with our timing. According to *The New York Times* (quoting anonymous directors of Time and Warner), it would take Paramount at least eight months to take over your company because that is how long it would take to negotiate deals with the hundreds of cable franchises owned by *Time*. Frankly, we believe it would take Paramount eight months because that is how long it takes Paramount to make a movie. As America's oldest continuously published weekly, nothing we do takes more than a week—thus, we could do the deal in seven days.

That's because of the unique deal we propose: As soon as we have taken you over, we intend to give *Time* and all your other properties—the Book-of-the-Month Club, Home Box Office, *People*, et al.—their independence. Paramount undoubtedly would sell off some of these subsidiaries to other conglomerates, but as a magazine founded by abolitionists, we believe in freeing the corporate slaves.

This plan should appeal to your stockholders, who will retain proportionate shares in each of these spin offs. But it will also please the editors and publishers of your various publications, since they won't have Paramount or Warner or even *The Nation* looking over their shoulders. Speaking of *The Nation*, we are even prepared to consider having the various sections of *Time* ("Nation," "World," "Milestones," etc.) spun off as independent entities. But all of that is subject to negotiation.

We were, of course, moved by statements in the press attributed to you and Steve Ross, chair of Warner, about how the Time-Warner merger is good for the economy and the country. Indeed, those lofty sentiments inspired this offer. Ever since the Reagan Administration abandoned its enforcement of the antitrust laws and the Congressional Democrats abandoned their plan to put a cap on conglomerate size, we have been looking for a way to do our part to protect the free enterprise system. Now we have found it.

> Yours truly,
> Victor Navasky, Editor
> *The Nation*

When I asked Arthur Carter what he thought of my letter, he said it was okay. Maybe the reason Arthur didn't find it funny (okay, it wasn't *that* funny) was that had he wanted to put his capital and his old Wall Street expertise behind such an offer, he might have pulled it off.

But I did get a letter back from Munro saying he liked our offer better than that of "Engulf and Devour," and he would give our proposal "all the attention it deserved."

On March 5, 1989, Time, Inc. announced its merger with Warner Communications. Who took over whom, to this day I'm not quite sure. At the time the message went forth that for synergistic reasons this was great for both companies. Eleven years after that, Time Warner took on AOL, or was it the other way around? Even though I wasn't sure, I knew I agreed with the late Justice Louis Brandeis that "bigness is badness." And so when Walter Isaacson, *Time*'s Managing Editor, asked me if I would write 1,000 words giving *Time* my thoughts on these matters, my first thought was Why not ask Ben Bagdikian? But after I figured out, given the lateness of the hour and the closeness of the close date, that they had probably already gone down the list of usual suspects and struck out, my second thought was Why not? I knew I was being used as some sort of token dissenter, but while I am an opponent of to-kenism, I am a believer in dissent, and so I wrote about the dangers posed by mega-communications conglomerates that are already bigger than the economies of countries whose monopolistic information poli-cies we condemn as a violation of democratic values.

It was, in any event, the biggest media deal ever. As Robert McChesney, author of *Rich Media, Poor Democracy* reported in *The Na-tion*, the deal was valued at around $160 billion. "That was 470 times greater than the value of the largest media deal that had been recorded by 1979. The nine or ten largest media conglomerates now almost all rank among the 300 largest firms in the world; in 1975 there were only a couple of media firms among the 500 largest companies in the world." And by 2002, AOL-Time Warner stock was in big trouble. First Bob Pittman of AOL was fired, then Gerald Levin of Warner was fired, and the papers were full of speculation about who or what was really re-sponsible for the way that AOL-Time Warner stock had tanked. In 2003, AOL's CEO was fired, and the speculation continued (not in the stock but about who and what was responsible for its dive).

McChesney is a research professor at the University of Illinois, but the problem of media concentration is so pervasive that students as well as professors can spot it. Consider the work of Michael Scherer, now the Washington editor of *Mother Jones*, but in 2002 a student of mine at the Columbia University Graduate School of Journalism, who documented scores of articles in one or another AOL-Time Warner publication that concerned one or another Time Warner product without disclosing that the editors worked for—and owned stock in—a company that the article might affect. For example, *Entertainment Weekly* is known for its lists: the best-dressed at the Oscars, the top-selling music, the most critically acclaimed blockbuster movies.

> So a January cover package that listed the "100 most important movies on DVD" was a perfect fit for a magazine founded to help consumers wade through the weekly tidal wave of entertainment offerings. There was just one problem. To do the story the magazine would have to judge hundreds of products of its corporate parent, AOL-Time Warner, the world's largest marketer of DVDs and a major *Entertainment Weekly* advertiser. Probably because of the company's sheer size, the idea of disclosing every relationship every time, an unimaginable burden, never occurred to them.

What had these various mergers done to democracy?

At first these mega-communications conglomerates always try to justify themselves in terms of economies of scale. But here, it sometimes looks as if the bigger they are, the sooner they fall. Every week AOL-Time Warner seemed to lose another part. In 2003, it dropped AOL from its corporate name. Whatever the company is called, however, AOL-Time Warner had a lot of parts to lose. The last time I looked, these included Warner Bros. Pictures, Morgan Creek, Regency, Warner Bros. Animation, a partial stake in Savoy Pictures, Little, Brown & Co., Bulfinch, Back Bay, Time-Life Books, Oxmoor House, Sunset Books, Warner Books, a joint venture with the Book-of-the-Month Club, Warner/Chappell Music, Atlantic Records, Warner AudioBooks, Elektra, Warner Bros. Records, Time-Life Music, Columbia House, a 40 percent stake in Seattle's Sub Pop Records, *Time* magazine, *Fortune*, *Life*, *Sports Illustrated*, *Vibe*, *People*, *Entertainment Weekly*, *Money*, *In Style*, *Martha Stewart Living*, *Sunset*, *Asia Week*, *Parenting*, *Weight Watchers*, *Cooking Light*, DC Comics, 49 percent of the Six Flags theme parks, Movie World and Warner Bros. parks, HBO Cinemax, Warner Bros. television, partial ownership of Comedy Central, E!, Black Entertainment Television, Court TV, the Sega channel, the Home Shopping Network, Turner Broadcasting, the Atlanta Braves and Atlanta Hawks,

World Championship Wrestling, Hanna-Barbera Cartoons, New Line Cinema, Fine Line Features, Turner Classic Movies, Turner Pictures, Castle Rock Entertainment, CNN, CNN Headline News, CNN International, CNN/SI, CNN Airport Network, CNNfi, CNN radio, TNT, WTBS, and the Cartoon Network.*

Even though I got some laughs out of our attempt to buy Time, Inc. with its own money (and I still believe it could be done), I know it is no laughing matter. Getting serious about media reform, as McChesney and our own John Nichols have written in one of *The Nation*'s series of special issues on the dangers to democracy of big media, is serious business, especially given the contradiction between our for-profit, highly concentrated, advertising-saturated, corporate media system and the communications requirements of a democratic society.

Granted that concentration and consolidation make for homogenization, and granted that the corporate media system, in McChesney's terminology, distort or miss the story, what is to be done? The late Herb Schiller proposed in *The Nation* that all candidates for national office ought to have an information policy, the way they have a foreign policy and domestic policies. I like that.

One of the myths about journals of opinion is that they are shrill, that all they do is criticize, and that they are not constructive. Although I have on occasion claimed to be a lobbyist for affirmative action at *The Nation* on behalf of constructivity—each issue, I believe, should contain at least one constructive idea—in the area of media concentration I think *The Nation* has done its share. In the early summer of 2003 at Chairman Michael Powell's initiative, the FCC was about to implement changes in media ownership limits that would relax limits on media concentration. As a result of the media and democracy movement (whose Marx and Engels are McChesney and Nichols, if not Bagdikian and Mark Miller, all of whom *The Nation* has been privileged to publish), the FCC received more than 700,000 letters opposing the change. Eventually more than 3 million people objected, and the Senate passed a bill that would nullify the changes. MoveOn.org, a left-liberal citizens lobby, moved in, and Free Press, a McChesney-founded nonprofit that describes itself as nonpartisan, seemed to provide a small army working

*See Eric Alterman's *What Liberal Media: The Truth about Bias and the News.*

for "a media system that fosters diverse, independent, and competitive media."

And don't let me get away with pretending that media concentration is a left-right issue. Along with *The Nation*, the NRA opposed the FCC rules, and *The New York Times*'s William Safire, a self-advertised conservative, has himself fulminated against "the concentration of power" at stake:

> Does that sound unconservative? Not to me. The concentration of power—political, corporate, media, cultural—should be anathema to conservatives. The diffusion of power through local control, thereby encouraging individual participation, is the essence of federalism and the greatest expression of democracy.

When one thinks of these behemoths, it's hard not to conjure up a privatized version of Orwell's Big Brother beaming (corporate) agitprop to passive news consumers. It is, of course, more complicated than that. Conglomerates, which almost by definition put commercial values ahead of democratic values, can suppress as well as propagate news. And occasionally an independent David can derail the best-laid plans of a conglomerated Goliath.

After I had returned to *The Nation* as publisher, complete with my certificate from the Harvard Business School, I got an inkling of how that can happen in an unexpected encounter with the number-two giant on Bagdikian's list, Bertelsmann AG, the German firm that until the AOL-Time Warner merger may have been the largest media corporation, and was still the largest publisher of English-language trade books in the world. It had annual revenues of $14 billion and it operated in more than fifty countries. The company owned or partnered with almost all the book clubs in the world. It owned magazines, newspapers, and music labels such as RCA; it co-owned CLT-UFA, Europe's biggest TV and radio company; and it had a major stake in America Online. In the United States it also owned Random House, Alfred A. Knopf, Doubleday, Crown, the Literary Guild, Ballantine Books, and much, much more, including a partnership with Barnes & Noble in a new Internet bookstore.

One day my assistant Mary Schilling called me at home, where I was working on deadline for I forget what, to ask whether I planned to attend Bertelsmann's annual meeting. I had been to this meeting the previous year, where I had been fascinated to observe that this privately held company held what appeared to be a press conference at a shareholders' meeting. They had started with cocktails, then served a modest lunch (at the Park Avenue building that houses the Council on Foreign Relations), then presented financials for the previous year and projections for the coming one, complete with elaborate charts and a slide show, then took as many questions from the reporters present as they cared to ask. On departure you were handed the equivalent of an annual report.

Nevertheless I was on deadline, so I told Mary to give my regrets.

"That's too bad," she said. "They said Mr. Middelhoff wants you at his table."

"I'm going," I said.

Thomas Middelhoff, in case you were wondering, was chairman of Bertelsmann. "But first send up copies of that article *The Nation* published on Bertelsmann," I added.

On December 28, 1998, we had published an article, "Bertelsmann's Nazi Past," by a German researcher, Hersch Fischler, and John Friedman, a regular *Nation* contributor and filmmaker with a special interest in the Holocaust. In its official history Bertelsmann claimed it was "closed by the Nazis" for refusing to "toe the party line." In fact, Fischler and Friedman documented that as early as 1934 the firm issued a book intended for the Brownshirts titled *Dr. Martin Luther's Little Catechism for the Man in Brown*, edited by Werner Betcke, which praised Hitler and the Nazi movement; throughout the 1930s it published books favored by Goebbels's propaganda ministry, anti-Semitic works and books that glorified battles and deaths and primed the Germans for war. The article, which also dealt with Bertelsmann's Nazi connections, made worldwide news. As a result the company announced that it had asked "the historian and publicist Dr. Dirk Bavendamm to look at the new information and begin to investigate the role the publishing house played in those days." After which Fischler-Friedman did a follow-up story about Dirk Bavendamm, the sixty-one-year-old German historian and alleged Nazi sympathizer who it turned out had written the earlier ersatz corporate history for the Bertelsmann Foundation. (In one of his books, published in 1983, Bavendamm stated that Roosevelt, not Hitler, had caused World War II; and that American Jews "controlled most of the media," hence Hitler's bad press.) The Fischler-Friedman revelations caused such a ruckus that with much fanfare Bertelsmann then proceeded to appoint an independent commission headed by the historian Saul Friedländer to look into the matter and report back.

My theory was that Mr. Middelhoff's desire to have me at his table might have more to do with the Fischler-Friedman revelations than my natural charm, or any interest he might have in joining *The Nation's* small group of shareholders, or in trying to sign me up for a book, although you never know. I also was interested in how the old Random House and Doubleday cultures were meshing with the Bertelsmann culture. Shortly after Bertelsmann bought Doubleday in 1986, my friend Sam Blum, editor of the Doubleday Book Club, then the largest book club in America, told me that a meeting had been called of all the editors of book clubs owned by Bertelsmann worldwide. For this meeting the head of Bertelsmann's book-club division had flown into town, a very formal individual dressed in a three-piece suit. According to Sam, the first question out of his mouth had been "Tell me, how are Jewish books selling?" Sam, who looked and dressed like Woody Allen playing a Woody Allen character, pondered to himself, Does he mean books by Jewish authors, books on Jewish subjects, or books selected by Jewish editors of the Doubleday book clubs? An embarrassed silence descended on the room, and they moved on to the next question.

Mr. Middelhoff, whose collar was also starched and whose double-breasted suit was suitably formal, seemed to have a knack for getting to the point. The man from *The Wall Street Journal* was on his left, and David Kirkpatrick from *The New York Times* was across the table, but no sooner had I sat down than he turned to me and asked, "So, Mr. Navasky, you are a friend of Mr. Fischler?" I told him that actually I had talked with Mr. Fischler only once or twice on the phone, but I was a friend of his co-author, Mr. Friedman. Mr. Middelhoff wanted me to know that Mr. Fischler kept calling to find out when the Friedländer commission would issue its report, that Mr. Fischler seemed to think that Bertelsmann was stonewalling, but that the truth was that the commission was working away and *was* independent, so independent that it would have been inappropriate for Mr. Middelhoff even to ask for its timetable. "You call Mr. Friedländer and you will see. You can call him, I can't."

I promised to bear this message back to Fischler and Friedman, which I did. Then in January 2000, two years after the commission was appointed, it issued a preliminary report indicating that Bertelsmann's earlier statements (about its having been shut down by the Nazis because it was a subversive company that had clashed with the regime) were not true. (They were forced to close in 1944 for hoarding paper illegally.) And in October 2002, the commission's final report documented the company's collaboration with the Nazis and confirmed an earlier report that Bertelsmann's family patriarch, Heinrich Mohn, had donated money to the SS. Far from resisting the Nazis, Bertelsmann had used its ties with the regime to transform itself from a provincial Lutheran publishing company into a mass-market publisher. It was the largest supplier of books to the German Army, at least fifty of them with clearly anti-Semitic themes, and Bertelsmann's religious literature contained anti-Jewish themes that included Nazi terminology. It had probably profited from Jewish slave labor at a handful of printing plants in Lithuania, where it contracted work. Bertelsmann expressed its "regrets." Middelhoff, who by this time had been relieved of his duties, complimented his former employer for uncovering and facing up to its dark history.

How had *The Nation* gotten this worldwide scoop? It hadn't. As it happens, Fischler, a Düsseldorf-based researcher, had been on the case for some years and published his report (without John Friedman's input or co-byline) first in a Swiss magazine, *Die Weltwoche*. Why had Germany's major media not picked it up? After all, it was a story ripe for *Der Spiegel* and/or *Stern*, each famed for its investigative capacities and interest in exposés and scoops centered on Germany. (Indeed, *Stern* had in the past been so eager to make news about the history of the Third Reich that some years earlier it had published excerpts from *Hitler's Diaries* before discovering that they were a hoax.) The answer, no surprise, was that Bertelsmann held a controlling interest in both periodicals. Bertelsmann, by the way, is itself owned by an entity (called the Bertlesmann Foundation), the largest of its sort in Germany. Since *Der Spiegel* and *Stern* weren't available, why didn't *Die*

Zeit, another German publication known for its critical commentary but also for providing occasional investigative information, pick the story up? It was patiently explained to me that *Die Zeit* is partly owned by a foundation controlled by Bertelsmann. *Got it?*

Whereas I thought I had left the law for journalism, as *The Nation* became enmeshed in covering the increasingly acrimonious extra-national-political and cultural conflicts of the late 1980s and 1990s, at times it felt like I had never left the law, after all.

I will do no more than mention the lawsuit by the former Soviet dissident Vladimir Bukovsky, whose 1979 memoir, *To Build a Castle*, had been celebrated in the pages of *The Nation* by Terence Des Pres, a scholar of the literature of death camps, as a "brilliantly rendered account." In May 1988, Bukovsky, now living in London but in touch with the right-wing American Heritage Foundation and the conservative American Enterprise Institute, sued *The Nation* over an article written by Kevin Coogan and Katrina vanden Heuvel criticizing the Center for Democracy, an organization of exiled Soviet dissidents, including Mr. Bukovsky. The article quoted from an internal memorandum proposing that the center collect military and other intelligence in the course of its human rights work; Katrina and her co-author contended this was a bad idea which would undermine its human rights work. Bukovsky, with the support, we believe, of a plaintiff's libel group funded by the late right-wing international financer Jimmy Goldsmith, sued *The Nation* for libel in the U.K., where libel laws favor plaintiffs (and where *The Nation* had fewer than 150 subscribers), and the suit bounced around the English courts for five years until it was finally withdrawn and settled in *The Nation*'s favor. But not before Katrina and I had to file lengthy affidavits, make trips to London, and the rest. (Des Pres, in his 1979 review of Bukovsky's book, had delineated with admiration the way this particular dissident conducted what he called his "war" against the state by turning his every grievance into an "opportunity for legal complaint." At the time it never occurred to me that nine years later he would deploy this tactic against those he regarded—wrongly—as his enemies in the West.)

That, however, was small mashers compared to another suit that was commenced just before Bukovsky's action was dropped. Incidentally, I should mention here that *The Nation* carried libel insurance, but it had a $50,000 "deductible" clause, which in practice means that even a frivolous suit brought for purposes of harassment could cost up to $50,000 out-of-pocket before the courts got around to throwing it out. (Not to dwell on the greater costs in time, energy, and diversion for those involved.)

Even though we eventually lost, the Ford case seemed worth it, not merely because it brought us valuable publicity, but because we had defended the First Amendment and challenged the idea that former public officials "own" public history; and perhaps most important although not apparent to me at the time, the law of intellectual property was changing in a way that should worry anyone who cares about the public sphere. More on that later.

No such worthy cause animated the suit that began in the wake of a call from Christopher Hitchens early in 1993. At the time he was still a *Nation* columnist and in transition from being a *Harper's* columnist, too, to being a *Vanity Fair* columnist (with what he called a "most favored *Nation* clause," which meant that in order to secure *Vanity Fair's* largesse, he had to cease and desist all other column writing except for *The Nation*). He had been on a panel with one Kanan Makiya, an Iraqi dissident who had written a book, *Republic of Fear* (1989), about Saddam Hussein's regime, which among other things had defended the Gulf War, which *The Nation* had opposed.

"He has a new book coming out," said Christopher, "*Cruelty and Silence*, which documents the failure of the Arab intelligentsia to condemn Saddam Hussein's brutal massacres and human rights abuses of Arabs and Kurds." Christopher said Makiya was most impressive on the issue of double standards. He had taken the liberty of asking Makiya whether any part of his book might be appropriate for magazine serialization, and the answer was yes. Christopher suggested that if I were interested I should give Makiya a call, which I did. We settled on a section of his book called "Cruelty and the Arab Woman," which vividly documented the barbarism of a state that employed people as rapists and traced the transition from cruelty in the home to public cruelty in the street and by the state. It was powerful reporting and analysis.

No sooner had we scheduled publication of Makiya's article than I received a call from Edward Said, by now perhaps the preeminent Palestinian intellectual in the West, *The Nation*'s opera critic, and a friend of so many of my friends that I thought of him as a friend of mine. Here is the background to my Said connection: One morning in 1981 I had awakened with what I was certain, despite my well-known modesty and humility, was the solution to the crisis in the Middle East. If the Palestinian community would adopt the Gandhian tactic of non-violent or passive resistance, substituting civil disobedience for terrorism, peace would have a chance. Passive resistance works only under certain conditions: You need a highly civilized population a portion of whom sympathize with the just cause of the resisters, and Israel, with its Peace Now activists seemed to me to fit the bill.

I arranged to have a drink with Edward at the old McGlade's pub, across the street from ABC Television, where he was making one of his increasingly frequent TV appearances. I put my proposition to him. What did he think? He pointed out that civil disobedience had already been tried—opening stores on the Sabbath in contravention of Israeli law, that sort of thing—but it didn't seem to have done that much good. But I explained that I had something more ambitious in mind. Nothing less than a movement. The problem was that such a movement could not and should not be proposed by a New York Jew. It needed a Palestinian identified with the cause, someone with the stature, prestige, credentials, intellect of a Said (who was then sitting on the Palestine National Council). In fact, it needed not someone like Said but Said himself. Would he consider it?

Edward liked the idea, we went our separate ways, and some weeks later a thick envelope with Said's return address on the outside arrived at my office. Usually when a manuscript comes in I give it to my secretary, who makes copies to be read by various other editors, but this time I couldn't wait. I opened the envelope and began to read. And what I read—on the need for the Israelis to put aside their "bankrupt" policy, the United States to stop calling for "stability," and the Palestinians to define what they mean by "self-determination"—was learned, nuanced, contextual, combative, and persuasive, like much that Said wrote. But the clarion call for civil disobedience, for passive resistance, for Gandhian nonviolence was nowhere to be found. I was grateful to Edward for his tough-minded intelligent analysis, but of course disappointed that he had chosen to put aside the original idea. When I called Edward to thank him for his eloquent piece, I asked him, gently, diplomatically, why he had decided not to go forward as planned.

"What do you mean?" he asked.

"You know," I said, "the Gandhian call to Palestinians to put down their arms. What we talked about."

"But didn't you read the piece?" he asked with genuine puzzlement. "It's all there on page 8."

I turned again to page 8 and found: "The time for hiding behind phrases like 'the liquidation of Zionism' is past. We must say clearly and directly to the Israelis what we propose to share with them as inhabitants of Palestine . . . the time for speaking clearly has arrived."

"Every Palestinian will know exactly what that means," Edward assured me. Given *The Nation*'s paucity of Palestinian subscribers, I nevertheless worried that the point might pass our readers by. Kai Bird, then *The Nation*'s associate editor, told me that "speaking clearly" indeed was the code phrase for accepting the existence of the State of Israel (or, as Palestinians preferred to call it, the Zionist entity). Issam Sartawi, Yasir Arafat's associate, had recently been murdered for saying as much. But somewhere the notion of a Palestinian protest movement of civil disobedience got lost in the shuffle. So much for my brilliant idea.

Now, twelve years later, Edward was calling about Makiya. He had heard "via the grapevine" that we were publishing part of Makiya's new book. Don't do it, he advised. This fellow Makiya is a mischief-maker, an unreliable reporter, and has written false (and libelous) things about Arab intellectuals, including not least Said himself.

Culture alert! I didn't ask Edward who this grapevine was, because it was irrelevant and because I thought I knew—"grapevine" being a code word for one of our editors, who undoubtedly shared Edward's concerns about Makiya's political reliability. In the ideal magazine or publishing office, editorial processes should be open among staff and simultaneously sacrosanct to the outside, so as to protect editors against extracurricular lobbying, second-guessing, and mischief-making. I believed, in other words, in the open exchange of ideas behind closed doors. (I guess leaks in office security are the price of openness.) I heard

Edward out and then said that the section of Makiya's book we had chosen dealt not with the issues he was raising or personalities he was concerned about but rather with the abuse of women in the Arab world; that it contained new and shocking information; that it had been fact-checked; that in any event it would be inappropriate for us to quash it as a favor to a cherished friend of the magazine (which I told him I knew was not what he was asking for). Besides, the article was already in galleys, and if we did kill it at this stage in the process, it would become one of those minor scandals of left political correctness that would only embarrass everyone involved.

Edward took the point but expressed his hope that whoever eventually reviewed Makiya's book (assuming it was reviewed) would do it justice (or perhaps injustice, depending on how you look at it).

I then made the mistake of asking Edward who he thought could give the book a fair and informed review. He rattled off a list of names, which I passed on to our literary editor. Given the review that *Cruelty and Silence* got, I would like to be able to confess that the fix was in. It wasn't. Elsa Dixler, who very much has a mind of her own, invited Eqbal Ahmad to review Makiya's book, not because his name was on the list I passed on to her (it was), but because for some time she had been trying to persuade Eqbal, who was a friend of the magazine and of mine personally, to write for us. He was an anti–Vietnam War visionary Pakistani radical who later taught at Hampshire College, had been indicted as one of the Harrisburg 7,* and was one of those rare scholar-activists who brought his own global vision and original perspective to any issue he tackled. I always learned something new from Eqbal's writings. And when Elsa mentioned to me that Eqbal would be reviewing Makiya, I thought I could predict more or less what he would say: that while Makiya was unfair in his depiction of certain Arab intellectuals like Said, his main points were well taken;

---

*Eqbal, who was himself a nonpracticing Muslim, had been indicted in November 1970, along with the Berrigan brothers and four other Catholic radicals, on the bizarre charge of conspiring to kidnap Secretary of State Henry Kissinger, among other plots against the government. Eqbal's contribution to the "plot," it turned out, had been to suggest a nonviolent "citizen's arrest" of Kissinger. When the verdict came down exonerating Eqbal (and finding Father Philip Berrigan and Sister Elizabeth McAlister guilty only of smuggling prison letters), even *National Review* called it "the greatest federal fizzle in recent years."

that human rights were not a culture-bound issue; that, as Makiya says, Arab states like all sovereign entities ought to be held accountable; and that Arab intellectuals, especially in the West, where they are free to speak out, ought to speak out.

I was only half right. Eqbal's review came in, and it was what is technically known as a hatchet job. I was not usually shown reviews before they were in galleys, but in this case Elsa thought I might be interested and made me a copy. As expected, Eqbal challenged as unwarranted Makiya's derogation of Said, whom Eqbal identified as "my friend." He also found that *Cruelty and Silence* fed anti-Arab and anti-Muslim hate-mongers in a way that did not help Makiya's stated mission of "bringing a democratic order to the Arab world." He disputed Makiya's facts, reported Noam Chomsky's conclusion that "he is a consummate liar," and quoted *The New York Times* to suggest that one of Makiya's key sources, a London-based fellow with the pseudonym of Khalil, was "under investigation" for "the possible theft of $4 billion to $5 billion of public money." And *en passant* he took a swipe at *The Nation* for publishing an excerpt from a book that "treats documents carelessly."

I was about to take off on my summer vacation in upstate New York, and I told Elsa just one thing: Since he not only attacks Makiya and his facts and character but specifically attacks *The Nation* and the facts in the section from Makiya's book that we published, make sure you put our best fact-checker on this. Whatever happens, we don't want our letters page to be subjected to an interminable wrangle about the facts.

Our state-of-the-art fact-checking system notwithstanding, some articles are easier to fact-check than others. The most difficult articles to fact-check, especially before the advent of the Internet (which itself is not fact-checked), were ones like Makiya's or Eqbal's, concerning overseas events and personalities. Some magazines check direct quotations taken from interviews. *The Nation* doesn't do that, partly because we trust our writer-reporters and think it is wrong and wasteful to go back over their work in this way, but also because when people hear what they have said repeated back to them, especially if it is controversial or includes an unintended self-inflicted wound, they are apt to deny they said it or to try to qualify it. On the other hand, we do fact-check quotations from printed material, such as Makiya's book.

In those days the magazine went to press on Thursday night and into the mails on Friday, so it was probably on Monday that I received a call from Makiya. "I will not say what I think about the review," he said, "but Khalid Nasser al-Sabah has hit the ceiling. He is fit to be tied. Ahmad has confused him with another al-Sabah. You should know that he will not let this stand."

Well, I said, if that is the case, we will of course print a correction. Give me his phone number and I will call him, talk with Eqbal, and set the matter straight.

Makiya was reluctant to give us al-Sabah's number, but said he would pass on my message and would have al-Sabah call me. Al-Sabah didn't call. Meanwhile, I asked Elsa to check into all this; assuming Makiya was right (which I did), we would print a correction in the next issue. Things were not so simple. The article had indeed been carefully fact-checked, including Eqbal's information discrediting Makiya's first and most ostensibly prestigious source, the Kuwaiti prince al-Sabah. (We even had *The New York Times* clipping which reported that "Kuwait has asked Interpol to arrest two members of the royal family," one of them named al-Sabah; and among the charges were mismanagement of a fund worth up to $100 billion in savings and the possible theft of $4 to $5 billion.) The problem, Elsa patiently explained, was that there were two al-Sabahs, both of them members of the far-flung royal family and both of them young, London-based investment bankers, and Eqbal seemed to have confused one with the other. Our fact checker had not discovered the confusion because he had relied on the same *Times* article as had Eqbal.

It seemed to me that while the mistake was unfortunate, the solution was simple: print a correction. Although we never received a call from any al-Sabah, we did receive a letter from one of the al-Sabahs' attorneys threatening legal action if we did not print a *front-page* apology and correction. When I informed Eqbal of these developments, he refused to believe there was more than one al-Sabah. "The man's a liar," he insisted. "It will make me very unhappy that I had any dealings with *The Nation* if you print a 'correction' of any sort." Eqbal, I explained, if it turns out there *are* two al-Sabahs and we got the wrong one, and if we don't print such a correction ASAP, our lawyer will be very unhappy. I explained that our libel insurance policy included a $50,000 deductible and the magazine couldn't afford it. Eqbal offered to indemnify the magazine—anything in order not to allow this "liar" to win a round.

I knew from the Bukovksy case and other threats of suits for defamation which never panned out that truth was a defense, but even if we had made a mistake, and were dealing with a public figure, unless we had acted with "malice and reckless disregard" under the law we should prevail, and a timely correction would be taken into account as evidence of our lack of malice.

Meanwhile, Elsa sent me a fax:

The official al Sabah genealogy lists three [al-Sabah] Khalid Nassers . . . the first Khalid Nasser is positively identified . . . as the head of the Kuwait Family Development Fund—that is as the man arrested by Interpol as an embezzler. In addition he is identified as a close relative of the Emir, information that was included in the *Times* clip. The genealogy shows that the two other Khalid Nassers are distant relatives of the Emir . . .

In *Cruelty & Silence*, Makiya tells us that his friend is a distant relative of the Emir. That could be Khalid 2 or Khalid 3, but not Khalid 1. He does mention the names of 4 of his friends, relatives—an Uncle X, brothers Y and Z, and an Aunt Sarah. Khalid 1, whom we know to be the embezzler, has an Uncle X and a brother Y, but not brother Z, or an Aunt Sarah . . . Khalid 2, who the process of elimination tells us is the best candidate to be Makiya's friend, has an Uncle X, brothers Y and Z and an Aunt Sarah, just as Makiya says he does. We recognize that this is not proof positive that Khalid 2 is Makiya's friend, but it strongly suggests that he is.

The other argument that persuaded us is that we have testimony from 3 or 4 reliable sources that the head of the Kuwait Family Development Fund was in London at the time of the invasion of Kuwait and remained there for the duration of the occupation. Makiya claims that his friend was in Kuwait during the occupation. Thus his friend and the embezzler must be two different people.

Over Eqbal's vociferous objections—he argued that it was Makiya's responsibility to prove his friend was not the embezzler—we published a correction, after which we were nonetheless served with legal papers demanding that we print a front-page apology taking as much space as

Eqbal's original review. Once again, the country's leading First Amendment attorney, Floyd Abrams of Cahill Gordon, who had represented
us before on a pro bono basis, offered counsel in the Washington office
of his firm to represent us in this case, although not pro bono. Floyd
believed that if al-Sabah was judged to be a public figure (and as a
member of the royal family who had agreed to be quoted in Makiya's
book, we thought he met the public figure test), then he would have to
prove "malicious intent and reckless disregard" on our part; and since
by any standard we had been neither malicious nor reckless, we assumed we would win the case.

Even with pro bono representation, costs can quickly mount up, as
our previous litigation experience had showed us. So after consultation
with counsel and to save the magazine from a crippling, needless
$50,000 expenditure, we decided to settle the case. Under the terms of
the settlement neither side was permitted to speak of its terms.

There are First Amendment absolutists, among whom I had previously counted myself, who believe it is unprincipled ever to "back
down" and settle a claim when the First Amendment is at stake. I don't
have much to say in my own defense, except to repeat the story
Michael Kinsley told at a *Washington Monthly* conference on neoliberalism about the time he and Nicholas Lemann went to small claims
court to defend the *Washington Monthly* and its editor against a suit by
a freelance writer. While waiting for their turn, they listened to a series
of cases during which the judge would say, "The purpose of small
claims court is to make an earnest effort toward settlement," and follow with a pep talk on the need to avoid litigation, which, as it happened, was the neoliberal position on most civil law suits. Then the
judge called Kinsley and said, "Young man, have you made an earnest
effort toward settlement?"

Kinsley said, "No, Your Honor." He was under instructions from his
boss Charles Peters. "We feel this is a matter of principle."

The judge turned beet red and said, "Young man! Small-claims
court is no place for principles!" He ordered them out into the hallway
to settle with the writer for $82.

"I went out and I told Charlie, 'Look, we're just going to have to settle this case. I have to get back to work!' And Charlie said, 'I can't believe it! I thought the courts were for justice!' And I said, 'Now, Charlie,

small-claims court is no place for justice.' The only way I could get him to settle with the writer was to agree to write him an article for free. There is a small moral here: it is very easy to be contemptuous of the law, of lawyers, of justice, of courts until you want something, and then even the staunchest neoliberal suddenly wouldn't mind a little bit more procedure."

8

THE EDITOR AS PUBLISHER

It used to be said that book publishing was a gentleman's profession. After sixteen years editing *The Nation*, I could see why nobody ever said that about publishing journals of opinion. So after sixteen years of meeting weekly deadlines, picking pockets, answering letters from complaining subscribers, keeping the peace between the proprietor and the staff, presiding over feuding columnists and contributors, negotiating with an increasingly militant Newspaper Guild, writing direct-mail copy, making no progress on a book that was decades overdue, I decided it was time to take a sabbatical and write my long-postponed essay on the role of the journal of opinion. I felt that one way or the other it would be good to put some distance between me and the magazine as I tried to figure out what it all meant. I applied for fellowships at the Institute of Politics at the John F. Kennedy School of Government at Harvard and also at the Freedom Forum Media Studies Center, then located on the ground floor of Columbia University's School of Journalism. I had given a brown-bag lunch talk on the role of the journal of opinion at the Joan Shorenstein center at Harvard, just across the courtyard from the Institute of Politics, and I had given a similar talk at a seminar at the Freedom Forum.

I talked first with Katrina vanden Heuvel about her sitting in the editor's chair in my absence. Katrina had started as a *Nation* intern (from Princeton) two years after I arrived; she had been the super-efficient organizer and archivist of Carey McWilliams's papers as part of her intern project; she had written her senior thesis at Princeton on the anti-Communist crusade of the 1950s, a subject dear to my heart, and at the core of *The Nation*'s postwar and 1950s concerns; she had left a job in television working on an ABC documentary about Mc-Carthyism to come back to *The Nation* as an assistant editor; she had married "Sovieticus," our Soviet affairs columnist, her old Russian politics professor Stephen Cohen, who saw Gorbachev for the radical reformer he was long before most Russia observers understood what he had wrought; and at my invitation she had assembled and edited a Best-of-the-*Nation* anthology for which E. L. Doctorow wrote an introduction: "You can dig through this anthology as you would a hope chest, finding and holding up to view its mementos, treasures, jewels—laces and old valentines. You begin smiling and then you catch your breath. This is your family's life and you have it in your hands." But more important than that, she seemed to me to have the character, values, and not least the temperament for the job; and to understand that, as Robert Borosage once put it, "*The Nation* walks on two legs—one inside the establishment and one outside." I knew that unlike anyone else in the office, with the exception of Richard Lingeman, who was too reticent for the job, she would not cause factional grumbling if she were made acting editor. And without saying anything about it, I knew that down the road I was not as indispensable as I thought I was; as a matter of fact, at some point I would move on, and here was an ideal opportunity for an audition—by a woman not yet in her forties. Not only that, but I knew, or believed I knew, that Arthur Carter would like the idea of Katrina sitting in for me.

By coincidence or the alignment of the stars, on the day I was to see Arthur to tell/ask him about my plan, I received a formal invitation from Harvard and later a similar letter from the Freedom Forum.

So my plan was to spend a semester starting in January 1994 as a fellow at the Institute of Politics in Cambridge, and in the fall I would move to the Media Studies Center at Columbia for my second "semester" off.

I was looking forward to Cambridge. My daughter Miri was on the staff of *Frontline*, the public television weekly documentary program originating in Boston, and had worked her way up from switchboard operator to researcher to head researcher to production assistant to assistant producer (she ignored my advice to stay on as switchboard operator, since that, I explained, was "where all power is"). At the Institute of Politics my own duties would be to run a seminar on the role of the journal of opinion, where members of the Harvard community would discuss the subject with speakers from the "real" world. I called it "The Case Against Balanced Journalism: The Magazine of Opinion, Counterforce to the Mass Media." (Once, when the English writer Jessica Mitford came to *The Nation* office, her husband, the attorney Robert Truehaft, introduced her by saying she was going to talk on pornography and constitutional law. She said, "Yes, but I prefer to call it 'Sex and the First Amendment.' It sounds much jollier that way.") My obvious premise was that these magazines' influence—through advocacy, analysis, interpretation, investigation, protest, prophesy, celebration, consternation—is greater than their circulation figures suggest.

My other "obligation" was a weekly dinner with my fellow fellows—Alice Wolf, former mayor of Cambridge; Kim Campbell, former Prime Minister of Canada, who had gotten in trouble for posing in the semi-nude for a book of portraits of Canadian women; two former congressmen—Beau Boulter, head of the Jack Kemp for President campaign in Texas, and Don Fraser, former National Chairman of ADA; Kate Michaelman, the passionate president of NARAL; and Florence Graves, founding editor of *Common Cause*.

If the plan worked, I would unwind and complete my research at Harvard and write my book at Columbia. James Hoge, former publisher of the *Chicago Sun-Times* and then editor of the *New York Daily News*, had made the same trajectory and told me that at Harvard I would have all the fun (appearing on panels, attending classes, putting up visiting speakers either at the elegant Charles Hotel or in J.F.K.'s old suite at Winthrop House), and at the Freedom Forum I'd get my book done. That's more or less what happened, except that I didn't get my book done.

I had a momentary setback my first day, when I stopped off at the Harvard Book Store and there in a section called Cultural Studies were hundreds of books on shelves taller than I, written in a language I didn't speak, the language of postmodernism, on a subject that did not exist when I went to college in the 1950s but one that even I could understand was somehow related to my quest—to assess the relevance of the journal of opinion in these, ahem, postmodern times. The only bright spot for me were the half-dozen volumes by and about Jürgen Habermas.

On my second day, while I was pondering whether to immerse myself in Cultural Studies, an undergraduate affiliated with the Institute of Politics further complicated my meditations. She chirpily pointed out to the Institute's fellows that they had a "once in a lifetime" opportunity to take any course they wanted at the "greatest university in the world" and they should make the most of it. Navigating between the Charybdis of graduate-school impenetrability and the Scylla of undergraduate hubris, I decided to split the difference: I would take some courses by day and browse by night.

As a gesture to Cultural Studies, I signed up for a lecture course called Mass Culture, taught by a brilliant young man named Thomas Richards, who looked like a cross between a matinee idol and Count Dracula with his black cape and flowing hair. He started with the famous (although not to me) Crystal Palace Exhibition of 1851 and the *London Illustrated Graphic* of 1850, and traced the way the images projected into the culture by them created a commodity culture before there was a commodity economy. I had hoped that by studying how the mainstream culture "commodified" art and ideas, I would gain insight into the opportunity for magazines of critical opinion to provide what the language I didn't really speak called a counternarrative. What I really learned, however, was that it was possible for Professor Richards, who was at home with semiotics and deconstruction, to give his students the illusion that we understood what he was talking about. I also came away with an inventory of aphorisms that I tried to capture in my notes so that I could decipher them later. My favorite: "Kitsch is the miniaturization of charisma." Yeah, sure.

I chose as my second course a seminar on American Dissent—one-third because of its title, one-third because its reading list included Tom Paine, Emerson, Thoreau, Frederick Douglass, W.E.B. Du Bois, Edward Bellamy, and others whom I treasured in memory, meant to revisit, and/or had never got around to getting around to; and one-third because of the name of the professor, Sacvan Bercovitch, whose Yiddish-speaking Canadian parents had named him after Sacco and Vanzetti. (When we became friends, I never knew whether to call him Sac or Van, so I called him Professor.) Sacvan's message, to the extent that I understood it, was that dissent implies assent, because after all, if Americans care about something enough to go to prison for it or fight a civil war over it, there's a value there. Sacvan was also interested in consent, and somehow between his notions of assent, dissent, and consent he persuaded me that I should not too quickly abandon the idea of objectivity as an ideal.

When I asked him to say a little more, especially about how it related to my notion of ideology, he referred me to cultural anthropologists for further enlightenment.

My third course, with the perfectly conventional title of Moral Reasoning, was a philosophy course required of all freshmen, but each professor taught it in his own way, and Stanley Cavell's way of teaching it was to show and talk about movies from the 1930s and 1940s—in particular what he called remarriage comedies (these included *Adam's Rib*, *The Awful Truth*, *The Philadelphia Story*, *It Happened One Night*) and those he called melodramas of the lost woman (*Stella Dallas*, *Camille*, *Now, Voyager*). Actually on Tuesdays he would talk about philosophical texts (Plato, Aristotle, Locke, Kant, Mill, Nietzsche, Rawls, etc.), and he would devote Thursdays to his favorite movies (which would be shown in the evenings). Oh yes, Shakespeare, Milton, Freud, and Ralph Waldo Emerson, whom he also considered to be philosophers, would make frequent guest appearances on both Tuesdays and Thursdays. At first I thought that parents of the country's future philosophers might be forgiven for wondering whether their sons and daughters were getting their money's worth even though the films were free. Was this really the best way of introducing college freshmen to the intricacies of philosophy? But any reservations I might have were quashed the day Professor Cavell got around to discussing the social contract.

In my political theory seminar at Swarthmore I had learned about the social contract by reading *The Second Treatise on Government* by Locke, *Leviathan* by Hobbes, and *The Social Contract* by Rousseau. Cavell, too, assigned these texts but he didn't stop there. Don't accept my paraphrase of Cavell's exquisitely nuanced attempt to use what he calls the remarriage comedies to teach moral perfectionalism (he wouldn't), but in the interests of moral transparency, here is the way I understood it at the time. As any college freshman knows, the social contract has to do with the relationship between the citizen and the sovereign, the instrument by which the citizen grants his consent to the sovereign. And when the citizen agrees to cede certain rights to the sovereign, he is making what philosophers call a utilitarian calculus: He agrees to give the sovereign these rights only in exchange for the sovereign agreeing that the state will provide in return some minimal condition of happiness.

Of course, Cavell acknowledged, there is no such thing as a social contract. It is a metaphor. So let's compare it to a *real* contract, the marriage contract, for instance. "When we say 'till death do us part' do we really mean it? Or do we mean under certain *conditions* 'till death do us part'? And what are those conditions? Don't they entail some minimal condition of happiness?" In the world according to Cavell, there are two critical institutions: marriage and government. Each involves a covenant designed to promote happiness. The private happiness that marriage can make possible requires a "meet and happy conversation." Its public equivalent requires the express (as distinguished from tacit) consent of the governed (Locke). And that means it requires free speech, debate, argument (Mill). They both involve the mystery that men and women and therefore society can be moved to change by speech. "Marriage is entry into the unknown," he was quick to note, "whereas remarriage [to the same person] is reentry into the known." What is it that these characters now know that makes them think they are going to enjoy that minimal condition of happiness? And what do we mean by happiness, anyway? What did Rousseau mean? What did John Stuart Mill and the utilitarians mean? What did Dexter (the Cary Grant character) mean in *The Philadelphia Story* when he rebuked Tracy (Katherine Hepburn), his former wife, for her moralism over his tippling? When she replies that his drinking made him unattractive, he accuses her of having been a scold. Isn't he really saying that one can't have a "meet and happy conversation" with a scold? If marriage depends on a covenant between those who are to govern each other, perhaps remarriage has to do with the discovery that one's former mate and oneself speak a common language.

Remember, Aristotle's conception of happiness involves the notion of friendship, and if we are interested in friendship (and marriage, by the way, is a metaphor for friendship), then we must examine conversation or the sharing of thoughts, for the goal of conversation is the highest form of friendship and it is only through friendship that we can realize our best selves (Emerson's moral perfectionism).

Cavell's classes were a cascade of questions: If the only hope (for society and marriage) is a mutual responsiveness, what does this conversation sound like? Can the state require happiness or the expression of happiness of its citizens? And what about the public happiness? Is it expressed most purely in the patriotic ritual or is it expressed in the robust debate, argument, conversation, and is this what we mean by consent of the governed?

My question was how to link Cavell's film festival and the endless verbal intercourse of its central couples to John Dewey's theory of the national conversation as the key to democracy, a happy state. If the national conversation is the key, then certainly the journal of opinion, which carries on, informs, enriches, tests, embodies this conversation, is a critical artifact as well as a critical journal.

What I hoped to do in my study-group seminar was to ask contributors to and editors of journals of opinion to introduce the students to the unique power and influence of journals of opinion, and to engage members of the group in genuine critical discourse about them. I also wanted to question the idea that such journals were mere relics of the eighteenth century and to dispel the myths that perpetuated this image of fragility: that their circulations are too small to be significant, that they preach only to the converted, that they are perpetually on the brink of bankruptcy, that their shrillness limits their audience, that they lack credibility because they take ideologically driven positions.

Even before the guest speakers arrived, I myself did my best to demolish these myths. The idea that circulation is a measure of influence is a misconception. Every small magazine has its equivalent of Frank P. Walsh's famous story about *The Nation*: In the 1920s he wrote a series of articles about railroads for the Hearst papers, which reached 10 million people, and not one reader said a word to him; but then he published the same material in an article for *The Nation*, whose circulation was then 27,000, and "The day *The Nation* went on the Washington newsstands my telephone started ringing. I heard from editors, broadcasters and Congressmen." Beyond the quality of the readership is the intensity with which these publications are read. Dwight Macdonald made this point when he wrote in 1957:

> While I was editing *Politics* I often felt isolated, comparing my
> few thousand readers with the millions and millions of non-

readers—such is the power of the modern obsession with quantity, also of Marxism with its sentimentalization of the "masses." But in the last eight years I have run across so many nostalgic old readers in so many unexpected quarters that I have the impression I'm better known for *Politics* than for my articles in *The New Yorker*, whose circulation is roughly seventy times greater. This is curious but should not be surprising. A "little magazine" is often more intensively read (and circulated) than the big commercial magazines, being a more individual expression and so appealing with special force to individuals of like minds.

As to the widespread notion that, as *Time* has put it, "traditionally, the opinion magazines have preached to the converted, offering the dependable pleasures of a party line," it of course is false—and not just in *The Nation's* case, as I have already suggested. These magazines as a class are read by diverse publics. In the early 1980s, when I visited James Curran, editor of *New Socialist*, a British publication in the orbit of the Labour Party, he seemed to speak for us all when he said, "We perform a knitting function, bringing together groups with very different ideas." (In his case it was the peace movement, feminists, trade unionists, civil libertarians, and Labour Party members.) Each of these groups has its own belief system, and their agendas are frequently at cross-purposes. And even if it were true that these magazines always tell their readers what they want to hear, there would still be some value in that, since many readers need and want facts, figures, and a vocabulary to document and articulate their sense of the world.

The truth that small-circulation journals are perpetually on the brink of bankruptcy was certainly incontrovertible, but the real point was that so many of them nonetheless seemed not to go out of business. As for the complaint that journals of opinion are shrill, captious, or carping, it is usually a euphemism either for a policy disagreement or for the acknowledged truth that critical journals of opinion are critical. Precisely because writers openly declare their biases, opinions, assumptions, and attitudes, the magazines can be described as non-objective, non-neutral, and therefore noncredible. But as we saw with *Iron Mountain*, it is a mistake to equate credibility with moderation of tone and the appearance of "evenhandedness" is to make a false equation.

There are those who say that magazines of critical opinion had more influence in earlier times. One reads, for example, of Kingsley Martin, editor of the *New Statesman* from 1931 until 1945, of whom it was written: "His influence on the generation which came of age in the 1930s is incalculable. It is probably no exaggeration to claim that for better or worse, it changed the course of history as well as the patterns of dissenting thought throughout the British Empire." And in 1939 Charles Beard credited *The Nation* and *The New Republic* with helping to bring about women's suffrage, old-age pensions, state and federal housing, the regulation of securities, wages, and hours, and public ownership of water sites, among other reforms.

But how does one define influence, and what are its indicators? Erwin Knoll, late editor of *The Progressive*, once told of a woman who approached him brandishing an umbrella and shouting, "I hold you and your magazine responsible for my son failing to register for the draft." (His response was: "I hope you are as proud of him as I am.") Some think that if an article in a small-circulation journal finds its way into the mass media, that is influence. Irving Louis Horowitz took satisfaction from the fact that a report on the transportation of prisoners which originated in his *Transaction/Society* was picked up for a twenty-minute segment by CBS, was seen by 25 million people, and led to new actions related to prisoners' rights. And then there is what we might call the Loom Factor: The looming presence of a muckraking magazine like the *Texas Observer*, for example, forces other Texas publications to publish material they might otherwise avoid.

When I set off for the Kennedy School, as far as I knew there was no history of the journal of opinion, critical or otherwise. That shows how much I knew. In fact I was to discover that the journal of opinion had an unlikely Boswell, who had traced its history all the way back to sixteenth-century Europe. I'll get to him in a minute. It was not as if I had not done my homework. I knew all about Frank Luther Mott's magisterial five-volume history of American magazines from 1741 to 1938. And I knew about John Tebbel and Mary Ellen Zuckerman's *The Magazine in America* and Dean Theodore Peterson's *Magazines in the Twen-*

tieth Century. But they were about American magazines. I had read Hendrik Hertzberg's essay on the journal of opinion in the *Media Studies Journal,* in which he argued, "The magazine as a medium of modern social expression was pretty much invented by one man—Daniel Defoe." Like most American boys and girls, I knew Defoe only or primarily as the author of *Robinson Crusoe,* but Defoe's magazine, which he called *The Review,* came out three times a week between 1704 and 1713. Each issue contained a 2,000-word essay on politics and trade which, according to the historian James Evans, was meant to "educate the rising trading class about its importance in England." It also answered readers' queries on matters such as dueling, drinking, love, marriage, and the union of England and Scotland. It even published fiction. And I knew that today if a journal of opinion loses a libel case, it has to pay court costs and a fine, whereas Defoe's exposé of the Church of England ("The Shortest Way with Dissenters") landed him in Newgate Prison for seditious libel. As Hertzberg said, "Every magazine writer and publisher should honor Daniel Defoe. He is the father of us all."*

Not long thereafter came the most famous and influential of England's new periodicals: Steele's *The Tatler* (founded in 1709), Swift's *The Examiner* (1710–14), and Addison and Steele's *The Spectator,* which began in 1711, whose essays and satires criticizing Parliament and the crown inspired America's first citizen of print, Benjamin Franklin. But the Whiggish *Tatler* and *Spectator* emphasized moderation in most things, and although their critical spirit did much to animate parliamentary democracy, our own colonial press was more opinionated and militant, and Franklin wrote: "The press can not only strike while the iron is hot, but it can heat it by continually striking." What the colonists feared, one historian wrote, was "not a society riddled with political publications, but a society without them." "Had it not been for the continual information from the Press," wrote one who signed himself a

---

*Actually, there is a dispute about whether Defoe's *Review* was really the first magazine. There are any number of prototypes. In 1691 J. de la Crose, a Huguenot, published *History of Learning,* which anticipated magazines like *World Press Review, Atlas, Intellectual Digest*; it was a sort of *Utne Reader* of its day, reprinting, summarizing, and criticizing new works from abroad.

Countryman in the *Providence Gazette*, "a junction of all the people on this northern continent . . . would have been scarcely conceivable."

My nomination for most ingenious editor-publisher is the man behind a magazine called *The New World*, which didn't appear until 1840 but which earned the wrath of Charles Dickens by publishing installments of Dickens's novels without permission or payment. That of course is not why I admire him, rather it is because he figured out a way to get around the onerous postal charges, which in those days were computed on a per-page basis; he did it by printing pages four feet long and eleven columns wide. A man after my own heart.

Neither of America's two monthly magazines, *Harper's* (founded in 1850 in New York) and *The Atlantic Monthly* (1857 in Boston), was a journal of opinion as such, but both were magazines of ideas, born as far as I can tell without a jot of preliminary market research, and although they have lost money for most of their lives, they are both still around, causing more than their share of constructive literary and political trouble.

But it was not until I read the philosopher Jürgen Habermas that I began to see these journals in their historical context. I had previously regarded Habermas as indecipherable, both because of his jargon-ridden, translated-from-the-German prose and because of his historic connection to the Frankfurt School, the first bastion of critical theory, which I found indecipherable in its own right.

Habermas had set forth his notion of the public sphere (which I put halfway between the political or governmental sphere and the private and personal sphere) in 1962, and it turned out that he identified the journal of opinion as a sort of house organ to the public sphere. But none of the so-called scholars of American magazines cited it, possibly because it was published in Germany under the title *Strukturwandel der Öffenlichkeit* and not translated into English until 1989, when the MIT Press brought it out under the jaunty title *The Structural Transformation of the Public Sphere: An Inquiry into a Category of Bourgeois Society*. By then so much attention was being paid to Habermas for his notion of the public sphere that the first half of his book, an ambitious analytic history of the organic connection between these journals and opinion formation in a democratic society, was largely overlooked.

Even before I knew about the journal part of his thesis, my hope had been to find in Habermas's conception of the public sphere a cul-

tural framework for thinking about the function of these journals—
something neither the market nor the state provided.

Capitalism assumes that the profit motive drives the market, so while
the market (or lack thereof) might explain why some of my favorite journals of opinion (*Furioso, The Masses, Blast,* Dwight Macdonald's *Politics,*
T. S. Eliot's *Criterion,* Albert J. Nock's *Freeman*) went under, it could not
explain the staying power of the journal of opinion, or of the genre itself,
which repudiates the profit motive. The market's opposite, its nemesis,
its alternative—the state, the government—also did not contain and was
not the answer to my question. In other nations and political cultures,
where a single political party controls the government, for example in the
former Soviet Union and throughout Eastern Europe, the state/Party
subsidized journals of opinion like *Novy Mir* and *Literatura Gazeta.* But
these journals of *official* opinion handed down a line—which is precisely
what an authentic journal of opinion is not, or should not, be doing. The
case for the journal of critical opinion, as I understand it, has always
been made in social, political, or cultural terms, never in financial ones,
and it has also been assumed that part of their work is to question the official line. In 1965, on the occasion of *The Nation's* 100th anniversary, the
historian Christopher Lasch wrote in *The New York Times* that these
magazines, which almost by definition inspire dissent, hostility, and suspicion in high places, "by default have come to serve as the only instruments of debate but also the only surviving media in which scholars can
still talk to one another. They give the intellectual community what little
unity and coherence it retains." With the advent of cable television and
the Internet, that is no longer true, but his larger point still stands: "If
they serve no other purpose, the magazines of dissent would still be valuable for the enemies they have made."*

---

*Other students of the genre, like the critic Casey Blake, agree that these journals are
places where intellectuals discover one another, explore unconventional political and
cultural positions, expand the debate, and contribute to "formation of public opinion as
a moral and political authority." And Blake would argue that historical forces rather than
the prospects for profit laid the predicate for these beasties: a non-ideological party system, a newly marginalized partisan press; the emergence of a salaried middle class;
expanded higher education, the new power of the corporation and the state, and the di-
minishing allegiance of the educated classes to religion and party politics. "Collectively,"
he asserts, "these set the stage for the simultaneous creation of the intelligentsia as
a social group and the journal of opinion as its chief organ of expression."

Habermas's idea of the public sphere as a category somehow related to a "civil society" that was neither market-driven nor dominated by the state seemed to me to be organically linked to the journal of critical opinion. Habermas's theory, in the Enlightenment tradition, is based on the idea that to flourish, democracy requires a continuous conversation, open argumentation, and debate. This happened (at least for white males) in the city-states of ancient Greece, and it happened again, Habermas the Frankfurt School Marxist observes, in sixteenth-century Europe, when conditions favoring mercantile capitalism also brought private citizens together to debate public issues in an open way—he calls this the "bourgeois public sphere." He traces this development to the coffeehouses that sprang up, beyond and yet next to court salons, and also to the periodical press, which set the agenda of coffeehouse debate. Especially in England, where censorship was minimal, by the beginning of the eighteenth century there were an estimated 3,000 coffeehouses in London alone. Earlier newsletters had reported on the journeys of princes and the arrival of foreign dignitaries, on balls, appointments, "special events," and other news of and from the court, and on the Continent. These came close to being PR handouts. Thus a March 1769 Viennese government press ordinance proclaimed: "In order that the writer of the journal might know what sorts of domestic arrangements and other matters are suitable for the public, such are to be compiled weekly by the authorities and are to be forwarded to the editor of the journal." But in Britain, where the court did not dominate the civic culture as fully as it did in, say, France or Spain, new periodicals like *The Review*, *The Tatler*, *The Examiner*, and *The Spectator* flourished.

Habermas's theory had particular resonance for me. I was already persuaded by another Christopher Lasch essay, this one "The Lost Art of Argument," in *The Gannett Center Journal*, bemoaning the transformation of American politics into a spectator sport. In the old days, he argued, journalism was characterized by and stimulated serious deliberation and public debate. But today television and the false ideal of "objectivity" in news reporting had changed all that, causing the atrophy of the virtues associated with public debate. Lasch's list of these virtues ("judgment, prudence, eloquence, courage, self-reliance, common sense") reminded me too much of the Boy Scout oath, but Habermas's historical survey and analysis took the matter to a deeper level.

I also made a more personal connection. Two minutes down the street from the old *Nation* offices at 333 Sixth Avenue and right next door to the old *Village Voice* offices, where Christopher Street meets Sheridan Square, stood the closest thing to a twentieth-century version of an eighteenth-century coffeehouse—the Lion's Head Tavern. It was known for the political graffiti in its bathroom, its rare cheeseburgers, and the overcooked political and literary arguments of its denizens, many of whose book jackets brightened its walls. Although I spent far too many hours there engaged in, ahem, public discourse, from Habermas I learned that I was carrying on an honorable tradition. In eighteenth-century London, Button's Coffee House contained a lion's head, and readers threw letters through its jaws. From then on, they were published weekly as the "Roaring of the Lion." So Habermas gave me both a philosophical analysis of my calling and a reminder of one of my hangouts. We had much to discuss, and I thought I had figured out a way to build that discussion into my sabbatical.

According to Habermas, the journals performed yet another service for a middle class newly exposed to higher education. Readers of their articles, arguments, and essays became engaged in the art of critical-rational public debate. Instead of royal authorities or the church being the authority, what Habermas likes to call the "authority of the better argument" asserted itself. Subjects previously controlled by church and/or state, and hence not subject to dissent, were now fair game, all of which gave rise to an expanded public sphere (still mostly barred to women).

Here, then, was the theoretical framework for thinking about critical journals, a set of abstract propositions against which to test the hands-on experience of and theories of our guest speakers.

I lined up Hendrik Hertzberg, who in addition to having written his essay on journals of opinion, was former editor of *The New Republic* and now at Tina Brown's *New Yorker*; Robert Kuttner, editor of *The American Prospect*; Rea Hederman, publisher of *The New York Review of Books*; Barbara Ehrenreich, whose writing appeared in *Mother Jones*, *The Progressive*, *The Guardian*, and everywhere else; John O'Sullivan, editor of Bill Buckley's *National Review*; Randy Kennedy, editor of *Re-*

construction; and *The Nation's* own Christopher Hitchens. And then I had another idea: Why not bring in Habermas himself? We didn't have the budget to bring him to Cambridge, and e-mail was not yet in wide enough use (by me, among others), to attempt contact that way, so I made him a proposal by FedEx: If he would answer a set of ten questions (which I included for his perusal), either on tape or typewritten, we would transcribe and translate his responses, and use the questions and answers as the basis for a special seminar, which we would in turn tape, transcribe, and translate for Habermas. He didn't answer either my questions or my letter.

The workshop, through no fault of my own, worked. When I say through no fault of my own, I am not engaging in false modesty. I had the wit to invite engaging, informed, fluent speakers. But in each case what they had to report was not the reason I had invited them.

From Christopher Hitchens I had hoped for a comparative analysis of the difference between the *New Statesman*, with its special relationship to the Labour Party, and *The Nation*, which prided itself on not being the organ of any party, movement, or sect. Instead, what we got was an elegant theory about why it is that for the most part what these journals do, whether British or American, is keep their readers amused, their critical faculties aware and awake for when they're needed, in a sort of holding action; they also provide stipends, however modest, space, and encouragement to write, for many people who would never otherwise survive as writers or would never otherwise write the article or book that makes the difference.

"When I used to travel around the world for the *New Statesman*," said the peripatetic Hitch, "it was a remarkable fact that in any of these countries the mention of the *New Statesman* was enough to ignite the fraternal flame. They felt it represented the English conscience." He told us that was an odd compound made up partly of puritanism, philanthropy, the antislavery movement, and internationalism, with a dose of political nonconformism. "Daniel Patrick Moynihan, in his book about the United Nations, said that the *New Statesman* and its ally, the London School of Economics—founded at the same time and by Beatrice and Sidney Webb—gave the newly independent countries the idea that there was such a thing as democratic socialism and political independence. This thoroughly inconvenienced those who thought that the imagination should be formed by the great powers. When I read that, I thought, Well, I haven't completely wasted my time."

Occasionally, he said, one can see a journal essay making a big difference, having a catalytic effect. Such was the case with "Britain and the Nuclear Bomb," a 1957 essay by the playwright and novelist J. B. Priestley. This extraordinary polemic against nuclear weapons as the most frightening and least understood new threat to civilization led directly to the formation of the Campaign for Nuclear Disarmament (CND), which through various metamorphoses survived into E. P. Thompson's movement of civic resistance for democracy against the Cold War bloc system that then divided Europe, and eventually helped in the germination of the events of 1989. "You have to trace a slight sort of reddish thread through the labyrinth, but," said Christopher, "I think it can be done and without immodesty to say that it caused a real change. As Marx used to say, the mole works a long time underground before making any visible difference, but that was a traceable mole."

Then there was Hendrik Hertzberg. I knew or thought I knew that he had quit *The New Republic* for political reasons, and I hoped he would elaborate on this. And indeed he did. For example, he had been profoundly offended by a very influential article that had recently appeared in *The New Republic*, a negative critique of Clinton's health-care plan written by one Elizabeth McCaughey. (Largely on the strength of this, George Pataki later selected her to run on his ticket for lieutenant governor of New York State.) Rik thought it was "a fundamentally dishonest piece of work," because 80 percent of her criticism could apply to every kind of health insurance, but, he pointed out, "it had a tremendous impact for one reason and one reason only—because even the liberal *New Republic* was attacking Clinton's bill. It's amazing to me how once you get a reputation as an early riser you can sleep till noon for the rest of your life."

But what I hadn't expected was his comparative assessment of the influence of *The New Republic* and Tina Brown's *New Yorker*, where he then hung his hat. Rik made a significant distinction between the influence of a magazine and the influence of articles published in it. Journals of critical opinion like *The New Republic*, *The Nation*, and *National Review* themselves have influence, but *The New Yorker*'s influence is often felt with single articles that appear in it, like James Baldwin's "The Fire Next Time" or Jonathan Schell on "The Fate of the Earth."

Once, I asked Irving Kristol, co-founder of *The Public Interest*, for his list of the most influential articles he had published in any of the magazines he had been connected with. He listed some that "caused a tizzy," such as Francis Fukuyama's "The End of History" (in *The National Interest*) and Nancy Mitford's "U and Non-U" (*Encounter*), "but tizziness isn't necessarily associated with enduring influence," he added.

Still, it seemed clear to my students that far from being eighteenth-century relics, the influence of journals of opinion was growing, if anything. They were read by people whom Hertzberg called "the secondary distributors of opinion, the factories of origin" of opinion. Columnists read them and TV news readers read them and newspaper editors and newspaper reporters read them. Their influence was hard to measure, but it spread out in waves from the center. "There are more Op Ed pages than ever. There are more radio talk shows than ever. There is more opinion being expressed in our society than ever before." The opinion industry was riding high.

When Rea Hederman, publisher of *The New York Review of Books*, the only journal of opinion to my knowledge that was actually making money, agreed to join us, I naïvely thought the class would glean some of the nuts-and-bolts wisdom of a canny capitalist. For me, however, the most memorable moment came when Hederman was asked something about his hopes for the *Review*, and he said he hoped that it would earn more money, so that its editors would have more resources to put at the disposal of their writers. I guess it would be even more naïve to say there appeared to be no editor-publisher tensions, but Hederman seemed slightly offended or rather surprised at the idea that he would even think of giving his editors editorial advice.

Since *The American Prospect*, founded in 1990, was the only foundation-funded magazine represented, I hoped that Bob Kuttner, its editor (and also an economist and newspaper columnist), would enlighten the class on the differences between working at a for-profit magazine and at a nonprofit one. But Kuttner's original contribution was to provide some shrewd insights into the politics of niche publishing.

Starting in the late 1980s, he told us, he and the writer Sidney Blumenthal (then working for *The New Republic* and subsequently *The Washington Post*) had been meeting with James Chace, editor of *World Policy Journal*, to talk about starting yet another journal of opinion. The only problem was that from Kuttner's viewpoint they were the wrong opinions. As Kuttner saw it, the 1980s had been a period of glory for the journal of opinion. The rise of the right wing had been prefigured and assisted by a generation of intellectuals who cut their teeth writing for *The Public Interest*, a small-circulation journal with an enormous amount of influence, which specialized in connecting first principles to policy particulars. *Commentary* had become neoconservative. *The New Republic*, like *Washington Monthly*, was becoming neoliberal, and the principal overlap between neoliberalism and neoconservatism shared the view that big government was the bad guy, the welfare state didn't work, public intervention, no matter how well intentioned, backfired and harmed its intended recipients.

The magazine that Kuttner, Blumenthal, and Chace envisioned would fill what they saw as a "tremendous niche" between, if you will, *The New Republic* and *The Nation*. "Those of us who were self-identified liberal—sort of the F.D.R. liberal— rather than radicals felt that there was no journal, no magazine occupying that realm, a huge expanse of ideological territory, the politics of what Mike Harrington used to call the left edge of the possible. That is where I would identify myself," said Kuttner.

I was too polite to interrupt and make the case for *The Nation* as a left-liberal big tent, with room for both radicals and F.D.R. liberals, but I also knew he was partially right. What he didn't know and I didn't say was that I believed (and still do) that Katrina vanden Heuvel's *Nation* would fill that niche.

"We felt that the absence of such a magazine was allowing the right to win by default, was allowing liberalism to be pushed to the right, and was helping the premise that this was a conservative era to become a self-fulfilling prophecy." Surveying the undergraduates around the table, he mentioned it was also making it very difficult for young people, who intuitively gravitated to this set of values, to validate their intuitions.

This was the impulse that ended up with *The American Prospect*, which was a quarterly, now a monthly. My own theory is that for anthroposociological reasons these journals maximize their influence as weeklies, but Kuttner commonsensically reported, "We just decided the frequency of the magazine would be a function of how much money we could raise."

When editor-writers like Kuttner give what, let's face it, are commercials for their periodicals, I find it inspiring. "Launching a magazine," he said, "is worthwhile because the whole can be greater than the sum of its parts. And there are nineteen- and twenty-year-olds growing up for whom this five-year-old journal is already part of the landscape. Not to be presumptuous, but it creates a role model. It shows there are serious people who think it is not a silly thing to be a liberal, and there are articles and specific analyses of a policy or a dilemma. So that's worthwhile."

One of the students in my class wanted to know what Kuttner thought of television as a forum for opinion, and I, being conservative by nature, was glad to hear him make the case for print. But he had another thought perhaps by way of explaining why he didn't go on television much himself: "If you appear on television you think of yourself as someone sort of above the drudgery of actual reporting, and you think of yourself as a kind of celebrity." I myself don't appear that much on television because I am not invited, but I have always thought that if you were good at it, it was a good thing to do, to get out the word about your magazine. But, argued Kuttner, "an awful lot of the actual analysis done on television skates on the surface, because you're too busy promoting your lecture bookings, you're too busy being a celebrity to go back to the dog work of reporting, or you're relying on the same elite sources. This is why a lot of television talk-show journalism is junk."

Our next guest was John O'Sullivan, who in September 1988 had replaced William Buckley as editor in chief of *National Review*. When I asked O'Sullivan about Buckley's relationship to his old magazine, he said, "It's very simple. I run the magazine on a day-to-day basis. I make all the decisions except when he wants to make one." My thought had been that even if Kuttner proselytized on behalf of F.D.R. liberalism, the editor of *National Review* would either present the case for the radical right or give us an old-fashioned dose of traditional conservatism.

But no, O'Sullivan preferred in effect to talk about what *The Nation* and *National Review* had in common. For starters, he has a theory as to why journalism aspiring to objectivity is less likely to have real influence than the journalism of opinion: "It ignores the psychological truth that an admitted set of opinions is less likely to influence the writer and is more capable of being corrected by the reader than an unadmitted set of opinions." Then he identified three distinguishing characteristics of the journal of opinion, each of which relates to its influence:

1. It represents a passionate constituency. But it does more than represent. "It rallies and defines. In bad times it gives it a voice in the body politic," said O'Sullivan. "When Reagan came in, the first thing *The Nation* did was to hold a huge rally in New York, which got an enormous lot of attention. It was in a sense raising the flag of resistance to Reagan. We wrote an attack on it, pointing out that some of the money for the thing had been provided by Mobil. We called it 'Masterpiece Hatchet.'" I hadn't thought of this before, but perhaps it was *National Review*'s editorial that caused Mobil to let it be known that it wanted its money back. I had favored inviting the head of Mobil to a press conference where we would hand him a big rubber check.

2. A journal of opinion encourages debate and the evolution of some kind of coherent philosophy within its own constituency. This is what Buckley did when he initially persuaded *NR*'s varied constituencies to cohere under the banner of fusionism. O' Sullivan confided, "We think we will see a convergence between moral traditionalists and libertarians around opposition to the radical bureaucracy. Thirty years ago moral conservatives counted on the state to promote prayer in the schools, ban pornography. Now I think they increasingly see the state as a radical bureaucracy pushing moral neutrality, delegitimizing traditional values, and libertarians don't think that there should be any role for the state in moral questions. So they are able to converge in opposition." (This was a prophecy that failed to come true, with a vengeance.)

3. A journal of opinion breaks new stories and puts new issues on the agenda. To my dismay, O'Sullivan cited "Troopergate" as a good example, for two reasons: "The lesser reason is the story itself, the issue of Bill Clinton's character, his moral qualities and infidelities. The much more important effect was that it alerted the public and the press itself to the fact that the press had been notably reluctant, partly because it sympathized with Clinton, to follow up any stories that served to discredit or to damage Bill Clinton. It was the Troopergate story which was in a sense the booster rocket for Whitewater in the

mainstream press. It forced them to look for critical stories about Clinton to avoid the charge of media hypocrisy."

Since so-called Troopergate was for me a mélange of half-truths, speculation-in-the-guise-of-fact, and hatchet job, I thought it was significant that *National Review*'s editor acknowledged it as the basis for the mainstream media's anti-Clinton campaign. But then again, as the convener of this seminar, I considered it my duty neither to praise this particular hatchet job nor to bury it, so I kept my mouth shut.

As the one guest speaker I failed to lure to my study group, Jürgen Habermas, wasn't available, his schedule being what it was and all that, the week he would have appeared I asked Shelly Cohen instead. Shelly was proprietor of the great Out-of-Town newsstand smack in the middle of Harvard Square. I wanted him to give us a report from the trenches. Shelly seemed to have helped launch as many new magazines as my friend Jim Kobak, the public-spirited magazine consultant—by giving them highly desirable display space—and I know this because he had done it for *Monocle* thirty-five years earlier. While it was nice to bring Shelly's newsstand to the academy, he was no Habermas.

So when I received an invitation to deliver a paper in June at the Louisiana Museum, outside of Copenhagen, I accepted on condition that the round-trip ticket include a stopover in Frankfurt. Luckily for me, when I called Habermas's office to see if he could spare me half an hour, Habermas was on the road but his secretary wasn't and she booked me in.

I was in the midst of packing when the phone rang. It was Habermas himself. There must be a mistake, he explained. He couldn't possibly spare the time, he hadn't answered my letter because he was traveling, he was overwhelmed, he had no time to compose answers, he didn't like to talk into tape recorders, he was otherwise occupied, and even if he wasn't, the last American journalists who had passed through had betrayed him. He hoped that in all other respects my stopover in Frankfurt would be productive. When I told him there were no other respects and asked if perhaps we could have an informal conversation, he relented, "but just for half an hour."

In the hour and a half I eventually spent with Habermas, in his spare two-room suite in a run-down gray university structure populated by cigarette-puffing students, he made a number of Habermasian points. Among them was this one: When I asked what he thought about

Lasch's lament for the institutions associated with public debate, he said, "Breakfast." Say what? "Breakfast is a critical institution," he said, "by which I mean that reading the morning paper at breakfast—and remember, *Die Zeit* and other European papers are closer to what Americans mean by the journal of opinion—gives you more time to consider rational argument. The morning paper is embedded with deep-seated cultural attitudes calling for time and attention—the scarcest of resources."

The journal of opinion in the public sphere may have been critically important in the past, but where does it fit in the new information age? What did Habermas have to say about prophesies that electronic data banks would replace magazines and books and relegate them to a bygone age of print? Habermas described himself as old-fashioned, in the sense that he believes in texts rather than oral presentations. He said he thought that print (which he quaintly called "the Gutenberg medium") put certain healthy restraints on the processes of the mind. As a result, Habermas said, "the print media are still at the core of any media we have now," and print media are the primary source from which television and movies draw their substance. "A world without print—imagine it," he said. "Articulation and analysis would be left to drown. Print is a necessary source for maintaining the public sphere."

Do left- and right-wing journals do the same thing in the public sphere, or do they have fundamentally different missions? "Conservatives feel they already have the answers, which are to be found in tradition." Without minimizing the differences, he advised me "not to moralize them," and he said, "I don't believe virtues and vices are unequally distributed on both sides." Thirty years ago he shared this pessimistic view, but the younger generation persuaded him otherwise. They were better informed than his parents' or his own generation on many issues, such as anti-Semitism, and he credited the left with this advance. "The left is endowed with the capacity to feel nervous. It feels an obligation to provide innovative answers."

I asked him whether he thought we might be in the middle of a paradigm shift that perhaps accounted for the civil wars within the various ideological camps. "To use the label of 'paradigm shift' makes it too easy," he said. "Remember that paradigm shifts are discovered only after they come about."

Since many radical theorists applauded opinion journalism on the postmodernist ground that facts were constructs, meanings were indeterminate, and objectivity was impossible, I asked the great man (and by this time I was certain he was a great man) how he felt about the idea of objectivity. "Objectivity is the wrong question. What's important is extending the range of arguments. It's less important to what conclusion the writer comes. It is the auditorium [the audience] who decides. That is the critical thing." Granting all the caveats about the impossibility of objectivity, he added, shaking his head, "you should never drop the ideal of reliable information. If you do, everything is lost. Which is not to say that reliability is enough. In our business the requirements are beyond reliability. What is required is the highest level of discourse. You should try to collect the best arguments for the most precisely stated position on the issue under discussion."

And then I asked the question that had brought me to Frankfurt: What is, what *should* be, the role of the journal of critical opinion in the next period? Although it may seem trivial or obvious when set down in black and white in the, er, Gutenberg medium, let me assure you that as it emerged in our conversation, it had all the clarity of the Liberty Bell. For anyone who entertained expectations of the public sphere, Habermas said, these journals become extremely important. "At the core of their mission is to maintain the discursive character of public communication. Who else, if not this type of press, is going to set the standards?"

Who else, indeed? And there you have it: "The key thing from the democratic standpoint is a critical audience which says yes or no. The question is how to keep the audience informed, how to keep it critical, how to keep it attending, how to keep it investing energy." In Habermasian terms, these important functions should be fulfilled by the actors in the public sphere. "And in the division of labor, those who are responsible for the journal of opinion, readers as well as writers and editors, should maintain that certain level of discourse."

By putting the contemporary case for these journals in terms of their arguments rather than the quality of their audience, Habermas (whom you already know believes that every subscription list is a political organization) exposed as irrelevant the objection that opinion magazines preach only to the converted. And his notion that the contemporary mission of these periodicals transcends their traditional ideological image has particular relevance today.

Six years later, in the immediate aftermath of September 11, 2001, Richard Falk, a longtime member of *The Nation's* editorial board, scholar, and peace activist, wrote a measured analytic reflection calling for and defining the elements of "A Just Response" to the attacks on the World Trade Center. "In our criticism of the current war fever . . . we should not forget that the attacks were massive crimes against humanity in a technical legal sense, and those involved in carrying them out should be punished to the fullest extent." To the dismay of old peace-movement comrades like Howard Zinn and Peter Weiss, three weeks later Falk wrote that "the war in Afghanistan against apocalyptic terrorism qualifies in my understanding as the first truly just war since World War II." But some weeks after that, he was in our pages yet a third time reporting that "with each passing day, my assessment shifts to reach the conclusion that the United States is waging an unjust war in Afghanistan, and it is doing it in a way that will have severe blowback consequences."

One of our contributing editors proposed that we have a new column called "Richard Falk Changes His Mind," but to me, having this thoughtful, learned, and committed peace and justice advocate think out loud in our pages about these momentous issues of war, peace, and justice was a classic Habermasian case of a journal of opinion doing its job—providing analysis, information interpretation in search of the most coherent framework to help the audience decide where justice and truth or simply the better course of action may be found.

By the spring of 1994, when Arthur Carter called me at Harvard's Kennedy School and sold me the magazine for money I didn't have, *The Nation's* circulation had not yet reached a million. It had briefly gotten up to 100,000 but seemed to be settling back into the high 80,000s. I did sign with Arthur, not by "Friday," but within a month, by which time I had not raised a penny of the $3 million I thought I needed. I had until the end of the year to take over as publisher, but my legal responsibility for its fortunes was now upon me.

On the one hand, the prospect of raising $3 million was daunting. On the other, it seemed to me that the money was out there and that this great cultural treasure, a part of America's heritage, was worth more than $3 million. No matter how formidable the task, we were better off than the *New Statesman*.

Over the years a number of well-heeled well-wishers had told me that if Arthur Carter ever wanted to sell the magazine, they were interested in buying. Of course they didn't mention—and naïf that I was, it didn't occur to me—that their interest was premised on the assumption that they would be in control. And my plan was to be in control myself, which the limited partnership my brother-in-law the lawyer had set up guaranteed. (If limited partners attempted to get active in the business, they risked losing their immunity from libel and other lawsuits.)

One of the first calls I made was to my old friend Ed Doctorow. I first met Edgar, you will recall, when he was editor in chief at Dial Press and agreed to publish *Iron Mountain*. Out of such adventures lifetime friendships are forged, and so I felt free to ask Ed (one of whose books *The Nation* had naturally savaged) for a favor, "just one." Since I had been asking Edgar for favors, "just one," for twenty-five years, I knew the drill.

"Edgar," I said, "I need a favor."

"Just one?" he asked.

Just one. I told him about my deal with Carter and said, "All I want from you is an introduction to Paul Newman."

The actor had well-known liberal political sympathies. I had read that he dedicated the profits from his popcorn and salad oil business (Newman's Own) to all sorts of worthy causes, and a friend of mine had told me a story about a group from his hometown in Connecticut visiting Newman to seek his help in the purchase of a new fire engine. How much does it cost? he had asked; $60,000, they told him, and according to my friend, he had written out a check for $60,000. Also, I knew that Doctorow had overlapped with Newman at Kenyon College and they were acquaintances.

Edgar said he would try. My hope had been to see Newman by Friday, as it were. A couple of weeks later, Edgar called with the good news. He had an appointment. That's great, I said. Not so fast, Edgar said. It's an appointment for next Thursday at 4:30 p.m. Newman was on location filming a movie.

"I'll be there," I said.

"It's an appointment for him to call me next Thursday at 4:30 p.m," Edgar explained.

The next Thursday at 5:00 p.m. Edgar called to tell me that at 4:30 Newman's office indeed had called, to say that Newman was in the middle of filming a movie and on location and could not make the call.

Two and a half months later, on a balmy evening in August, at long last Edgar and I were on our way to dinner with the great man. By now I had moved my files from Cambridge to the Freedom Forum at Columbia and had moved my head from Habermas to more mundane matters, like the fact that thus far my fund-raising batting average was 000.00. The reservation at a small Italian restaurant on the Upper East Side was for four, and although I had nothing but admiration for Joanne Woodward, aka Mrs. Paul Newman, and on any other occasion would have killed to be in her company, I worried. Based on past fund-raising experience, my view was that often the function of the accompanying spouse was to make sure no funds were raised. The other bad news was that although the restaurant served wine and beer (including red beer, Newman's favorite), there was no hard liquor. Although not vodka-dependent myself, after extensive research I had discovered that nothing disarmed or facilitated the potentially reluctant investors (funders) better than a few belts of Stolichnaya on the rocks.

As I feared, the dinner quickly took on the aspect of a social occasion. Doctorow and Newman kept topping each other with Kenyon stories, and Ms. Woodward and I had a fascinating discussion about the Group Theatre, about which she had made a quite wonderful television documentary, whose filming I had chanced to see. As a matter of fact, as the inquisitive Ms. Woodward drew me out on which members of the 1930s Group had during the 1950s named each other as Communists, a subject on which I felt I could speak with authority, I became more and more fascinated with what I had to say. I even almost got to the point of silently forgiving her for being there. I mean, if you have to change the subject, what better subject could I have hoped for? Then Newman turned to me and said, "So, Professor, what's the damage? What can I do for you?" I talked for about half an hour, going through the political situation, the cultural situation, the economic situation, the mass-media situation, the independent-media situation, and *The Nation* situation—with its virtual monopoly on weekly, progressive magazine journalism. He listened, nodded, asked some questions. The last one was: How much?

In a manner reminding me of the late Senator Joseph McCarthy ("I have here in my hand . . ."), I began waving about our inch-thick prospectus. According to projections prepared by James B. Kobak, I said, if we merely continued growing in the next three years at the same rate we had been growing over the past sixteen years (an average of 5 percent a year in circulation, advertising, and gifts from those we called Nation Associates), we could hit and pass the break-even point somewhere between years three and four (1997 and 1998). And all this could be done with an investment of $1.5 million. Being the prudent businessman I was trying to learn how to become, however, and aware of the need for a cushion to protect us against unforeseen contingencies, and because once I was in place, I didn't want to have to spend all my time fund-raising, my goal, I bravely announced, taking a deep breath, was to raise twice that—to find three or four individuals who would each invest a million dollars over the next four years.

"Is it tax deductible?" Newman asked. He told me his salad dressing and popcorn business was making more money than his movies. I explained that *The Nation* was not a nonprofit and why. I also told him about our institute, a public charity that runs an intern program and conferences, and supports research but is not allowed to pay the salaries of editors, or pay the printer, or fund subscription solicitation campaigns.

Newman nodded his head. He said I was asking for a lot. Couldn't I broaden the base of potential donors?

Investors, I said, correcting him with a smile. Yes, I said, I probably could, but to do that I would have to spend more than half my time fund-raising, and that would be too bad, since to make this work, I really ought to devote full time to the magazine.

He nodded again and stroked his chin. "It's very rich," he said.

Joanne Woodward piped up, observing chirpily, "You're very rich."

"So are you," said Newman.

"Not as rich as you, dear."

Maybe having the spouse there wasn't such a bad idea, after all.

"Well, I'm interested," Newman said. "Give me your prospectus. I'll let you know."

"Of course I will give you our prospectus," I said, as I took the thick spring binder I had been waving and handed it to him, but I didn't quite let go. "Let me tell you something. All the numbers describing our past history are 100 percent reliable. And all our numbers projecting future costs and revenues are conservative, although as you know, one can never predict the future. And if you ask anyone in the business, they will tell you that James Kobak, who helped us prepare these projections after studying our circulation history, is a consummate professional who invented a state-of-the-art magazine economics forecasting program. But anyone who knows the business will also tell you that projections are nothing but projections, that given our history of 130 years of losses, the chances of our turning this thing around are long-shot at best. If you are looking at this as an investment opportunity, you can do better by throwing a dart at the stocks listed on the over-the-counter exchange in *The New York Times*."

On the other hand, I said, if you agree with our social, political, and cultural analysis about where America is and is going, and the important function a magazine like *The Nation* can serve, then the numbers aren't going to tell you anything you don't already know. So if you take my prospectus home, share it, mull it over, ask all the right questions—and I know you will have many—and in December tell me you are in, I will be overjoyed. It will be the best thing that has ever happened to us. But if you tell me right now, tonight, here, before dessert, that you are in because of who you are and what you symbolize, you will have made the deal happen. You will be a magnet for the other partners. You—

"Oh, Paul," said the beautiful woman on my left. "This is for you. You know that."

Newman's eyes narrowed ever so slightly, and he looked at me like Fast Eddie having a pre-game negotiation with Minnesota Fats. What about half and half? he said.

Half and half? I asked.

"Yeah. Half in the Institute and half in the magazine. And over four years."

A whiz at the old math, I quickly figured out that came to $250,000 per annum.

"Deal," I said, extending my hand across the table.

"Deal," he said, taking it.

"A toast!" Doctorow said, adding something eloquent about "perfect casting" as four glasses clinked.

I know there is something called the law of unintended consequences, but I hadn't really experienced it until Newman got involved in *The Nation*.

Prior to this dinner with the Newmans, I had two $1 million investor candidates with whom I was in serious negotiation. Once Paul Newman was on board, what I hoped would happen did, and both eventually came into the partnership. But because he was putting only $500,000 into the magazine, my once million-dollar prospects became $500,000 prospects. (My brother-in-law the lawyer had said to make sure we didn't intermingle Institute and magazine funding.) If Newman with his countless millions was in for "only" a half mil, how could I expect my other partners to do more?

So here I was with half my capital. What to do?

"Do you think Harold Willens could help?" Newman asked one day in his sunny Fifth Avenue apartment. "If you would like, I could call him."

To me, Willens was only a name. I knew that he had organized Business Executives Against the War in Vietnam. I knew that he lived on the West Coast. I had heard he was not well. Newman recited his phone number by heart (despite the fact that they had not worked together for twenty-odd years) and we were in business. With Harold's help, we announced as a goal a "Circle of 100" mini-shareholders, each of whom would commit to $5,000 a year for three years. That way we would secure our $3 million by raising one-half from a small group of large investors and one-half from a large group of small investors.

The capitalization of *The Nation* is no model for the financing of start-ups, I should quickly add. If it is the model for anything, it is the model for the refinancing of 130-year-old magazines of a certain sort. And the truth is, there are as many different ways of capitalizing a magazine as there are magazines, and ideally the way you choose should be related to your magazine's mission.

During this period, a recent *Nation* intern, Phil Boroff, now working for public radio, asked if he could do an interview. Never one to turn down an opportunity to recruit new subscribers, I said sure. And Phil's first question showed that his intern training had not been for naught: Over the last 130 years *The Nation* has lost millions of dollars. What makes you think you can change that?

That's the point, I said, without batting an eye. Over the years, millions of dollars have been invested in *The Nation*. We are going to cash in on that investment.

At the time I thought I had made a joke, albeit a lame one. But as I was eventually to discover, the business of branding (that's what they call it at the Harvard Business School) was no joke, and while fewer than 100,000 people subscribed to the magazine, because of its tempestuous, noble heritage, millions of citizens knew or thought they knew what it stood for.

And speaking of the Harvard Business School, with Newman in tow, I decided it was time to go back to Cambridge and give my HBS faculty friend Sam Hayes an update: I had signed the deal with Arthur; with the help of Jack Berkowitz, a magazine consultant whom I had hired to run the day-to-day business, we had persuaded the Newspaper Guild to postpone negotiations on our about-to-expire contract for a year. This was not that hard to do, since with the exception of Newman's commitment (and strong expressions of interest from Katrina, whom I had asked to stay on as editor, and our old friend Alan Sagner), we had no money in the till; besides, we guaranteed the Guild that any settlement would be retroactive to the previous year. We had launched our Circle of 100 potential smaller shareholders, and with Kobak's magic magazine spread-sheet program we were putting together our strategic plan. I had finished my sabbatical, so prior to plunging in, in early 1995 I gave old Sam Hayes my progress report and renewed my proposal to open our impoverished books for a case study.

While I had given much thought to my sales pitch—how Harvard's M.B.A. students converting the money-losing *Nation* into a capitalist success story would be great PR for Harvard, for *The Nation*, and for Sam—it never occurred to me that Sam himself had a better and far more subtle sales pitch than I.

At our follow-up lunch Sam listened to what I had to say with polite interest and then gave me the happy news that the Harvard Business School would help us. He was, he said, impressed that Paul Newman had agreed to invest in our cause, he had "run" our numbers, and he allowed as how *The Nation* might make a fascinating case study—not for the M.B.A. program, but for a special course given for owners, presidents, and CEOs of companies with annual sales ranging from several million to several hundred million dollars: the Owner/

President/Management Program (OPM), whose initials coincidentally also stand for "other people's money." It was an apt acronym, since the course—offered in three units of three weeks each over a three-year period, to accommodate the busy schedules of its students—cost an astronomical $12,000 a year.

Sam described the kinds of students that OPM tends to attract (and I immediately began to think of them of as unpaid consultants): self-made entrepreneurs who have had a successful business idea and want to learn how to run the business; sons and daughters who went into the family business and now wanted to professionalize it; folks catapulted from middle management to the tops of their companies; and foreign entrepreneurs who wanted to see how the Americans do it. The course was a case-study one, using the "learning by analogy" method, and *The Nation* could be one of the cases. Sam explained that although raw IQ scores of the M.B.A. candidates might be higher, the OPMers were livelier, cockier, and, because of their varied experience, in a unique position to make informed, creative, and perhaps even constructive suggestions. I would be invited on the day *The Nation* came up for discussion—not quite what I had had in mind, but not bad.

Sam explained that OPM had three phases: Unit I dealt with management skills; Unit II with profitability and growth; Unit III with harvesting the wealth that OPMers had learned how to maximize in Unit II. A diabolical smile crept over his face, and his eyes narrowed. "You know," he said, "we can do the case study, but whether or not we do it, you might want to take this course yourself." Only good breeding, one assumes, kept him from adding, "You don't know what the fuck you're doing."

There was, of course, no way I could or should take this course. My sabbatical had kept me away from the office for too long as it was. Although by the standards of our slice of the industry I had had some fund-raising success, I had put together only a third of the capital I believed *The Nation* needed. It was going to be labor-intensive work to get the rest. Moreover, the magazine was continuing to lose around $50,000 a month. We were changing printers, redesigning, and computerizing all at the same time: a triple trauma. Our union contract had run out and renegotiation time was upon us. The Harvard OPM course tuition was unaffordable. And besides, the deadline for application had passed. So, naturally, I applied.

As I was subsequently to learn, a balance sheet has two sides, and Sam, who served as a reference and used his pull to get my deadline extended, was right: Essentially I was an immigrant to the land of high finance. But here, at a minimum, was a chance to learn the language—how to read balance sheets, keep track of cash flow, talk to potential investors, find out what "goodwill" really meant, master such tools of business analysis as price-earnings and other ratios, become an effective manager, and all the rest. Besides, I would get to see my Cambridge daughter. And maybe it was a good omen that I was hoping to recruit a Circle of 100 for *The Nation* and OPM that year had 101 students, not including me. Perhaps some of my self-made multimillionaire classmates would see the virtue of investing in a business with a social mission (once I learned how to write a mission statement). Even if I averaged only one new Circle member a year, I would cover my Cambridge costs and then some.

On a windy Sunday in early March, along with fellow OPMers from eighteen countries, I arrived at George Baker Hall in time to be shown to my monastic dormitory room. (We had been told to leave our spouses behind, because this was to be a "total immersion" experience. A honeymooning classmate took this injunction so seriously that he left his bride in California.) It included a single bed, one window, a computer, a clock radio, a small bathroom, and a narrow shelf stocked with case studies in five areas—financial management, general management, human aspects of business, accounting and control, marketing strategy—and an "HBS Executive Education" book bag in which to carry them.

I put on the name tag each of us was required to wear at all times and joined the welcoming cocktail party in the Baker Lounge below, with only mild trepidation. It seemed to me auspicious that the first person I met, clad in a University of Florida basketball jacket, was Nathan S. Collier, a man with an open, friendly smile and tousled blond hair. He told me that his granduncle had founded the late *Collier's* magazine, although he himself was in what he called the apartment-ownership-management business. In fact, after the second—or was it the third?—vodka on the rocks, I concluded that a surprising number of my new classmates might see the business potential in America's oldest weekly magazine, if they were only given a fair chance. Besides Nathan, there was Richard Elden, a Chicago-based investment manager of $2 billion who had started out as an International News Service reporter. On the side, he had recently helped to found a small company that hired investigative journalists to prepare in-depth reports on targeted industries and corporations. David Karam, president of an Ohio company that owns and operates seventy-five Wendy's Old-Fashioned Hamburgers franchises, told me that his Lebanese father would be thrilled to know that his son had a classmate whose magazine, *The Nation*, had been the first to publish his personal hero, Ralph Nader, also of Lebanese extraction. And there was Maximiano A. (Max) Goncalves, president and chief executive officer of Fenasoft, located in São Paulo, Brazil, which produces the largest computer show on the planet. He had a particular interest in U.S. journalists, and could we have dinner to talk about it?

Clearly, I had more in common with my fellow businessmen (I now for the first time began to think of myself as a businessman) than I had anticipated, and I could hardly wait for the next day's program to begin. I set my clock radio for 6:30 a.m., so that I'd be up for the 7:00 breakfast in the Baker Lounge and still have time to scan the papers that OPM provided gratis—the *Financial Times* and *The Wall Street Journal* among them—before the morning study group to which I had been assigned convened at 7:45. Fortunately for my study habits, the clock radio in the room next door sounded off at 5:30, as it would every day of the course, which gave me an extra hour to read and reread my cases.

Over those three weeks we read and discussed something like 150 cases, so it doesn't surprise me that I don't remember which case it was that Professor Norman Berg, who headed OPM, taught in the opening 9:00 a.m. class on general management. But I should have seen the handwriting on the wall, even if it was disguised as chalk marks on the electronically manipulated blackboard, which he kept sending up and down like an elevator. Norm had asked the class to list the pros and cons confronting the company under consideration. A forest of hands went up, and we had our first con. The company had a union. What could be worse than that? Norm wrote UNION in big letters at the head of the con column, underlined it three times, and chalked in an exclamation point for good measure.

I got a big laugh and a lot of little snickers when I mentioned that unions can increase productivity. I should have realized then and there that I'd have to decide about a basic issue: Did I want to spend my valuable classroom hours scoring political points against my (mostly) free-marketeer classmates, or did I want to concentrate my energies on learning how to bring *The Nation* to the break-even point? Though I had signed on with OPM to learn to think like a businessman, I was not ready to abandon *The Nation*'s tradition of dissent and its anti-business bias, if you will. (And, of course, it would have been bad for business.)

Case after case underlined the dilemma. One day OPM took up Wal-Mart. It was just after 3:00 p.m., and class was out, but the conversation flowed on. I was on the Lars Anderson Bridge, headed back across the Charles River to Cambridge. On my left Pedro Salles, who ran the fourth-largest bank in Brazil, was zipping along in the electric wheelchair that took him from class to class. On my right was Tim Erdman, chairman, president, and CEO of this country's oldest and largest designer-builder specializing in outpatient medical facilities. Tim, in his late forties, was on Rollerblades. I was in the center, huffing and puffing and not quite keeping up. Our destination was Cybersmith, a store that featured the latest in technology before it became generally available. But what really seemed to propel my fellow OPMers was the inspiring tale of Sam Walton, a JCPenney trainee who had had the idea of building discount department stores in small towns across the country that would all operate on small-profit margins, and who converted this "niche marketing" concept, as they liked to call it, into one of the greatest business successes of all time. When he died, *The New York Times* put his family fortune at $23.5 billion, but the professor had suggested that Walton was the kind of guy who would have cared more about the Wal-Mart cashier who had $262,000 in her retirement account after working for the company for twenty-four years.

I pondered whether to mention a *Nation* article, published the previous year, that had portrayed Sam Walton as the main threat to Main Street U.S.A., the man responsible more than any other for the malling of America, for the destruction of community upon community. But before I could decide, we had arrived at Cybersmith, I was out of breath, and why spoil a good party?

By the time we considered the case of Cash America, I was less reticent. As it happened, that morning I was the leader (owing to daily rotation) of my 7:45 a.m. study group, and since I'd been up since 5:30, I had had plenty of time to prepare. Cash America made its money from a chain of pawnshops charging steep rates of interest. A prime purpose of the case was to assess the CEO's new strategy of trying to destigmatize pawnbroking and simultaneously change what HBS likes to call the "value equation." Instead of lending as little as possible on collateral and selling it for as high a price as possible if it was forfeited, his revolutionary idea was to lend as much as possible and sell as inexpensively as he could, on the theory that he could make up in volume (from repeat customers, who were the most profitable) what he lost on the margins.

When I reported that according to a forthcoming *Nation* article (called "Cashing In on Poverty"), Cash America's typical loan rate hovered around 200 percent, I naïvely assumed that we would have an interesting dialogue on the morality of the pawnbroking business, especially given the *Nation* writer's assumption that it was immoral to exploit the poor merely to increase return on investment ("ROI," I had learned to call it) for the rich. Instead, the study group immediately divided into those who believed that the poor were deadbeats who deserved what they got and those who felt that Cash America was giving the uncreditworthy poor a valuable service. Let the market decide!

The bottom line of the HBS/OPM mentality seemed to be that the bottom line is the bottom line. One morning in Professor Ben Shapiro's marketing-strategy class we discussed the marketing of a product subject to government regulation. Spotting David Karam's hand in the air, Ben made a beeline in his direction and asked whether he thought the regulation was appropriate. "It all depends on whether you believe Adam Smith or Karl Marx," David said. "Do you mean to tell me," the consternated professor shouted, "that this case has something to do with *Communism?*" He then turned, looked at me across the room, and said with a sweet smile, "Sorry, Vic."

I didn't mind my status as class foil. And although we had our disagreements, my classmates and I gradually developed mutual respect. When Dan Roche absented himself from class during Unit II for all of two days and returned $36 million richer, having sold his software business, I enthusiastically joined in the applause despite my by now well-known antipathy toward corporate takeovers. When a small-town banker commiserated with another classmate, saying, "You're in a family business? I wouldn't wish that on anybody," my heart went out to both of them.

Note from my learning journal (we were instructed to make entries after each class about how the case applied to our own companies):

> Everyone gets a great kick out of Sam Hayes's favorite trick—to dramatize the principle that financial leverage always involves risk, he spreads his arms like an acrobat attempting to keep his balance and then tiptoes out on what he calls "the debt limb." He explains that his financially conservative wife, Barbara, who disapproves of going into debt, "hugs the trunk," whereas he is generally inclined to go as far out on the limb as financial prudence permits. Today he is out "on the twigs." My problem is that every time Sam does his balancing number, it reminds me of my own delicate balancing act—the attempt to absorb HBS know-how without succumbing to HBS values. I am persuaded that if the HBS faculty ran the world, it would be a better, more humane and efficient version of the status quo. But what attracted me to *The Nation* in the first place was its commitment to challenge the status quo. I'm not sure that it is possible to apply the lessons of the typical HBS case to a company like *The Nation*.

I did my nightly homework and read all about MBO (Management by Objective), MBWA (Management by Walking Around), TQM (Total Quality Management), the New Intimacy (a catchphrase to describe the relationship between customers and vendors), the Price Performance Curve, the Value Chain, the Magic Matrix, the Order Cycle, Market Segmentation, and Market Share (said to be the management mantra of the 1980s—by the 1990s it was New Economics of Service). I kept in mind Professor Shapiro's maxim "There is only one reason to lose a lifetime customer and that's death. His!" But I still had trouble analogizing case studies of Steinway pianos, Southwest Airlines, Mrs. Fields Cookies, and such to my venerable company.

This was partly because of *The Nation*'s status as a nonprofit sheep in for-profit wolf's clothing, but also because my *Nation* self still tended to regard the profit motive as avaricious indifference to social consequences, while OPMers saw it as the key to business success. Not that my classmates were against doing good—they were all for it. Well, most of them were for it, but that had to do with the Service-Profit Chain (treat employees well and they will treat customers well). Even language compounded the problem. At OPM, "downsizing" was a synonym for efficiency and savings, whereas at *The Nation* it signified misery and unemployment. A word like "empowerment" in *The Nation*'s pages means granting the disenfranchised and the dispossessed more say over their destiny; at OPM it meant getting rid of middle management.

One day we took up the case of L.L. Bean. What impressed me about L.L. Bean, founded in 1912, was not the innovative systems that were the ostensible focus of our study but, rather, that the company's founder, against advice, had stuck to his idiosyncratic ways. Maybe there was something to this learning by analogy, after all.

To this day an L.L. Bean customer can return a product at any time, day or night, and get, at his or her option, a replacement, a refund, or a credit. If a customer returns a pair of boots after ten years, the company will replace them, no questions asked. This seemed to me a tribute to the maverick who started the business in his brother's basement in Freeport, Maine (which is how it came to be open twenty-four hours a day). He sold his first hunting boots (based on rubbers his wife bought him, with leather tops stitched by a local cobbler) to friends and relatives (hence the no-questions-asked returns policy), and then he refused to automate or adopt any of the efficiency measures advocated by his financially ambitious grandson.

When asked to put a value on the company (whose sales in 1965, the date of the case, were $3 million a year), classmates—especially the contingent from Latin America—expressed skepticism about the old man's unwillingness to move into the modern era. I thought that his lesson of self-reliance deserved a premium. Philip Adkins, a London-based investment banker who owned the J. Boag & Son brewery in Tasmania and who had arranged the financing for a Disney theme park in Japan, piped up: "I agree with Vic. This image of Emersonian self-reliance adds untold value to the Bean brand name." His estimate of the company's value was ten times higher than anyone else's. The professor ended the class by reporting on the current market value of L.L. Bean stock—more than a billion dollars.

At lunch I asked Philip whether he thought there was an analogy between the "brand recognition" of *The Nation*—which, after all, had a 135-year-old reputation for its nonconformist politics—and L.L. Bean. Yes, he said; in fact, as he thought about the worldwide possibilities for exploiting *The Nation*'s "brand name" in the new electronic media, he decided that I was "sitting on a gold mine."

I generously offered to share with him my prospectus for the gold mine. He said he would review it with interest and asked me whether I knew that when Rupert Murdoch bought *The Times* of London, the first thing he did was to enter on its balance sheet a goodwill item of as much as $50 million. When his solicitors said he couldn't do that, Murdoch asked, Why not? Why do you think I paid $27 million for it? For its printing plant? I'm shutting that down. For its staff? I'm getting rid of half of them. Talent is for hire. I bought it for its name. I own *The Times* of London.

Philip had all sorts of ideas about what I might do with *The Nation*'s name, not to mention its balance sheet, pointing out that a goodwill item of $10 million for the name (more than three times what I had listed) would impress potential investors. He said that he, at any rate, was impressed, and that I should consider him a potential investor. (True to his word, he's still a potential investor.)

Of course, the big day for me was the last day of Unit II, when the *Nation* case was on the agenda.

Aside from my strategy of importing my wife, Anne, to sit by my side as a buffer against those classmates who tended to see visiting CEOs as an occasion for target practice, the class began like any other. Sam immediately put my wife the stockbroker at her ease by introducing her to the class, and then he added, "You all know what a stockbroker is, don't you? It's someone who invests your money until it's all gone."

Sam proceeded to the case at hand. "If you were the CFO of another magazine," Sam asked as his opening question, "what are the financial dimensions you would be looking for on a day-to-day basis?" He drew from the class the difference between *The Nation*'s fixed costs and its variable costs. He had the class inventory our assets, intellectual as well as physical, and then diplomatically observed, "In terms of the balance sheet, this is not an asset-intensive business." I nudged Anne when Sam described Carter's note as a "very friendly arrangement." Perhaps I was not such a dummy, after all.

But just a minute. There were not enough assets to cover obligations. How would the balance sheet handle that? As he referred the class to the goodwill item on the balance sheet, Sam asked, "What is the kernel of value inside the husk?" Philip Adkins could have told him, but Philip had dropped out of Unit II for personal reasons. Sam called on Mitch Dong, who had been waving his hand for some time now, as was his wont. Mitch lived in Boston and embodied the entrepreneurial spirit that OPM did its best to cultivate. He had merged his environmental company with a publicly traded company, sold his interest a year later, and started a hedge fund that traded gold equities based on esoteric statistical models, all of which enabled him and his family to alternate vacations between a boat in the Galápagos and a villa in Tuscany. Mitch didn't have the answer to Sam's question, but he did, he said, have the solution to my problem. As he saw it, I had it made. *The Nation* had a $1 million sweetheart loan from its former publisher. It had a subscription list now approaching 100,000 names, worth $10 to $20 a name in the marketplace—maybe as much as $2 million. And it was bleeding $50,000 a month.

His solution: Kill *The Nation*. "That way," he happily explained, "you cut your losses to zero. You sell the subscription list to J.F.K., Jr.—he's started a new political magazine, hasn't he? And with the $2 million you get from the sale you buy long-term Treasury notes, which pay 7.5 percent interest [this was 1996, remember]. And you use the difference between the 7.5 percent you receive and the 6 percent you owe to settle your obligations, your severance payments, and your accounts payable. And on the difference you retire to the Galápagos, sipping piña coladas. If you get bored, Machu Picchu is right next door."

Lots of other ideas were generously offered. Carlos Adamo, an Argentine banker, said we should raise the subscription price: we had loyal customers and nothing to lose. Chris Bergen, who with his wife ran a pharmaceutical-testing company, thought we should consider going biweekly. Sam proposed that we find a way to segment the market, charging more for those willing to pay more. I liked this idea, not least because it reminded me of a doctrine I had studied in a political-theory seminar at Swarthmore: "From each according to his abilities, to each according to his needs."

On March 21, 1997, Tom Potter, the managing director of Eagle Boys Dial-a-Pizza, in Queensland, Australia, who had never been to college, gave the graduation speech and got his Harvard certificate, along with the rest of us. As I sat there listening to Tom, I did a reckoning of my OPM experience.

The Nation had not yet passed the break-even point, and if I didn't take up Mitch's proposal to kill the magazine, perhaps it would be a while before we turn a profit, but OPM was not a total loss. I failed to enlist any of my classmates as *Nation* shareholders, but . . .

I went to Harvard thinking that ROE was *Roe v. Wade.* Now I know it is Return on Equity.

I went to Harvard thinking that the year was divided into seasons. Now I know it is divided into quarters.

I went to Harvard not knowing the difference between the quick ratio and the acid-test ratio, and now I know they are the same thing (the sum of cash, current marketable securities, and receivables, divided by current liabilities—so there).

Finally, I went to Harvard believing I was a buffalo and came back hoping I could become a goose. Before OPM I had assumed that in my new position as the company's leader my job would be to lead. Then, in Unit III, I read a book called *Flight of the Buffalo*, which summarized what I had already begun to learn from my more enlightened classmates: that a good business doesn't function like a herd of buffalo, with loyal followers doing what the lead buffalo wants them to do, going where the leader wants them to go. (That's how the early settlers were able to decimate the buffalo herds. They'd kill the lead buffalo. Then, while the rest of the herd stood around waiting for the leader, the settlers slaughtered them, too.) What a business needs is not buffalo but responsible independent workers, like a flock of geese, who fly as a team in a V formation, the leadership changing all the time.

By the time we graduated, Nathan Collier, who was forty-five, and I had become good friends, and he shared his ambition with me: "It has three elements. I want to earn my first billion by the time I'm sixty.

I want to have a helluva good time getting there. And if I can help mankind a little along the way, so much the better."

And I learned from the OPM bulletin board that between Unit I and Unit II Nathan had made a $10 million bequest in the form of adjacent property to his alma mater, the University of Florida at Gainesville. He also took out a one-year subscription to *The Nation*.

I count David Karam among my new friends, too, although his father's admiration for Ralph Nader was put in perspective on the last day of class, when David made a rousing speech denouncing unions, to enthusiastic applause. David is a member of the libertarian-conservative Cato Institute, and hopes down the road to run for high political office on what I suspect will be an anti-government, anti-union platform. Early on I crossed David off my list of potential *Nation* shareholders, but I was moved when one day he articulated his business philosophy: "To provide a high-quality product and service, to make a fair profit, and to improve the lives of our employees." If he does run for the Senate, I'll probably disagree with 90 percent of his platform and send him a campaign contribution.

When Richard Elden invited me to dinner, I thought at first that it might be the moment to make my subtle pitch. I would tell him about the good luck I was having rounding up my Circle of 100. But before I got to it, he told me about the good luck he had had rounding up a Circle of Four or Five for his investigative-reporting enterprise. We still get together when we are visiting each other's city, and maybe if I ever make a financial success of *The Nation*, he will let me buy into his business with my profits.

Max Goncalves's interest in American journalists turned out to be an interest in recruiting five of them to serve as journalist-judges for his high-tech expo in São Paulo. Happily for me, I turned out to be one of them, despite the fact that, as I made clear, I spoke neither Portuguese nor computerese. Our job was to give a "Max" Award to "the most innovative exhibit of Brazilian computer technology that has the best potential for export sales." As it turned out, my contribution was to add an additional criterion—social benefit. And I guess that if *The Nation* ever puts out a Portuguese edition, Max might want to subscribe.

Actually, I did come back to New York with some Circle members from the Cambridge area. None of them were OPMers, but I had more than enough to cover my tuition. One day at the local Laundromat I ran into Abby Rockefeller, David's daughter and a radical philanthropist. She and her husband, Lee Halperin, are now shareholders, friends, and co-chairs of *The Nation*'s Circle of 100. And OPMers did account for twelve new *Nation* subscriptions. As an unexpected bonus, when Peter Norton, who created Norton Industries and, with Paul Newman, is one of *The Nation*'s principal shareholders, discovered that I had enrolled in OPM, he told me that he, too, had attended the program. "I was in hog heaven," he said. "Until then I had never had a male-bonding experience, and in terms of intellectual challenge it's one of the highlights of my life." By the time I graduated, Peter had significantly increased his *Nation* investment.

But on my return to the office after my first three weeks in the spring of 1995, Teresa Stack, then associate publisher and now our president, asked me to give an example of what I had learned at Harvard, and I told her. Before, when a subscriber wrote in to cancel his or her subscription, the loss of the $48 never really bothered me. I agreed with E. L. Godkin, who once said, "If I don't get my requisite share of cancellations every week, I fear my editorial hand must be slipping." But I did hate to lose an old friend, so I'd send a note asking, Are you sure you really want to do that? About half of them were so thrilled to get a personal note from the editor that they would agree to keep their subscriptions.

But after nine weeks of Ben Shapiro, who among other things introduced me to the concept of "the lifetime value of the customer," I developed a whole new calculus for cancellations, I told Teresa. Subscribers who have been with us four years or more renew at an average rate of 80 percent. The average age of our subscriber is 47.5 years. The average life expectancy of a 47.5-year-old is 31.6 years. So instead of saving the magazine $48 by preventing a cancellation, I am saving 80 percent of $48 times 31.6, and when one factors in the fact that 15 percent of our subscribers send gift subscriptions and extra money, and so forth, it's clear that the "value" of a *Nation* subscriber is well over $1,000 rather than a mere $48. Teresa nodded and smiled, and was obviously impressed, and then she asked, So what can we do about it? Well, I said, we can write a letter to anyone who tries to cancel and explain why he or she shouldn't. But you already do that, she pointed out.

Yes—but as Sam implied at the outset, I didn't know what I was doing.

Until I became an owner, a publisher no less, like most editors I took for granted that in disputes between editors and proprietors the editor was always right. As Thomas Carlyle had once written: "Is not every able editor a Ruler of the World, being a persuader of it; being self-elected yet sanctioned by the sale of his numbers?" But once I became a proprietor, it occurred to me that while editorial independence might be sacrosanct, even Carlyle seemed to understand that if the numbers aren't there, after a while the editor won't be either.

As editor I had had a number of business ideas that I could never persuade my publisher to try, for example, to take out a weekly front-page classified ad in *The New York Times*. Ham Fish had tried it for a while, but when after six weeks an analysis showed that the numbers weren't panning out, over my objections we stopped. (I argued that we needed to test it for a full year, and that way it could become a point of reference for publicity.) Now that I was publisher and I saw what a year's worth of front-page classified ads cost, I didn't do it.

Then there was *The Nation*–Mobile. For years I had unsuccessfully tried to persuade first Ham and then Arthur that we should send a couple of college kids around the country to visit the *The Nation*'s retail outlets. Was our distributor sending too many or too few copies? Were *Nation*s given proper display or (as I suspected) languishing in warehouses? Were we charging too much or too little? Did covers really affect sales, and if so, how? Now I ran a classified ad in *The Nation* promising a "free cross-country trip" (thinking our intrepid travelers could stay in Nation Associate homes). Imagine my thrill when the first people to answer the ad were Jack Kennedy's old advance man Jerry Bruno (whose book, *The Advance Man*, I had reviewed—favorably, he reminded me—for *Life* magazine many years before). He and his wife, Kathy, a former book PR person, had retired to Maine, but this sounded like something they would like to do. Our goal was to double newsstand sales. For the next three months they and the Associates who housed them had a helluva good time (even though *The Nation*–Mobile kept breaking down) and made news in the towns along the way. But the Brunos and we got a brutal education in the growing power of the chain bookstores, the perils of independent bookstore economics, and the new consolidation among magazine distributors (most of whom were absorbed by four mega-national distributors over the next two years), in why the independents were not the answer to our problem. We didn't reach our goal, but it was a noble experiment.

I tried to excavate McWilliams's old idea of holding *Nation* dinners across the country (like the one Nation Associates dinner in the late 1960s at which Martin Luther King, Jr., came out against the war in Vietnam), where the price of admission included a fully paid subscription. Everyone was ultra busy, and such dinners take time, planning, and expertise (events planners, no less). I'm still trying.

I also excavated from among Carey McWilliams's papers a barely legible copy of a memorandum dated January 7, 1971, which seemed as true when I read it twenty-five years later as the day he wrote it.

> Whenever the problem of *The Nation* comes up for discussion, it is usually sidetracked. The topic then becomes: what about using a better paper stock . . . what about adding a column on rock music or a travel editor . . . what would a color cover do for us . . . what about publishing twice a month instead of weekly . . . what about merging with *The New Republic* (which would compound the problem) . . . what about sending Cardinal Cooke to cover the superbowl game in Miami . . . and, the ultimate cop-out, what about changing the character of the magazine? These are all evasions.
>
> The problem is that *The Nation* happens to have a marvelous editorial policy, formulated by a genius, E. L. Godkin. But the format, the policy, limits circulation, always has, always will. The magazine can never expect to get the readership which would enable it to get the advertising which would enable it to be self-sufficient, even profitable *through advertising*. That is, it can't expect to do that and remain *The Nation*. But this is a rare piece of good fortune. If *The Nation* ever became dependent on advertising, it would cease to be *The Nation*.
>
> All of which means that the problem is getting enough full-

price regular subscriptions—from readers who are natural *Nation* readers—to carry the load. The task is not unmanageable; it can be licked. And if it can be licked, it insures the future of *The Nation* in the mercilessly competitive world of magazine journalism today when the bigger they are (those who rely on advertising) the harder they fall. Concentrating on the essential problem—not evading it by wishful thinking or fantasy—as by diverting to some other problem—is the key to survival.

No matter how many bright ideas I thought I had, one thing was clear: The key to *The Nation*'s future, to the success of our business plan, was more subscribers. And the key to acquiring more subscribers at an affordable rate was our old friend second-class mail, which delivered the magazine to subscribers at the special lower rate for periodicals.

Imagine my consternation, then, on discovering my first day back from my first three weeks at the Harvard Business School in the spring of 1995 that the U.S. Postal Service had recommended the abolition of second-class mail. All my projections, I feared, would go up in smoke.

Ten years earlier, at our California conference, I had made a point of putting matters postal at the top of the agenda, since keeping postal costs under control was one of the few issues around which journals of the left, right, and center might organize to mutual advantage. Robert Myers, a former publisher of *The New Republic*, told us about how in the 1960s he had put together a group of small-circulation magazines whose purpose was precisely to promote their common postal interests, and he even had a constructive proposal that he persuaded Congressman Morris Udall to introduce as legislation: that the first 250,000 copies (in Udall's bill, it was only 25,000) of all publications be mailable at reduced rates. That way, smaller publications, journals with heavy content (perhaps for reasons of high seriousness), would get the largest proportional benefit, but all magazines would get *some* benefit. The legislation never got anywhere, alas.

The most articulate opposition to government help for small magazines came, surprisingly, from our friend Michael Kinsley. Kinsley had come out against the second-class mail "subsidy," as he called it, in 1975, in an article in the *Washington Monthly*. At the conference he boiled his continuing objections down to three: Since the readership of journals like *The Nation*, *The New Republic*, and *National Review* were the highly educated elite, their income was above average and the second-class subsidy therefore amounted to "a transfer of wealth from the poor to the rich"; once the camel's nose of government got into the tent of "subsidizing" opinion journals, it was inevitable that they would end up hooking content requirements to the subsidy, raising profound First Amendment concerns; and since opinion journalists were supposed to be watchdogs against special interests, it was wrong for us to become one ourselves, demanding a share of the federal money pie. Kinsley observed that right-wingers should oppose such subsidies because they interfered with the free market, and left-wingers because they were regressive.

It was a virtuoso performance, and Kinsley, his forensic skills sharpened by hundreds of hours on *Crossfire*, had my vote as captain of the debate team. But the lawyer Tom Silk, who successfully defended *Mother Jones* when the Reagan administration challenged its nonprofit tax status, made a telling point. Some things are too important to leave to the vicissitudes of the market, like national defense and clean air—even Kinsley conceded that these two were "public goods"—and public discourse and the dissemination of literature were two more.

Now, in 1995, when the trade press reported that the USPS wanted to abolish second-class mail, my first impulse was to write an Op Ed piece denouncing the USPS. But that, I quickly realized, was the writer in me wanting to be heard sounding off. Now that I was a publisher (ahem) I had bigger guns to bring out. As a member of the Magazine Publishers Association, I assumed my trade association would be up in arms. So imagine my further consternation when I discovered that not only was the MPA not interested in challenging the USPS proposal, they were supporting it.

I had foolishly believed that since the MPA has a membership of 250 magazines and most of these magazines have circulations of 250,000 or under, they would represent their members' interest. No such luck; 20 percent of the MPA's members are responsible for 80 percent of its budget. Karl Marx was out of fashion, but he would surely have reminded me that if I had simply looked at the economics, I could have predicted MPA's position, the position of the mega-publishers, the position of Time Warner and Dow Jones.

Lacking a trade association to make my case, I reverted to my old writerly habit and went to the local library to see whether there was indeed a case to make. I discovered a great deal of interest. First, Americans are lucky that when the British decided to clamp down on the colonies they did it via the Stamp Act. This provoked opposition from angry printers, because it curtailed their civil liberties and cost them money. Print was so central to the routine of colonial life that the public sphere itself—civil society as they knew it—seemed at stake. It was a happy accident that Benjamin Franklin was simultaneously a postmaster, a printer, and the founding publisher of America's most famous early magazine, *The Saturday Evening Post*. Early American governments spent a great deal of money building and maintaining the post roads, and politicians from all camps agreed to sustain the preferential low postage rates for newspapers that Franklin had established. Many wanted *free* distribution of newspapers, which were in those days highly partisan—the notion of an *objective* colonial press would have been truly revolutionary. (The term "objectivity" didn't even exist until 1817 when Samuel Taylor Coleridge, who also gave us in his *Biographia Literaria* the concept of "the willing suspension of disbelief," invented it.)

I also discovered that an organization called the American Business Press, representing mostly trade magazines, the vast majority of them with circulations well under 250,000, was pressing to retain the second-class category and keep the periodical subsidy, as Kinsley had called it, alive and well. I contacted their attorneys to find out what there was to find out, and to see whether there was a way *The Nation* and other journals of opinion might be heard.

The Business Press and our little anti-business magazine had, as Jesse Jackson might have put it, common ground. Not only were the attorneys for ABP willing to share their research, leak the other side's documents, and generally connive and conspire to help us bolster our case (though the proceedings were well under way before the Postal Rate Commission, which was charged under byzantine rules with holding hearings on the USPS proposals and then making recommendations to a board of governors, most of them Reagan and Bush appointees, and many hours of testimony already had been taken), they explained that if I were willing to testify as a "rebuttal" witness on behalf of ABP, I could appear before the Rate Commission myself and make my case on behalf of journals of opinion as a class.

How could I say no? As I prepared for the big day, I was told that the commission had scheduled nine witnesses for that day, and my own appearance would probably take no longer than twenty minutes, a half hour at most.

I had previously testified before one congressional committee (as a witness on behalf of the ACLU), urging the adoption of a national shield law that would protect book authors as well as reporters from having to reveal their sources. My testimony was received and read into the record, I was thanked by the chairman, asked a few desultory questions by the late Representative Ben Rosen, a friend of a friend, and dismissed. It took all of ten minutes. But my appearance before the PRC lasted three hours, for as the chairman announced, as soon as I had finished my testimony, that among those participants who had requested oral cross-examination of witness Navasky were the Office of the Consumer Advocate, Time Warner, Dow Jones & Co., the Magazine Publishers of America, and the U.S. Postal Service. Bingo.

What followed helped remind me why I was glad I had never practiced law, and why they call it an adversary system. The thrust of my testimony had to do with why I believed the proposed elimination of the second-class-mail category would wound all journals of opinion, regardless of creed. In dollar terms the so-called reform would save millions in costs for magazines with mega-circulation like *People* and *TV Guide* (because of their ability to "pre-sort" and "drop-ship"—by this time I had internalized and incorporated the postal lingo into my pitch), but it would cost magazines like *Commonweal* or *Human Events* or *The Nation* something like 20 percent more than they were already paying (in *The Nation*'s case this came to an extra $160,000 a year).

My strategy was to try to seize the high ground and give a brief lecture on postal history.

The Founding Fathers saw the dissemination of opinion as a precondition of self-governance. And they saw the postal system as the circulatory system of our democracy. That's why Benjamin Franklin agreed to serve as Postmaster General. That's why Thomas Jefferson sought to persuade President Washing-

ton to appoint Tom Paine, author of such polemical masterpieces of opinion journalism as *Common Sense* and *The Rights
of Man* as Postmaster General. That is why George Washington
himself believed that all newspapers, which in those days were
the equivalent of journals of opinion, should be delivered free of
charge. That is why in 1879 Congress established reduced rates
for newspapers and magazines which, because they were understood as critical to the enlightenment of the Republic, were
never expected to pay their own way.

For nearly two centuries this philosophy prevailed. Only in
recent decades has the notion that dissemination of independent opinion is essential to make democracy work begun to give
way to bottom line considerations.

It would be a tragedy if at this moment of unprecedented
concentration in communications conglomerates, one of the
few remaining institutions dedicated to the creation, propaga-
tion, circulation and testing of new policy ideas—the journal of
opinion—were the casualty of lobbying by the very forces which
make it more important than ever before that these independent voices—whatever their politics—be heard.

I did not expect but I got a detailed interrogation on Ben Franklin's
motives and Tom Paine's employment history. I don't know how to convey the flavor of the exchange without reproducing it.

KEEGAN (lawyer for Time Warner): Do you think Jefferson's recommendation of Paine might have had something to do with the
fact that Paine was an ardent Republican and an ardent admirer
of France, that is, of Jefferson's party?
ME: Absolutely. But there were many ardent Republicans and
none of them wrote *Common Sense* or *Crisis* except Tom
Paine . . . (At this point I self-aggrandizingly noted that I had
been the recipient of the Tom Paine Award for civil liberties fifteen years earlier so I harbored a special affection for him. I
didn't mention that the award was bestowed by the National
Emergency Civil Liberties Committee, which in 1961 had
been—falsely—named by HUAC as a "Communist front.")

KEEGAN: If it eventuated to be the fact that at the same time Jefferson made that recommendation, he was actively trying to get Washington to transfer authority over the postal service from Secretary of the Treasury Hamilton to Secretary of State Jefferson, would that lead you to suspect that his motives for trying to persuade Washington to accept a Republican Postmaster General were at least more complicated than . . .

ME: I think all human motives are complicated and Jefferson's were more so than most . . . But the reason that Tom Paine was singled out was that he probably was the foremost pamphleteer and passionate exponent of opinion journalism of his day and was famous for mobilizing sentiment in the colonies against the crown.

I also think one of the reasons he published *Common Sense* as a pamphlet was because there were problems with the postal system in getting it [distributed]. That is why Jefferson thought he was sensitive to [postal matters].

KEEGAN: Do you know whether Paine ever held a job he was not fired from or did not have to abandon in disgrace?

ME: He was a troublemaker, a dissenter with a fiery personality, and it took those kinds of people to make the revolution that gave us our independence from the British.

Then Keegan asked me, as I expected, "It is a fact, isn't it, that newspapers were given preferential rates initially and magazines and other periodicals were not?" I noted that the acknowledged authority on these matters wrote that Congress reserved the most privileged rate for newspapers, many of them avowedly political *journals*, and that the reason he used the word "journals" was that there was an ambiguity about the difference between newspapers and magazines, and in fact a lot of magazines disguised themselves as newspapers to get the benefit of the lower rates.

When I mentioned that the young apprentice printer Ben Franklin consciously set out to imitate Addison's writings from *The Spectator*, Keegan asked me, "Is it your understanding Addison's *Spectator* would have qualified for second-class rates?" This was a trick question, since magazines got no preferential treatment until 1852. So we sparred, and

I repeated, "The preference did not include magazines, although newspapers, as I said, were modeled after a magazine, *The Spectator*. This was an oversight they finally got around to correcting. During that period you had this strange thing where a lot of magazines presented themselves in the format of newspapers."

Keegan sought to reassure the commissioners that he had only one more page of testimony on which to cross-examine me, and the chairman, who was clearly having an okay time, demurred: "Please, Mr. Keegan, this is probably the most interesting and understandable cross-examination that any of us have ever been party to here. And the only problem I find with it is that it encourages me to want to leave and go home and read books rather than stay here and read testimony."

Next came Mr. McBride from Dow Jones. Mr. McBride had earlier let me know privately that it was his brother Joseph who had written the newsmaking *Nation* article about the possibility that President George H. W. Bush had been in the CIA prior to becoming its director, in which case he had perjured himself at his confirmation hearing, where he denied previous agency involvement. McBride's goal, if I understood his badgering questions correctly, seemed to be to use *The Nation*'s ratio of advertising to editorial content to catch me out. My general defense was that "it costs us 10.4 cents to physically produce a copy of our magazine and it costs us 16 cents to mail it."

> MS. GORDON (the consumer advocate): Do you think the editorial matter in your publication is more valuable to society than, say, the editorial matter in *People*?

Well, of course I do, but not even I was stupid enough to say so. What I said instead was:

> I'll put it this way. My wife reads *People* before she reads *The Nation*. We get along very well and I respect that interest of hers and it enriches her life to know what's going on. It doesn't happen to be my interest, and so we benefit from each other's different reading patterns. Sure, I prefer policy journalism, and I am more interested in reading Bill Kristol's new magazine [*The Weekly Standard*] than in reading *People*. It is a complicated

question because . . . to me it is critical that the print culture survives. To the extent that people read *People* rather than watch television, I think our culture is better off. It is a personal prejudice.

I quote these colloquies to show the harassment which citizens who, rightly or wrongly, believe they are testifying in the public interest can be made to suffer. Commissioner LeBlanc wanted to know whether *The Nation*, like another small publisher who testified earlier, would consider dropping some of its subscribers to avoid the extra cost if new regulations went into effect that charged higher delivery rates to magazines with fewer than twenty-four readers in any zip code area?

> ME: I would do everything in my power not to be driven to do that.
> COMMISSIONER LEBLANC: Very tactful answer. That was good . . . My personal reading is "binding the nation together" is still important. So if you drop someone from a list like that, is that necessarily "binding the nation together"?
> ME: No . . . and it is not just a matter of dropping one person. It is really dropping either the least advantaged or the people who are most isolated. To me these are the people for whom journals like this are a lifeline.

In the end, after months of hearings, briefs, witnesses, rebuttal witnesses (me), reply briefs, and such, the PRC made its recommendations to the Board of Governors, which agreed with them. For the first time in the history of the U.S. postal bureaucracy, the PRC, recognized the importance of the journal of opinion as a separate category. To make a complex ruling simple, they changed the name of second class to periodicals class, but did not break it up to give the mega-few an advantage over the small-circulation many. It was a mini-victory for our side!

But the real philosophical point—that journals of opinion should not be required to pay their own way—had not yet re-entered the national dialogue. Bob Sherrill had explained way back in 1970 in *The Na-*

tion that the so-called efficiency that market economics is supposed
to provide often works against the poor:

> Excusing themselves on the ground of efficiency, the railroads
> cut out "unprofitable" passenger service, telephone companies
> avoid so far as possible the servicing of any but the more popu-
> lated areas, and airlines drop routes and schedules.
>
>   At present the postal service costs the taxpayer about $1 bil-
> lion above the costs they are paid by stamp sales. This is hardly a
> drain, when compared to the $3 billion in agricultural subsidies
> and the $120 billion in defense subsidies. And yet the great cry
> from postal references has been the need to "break even."

In the ten years since those hearings, the Independent Press Association, a San Francisco–based MPA-type outfit for the little guy, has
signed up four hundred small-circulation magazines, and the IPA now
appears before the PRC on behalf of all of them. *The Nation*, along with
Mother Jones and *Harper's*, is one of their largest-circulation members.

The 1970 legislative decision to have every class of mail pay its own
way was not only a draconian reversal of two hundred years of public policy but was yet another instance of the privatization of the public sphere.
Nevertheless, the powers that be retained the discretion to allocate costs
and benefits within each mailing class, and if journals of opinion, ideas,
and literature didn't lead the way in pressuring them to exercise their discretion on behalf of the freest flow of ideas, we had only ourselves to
blame—and were blameworthy. I thought back to my failure at our California conference to persuade my fellow practitioners that now was the
time for small-circulation journals to organize as a class, a counterforce.
Until we did so, until we made our case within, before, and on behalf of
the public sphere itself, we would never begin to return it to what
Habermas, and the Founders themselves, knew it could be.

Many publishers make up what they lose in rising postal rates by
increased ad rates. And for sure they spend much if not most of their
time selling ads. But since advertising made up at most 10 percent of
The Nation's revenue, it did us little good, and as publisher I didn't
spend much time on ad sales. To make up the rest, we used our wits.

I'll give you an example. When Reagan became President, we got a call from the White House. They told me that as a cost-saving measure the White House library's magazine subscription budget had been slashed. Could we donate a free subscription? I talked to my colleagues and we decided to give President Reagan a subscription at our special student rate, on the theory that he could use the education that we could supply.

Then there is the Nation Associates. When I arrived at *The Nation* as editor, the magazine was getting something like $7,500 a year in the way of gifts from our readers. We turned it into a program, recruited new members from the ranks of *Nation* subscribers with biannual mailings, and the last time I looked we had 22,000 Nation Associates contributing more than a million dollars a year.

Every once in a while the Nation Associates get a big check. For example, Joe Edelman's. The story began in February 1985, when we received a check for $500 from one Joe Edelman in Oakland, California, whose accompanying note said that he intended to remember us in his will.

I sent him a thank-you note and said the next time I was going to be in his neighborhood, I'd give him a call. And one day I telephoned Mr. Edelman and we arranged to have tea. Joe and Ann Edelman lived in Oakland in a beautiful home, their walls filled with modern art of considerable value. He was in his eighties and vigorous, and she, not quite as spry, the perfect hostess. Some weeks later, a thick envelope arrived with Edelman's return address on the upper-left-hand corner. It contained a manuscript. Joe, it seemed, was a writer. I forget the subject, but I remember the piece was not great, though not bad. I explained to Joe that we couldn't use it, but urged him to keep us in mind. A few months later, a slightly less thick envelope arrived from Oakland, this one containing a group of poems. Edelman was a man of many talents. Without saying anything about their author, I passed them on to our poetry editor, Grace Schulman. Grace said she particularly liked one of them, but there was no way we could use any of them, since we were sitting on two years' worth of not-yet-run poems by the likes of James Merrill, W. S. Merwin, and Adrienne Rich. I wrote Joe again, explaining our decision.

Then one day another thick envelope arrived, this one containing a strong, first-person article from Joe on what it was like to live directly on the fault line during San Francisco's most recent earthquake. The article was publishable, but he hadn't gotten around to sending it until two months after the earthquake, by which time we had already had our earthquake say. However, I asked him if he would let us run a few paragraphs of it in the sometime newsletter that we sent to Nation Associates. Yes, he would.

A few months later I received a legal document from Joe, which—despite my Yale Law School studies in Freud and jurisprudence and all the rest—I could not decipher. It was something about a "third amendment" to a charitable trust. *The Nation* was listed as a beneficiary, along with the American Friends of the Hebrew University, *Jewish Currents*, the American Friends of *New Outlook*, and Common Cause. An accompanying note referred to a "fourth amendment now being processed." I never did receive that "fourth amendment."

Apparently some of his poems, including one called "Deuteronomy 18" about Nancy Reagan's astrologer, subsequently went to our poetry editor and were rejected with a form rejection slip. Nevertheless, in January 1990, he sent a note saying his accountant had advised him that *The Nation* would still be "a beneficiary of the Edelman Charitable Trust when I depart this earth. As *pro quo* I neither desired nor invited special consideration although a minimum of human courtesy would seem appropriate. You may wish to review our previous correspondence. Please tell me what is wrong with your utter lack of appreciation. Is *The Nation* so well provided that my pittance is scarcely noted?"

I responded with alacrity and what I thought was a maximum amount of courtesy.

Many months and years went by with no word from Joe. But I did notice in an issue of Michael Lerner's *Tikkun* magazine, which originates in San Francisco, a not bad short story by one Joseph Edelman, who, according to the author's ID, lived in Oakland. So be it.

After Arthur sold me the magazine, when I made a list of potential investors, I put the Edelmans' name on it, but they had moved, left no forwarding address, and even stopped contributing to Nation Associates.

And then, out of the blue, in 1996 I received a call from an attorney in Los Angeles. "Is *The Nation* a nonprofit?" he wanted to know.

"No, it's not," I told him. I gave him the usual explanation about not wanting to be subject to the IRS's stringent rules about what we could and couldn't publish or hostage to hostile administrations.

"That's too bad," he said. "I have a client who wants to remember you in his will. But he has a charitable remainder trust and can only leave his money to a bona fide 501(c)(3)."

"That's too bad," I agreed. "But perhaps he would consider leaving something to The Nation Institute, which is a public charity."

"What's that?" he asked. I explained how The Nation Institute worked, that it runs an intern program, conferences, an investigative reporting fund, InterNation. "All of its programs promote the same values as *The Nation* magazine does," I said.

Well, he said, sounding somewhat skeptical, he would consult his client.

"If it's not confidential information," I said, "could you tell me your client's name?"

"Sure," he said. "It's not confidential. His name is Joe Edelman."

"I know Joe," I said. "If it's the same Joe." (It was.) Could I write him? I could and I did, telling him about the Nation Institute internship program and how it could be the Nation Institute's Joe and Ann Edelman Internship Program should there be an appropriate bequest in the offing.

Eighteen months later the lawyer called. "Mr. Navasky, I have some bad news and some good news."

"What's the bad news?"

"Joe Edelman died."

"That is bad news. I'm sorry to hear it. I liked Joe. What's the good news?"

"The good news is that for the last fifteen years he's been putting you into his will and taking you out of it, along with the ACLU and a dozen other organizations, and you won the toss."

"You mean—"

"Under the terms of his bequest, either when Mrs. Edelman, who is in a nursing home and in her nineties, passes on, or in the year 2000, whichever is first, the Nation Institute will receive one-half of Mr. Edelman's estate."

I wrote Mrs. Edelman, who was not well enough to answer.

In 1998 we received word of Mrs. Edelman's demise, and after pro-
bate the Nation Institute received a check for $2 million and change.

But remember, for reasons I have already rehearsed at considerable
length, *The Nation* is not a nonprofit (despite the cost of hundreds of
thousands of dollars in postal savings), and my brother-in-law the
lawyer continues to insist that the Nation Institute, the beneficiary of
the Edelman millions, is not permitted to put its loot at the behest of
The Nation. So how to make up the annual deficit? In the long run, the
best way to do that, if possible, is to find new subscribers, but at what
cost?

If you don't have much of an ad budget, and we don't, the trick is to
get all the "free media," as they call it, you can.

Once I kicked myself upstairs to be publisher, *The Nation* was
blessed in Katrina vanden Heuvel with an editor who was articulate,
photogenic, and energetic, a combination which made her a natural for
the new television chat shows on the new cable channels made possible by the new technology. Other *Nation* writers, Jonathan Schell, Eric
Alterman, Naomi Klein, David Corn, Katha Pollitt, and Bill Greider
among them, were also invited to partake in the sound-bite society and
to air their dissent in a way that would have been unthinkable during
the dark and overheated days of the Cold War.

One night I even found myself on Fox News's *The O'Reilly Factor*.
Since *The Nation* had run more than one article documenting that Fox
was unfair, unbalanced, and not unbiased, you would be within your
rights to ask why I would do that. In fact, my Columbia Journalism
School colleague Todd Gitlin asked, Why would you want to do that?
(Actually, he asked, Why would you want to enter their cage?) I was embarrassed to tell him the real reason—to sell magazine subscriptions. So
instead I said we were shameless publicity seekers. But what I didn't
tell him was that even for us there are limits. Example: Early in 1998 I
found an "urgent" message from "Mr. Norman Sommer, a longtime subscriber," who had a "worldwide front-page story" he wanted to talk to me
about. I returned the call to his Florida-based area code.

It seems that thirty years ago his closest friend had a regular tennis
partner. They would play twice a week. That is, until his friend discovered that his tennis partner was sleeping with his wife. Now, here it is,

thirty years later. His friend is long divorced but ready to go public about the tennis partner who had destroyed his family.

Why bring all this up now? Or to put it another way, who was the tennis partner?

None other than Henry Hyde, the Republican congressman who would chair the House Judiciary Committee, which would draft articles of impeachment, should it come to that. In other words, the man who would be sitting in judgment on our allegedly adulterous President was an adulterer—the man who had destroyed his friend's family.

Were we interested?

As a general proposition we didn't run such stories. We thought public servants should be judged on their pubic positions and public conduct, and we had, as a magazine, been critical of those who were using President Clinton's scandalous private behavior to try to hound him from office; and/or simply doing their best to exploit it to sell papers.

Nevertheless, if the allegation proved true and if there was a substantial issue of hypocrisy involved (if, say, Representative Hyde had publicly condemned the President as an adulterer) . . .

David Corn, our Washington editor, spent the better part of a week tracking and checking the story, and then called to say that Sommer's story appeared to check out. Katrina talked with David, I talked with Katrina. We all talked with each other, and collectively we agreed that was not a *Nation* story. If Habermas had been around, we would have checked with him to ask did it meet the setting-the-standard standard, but he wasn't, and we decided on our own that the story was not for us.

Some weeks later the House convened its impeachment hearings under the chairmanship of Representative Henry Hyde, and Katrina told me she had had a call from David Talbot, the editor of *Salon*, the on-line magazine. It seems that after *The Nation* turned Sommers down, he went to *Salon*, and *Salon* now wanted to know whether we wanted to co-publish a print version. We didn't.

Salon went with the story and it was, indeed, front-page news across the country. Along with the story *Salon* ran an explanation of "why we took this extraordinary step" of publishing it: Like *The Nation*, *Salon* it-self had previously "strongly argued that the private lives of all Americans whether they are public figures or not, should remain sacrosanct . . ."

But Clinton's enemies, *Salon* observed, had changed the rules.

In the brave new world that has been created by the Clinton-Lewinsky scandal, the private lives of public figures are no longer off-limits . . .

Aren't we fighting fire with fire, descending to the gutter tactics of those we deplore? Frankly, yes. But ugly times call for ugly tactics.

We didn't think so. At least not that ugly. The whole episode reminded me of the time *Monocle's* tenant, Richard C. Neuweiler, did a public-radio interview with Elaine May during the 1964 Democratic convention, Ms. May playing a *New York Post* reporter. Asked what she was writing about, Ms. May replied, "I'm working on a fifteen-part in-depth series on Jacqueline Kennedy's quest for privacy."

Instead, we did our best to reduce the annual deficit and retain our independence by what the old left used to call "using the contradictions of the system against itself." We set up a *Nation* credit card—instead of free airplane miles, users got the satisfaction of knowing that .01 percent of their bill went into *Nation* coffers (and they also got a red, white, and blue Visa credit card featuring an Ed Sorel caricature of Uncle Sam reacting in horror to a *Nation* cover story).

After Eric Alterman took *National Review's* cruise at our expense and wrote a hilarious account of life at sea with Bill Buckley and Co., *The Nation* launched a cruise of its own, which seems to net a couple of hundred thousand dollars a year.

On the *Nation* cruise's maiden voyage I told the three hundred passengers, "When I arrived at *The Nation* in 1978, there were two things I knew to be true, two north stars in my universe: one, that the Soviet Union was not about to go under, and two, that *The Nation* magazine would never sponsor an ocean cruise."

And although as members of a partnership, *The Nation's* $5,000-per-annum investors would normally get a shareholder's agreement rather than a stock certificate, we commissioned the cartoonist Ed Koren (who draws those fuzzy creatures) to draw up a mock *Nation* stock certificate, one hundred of which he signed and numbered as if it were a limited edition. This enabled me to promise our potential shareholders, "The price of your stock may go down, but the value of your stock certificate is bound to go up!"

Who would have thought that in pursuit of the noble goal of editorial independence I would end up selling credit cards, cabins on a Holland-America ocean liner, and worthless stock (at least by Wall Street standards).

And yet, I'm not sure I know a better way. Well, let me amend that. If your father-in-law wants to found and turn over to you a magazine the way Walter Bagehot's father-in-law, the banker James Wilson, turned over *The Economist* to him in 1859, more power to you. If your father wants to buy you a magazine the way railroad baron Henry Villard bought *The Nation* for his son Oswald, my blessings upon you. If your wife is rich enough and loves you enough to acquire and help sustain a distinguished money-losing weekly, as was the case with the last two editors in chief of *The New Republic*, Gilbert Harrison (courtesy of his wife Nancy Blaine's McCormack Harvesting Machine Co. fortune) and Martin Peretz (courtesy of his wife Ann Farnsworth's Singer Sewing Machine fortune), I say go for it.

But nepotism requires a nepotist. And not all editors have one. Nevertheless, I am pleased to report, based on a lifetime of research, there are almost as many paths to founding or taking over or sustaining an independent journal as there are would-be editors to run them. Some dip into their own pockets. Others pick the pockets of more affluent would-be publishers. And still others, witting and unwitting, find sponsors.

The point was underlined for me a few years ago in the year 2000, when I received a call from Professor Marina Kotzamani of Columbia University's Hellenic Studies program. The Classics department had invited Christos Papoutsakis, the editor of the Greek biweekly magazine *Anti*, to visit Columbia. *Anti*, which Papoutsakis had founded with his own modest funds in 1972 as a protest against the Greek dictatorship, had modeled itself on the American magazine *Ramparts*. Would I agree to conduct a public interview with him?

Ultimately, individuals who found magazines, especially journals of opinion, probably do so because they can't help themselves. They are incomplete without one. I understand their affliction. I am visited by a stream of such people, young and old, and they all think the world is waiting for their periodical when, in fact, the need may be inner rather than outer. No matter. It behooves those of us in this so-called business to help each other. I said I would because I identified with Mr. Papoutsakis and his strugging little magazine, but also because I had an idea. The Columbia Journalism students concentrating in magazines struck me as alarmingly nonpolitical, except for a small minority. Their goal, for the most part: "to get a job on a consumer magazine" (preferably *The New Yorker*, but *People* would do). Here might be a chance to expose them to the glories, the passions, the non-material nature of the journalism of engagement.

Two years earlier, on the occasion of Elia Kazan's nomination for a lifetime achievement award by the Academy of Motion Pictures, I had served on a Hellenic Studies panel. The subject was controversial because of his notoriety as a McCarthy-era name-namer (my position was give him the Oscar because he was a great filmmaker but put on the back the names he named to remind him and everybody else how he had behaved when it counted), but the audience it drew was fewer than fifty people. So I had a counterproposal. Why not organize an evening at the journalism school, on the "Journal of Dissent." Papoutsakis and *Anti* could be the centerpiece, and perhaps we could persuade the rambunctious Warren Hinckle, the *Ramparts* editor after whose magazine Papoutsakis had modeled his own, to join us. That way the evening might even make a little history, since the Greek editor, now sixty-eight years old, had never met the black-eye-patched Hinckle.

Hinckle's *Ramparts* had come to national attention in the late sixties, when they ran a series of highly publicized exposés of the CIA, launched by full-page ads in *The New York Times* (something no non-establishment publication had ever tried before). "It was an attempt to break out of the circulation boundaries and audience of fellow basket weavers of the traditional left-liberal press," Hinckle later explained. "The goal was to escalate dissent from the soapboxes to the newsstands of America."

And in addition to Hinckle, why not, then, also invite Ms. Frances Stonor Saunders, whose book on the CIA and the culture wars was just being published? In it she describes how in April 1967 *Ramparts* exposed the CIA's sponsorship of the Congress for Cultural Freedom (and the various periodicals it secretly subsidized, including most famously

Encounter, the London-based monthly). But she also documents how in anticipation of the *Ramparts* exposé in early 1966, the CIA launched an investigation into *Ramparts*. The result: A week after the *Ramparts* exposé of the Congress appeared, the right-wing magazine *Human Events* ran a CIA-inspired article called "The Inside Story of '*Ramparts* Magazine.'" Its journalists were dismissed as "snoops," "eccentrics," "ventriloquists," and "bearded New Leftniks" who had a "get out of Vietnam" fixation. As it turned out, *Anti*, founded in 1972, had its own encounter, as it were, with the CIA, since it took as part of its mission the publication of the names of CIA agents working in Greece.

The evening soon took on a life of its own. Hinckle would be on hand to provide the hidden history; Saunders would fill in the context (the CIA helped subsidize something like twenty periodicals and over one thousand books to advance its Cold War agenda); I would interview Papoutsakis; and then because he was something of an expert on Greek politics, the CIA, and dissenting journalism, Christopher Hitchens would join in the fray. George Stephanopoulos, working as a commentator for ABC-TV but also a fellow at Columbia, agreed to serve as moderator.

Although Hitchens and Stephanopoulos were the main attractions, I was particularly looking forward to the Hinckle-Papoutsakis exchange. And I thought if Hinckle shared his fund-raising escapades, Columbia's surprisingly nonpolitical graduate students of journalism would get double their money's worth: an introduction to Cold War politics and an invaluable window on the paradoxes and attractions attending a politically engaged periodical, especially since Hinckle famously managed to pursue a radical agenda while literally traveling first class.

In his memoir, *If You Have a Lemon, Make Lemonade*, Hinckle takes umbrage at the story that once during an airline strike he flew from Chicago to New York by way of Paris. "It was San Francisco to New York," he said, "if it was Chicago I would have taken a cab."

A clue to Hinckle's modus operandi may be found in his relationship to *Ramparts*'s original owner, a wealthy liberal Catholic (or rather a liberal Catholic with a multimillionaire wife), Edward Keating, who had originally founded *Ramparts* as a Catholic magazine whose mission was to enlighten the Catholic community.

Hinckle had been trained as a Jesuit, but was working as a PR man

A Matter of Opinion

and reporter for the *San Francisco Chronicle* when he took a six-month leave to work for *Ramparts*, only to be told shortly after he had arrived that his publisher was broke or, as Hinckle put it, "that he had blown all of his wife's money on the magazine."

After his publisher asked him to find someone to help, Hinckle recalls the following exchange:

"You mean you really don't have any more money?"

"Well, I do have one shopping center left . . . It's only a medium-sized shopping center. It's in Santa Clara. It's got a mortgage on it, and there's a lawsuit I'd have to settle with one of its tenants, and I'd have to fix the air-conditioning before I could sell it. But still in all, it should net a little over a hundred thousand after that."

Hinkle demurred. He said he did not want to be the person who told his publisher to sell his last shopping center. He picked up the check, signed it, added a generous tip, and handed it to the waiter, who nodded in silent gratitude.

"Thank you," Keating said.

I thought he was being sarcastic; but no. He seemed genuinely grateful that I had signed the check.

"But it's *your* money, Ed," I said. "What are you thanking me for? I just signed my room number. You're paying the hotel bill."

"I know, I know," Keating said. "But I just like the way you do it. You just pick the check up and *sign* it. I could never do anything like that."

Hinckle tells us he shrugged and mumbled something incoherent about there being "nothing to it."

When the *Army Times* asked (on the occasion of a *Ramparts* cover featuring a Special Forces master sergeant quitting the Army and calling the Vietnam War "a lie") how could *Ramparts*, "with almost no advertising and a small circulation, afford a full-page ad in *The New York Times*, a massive mail subscription solicitation campaign, and the services of a New York public relations agency?" the answer was "nerve and credit." The *Times* ads paid for themselves in subscription revenues, and as often as not, to pay for the ad in advance, Hinckle "piggybacked on a friendly advertising agency's credit and paid off when the money came in." The year *Ramparts* went bankrupt, Hinckle, who had already made *Who's Who in America*, gained the additional honor of a listing in *Who's Who in Finance and Industry*.

I especially looked forward to meeting Papoutsakis; I was curious how much he knew about *Ramparts*, whose flame had long since burned out, and I was also curious to see whether Hitchens and Hinckle would try to take on the more establishment-oriented Stephanopoulos. There was only one problem. Unbeknownst to the overflow audience, at the last minute the State Department had denied Papoutsakis an entry visa. Despite protests from PEN, the ACLU, various Columbia deans, and me, the State Department was unrelenting and gave no reason for its action.

As Steve Shapiro, the ACLU attorney explained, if accusations of terrorism were involved, under the law—and remember, this was two years before September 11—the government is not obligated to give a reason for exclusion, and our best guess was that *Anti*'s anti-CIA stance was considered the aiding and abetting of terrorists.

The night of the big event, the journalism school's second-floor World Room was jammed with Greeks, Greek television, J-school innocents, Hellenic studies graduate students, and faculty. The Greeks who had come to see Papoutsakis were disappointed. Instead of the man, they got his remarks, a short history of *Anti* (which in Greek means "against" or "instead of"). I won't go into detail here (you can read it in English or in Greek, since Papoutsakis subsequently published his text in *Anti*), but it's worth noting that over the years this muckraking monthly, published on paper as cheap as *The Nation*'s, which covered and uncovered the dark side of Greek Society and whose offices had been bombed, had itself spawned two journals, *Polets* and *Pontini*, founded by disaffected *Anti*-ites.

Not only was Papoutsakis missing, however. At the last minute events in the Middle East caused ABC-TV to summon George Stephanopoulos to Israel, so rather than seeing George, those who came to see him saw instead the Greek Orthodox prelate Father Robert G. Stephanopoulos, who had come to see his son. And of course Hinckle and Hitchens, congenitally late, were nowhere to be seen. Which left Frances Stonor Saunders and myself to face the restless hordes.

After I explained the empty chairs and read an abridged version of

Papoutsakis's history, Frances gave a brilliant short course on how during the Cold War years the CIA used magazines to get across its message promoting the non-Communist left. Among her revelations: The
most famous and most effective piece of anti-Communist literature of
the Cold War, the book *The God That Failed*, started as a series of CIA-
sponsored magazine pieces by such prominent intellectuals and ex-
Communists as Arthur Koestler, Ignazio Silone, and Louis Fischer,
each detailing the process by which he became disillusioned with
Communism.

Mel Lasky, who went on to become editor of *Encounter*, had the essays translated in the offices of *Der Monat*, which published all but one
of them first in German. Then he arranged to publish the English version in 1950 with Arthur Koestler's English publisher, Hamish Hamilton, and had his close friend from the Office of War Information, Cass
Canfield (later CIA director Allen Dulles's publisher), arrange for an
American edition. "With this background," Frances concluded, "*The
God That Failed* was as much a product of intelligence as of the intelligentsia."

At which point, the high point of the evening actually, Hitchens
made his entrance. I'll let Frances tell you about it, since she took the
trouble to write it up for the *New Statesman*:

> It is all very theatrical. Like any good showman he keeps them
> waiting . . . and waiting. Forty minutes after the scheduled start
> time, he finally appeared, waving and nodding to people in the
> audience as he picked his way through the crowded aisles, the
> stale odor of booze and cigarettes trailing invisibly in his wake.
> His eyes were bloodshot and his crumpled clothes looked as if
> they had doubled as his bedding for the past week. And so this
> latter-day Swift entered the coffee house of student debate.
>
> In person, as on stage, Hitchens is in masterly possession of
> what he calls *saeva indignatio*, that combination of cheek and
> anger to point out how the world falls short of its pretensions.
> He is a skilled orator, working as far as I could see without texts
> or notes. He chooses his weapons carefully and is efficient ei-
> ther as a sniper or as a bombardier unloading the full arsenal of
> his invective. But he is also Barnum, of the type so congenial to

that quintessentially American tradition of cracker-barrel sales-manship. When an elderly woman rises to challenge Hitchens, he quips: "Mother, I told you not to do this!" Thus her question is deflected, amid general laughter of an audience who are be-having like so many valets to his lofty wit.

Shortly thereafter Hinckle burst into the room with his Labrador retriever (on a campus which bars animals), sauntering down the aisle and shouting inaudible responses to whoever was speaking from the podium.

Don't ask me who said what after that, although Christopher, for all his dishabille, was characteristically definitive on how the CIA had sabotaged dissident Greek journalists like his friend Elias Dimitri-copoulous, who had flown in from Washington to offer personal testi-mony, which he did during the question period. My only regret was that Papoutsakis was not there to share with Columbia's graduate stu-dents of journalism this unique educational event.

I don't doubt that some future scholar of small, dissident magazines will note that *Ramparts* exposed CIA sponsorship of *Encounter* and other journals, as a result of which they eventually went out of busi-ness. But it inspired Papoutsakis, as a result of which *Anti* went into business. At the same time, the CIA retaliated against *Ramparts*, as a result of which *Ramparts* went out of business, and the editor of *Anti*, doing his best to carry on in the *Ramparts* tradition, was banned from the United States. (Meanwhile, *Anti* limps along, while the anti-*Anti* journals it incited modestly thrive.)

There is a lot to be said about the role of the CIA in corrupting Amer-ican (and other) culture through its secret subsidies. (I myself spent a summer working for an old Swarthmore psychology professor who was doing a study of Hungarian refugees in the aftermath of the 1956 uprising. The study had been conducted under the auspices of the Free Europe Committee. Our joke was that the FEC, which was of-ficially surviving courtesy of the monies raised through President Eisenhower's Crusade for Freedom campaign, was in fact being secretly subsidized by the CIA. It later turned out that the joke was no joke.)*

But here I am concerned less with the CIA than with what may be learned about the magazine business by virtue of the Agency's involvement. The answer is, although its focus was on propaganda, because the CIA chose to enter the business of magazines, it had unwittingly, if I may use that locution, taken on all of the burdens, stresses, and strains of the nonprofit magazine-publishing business.

When the CIA gave birth to *Encounter*, along with twenty other periodicals, it knew what it was doing. Even though in this country the journal of opinion is the Rodney Dangerfield of magazines—it needs a little respect—abroad there is a general understanding that such magazines matter. One CIA-ster called *Encounter* "our greatest asset."

The purpose of *Encounter*, which was founded in 1953, was to address what Frances called "the perceived deficit in the bank of intellectual anti-Communism." *Encounter* and other CIA-funded magazines like *Der Monat* in Germany, *Preuves* in France, *Cuadernos* (launched in Paris, directed at Latin America), and *Tempo Presente* in Italy, were aimed at establishing and consolidating an anti-Communist, anti-neutralist, pro-American consortium.

I knew about the CIA's role vis-à-vis *Encounter*, because I had read about it when *Ramparts* and others broke the story.

And I knew about the CIA's more general interest in publishing, because back in 1976, when Frank Church's Senate Committee report on

---

*The study consisted of an analysis, based on in-depth interviews with something like sixty Hungarian refugees, of the factors that went into the Hungarian uprising of 1956. My job, along with that of three fellow "coders," was to rate each interview subject (on a five-point scale) on matters such as "education level," "attitude toward fascism," "anti-Semitism," "attitude toward communism," and "degree of involvement in revolution." When the study was completed each of us was asked to submit a memorandum on the significance of our findings. I forget my conclusions but I remember that Henry Gleitman, my Swarthmore professor and co-director of the project, congratulated me on my memorandum. In fact, he said, he and Joe Greenbaum, the other co-director of the study, wanted to incorporate my findings into the final draft of their paper and asked if I wanted a co-byline on the monograph, which would be published by the Free Europe Press under the title *The Romantic Revolution*. I decided that I did not want my first professionally published work to be a product of a committee over whose final editorial decisions I had no control, and so I thanked Henry for his generous offer but said no thanks. Had I not, I discovered some years later, my first published work would have been under the auspices of the Central Intelligence Agency, a credit the future editor of *The Nation* (and any other independent journal) could do without.

covert operations revealed that the CIA had subsidized "well over 1,000" books, I had contacted the Agency to get the list. In fact, after two CIA bureaucrats who promised to get back to me the next day forgot to return my phone calls, I made a third call, this one to Leon Friedman, a lawyer versed in the ways of the Freedom of Information Act. With his help, on November 10, 1976, I sent a formal letter to George H. W. Bush, then director of the Central Intelligence Agency. Under the law he was supposed to get back to me in ten days, but I guess he was too busy. And when I finally received my answer and the CIA denied my request, I went to court.

I will resist the temptation to belabor here the exquisite procedural, technical, and legalistic obstacles set up by the Agency to keep their publishing list secret (were they proud or ashamed of their sales record?). I did learn that whatever else the company was up to, the CIA was no marginal publisher. In declining to provide material, the Agency explained that even if it wanted to respond, the "request is staggering" because "files and materials relating to books subsidized or sponsored by the CIA . . . vary in size from two linear feet to approximately 200 linear feet. It is estimated that there are 2,000 pages of documents a linear foot."

I knew about the CIA's use in particular of the Congress for Cultural Freedom as a conduit for secret funding, because I had read the historian Christopher Lasch's extraordinary 1968 *Nation* essay on the way the Agency used Congress to influence the political culture. But it took Frances Stonor Saunders to uncover materials which show that although the Agency may have been a sophisticated if covert book publisher, when it came to magazines, they really didn't understand the editor-publisher relationship.

Generally I am against reading other people's mail. But I make an exception in the case of the correspondence leading up to *Encounter*'s very first issue, because I think it has something to teach us about the fundamental tension which lies at the heart of the editor-publisher nexus.

Encounter's London-based co-editors were the prestigious British poet Stephen Spender and the American intellectual Irving Kristol, who had come to *Encounter* after an editorial stint at *Commentary*. Since the main financial support for *Encounter* came via the Paris office of the Congress for Cultural Freedom, Kristol sent one Michael Joesselson, his Paris-based Congress contact, superior, and paymaster (and unbeknownst to him at the time a secret CIA agent), the prospective table of contents.

Joesselson made the mistake of replying that the lineup was not political enough, and Kristol—what did Joesselson expect?—got on his high editorial horse.

> I'm not sure about your cryptic remark about the "political contents" [not] living up to expectations. The magazine, obviously, should be a "cultural" periodical—with politics taken, along with literature, art, philosophy, etc., as an intrinsic part of "culture," as indeed it is. The ratio of specifically political to literary, etc. articles will naturally vary from number to number. In the first number, politics is relatively subordinate, since we are aiming to capture the largest possible audience. I have a very clear idea of what the Congress wants, and of how one should go about getting it. But I can't operate efficiently with the Paris office breathing down my neck, sending editorial directions, etc.

We can almost feel the frustration of editor Kristol leaping off the page as he wrote his complaining Paris handler:

> We here in London are not inept morons, and I sincerely believe that we can judge the situation better than you can in Paris. You and your colleagues in Paris think the cover is lousy. Well, maybe you're right. Then again, maybe you're wrong—magazine covers are not, after all, your specialty. I think the cover is good, though doubtless capable of improvement; Malcolm Muggeridge thinks it's very good . . . You think the first issue is insufficiently political? But then you obviously haven't studied the table of contents carefully . . . You think the issue is too literary? Well, you're wrong . . . Perhaps I'm deluding myself, but I really think that in *Encounter*, the Congress has hold of something far more important than even you realize. You, apparently, would be satisfied if we could achieve the standing of *Preuves*. My god, man, we're way past that (again, unless I'm deluding myself). Potentially, we have it in us to become, in a few months, the English language cultural periodical, and not only in England,

but for Asia too. Give us a few months and we'll be the idol of the intelligentsia, East and West—a magazine in which an Asian—or European and American!—writer would give his eye-teeth to appear. I mean this seriously and if I'm wrong, then you ought to get yourself another editor. But you've got to give us time, and editorial freedom, to achieve this.

Never mind that from Kristol's vantage point, publisher Joesselson was intruding on editor Kristol's prerogatives. Never mind that what should have been informal face-to-face give-and-take was carried on via snail mail (then merely called mail) between London and Paris. And never mind that the context in which the editor-publisher conversation occurred involved a lie—a journal dedicated to the promotion of openness, the free exchange of ideas, robust debate, political transparency was being secretly paid for by one side.

The core of the conflict, trust me, is built into the contrasting roles, which doesn't mean there aren't better and worse ways of handling it.

Oswald Garrison Villard once called himself the luckiest of men because he owned the magazine he edited. "Inherited means," as he put it, bestowed on him "the opportunity to be my own master; they enabled me to write as I pleased without ever having to wait upon another to get his orders . . ." Owning what one edits is indeed a foolproof way of guaranteeing editorial independence. But even Villard, who valued independence and the editorial freedom to fight the good fight, forgot what he knew when he was entrusted with the business responsibility for a periodical other than his own.

Consider the NAACP's magazine, *The Crisis*, and the experience of W.E.B. Du Bois, a man of towering stature and intellect. His title at the NAACP was Director of Publicity and Research, but his job, his vocation, his project was to serve as editor of *The Crisis*, which he created in 1914. Technically I guess one would have to call it a house organ, but in fact under his stewardship it put most other journals of opinion to shame. He and his magazine attacked the Negro press, white philanthropy, the colored clergy and church for not reaching out to the middle class. From the perspective of the NAACP's board, though, he was a source of constant frustration. He rejected the board's suggestions (e.g., that *The Crisis* should cover crimes committed by Negroes as well as those against them), and he resented the board's attempt to run *The Crisis* as a conventional business (keeping track of returns, bad debts, costs-per-issue). Things got so tense between Du Bois and the NAACP's treasurer that before the year was out, the treasurer resigned. This left him free to devote more of his time to his duties on the *Evening Post* and *The Nation*. The treasurer, in case you haven't figured it out, was Oswald Garrison Villard.

I don't know whether the American Jewish Committee studied the case of *The Crisis* before it set up *Commentary* in the 1940s. But it seems to me they did the right thing in letting their various editors (Elliot Cohn, Norman Podhoretz, and his successor Neil Kozodoy) alone. Especially under Podhoretz, in the 1960s and 1970s the magazine brought prestige to the Committee. It ran articles that were of interest to the intellectual community at large and not merely its own primarily Jewish constituents. For better or worse, even as President John F. Kennedy hired Dean Rusk as his Secretary of State after reading his *Foreign Affairs* article on the dangers of summitry, *Commentary* may take credit (or blame, if you will) for President Reagan's appointment of Jeane Kirkpatrick as Ambassador to the United Nations (after Reagan and his people read her *Commentary* article on the difference between totalitarians and authoritarians); and for bringing Daniel Patrick Moynihan's ideas on welfare policy to the attention of Richard Nixon, who proceeded to appoint him presidential counselor on domestic affairs. But by the 1980s, when *Commentary*, which under Podhoretz (who started as a liberal but from the mid-sixties on moved steadily to the right) became the leading neoconservative magazine, the AJC made its most interesting publishing decision. A significant segment of the Jewish intellectual community related to *Commentary*, another segment didn't. Instead of taking the suggestion of Stanley Sheinbaum, the West Coast liberal philanthropist and activist in Jewish affairs, who proposed that they fire Podhoretz, the AJC founded a second magazine, *Present Tense*, whose politics, while not radical, were far from conservative, neo or otherwise.

Not only that, but as the editor Murray Polner, an old-fashioned liberal, tells it:

> When I was approached to start a magazine for them, my question for them was what kind of magazine would you like? And

they said whatever magazine you would like to produce. I asked, would you like a popular magazine or would you like an academic journal or would you like one that's filled with ideas— sometimes confusing and sometimes inexplicable? And their response was whatever you want. I was amazed. And I had a brief chat with Podhoretz, and he said it's always been that way and it'll always be that way. And [this was thirteen years into the job] damned if it hasn't been. The one exception was that a former head of the organization called me in February 1981 or '82. Stephen Rosenfeld, the deputy editorial page director of *The Washington Post* and a *Present Tense* columnist, had written something critical about the war in Lebanon, and the guy who was heading the AJC called me in and rather uncomfortably he said to me he didn't like the article. I said nobody had ever said that to me before and that was not right. And he said well, you ought to join the club. And I said I don't know what clubs mean. All they can do is fire you, but in most cases bureaucrats back down. If they don't, well, at least you have your integrity and you can always get unemployment insurance.

I serve on the publications advisory committee at Swarthmore College. One would think that since the mission of the college alumni magazine is as clear as the snow on the lawn in front of Swarthmore's Parrish Hall—to promote the school, right?—and since the editor has no illusions about his independence, there should be no friction. House organs should be flacks for the house. End of story, right? Wrong. I won't tell tales out of school, but the observations of the editor of the alumni magazine at Johns Hopkins (which may be found on the Internet) are apropos. First, he acknowledges that the purpose of a university magazine is to continue the intellectual and emotional engagement of alumni with the institution. "It does this," he shrewdly notes, "not by promoting the university, but by exemplifying it with reporting and writing of high standards." What follows only hints at the complexities of the editor's relationship to the administration and doesn't even mention budgetary or political considerations or the fear by many academic bureaucrats of offending the alumni:

"By chronicling the accomplishments of people connected to the institution, it inherently promotes it, but does not descend to PR flacking or blatant marketing or solicitation." He adds that it must regard its institution with sufficient skepticism to maintain credibility with its readers, and yet it has to adhere to the standard of truth expected of an intellectual institution. Its goal: to foster a sense of active belonging among alumni and the rest of the university community. It should tell the truth and nothing but the truth, but occasionally, if the administration has its way, it will not tell the whole truth. As Jeff Lott, the editor of the Swarthmore alumni magazine, puts it, writing for an alumni magazine is like being a reporter whose only beat is your publisher. "Imagine if you worked for the *Times* and all your stories were about the paper."

The editor, in other words, needs elbow room. Presidents of liberal-arts colleges and boards of trustees, take heed! If you want your alumni to read the alumni magazine, don't censor or second-guess the editor. It's bad for morale and it's bad for the journal, and in the last analysis it won't be good for the institution. Only a fool doesn't know the difference between a house organ and an independent periodical. It's the difference between a propagandist and a journalist. Its purpose is less to tell the truth than to rally round the flag. Still, if you want your editor to put out a quality magazine, a lively magazine, a fresh magazine, an effective magazine, you should give him or her the policy guidelines (and if need be, a list of taboos, although I'd be very stingy with that), but then let the editor run the show. If you don't like what the editor is doing, then get another one, but don't undermine the one you have.

The paradox: If I am right, the publisher's interest will be best served by never (well, almost never) vetoing the editor. This, of course, does not take account of the case where the publisher believes it in the interest of the magazine—be it for political or economic reasons or both—to shut it down. Example:

A few years after Rabbi Michael Lerner appeared on the scene with his independent, relatively liberal Jewish journal of opinion, *Tikkun*, the AJC shut *Present Tense* down, presumably on the theory that *Tikkun* would do what *Present Tense* had been set up to do. That's too bad, because *Tikkun* (pronounced "teekoon"), which in Hebrew means "mending" or "healing," and *Present Tense* had quite different politics, although to be sure, neither was on the conservative side of the line. The difference between *Tikkun* and *Present Tense* is that while the latter would run articles pro and con the West Bank settlers ("because it was a complex situation, not on some equal time principle," Polner said), *Tikkun's* articles have been more consistent. They have run the gamut from a piece (on the occasion of the twentieth anniversary of the Six-Day War) titled "The Disastrous Occupation," calling Israel's presence in the territories "an unmitigated disaster for Zionism, the Jewish people and most Israelis," to an article which appeared the following year under the headline "The Occupation: Immoral and Stupid."

As for Lerner's relationship with his publisher, she divorced him. A last but not least point: When an editor and owner are on different pages, it may from time to time make for more interesting pages. Example: Martin Peretz, proprietor of *The New Republic*, was both Rik Hertzberg's and Michael Kinsley's tutor at Harvard. In each case he knew they were more left than he. Yet over a period of years he seemed to make a deliberate point of hiring Kinsley and Hertzberg alternatively to edit his magazine. Says Hertzberg, "It made Kinsley miserable and then it made me miserable; and then it made Kinsley miserable and then it made me miserable. There was a passionate disagreement between the editor in chief and owner (Peretz) and the editor. And that disagreement kind of split the staff. It was no joke. It was a real struggle. But it added something to the magazine—I really believe that. It resulted in a kind of sinuosity in the magazine, a sort of toughness. I mean, you could not get a piece in the magazine solely on the basis of massaging the prejudices of the editors, except when Marty was moved to pull rank, which he occasionally was. As a result, each piece went through a process of criticism that made it emerge stronger."

Hertzberg still worries that in many ways he did a disservice to his own politics during those years, because he took so many outrageously conservative pieces and improved them. Kinsley apparently had a different attitude. If he thought a piece was terrible, his assumption was, nobody will take this seriously, so print it and forget it. Peretz, of course, as owner–editor in chief, complicated the problem, since he was, in part, an absentee landlord. Again be it Willie Morris's money men, the CIA's handler, the nonprofit's board member or bureaucrat, the college's vice president of alumni relations, or the ad salesman identified on the masthead as publisher, each and every one of them will see the periodical as product and will want the product to maximize the goals—financial, political, or cultural—of the parent organization. The editor, if he's any good, will want to put out the best possible magazine (and in my opinion, both parties will be best served if the former gives the latter his marching orders and then leaves him alone).

Arthur has sold his interest in *The East Hampton Star*, did and undid a deal to sell his beloved *New York Observer* to the billionaire press lord Conrad Black (who later had his own comeuppance), and, remarkably, in his late sixties began a new career as a serious metal sculptor. I miss my weekly lunches with Arthur, because he always brought an unexpected perspective to the table. At our farewell dinner in his honor in 1994, he observed that *The Nation* of 1865 was capitalized at $100,000. "If we were to compute $100,000 from 1865 to date, compounded at a 6 percent rate, it would come to $240,000,000; of course that's before taxes . . ." I'm still thinking about that.

Hamilton Fish left the magazine to run for Congress (twice), and when Congress eluded him, he went to work for Human Rights Watch, where he founded the Human Rights Watch Film Festival, now an annual gala event. He then returned to *The Nation* by way of the Nation Institute, where he heads up the effort to establish an endowment.

Katrina seems to grow into the editor's job week by week, while simultaneously establishing a new and highly visible career as a television commentator. Don't tell her, but she's my designated successor. History will, I suspect, judge the success of one's tenure at a magazine like *The Nation*, one half by what happens on one's watch and the other half by whether one has passed it on into the right hands. Go, girl!

As for me, I divide my time between publishing *The Nation*, whose mission seems more urgent than ever, and teaching at Columbia University's Graduate School of Journalism, where the new dean, backed by the president of the university, is bent on transforming the curriculum (and using it as a lever to transform American journalism). He has asked me to take responsibility for the *Columbia Journalism Review*. This is ironic, since the last time I had anything to do with *CJR* was when I was helping Dick Pollak and Tony Lukas found MORE, whose mission was to challenge establishment journalism symbolized by, what else?, the *Columbia Journalism Review*. (And when MORE went out of business in the early 1980s, *CJR* picked up its subscription list.) We'll see.

The last issue of *Monocle* came out in 1965, although since our final price was "Ten dollars for seven issues, or five dollars for a life-time subscription," metaphysically speaking we may still be publishing. Who knows?

But if *Monocle* is no more, Jon Stewart's *Daily Show* and Al Franken and Wonkette.com seem to have moved in next door. It reminds me of a comment by the Polish philosopher Leszek Kolakowski (whose essay "What Is Socialism?" we published in the first issue of *Monocle*). What Kolakowski wrote (not in *Monocle*) had to do with the antagonism between the priest and the jester. He said that "in almost every historical epoch the philosophy of the priest and philosophy of the jester have been the two most general forms of intellectual culture. The priest is the guardian of the absolute who upholds the cult of the final and the obvious contained in its tradition. The jester is he who, although an habitué of good society, does not belong in it and makes it the object of his inquisitive impatience; he who questions what appears to be self-evident."

Maybe *Monocle* lives on after all.

The alliances of the late 1960s, like the brief one between democratic socialist *Dissent* and not yet neoconservative *Commentary* (united in their opposition to the counterculture) are no more. They have, as one scholar of the sectarian wars put it, "withered away."

With the founding of the *The Public Interest*, by the 1970s the conservative business community decided that intellectuals were a good "buy," and so they invested in them. From that point forward, it no longer remained the case that the right had the money but the left had the intellectuals. And the culture wars between the neocons and everybody to the left of them, which defined American journals of opinion in the last decades of the twentieth century, have now migrated into the mainstream media.

The sniping that went on between *The Nation* and *The New Republic* is, I keep hoping, a thing of the past. As Studs Terkel (and Jesse Jackson before him) says, "Keep Hope Alive!" But I wouldn't bet on it. Too many who identify with these ancient non-mergerees take too much sustenance from each other's misfortunes.

Internally things seem to have quieted down, but that may well be a temporary lull brought on by the near-universal desire in the *Nation* family to send the President packing (a desire that only heated up after he won the election).

On the postal front, the big magazines are still at odds with the littles—right now they are lobbying the Postal Rate Commission to charge more to magazines with higher editorial content (that means higher rates for *The Nation*, but also for *National Review*, right-wing *Human Events*, neocon *New Criterion*, etc.). Maybe Jim Hightower is right. Writing in "Hightower's Lowdown," his biweekly newsletter, he claims: "The most important—and the most radical—political perspective in our country is not right to left, but top to bottom, and most Americans today realize that they are no longer even in shouting distance of the economic and political powers at the top." Hightower, by the way, is in the tradition of "A Laborer" (aka William Manning), who wrote toward the end of the eighteenth century in his pamphlet, "The Key of Liberty," that the key of liberty was to give to the Many the knowledge and information only possessed by the Few (and to do it by way of a monthly magazine which would be available to all members of his proposed Society of the Many).

A factor in our business favor (but also helpful to publications like *Mother Jones*, *The Progressive*, *In These Times*, *Extra!*) was the threat that the Bush administration, with its war on Iraq and its civil liberties clamp down, appeared to pose to progressive values. The last time our circulation zoomed up was just after the election of Ronald Reagan; came Clinton-Gore and we took a hit. (On direct mail, renewals, single-copy sales, donations, all of it.) I told you earlier that for years our bad joke has been "If it's bad for the country, it's good for *The Nation*." After the U.S. invasion of Iraq in 2003, when people asked how we were doing, I could truthfully tell them, "Better than ever." But even I would have a qualm or two if I thought that *The Nation*'s business future depended on an imperial America's unilateral aggression abroad and suppression of civil liberties at home. Ultimately, I believe, a magazine like *The Nation* must incarnate, discover, and rediscover the case for its indispensability in the course of its weekly conversation with its readers. In the long run, rank exploitation of the short-run political situation is no recipe for success. (Unrank exploitation, however, like increasing the size of one's direct-mail campaign at the propitious political moment, is another matter.)

9

REFLECTIONS

In the good old days, when people of all ranks exchanged ideas in coffeehouses and taverns, you had what my favorite philosopher, Jürgen Habermas, has elsewhere called the "ideal speech" situation. Now TV is tabloidized, the mainstream press is Murdochized, and much of the information produced by the mega-conglomerates that dominate the media landscape, including most of the new media, is commercialized, bureaucratized, and homogenized. The received wisdom seems to be that serious journalism is yesterday's news unless it is digitalized and on a computer screen.

It used to be that taking potshots at the media was a right-left thing. From Agnew-Safire we got "nattering nabobs of negativism," and from Chomsky-Herman we got the manufacturing of consent and "the propaganda model." (Read it, a lot still holds up.) On the right was "Accuracy in Media" (AIM), and in the other corner is Fairness and Accuracy in Reporting (FAIR). Go, FAIR!

These days it's a little more complicated. The right complains about the liberal media, and (liberal) *Nation* columnist Eric Alterman pretty much disposes of the complaint in his book *What Liberal Media?* The left laments lack of media access, and "fair and balanced" Fox News's Bill O'Reilly invites "these pinheads" (that's me) to come on his program and be insulted and/or interrupted by him. And the Texas populist Jim Hightower adds that the most important political perspective "is not right-to-left but top-to-bottom."

Perhaps the most articulate exponent of the idea that journalism is in trouble is an outfit called the Committee of Concerned Journalists. Its thoughtful chair is Bill Kovach, former curator of the Neiman Foundation and Pulitzer Prize–winning editor of *The Atlanta Journal-Constitution*, and on its letterhead are some of the most prestigious and serious journalists in the business. I owe Kovach. When I was putting together the funding to acquire *The Nation*, over a beer at Casablanca, a Cambridge hangout, he gave me canny advice and an investor tip that actually panned out. Nevertheless, two years later I declined to sign his new organization's "Statement of Concern," because in the second paragraph is an assertion that seems to me to attack "opinion," at least by association—the very genre of journalism that I regard as the best hope for the profession, not to mention our democracy:

> As audiences fragment and companies diversify, there is a growing debate within news organizations about our responsibilities as businesses and our responsibilities as journalists. Many journalists feel a sense of lost purpose. There is even doubt about the meaning of news, doubt evident when serious journalistic organizations drift toward *opinion*, entertainment and sensation *out of balance with the news*. [my emphasis]

To me the problem is too little opinion, not too much. So I didn't sign the statement, but the question it raises is critical. Is opinion, open advocacy, moral and political argument, rational deliberation, critical analysis the problem, or is it part of the solution?

As you may suspect, I think it's part of the solution. But before I go there, I want to say a few words about objectivity, which is often (wrongly, in my view) posed as opinion's foe. As far as I'm concerned, when in 1993 Molly Ivins achieved the ripe middle age of forty-nine, she disposed of the objectivity question for all time: "The fact is that I am a forty-nine-year old white, female, college-educated Texan," she said. "All of that affects the way I see the world. There's no way in hell that I'm going to see anything the same way that a fifteen-year-old black high-school dropout does. We all see the world from where we stand. Anybody who's ever interviewed five eyewitnesses to an automobile accident knows there's no such thing as objectivity."

Here is what two other alumni of that ostensible paragon of objectivity *The New York Times* (yes, believe it or not, Molly, too, is an alumna of the *Times*) have to say.

First, the Washington columnist Russell Baker wrote in his memoir: "Objective journalism forbade a reporter to go beyond what the great man said. No matter how dull, stupid, vicious, or mendacious they might be, the utterances of the great were reported deadpan, with nary a hint that the speaker might be a bore, a dunce, a brute, or a habitual liar." And, I might add, as far as balance goes, canceling out the misguided quote of one great man with the misinformed quote of another gets the public no closer to the truth or even the issue.

Now, listen to David Halberstam, one of the best and the brightest practitioners of mainstream journalism: "In truth, despite the fine talk of objectivity the only thing mildly approaching objectivity was the form in which the reporter wrote the news, a technical style which required the journalist to be much dumber and more innocent than in fact he was. So he wrote in a bland uncritical way which gave greater credence to the utterances of public officials, no matter how mindless these utterances."

I am not the first or even the hundred and first person to observe that the objectivity that is supposed to guarantee a reporter's neutrality has a built-in presumption on behalf of keeping things as they are. But, actually, what Baker and Halberstam are talking about is pretend-objectivity; the rituals and conventions that are supposed to guarantee narrative neutrality but really end up reinforcing the status quo. In Baker's case it has to do with reliance on official sources, the experts, and you know what I (as co-director with Christopher Cerf of the Institute for Expertology) think of those; and in Halberstam's case, it has to do with the ban against editorializing or interpreting in the news columns, and you know what I (as an editor of a journal of opinion) think of that.

Which is not to say that objectivity is nothing more than factual accuracy. Remember, when I asked Sacvan Bercovitch in the middle of his seminar on American dissent what he thought of the way I thought about objectivity and ideology, he cautioned me not to give up on objectivity. "It's possible to keep both the objectivity ball and the ideology ball in the air at the same time," he said. When I asked him to say a little more, he suggested that the answer may lie with the cultural anthropologists.

And so it was that I came upon the cultural anthropologist Clifford Geertz's essay on why he was an anti-anti-relativist. He is not a relativist, but calls himself an anti-anti-relativist because he thinks more sins are committed by those who think they know the objective truth than by those who call themselves cultural relativists. Having identified with those denigrated as anti-anti-Communists during the late Cold War (in the sense that I believed that the countersubversives were doing more damage to the country than the alleged subversives ever did), in the argument between the relativists and the absolutists, I'm with Geertz.

He tells the Indian story about an Englishman who, having been told that the world rested on a platform which rested on the back of an elephant which rested on a turtle, asked, What did the turtle rest on? Another turtle. And what did that rest on? "Ah, Sahib, after that it is turtles all the way down."

Each culture does its subjective best to make sense of the world as it knows it, and Geertz seems empowered by his ethnographic studies to test his self-proclaimed subjectivities and biases in the classroom and in print. The implicit proposition: What democracy requires is a public debate rather than so-called objective information. Or to put it another way, the kind of information it needs can be generated only by Habermas's reasoned argumentation.

My colleague Jonathan Schell also distinguishes between pretend objectivity (the *appearance* of objectivity which comes from narrative neutrality and such) and the other kind. But he likes the other kind. To him every news story can be seen as the answer to a question. In that context, objectivity means setting aside one's predisposition (what I have called ideology, others call bias) in the conduct of the investigation. He likes the cold word "objectivity" because, he says, "it captures the self-restraint, the discipline required for the operation."

Objectivity, what Habermas called reliable information, then, may have its uses so long as it is not confused with the spurious objectivity that insidiously promotes conformity under the veneer of disinterestedness. I suspect even Molly would agree with that.

I had hoped to end this exercise with some findings, some conclusions, some tips, as it were. But as I look back on my journey, I find that I keep reprocessing it. Take, for example, my experience at the Democratic Convention in 1956. At the time, I saw my encounter with West-ern Union primarily as evidence of my own naïveté and incompe-tence. It never occurred to me to ponder the role of Western Union itself and to consider that in my failed and farcical attempt to transmit my copy to Alaska I was up against America's first bilateral monopoly—Western Union's monopoly of telegraph and the Associated Press's monopoly of wire service. Now the scholar and *American Prospect* co-editor Paul Starr, in an ambitious book, *The Creation of the Media: The Political Origins of Modern Communications* (2004), makes it clear that the former had much to do with the centralization of the media and the latter, for all its good work in bringing the news, contributed to the rise of so-called objectivity by encouraging a journalism which on the surface was non-partisan (so as not to offend its thousands of clients). Starr asks, "Could the news media do the job that democracy classically assigned the press—or did the commercially driven me-dia and new techniques of mass persuasion so distort public knowl-edge and degrade public discussion as to make popular government impossible?"

What's remarkable is that Starr's book stops in 1941, but sixty-four years later the question is more germane than ever. And that is be-cause, objectively speaking, you should forgive the expression, given the new media concentration, things have only gotten worse.

Another thing that didn't register at the time: All those '56 conven-tion "freebies" had a good old-fashioned capitalist purpose. The matter was brought home to me in 2004 at the Democratic Convention in Boston. This time, covering the convention for *The Nation*, as I con-sumed more than my share of the gallons of free booze and the tons of sumptuous hor d'oeuvres paid for by Bell South, Union Pacific, Edison International, and all the other sponsors of the convention receptions, I listened as the delegates and the press talked to each other about nothing so much as the influence of big money on politics, and it oc-curred to me that they knew whereof they spoke (and ate and drank).

Or take Harper & Row's 1978 suit against *The Nation* in connection with our story about President Ford's forthcoming memoir. At the time I saw it as a former public official and his book publisher trying to protect their propriety rights at the expense of our journal's First Amendment rights. What I now believe is that this was merely the latest in a long history of corporate incursions on the public sphere or, more legalistically, the public domain. These are documented in Lawrence Lessig's controversial 2004 book, *Free Culture: How Big Media Uses Technology and the Law to Lock Down Culture and Creativity*, where he reminds us that the Copyright Act of 1790 took a restrictive view of intellectual property and emphasized the importance of free expression and the public domain. His persuasive conclusion: "As a result of changing law, concentrated markets, and changing technology, never in our history have fewer had a legal right to control more of the development of our culture than now."

When, as a Yale law student, I wrote about Jack Benny's "Autolight" parody of *Gaslight*, I thought I was striking a modest blow for parody. Now it dawns on me that this was yet another case where in the name of intellectual property rights the courts were cutting off the creativity that our Constitution sought to enable in Article I, Section 1, Clause 8 ("Congress has the power to promote the progress of Science and useful Art by securing for limited times to Authors and Inventors the exclusive Right to their respective Writings and Discoveries"). For the first hundred years of the Republic, the copyright term was extended once. In the last forty years, increasingly powerful media corporations have persuaded Congress to extend it eleven times.

I think Groucho Marx had the right idea when Warner Bros. tried to keep the Marx Brothers from calling their film *A Night in Casablanca* because the studio deemed it too similar to its own *Casablanca* with Humphrey Bogart and Ingrid Bergman. Groucho sent off a letter: "You claim that you own Casablanca and that no one else can use the name without your permission. What about 'Warner Brothers'? Do you own that too? You probably have the right to use the name Warner, but what about the name Brothers? Professionally we were brothers long before you were." ("I am sure," Groucho added, "that the average movie fan could learn to distinguish between Ingrid Bergman and Harpo.")

What it adds up to is "permission culture" rather than a free culture. As a card-carrying member of the Author's Guild (a board member, no less), when I think of permissions fees as paying authors what they rightfully deserve, I'll fight for it. But when one thinks of permissions negotiation as a vast bureaucratic strategy by which mega-communications and entertainment corporations determine the content of the public sphere, then one thinks again. "Permission is not often granted to the critical or independent," Professor Lessig told me when we shared a panel at the 2004 Fine Print Conference at UC Irvine. I wish Justice O'Connor had been there to hear him when she wrote her decision in *The Nation* case.

The practice shows just how far the law has come from its eighteenth-century roots. Says Lessig: "The law was born as a shield to protect publishers' profits against the unfair competition of a pirate. It has matured into a sword that interferes with any use . . ."

As for Habermas, by the time I discovered him, he was fast losing favor with the academic left. Wouldn't you know? To start with, his public sphere, which he himself has conceded existed only briefly, "for one blissful moment in the long history of capitalist development," confined itself to the white landed male gentry. As helpful as I found and still find his notion of the "ideal speech situation," even I recognize that by focusing on this ideal type he is also ignoring class, he is ignoring media, he is ignoring all those books on the cultural-studies shelf at Harvard except his own. Maybe not ignoring exactly, but subordinating. And his case sounds suspiciously like the case for the marketplace of ideas, which is fine, but then one has to ask how does this marketplace deal with the power of the newly concentrated and consolidated media—doesn't that count for anything? And what about McLuhan, Freud, and their successors, who would argue that technology and the subconscious trump the rational? I know, I know, I'm oversimplifying here and leaving out all of Habermas's careful qualifications. And I also know that Habermas has posited that to achieve legitimate consensus, the state must immunize all speech against repression and all force except the force of the better argument.

So call me a rationalist (despite my exposure to theosophy at Steiner, to Marx and Dewey at the Little Red School House, to the inner light at Swarthmore). I'm still with Habermas and *Monocle* contributor and *Nation* contributing editor Neil Postman (even though, alas, he's no longer with us) who wrote, in his last book, *Building a Bridge to the 18th Century*: "It was no accident that the Age of Reason was coexistent with the growth of a print culture, first in Europe, then in America." Looking back to the eighteenth century, Postman asked how our enlightenment past can improve our future. I'm with him, especially when he talks about how language can be controlled by "the rigors of print." Who needs postmodernism when we've got Neil Postmanism?

If he had built his bridge to the nineteenth century, Neil could have cited Francis Jeffrey, who edited the *Edinburgh Review* from 1802 until 1829, and took it as axiomatic that "the greatest good that argument can do must be done by printed argument in a work read with some attention, by 50,000 people within a month after it is printed." The philosophical and sociopolitical questions raised by theorists like Starr, Lessig, Postman, and Habermas (even as qualified above) are critical to the future of journalism and the possibility of democracy.

But the matter of whether journalism will play a creative and constructive role in re-creating a democratic public sphere is not going to be resolved in the next ten pages.

That matter is part of a continuing conversation among philosopher-activists like Jay Rosen, founder of the movement for what he calls a public journalism; practicing journalists like Jim Fallows, who, in a manner akin to the slow-food movement, has called for a slower, more thoughtful journalism to replace the media's sweeping rushes to judgment; not to mention scholars, including any number of my colleagues at Columbia University.

Speaking of Columbia, Jim Carey, who runs the J-school's new Ph.D. program, has eloquently recommended that journalism ought to be conceived less on the model of expertise and objectivity and more on the model of conversation. This is appropriate, since as any habitué of the West End bar will tell you, Carey himself is always in conversation anyway. Every student of Communication 101 knows about the old debate between Walter Lippmann, who thought journalism was a science whose goal was to find and report the facts, and John Dewey, who argued (as Lasch and others did in later years) that the purpose of the press was less to develop information than to ask the right questions, to raise the level of discourse the public requires to make up its mind.

Carey, who once even proposed that we think of journalism as "an exercise in poetry," has recommended that we discard the idea that the job of the journalist is to bring the facts to a passive audience. Instead he has recommended that we say good-bye to the scientific conception of a journalism involving information, the experts, objectivity, and all the rest. "All journalism can do," he has written, "is to preside over and within the conversation of our culture: to stimulate and organize it, to keep it moving, to leave a record of it so that other conversations—art, science, religion—might have something off of which they can lead." The challenge is to persuade the public to come back to politics and cease to sit passively before a discussion conducted by experts and transcribed by journalists. I am all for having this particular conversation take place, even if, as the poet said, "Life is a conversation. When we enter it is already going on. We try to catch the drift of it. We exit before it is over."

The beauty part is that we don't have to start from scratch. This wheel has already been invented. Journals of opinion are not by themselves going to save the world. But they have been carrying on the conversation, arguing the world, for centuries. And opinion of course is not where the conversation stops. Opinions, it has been said, are to ideas as facts are to knowledge (and I, ever the optimist, might add, as knowledge is to wisdom). Once the ideas are launched, these same journals make it possible to study, assimilate, illustrate, criticize, modify, and project them out into the culture. That's what the conversation is all about.

As you know, I have wrestled like Jacob with the angel over the problem of which form of ownership is best suited to the journal of opinion. You will not be surprised to know that on this as on so much else, I don't have the answer. That may be because there is no single answer. There is a fellow in Cambridge, Massachusetts, Chris Mackin, who is the country's leading expert on employee stock ownership plans in union shops. I spent some time with him after I got Arthur's call, but I couldn't figure out how to do it in the *Nation* context.

The *Statesman*'s Bruce Page once noted that while democratic socialists may have many answers for dealing with the shortcomings of capitalism, worker ownership of a journal of the *Statesman*'s sort is not one of them. If the choice is a better health-care plan or money for an expensive investigative exposé that may or may not work out, the odds are that the shop will vote for better health care (and why not, the editorial idea was undoubtedly lousy to begin with). In the current American legal context, I don't love the nonprofit option for the reasons so eloquently set forth at our California conference. (The First Amendment and all that.)

I was and remain attracted to the notion of some sort of trustee-ship, but my pathetic experience as a *New Statesman* trustee is not lost on me. I was interested to note that just the other day, on the occasion of William F. Buckley bowing out as guarantor of *National Review*, that (with characteristic modesty) he replaced himself with five trustees.

I worry about having the editor serve at the whim of the market or of the *New Statesman*'s dreaded single proprietor, and yet, with an origi-nality worthy of Polonius, I do believe it sometimes does come down to the who—or is it the whom—you know? (I'm with Trillin that "whom" ought to be banished from the English language, because whom knows how to use it?) To put it another way, Villard's point about the advan-tages of the publisher and editor being the same person is well taken, depending on the person. But I would oddly add that the thing to worry about is less your proprietor's politics than his/her character and tem-perament. (I say this despite my questionable character given my well-known devotion to prizefighting and gambling on cruise ships.)

Bill Greider, whose book *The Soul of Capitalism* has some valuable things to say about all this, is most persuasive on the importance of workers feeling a sense of psychological ownership. When I asked him about nonpsychological ownership, he allowed as how "private enter-prise can't function as a democracy, which has the luxury of not decid-ing things. An enterprise like yours doesn't have that luxury. It has to come out every week. You do need an authority to make the last call."

He calls it an authority. I call it an editor. But I like Bill's idea that it wouldn't do any harm to have an annual nonbinding vote of confi-dence in the magazine's leadership among its various constituencies (writers, staff, subscribers, donors, owners). If the vote goes against you, it tells you something. I plan to recommend to Katrina that this practice be instituted as soon as I retire.

Whatever form of ownership is chosen, there are things that gov-ernment can and should do on behalf of these small-circulation, inde-pendent journals (and by implication on behalf of journalism itself), since they are indeed ideally situated to set the standard. These range from lower mailing rates for periodicals which are engaged in democ-racy's work (I know there are line-drawing and definition difficulties here, but that's true everywhere). And I cannot tell a lie. For reasons you have already heard, I favor George Washington's proposal for free deliv-ery of newspapers (and magazines); and I favor tax relief for family-owned periodicals, so that when the proprietor keels over, estate taxes don't force his or her loved ones to sell to the nearest chain; and legislation facilitating the start-ups of printing co-ops. The Independent Press Association idea of lower postal rates on the first 50,000 copies of any magazine sent through the mails makes sense, although now that *The Nation's* circulation is up to a record-breaking 184,296, I favor a cutoff at 184,297—but I'd be for IPA's proposal on principle (being the principled principal that I be).

Are these journals a relic or a counterforce? They are, of course, both. A relic couldn't force the world's largest book publisher to own up to its Nazi-publishing past, which it had previously denied. It's no accident that Fred Cook, writing in *The Nation*, and the rambunctious *Ramparts* and not an organ of the establishment, broke those stories on the CIA, or that small-circulation independents beat the mainstream media on stories about the human consequences of corporate malfeasance, media concentration, hunger in America, chemical poisoning of the environment, U.S.-sponsored torture in Third World countries; or that a small journal (dismissed by President Reagan as a "Lebanese rag") broke the Iran-Contra story, or that *Mother Jones* exposed de facto corporate murder by car manufacturers. " 'Tis strange the mind, that very fiery particle, Should let itself be snuffed out, by an article." So wrote Lord Byron, and so it is.

Although this journal might hire a world-class designer to give it a new look and that journal may move to an elegant townhouse, these journals are not, as a rule, about façade. A story is told that once during the sixties a group of Weathermen, the violent faction which split off from the Students for a Democratic Society, was dispatched to blow up the offices of *Dissent*, with whom they were in ideological conflict (*Dissent* being against the use of violence as a political tactic). They failed in their mission, but only because they couldn't find the *Dissent* offices, and they couldn't find them because there were no offices. The magazine was put out from the home of one of its staff.

That the often intangible influence of these journals is not quantifiable does not make it any less real. How does one measure their influence on intellectual currents, on cultural assumptions, on the sense of the possible, on the climate of opinion? The fight to exert influence is often a fight over the future. We have seen how *National*

Review's nourishing of the impossible, and I would add implausible if not insane, ideas of the radical right contributed to the nomination of Goldwater in 1964 and the election of Reagan in 1980.

Dick Crossman, when he was the editor of the *Statesman*, said, "The Socialist journalist must cultivate the art of the impossible—until a climate of opinion emerges that makes the impossible possible." Or as *The Nation*'s Daniel Singer used to say, "Be realistic. Ask for the impossible."

On February 1, 2003, just weeks before the invasion of Iraq, I opened my *New York Times* to an article by Todd S. Purdum of the Washington bureau titled "The Brains Behind Bush's War Policy." From the *Times*'s Washington bureau I expect the scuttlebutt, the inside word from the denizens of the war party. But what Purdum gives us is less inside dope from the inner circle of hawks than outside analysis from *The National Interest*, *The Weekly Standard*, from various (neocon) journals of opinion. He reports their common theme (in articles starting in 1997): "Saddam must go." And the essence of all their arguments in favor of war with Iraq? That the doctrine of containment no longer applies in a post-Soviet, post–Cold War world. (Containment, of course, was first set forth as policy in another journal of opinion, *Foreign Affairs*, which published George Kennan's history-making essay "The Sources of Soviet Conduct," under the pseudonym "X" in July 1947.)

So take it from me (or better yet, take it from the *Times*), the journal of critical opinion is here to stay.

Fifteen years after we came in for our share (more than our share) of contumely for inviting retrograde and/or politically incompatible journals to our California conference, I invited *National Review* editor Rich Lowry to lecture at the Columbia Graduate School of Journalism (see how ecumenical, fair, and balanced I can be). But he outfoxed me. Like *National Review*'s O'Sullivan had done at Harvard, instead of spewing right-wing propaganda, he talked about what our two magazines had in common. He said that like *The Nation*, *National Review* exists to make a point, not a profit; and that opinion journals are at their best when they are fighting for ideas that are out of favor, like the idea that the case for keeping drugs illegal is intellectually bankrupt, an idea in which both magazines concur. (Although I'm glad *The Nation* has also given space to Rev. Jesse Jackson's contention that decriminalization will amount to suicide for the boyz 'n the 'hood.) When and if the retrograde drug laws are changed, I guess it's true that it will be at least partly because these journals have been chipping away at them all these years.

Hitchens, you will remember, traced what he called a "thin reddish thread" connecting J. B. Priestley's article on the nuclear threat to E. P. Thompson's history-making Committee for Nuclear Disarmament. I don't know whether Thompson would have agreed with Hitch on the role of Priestley's article. I do know that as the British social historian and leader of the European nuclear disarmament movement saw it, by the early eighties America and Europe appeared to have drifted beyond the range of communication, and the drift seemed to be endangering both continents.

The Nation invited him to send his warning to his American friends— and devoted an entire issue to his message: "We must protest if we are to survive. Protest is the only realistic form of civil defense." This slogan of the British antinuclear movement may have sounded idealistic at the time, but Thompson's confidence that rhetoric could be turned into action proved prophetic. A decade before the disappearance of the Soviet Union and the self-transformation of its satellite East European regimes, he wrote that even though only courageous dissidents will, in the first place, be able to take an open part, protesting "will provide those conditions of relaxation of tension which will weaken the rationale and legitimacy of repressive state measures, and will allow the pressures for democracy and détente to assert themselves in more active and open ways."

I cite these prescient sentiments, not just because I *agreed* with them (although if I didn't I wouldn't cite them—you have me there), and not just because I believe them to be as compelling an explanation for the meltdown of the U.S.S.R. as the claim that the arms race bankrupted it (although I do), but because "protest and survive" is more than a stratagem. It is a philosophy, and as such describes more than the British antinuclear movement. Indeed, it is as fair an account as we have of the animating force behind the journal of dissent itself. When Thompson wrote about generating an alternative logic, an opposition that must be at every level of society, must win the support of multitudes and bring its influence to bear on the rulers of the world, his argument exemplified the case for a truly independent journalism.

Now consider again Godkin's injunction not to be the organ of any party, movement, or sect. A magazine like *The Nation* can inspire, it can mobilize, it can organize, but in the end it is not a movement, since it is also the job of our journal to deal with—not omit or ignore—inconvenient facts; to persuade, in Habermas's phrase, through the power of the better argument. There is a time to protest and a time to consider, to analyze. To me, this double life, this mixed mandate, the Garrison-Thompson tradition of protest and the Godkin-Habermas tradition of intellectual debate are not either-or. It is the job of the journal of opinion—postmodernism and that Harvard cultural-studies shelf to the contrary notwithstanding—to tell the truth (*pace* Lewis Bergman). And when there is no truth to tell, tell that, too. At least in the case of *The Nation*, although it doesn't always seem that way, the two traditions keep company.

Once, when Bob Sherrill quit for the umpteenth time, he sent me a four-page, single-spaced letter explaining why. I plan to donate my cache of Bob's I-quit letters to the Smithsonian, but I think the last half of the last page may help you to understand why, so even though he pays me some (insulting) compliments, I quote it here:

> Anyway, Victor, you and I aren't on the same wavelength. You are an eastern liberal—extremely clever, very intellectual, very reasonable. I'm not an eastern liberal; I'm a western anarchist; and I'm not clever, not at all intellectual, and very unreasonable. You talk over my head. I never can remember all the Borgean feuds and neo-liberal intellectuals who are supposed to be our enemies. You do that beautifully, and doubtless it is worth doing. But I think I hate corporations much better than you do, though I'll admit it is not a very sophisticated hatred; and I know damned well that I hate politicians better than you do, though the hatred is downright gutter. So we really don't have much to talk about and I guess it's just as well we didn't get together much.
>
> And don't make me a contributing editor. That is the dumbest and most meaningless title ever concocted by a profession that spends half its time doing dumb and meaningless things. Just take me off the masthead. You know I wish you well indeed.

Sherrill is definitely unreasonable (and a world-class hater of all corporations and most politicians). But that, along with his other qualities—including an overdeveloped sense of injustice, a passion for the good, the true, and the beautiful, an amazing intellect, spit-in-the-devil's-eye prose, an insatiable curiosity about this and that and the other thing, and an indifference to the dollar—are precisely the qualities one hopes for in a magazine of *The Nation's* sort. We didn't take Sherrill off our masthead, but we did persuade him to become our corporations correspondent (although I wouldn't be surprised if by the time you read this he has a new title).

I suspect that like Sherrill *The Nation* has survived all these years partly because it serves no party, movement, or sect, but also because of, not in spite of, its independence, financial as well as political. But it also has survived because its goal was the opposite of the goal of most of my fellow Harvard small-business men and women. What they were aiming for was/is a liquidity event, an IPO, an initial public offering. *The Nation*, of course, is a cause more than a business. So it is ironic that the small-circulation *Nation* has survived while any number of magazines with circulations in the millions have gone under. I believe there is a reason why *The Nation* survives as America's oldest weekly in a business where survival may be the ultimate test of success. And it has to do partly with the raison d'être of all journals of opinion, and partly with *The Nation's* values and ideals.

Protest against injustice, protest against the despoliation of the world's resources, protest against the arbitrary exercise of power, protest against prejudice and discrimination, protest on behalf of the dispossessed, the disenfranchised, protest on behalf of those who don't read us are only one part of *The Nation's* mission, but it is a critical part. Also, it is worth noting that, as Perry Anderson has pointed out, political journals have no choice: "To be true to themselves, they must aim to extend their real life beyond the generations that gave rise to them."

At first I thought it was an anomaly when Rupert Murdoch and his News World Corporation agreed to fund *The Weekly Standard*. Because by definition the journal of opinion, if it is to be politically and culturally free, must also be financially independent. The conventional wisdom tells us that in the world of mass magazines so-called stand-alones are a thing of the past. Not so in the world of opinion journals, where stand-aloneness seems to be something of a necessary condition.

But then I thought, Well, in the U.K. the *Spectator*, currently owned by the London *Telegraph*'s communications conglomerate, has survived a series of mega-corporate owners. And though like the *Standard*, only more so, it often values style over substance and is too quirky to be circumscribed by a party line, it is nevertheless an opinion journal of the right. These magazines are in the position of defending the powers that be, and so conglomerate ownership, which is anathema to the left, may be organically appropriate to their mission as magazines dedicated to free-market capitalism.

Either way, as *The American Prospect*'s Bob Kuttner has observed, one fundamental difference between left and right is that "the right is always floating downstream relative to economic power. And the left is always heading upstream. That helps explain why the right is always so well-funded. Because it is validating the world view of people who have a ton of money."

Nevertheless, I guess I still subscribe to the idea that those of us in the opinion industry have a stake in protecting each other's space. And if you're not already, you should become a subscriber, too.

We are told that because the new media quicken the news cycle— that the twenty-four-hour news cycle is now a twenty-four-minute one—the weekly will soon be, if it is not already, outmoded if not outmodemed. To the contrary, what the speeded-up new media mean is that the news is too often replaced by un-fact-checked hyperbole, and thoughtful debate, argument, and opinion by shouting matches.

What effect will the new communications technologies have on current cultural formats, artifacts, and institutions? Talkies put silent movies out of business. But the paperback extended the audience for the hardcover novel, and neither television nor videotapes put talkies out of business. Will the advent of on-line journals like *Slate* and *Salon* and the arrival of bloggers,* not to mention the availability of on-line versions of thousands—hundreds of thousands—of print opinion pieces in electronic form, negate the need for the classic, stapled journal of opinion?

I don't think so. But then I'm told by my mostly younger colleagues

---

*Blog is short for Web log, and a blogger is someone who has his own Web site and regularly sends out his views on, well, anything.

that I don't get it. I don't. It seems to me that despite the benefits, low costs, speed, and interactivity of the blogosphere, the depositing of prose in an electronic database cannot compete with the canonization, the legitimization conferred by these old-fashioned print journals, at least not in contemporary cultural terms. That an essay has survived the vetting process of a board of editors on whose political/cultural judgment the reader has come to rely (though not necessarily to concur in) tells the reader not only how to read a particular piece but that it may be worth the effort. Moreover, one's reading of, say, an Arthur Danto essay on the end of beauty may be influenced by its being sandwiched between Gore Vidal's requiem for an empire and Katha Pollitt on "Are Women Morally Superior?" (I forget where Katha came out, but of course that is not the point. The unhurried superior quality of her prose, her argument, her moral sensibility is the point. And the rhythm of magazine reading and mulling is the point.) Over the long haul, these magazines provide their own narratives, a long-running moral/political/cultural paradigm complete with its own heroes and villains. Which is not to say there is not room for an electronic republic of letters to supplement its print predecessor.

Perhaps I am a victim of my mail (not the hate mail of which I receive more than my share, but the other kind). Only today (I kid you not) I found this message on my voicemail from a woman who identified herself as a sixty-eight-year-old widow: "I need to ask a favor of you. I'm stuck in Abbeville, Louisiana, and I want to move, but I want to move somewhere where I can see a Democrat before I die. It occurs to me that you might be able to rummage up a place where people are actually subscribers to *The Nation*, where I would have somebody to talk to. I don't want their names or anything. I just want a town where there are a few kindred souls." And she added, "If you could call around noon I'd be grateful, I'm about to cut the grass." I have always believed that if Gallup or Roper or the latest public-opinion surveyor asked a representative sample of our readers, "Who are you?" any number of them might answer (never mind their vocation and religion, marital status, gender and/or sexual orientation), "I am a *Nation* subscriber." Just the other weekend in the Sunday Styles section of *The New York Times*, the featured wedding described how one Nina Rowe, the bride, met her groom-to-be. She found him on an Internet dating service under his handle, "nationreader." The readers of journals of critical opinion constitute nongeographical communities, whose self-identification and links with people they have never met are no less real for that. They are indeed kindred souls. Maybe it's no accident that the social anthropologist Benedict Anderson, who invented and elaborated the idea of the imaginary community, has a brother, Perry Anderson, who edits a journal of opinion, *New Left Review*.

My OPM Harvard classmates have an annual reunion at overpriced luxury resorts like that ranch in Scottsdale, Arizona, or the Oriental Palace in Thailand. I have yet to go, but this year I'm tempted. On the day I presented the *Nation* case at Harvard, one of my classmates demanded—rather emotionally I thought, as though he was really put out—to know the answer to the question "Are you or aren't you interested in making money?"

Maybe because I didn't want to flunk his exam I said something like "Sure, but that is not all I'm interested in." I wish he were around as I write this six years later, because we just received our financials and they say that last year we made a profit of $251,000. He would undoubtedly say, "You call *that* money?" But I'm proud of our turnaround, even though I know that while technically profitable, we're still subsidized by anonymous well-wishers and what with rising postal rates, rising paper costs, rising health-care premiums, and our inimitable capacity to offend our most generous donors, next year we will undoubtedly be back in the red. More important, short-run profit can contribute to survival, but it is no measure of mission. Every publisher of *The Nation*, and I am no exception, has understood that it is a public trust.

So I end where I began. You need to run one of these magazines like a business or else you will be out of business. But if business is all you are, you will be out of business, too. As the *Texas Observer*'s Ronnie Dugger wrote in Volume I, number 1 back in 1952: "We have to survive as a business before we can survive as a morality; but we would rather perish as a business than survive as an immorality." The tension between market and mission is unresolved, although the choice is clear. When in 2003 anonymous Disney executives were talking about shutting down ABC's *Nightline* because it had "lost its relevance," a part of me thought if relevance is measured by the bottom line, they are right. I was glad to be in the un–mass media.

The tension between independence (honoring the intellectual's role as truth-seeker) and commitment (honoring the activist's role as agent of change) is as alive as it was in the days of Garrison, Godkin, and Steffens, but I like to think that the two are not mutually contradictory. And what better forum in which to play it out?

Finally, a nagging question: Doesn't the fact that these journals are of, by, and for elites render them inappropriate vehicles for building a truly democratic culture? I would like to agree with my old friend and *Monocle* subscriber the late Dean Theodore Peterson of the University of Illinois, who wrote: "There is still a place in society for a cultural elite, open to whoever cares to join it. Just as there is an important place in society for tailors to custom-make suits for people who choose not to buy their outfits from the racks, so there is an important place for people who think that even primary assumptions should come in for some challenge and that *Camelot* is not necessarily America's answer to *Aida*." But I know it's more complicated than that. Listen now to one of Habermas's erstwhile Frankfurt School colleagues, Theodor Adorno. He might as well have been talking about the journal of critical opinion when he argued that art could be difficult and intransigent precisely in order to prevent commercialization. "High art by this token remains high, even austere, not in order to preserve in those who know about it their superiority, but in order to maintain an unanswerable and compelling criticism of the way things are, a picture of how they might be better, a call to humanity and its guardian intelligentsia never to fall into conformity and resignation. "Art," wrote Adorno (and for art substitute the journal of opinion), "always was, and is, a force of protest of the humane against the pressure of domineering institutions." He says it better than I could.

ACKNOWLEDGMENTS

It is customary in the course of acknowledgments to absolve the acknowledgees of any responsibility for the work in question. I don't feel that way about Richard Lingeman, E. L. Doctorow, Robert Snyder, and Scott Sherman, who took time from their overcrowded schedules to read earlier drafts of my manuscript. I'm indebted to them for their helpful comments, but if you have found anything offensive, unnuanced, wrong, or otherwise troubling in the book, blame them. The only reason I asked them to read it was to save me from such embarrassments.

I feel the same way, only more so, about my scrupulous editor, Elisabeth Sifton, whom I have dutifully followed from house to house over the many years it took me to complete this book. She was a constant source of constructive criticism but also of unwavering encouragement, so if you think this thing was one big mistake you know whose fault it is.

I was going to say don't blame my agent, Amanda "Binky" Urban of ICM, because she didn't sign this book up in the first place. Lynn Nesbit did that, but no sooner had she done so than she fled ICM and set up her own agency with Morton Janklow, so Lynn gets a grateful pass. But Binky has done her energetic and professional best on my behalf and thereby has earned her share of responsibility for what has gone before.

Others who have left their indelible imprint on this project include Mary Taylor Schilling, my longtime and long-suffering assistant, and her predecessor, the ever-cheerful Denis Selby; and Kathryn Lewis, who in the guise of typist served as secret editor. I also wish to acknowledge Scott Sherman for the six glorious years that he put in as my always indispensable kibbitzer, research assistant, and all-purpose advisor; Brian T. Gallagher, who ably succeeded him; and Peter Mayer, who over the years has been guilty of an abundance of small kindnesses.

When in the early 1980s I first signed up to meditate on the matter of opinion journals, I thought I could manage it because my duties as *Nation* editor would serve as the equivalent of research. But I soon found that *The Nation* had invaded my life to such an extent that I could no longer distinguish *Nation*-time from book-time from all-the-time. As a result, by my lights, there is no member of the *Nation* family who has not facilitated this enterprise in one way or another. This goes for everyone up and down the masthead from Hamilton Fish, my original partner; to Arthur Carter, his successor; to Katrina vanden Heuvel, who replaced me as editor and who magnificently piloted the magazine through the difficult post–9/11 years.

To the long line of *Nation* interns, many of whom have gone on to high-flying careers in journalism, publishing, the arts, and academia, not to mention at *The Nation* itself, I say I hope you learned as much from me as I did from you. If I have omitted you from the following list of those to one or another degree complicit in this project, please don't thank me. It was unintentional. Dustin Beilke, Martin Boer, Phil Boroff, Tim Bradley, Theresa Braine, Carl Bromley, Jennifer Buksbaum, Phil Connors, Kabir Dandona, Arne Delfs, Robin Epstein, Charles Forcey, Don Guttenplan, Paul Haacke, Jill Hamburg, Caleb Hellerman, Phil Higgs, Mitch Horowitz, Nicholas Jahr, Neil Jumonville, Josh Kornbluth, Ben Kunkel, Leon Lazaroff, Jim Ledbetter, Mark Lotto, Kevin McCarthy, Peter Meyer, Edward Miliband, David Montero, Morgan Neville, Jane Oski, Reed Richardson, Sumana Raychaudhuri, Peter Rothberg, John Rudd, Mosi Secret, Elizabeth Seay, Andrew Shapiro, Nina Shapiro, Ben Shouse, Micah Sifry, Peter Siskind, Sarah Song, Jim Spanfeller, Sam Stoloff, Daniel Swift, Michael Tomasky, Ari Weisbard, Marjorie Wentworth, Sandy Wood.

Tom Goldstein, Dean of the Columbia University Graduate School of Journalism, contributed to the delay of this project by inviting me in 1999 to join the J-school's extended family, and then, along with Associate Dean David Klatell, attempted to atone for this deed by granting me a series of fall semester leaves of absence to enable me to get on with it. Dean Nicholas Lemann kindly continued the tradition.

At Harvard's Institute of Politics, where I was a fellow in the winter and spring of 1994, Charlie Royer and Terry Donovan were particularly supportive, and at the Freedom Forum's Media Studies Center, where I was a senior fellow in the fall of 1994, Ev Dennis went way out of his way to assist me.

Parts of this manuscript have appeared in other forms in other places. This is especially true of my visit to Habermas, which Rob Snyder persuaded me to write up for the *Media Studies Journal*, and my time at the Harvard Business School, which I first put on paper at the behest of Randall Rothenberg when he was at *Esquire*. When he left *Esquire* so did my manuscript, which migrated to Bill Whitworth and *The Atlantic Monthly*, where he and his staff were gracious and hospitable, and where it probably belonged in the first place. I have also felt free to lift small and sometimes large chunks of my own prose from articles I did for *Holiday*, *The New York Times Magazine*, Jack Newfield's *American Rebels* (Nation Books, 2003), Katrina vanden Heuvel's and my *Nation* anthology (Thunder's Mouth Press, 1991), a reprint of Leonard Lewin's *Report from Iron Mountain* (Free Press, 1996), and occasionally even *The Nation* itself.

As I was headed down the homestretch, Miri Navasky took advantage of a temporary respite in her career as a documentary filmmaker to organize the last remnants of my files, thereby depriving me of yet another excuse for procrastination. The only member of my family who is 100 percent innocent of all blame is my daughter Jenny (she has yet to see a page of this), and I thank her for that.

Finally, I acknowledge that were this a bona fide history of *The Nation* I would have felt compelled to acknowledge by name and deed the dedicated and super-talented *Nation* staff that has, over the years, made that impossible magazine possible. It isn't, so I didn't.

INDEX